NATIONAL
GEOGRAPHIC
T R A V E L E R

prague &
the czech republic

NATIONAL
GEOGRAPHIC

TRAVELER

prague &
the czech republic

by Stephen Brook

National Geographic
Washington, D.C.

CONTENTS

Pages 2–3: Charles Bridge looking toward Malá Strana
Opposite: Dining Prague-style

TRAVELING WITH EYES OPEN

Alert travelers go with a purpose and leave with a benefit. If you travel responsibly, you can help support wildlife conservation, historic preservation, and cultural enrichment in the places you visit. You can enrich your own travel experience as well.

To be a geo-savvy traveler:

- Recognize that your presence has an impact on the places you visit.

- Spend your time and money in ways that sustain local character. (Besides, it's more interesting that way.)

- Value the destination's natural and cultural heritage.

- Respect the local customs and traditions.

- Express appreciation to local people about things you find interesting and unique to the place: its nature and scenery, music and food, historic villages and buildings.

- Vote with your wallet: Support the people who support the place, patronizing businesses that make an effort to celebrate and protect what's special there. Seek out shops, local restaurants, inns, and tour operators who love their home—who love taking care of it and showing it off. Avoid businesses that detract from the character of the place.

- Enrich yourself, taking home memories and stories to tell, knowing that you have contributed to the preservation and enhancement of the destination.

That is the type of travel now called geotourism, defined as "tourism that sustains or enhances the geographical character of a place—its environment, culture, aesthetics, heritage, and the well-being of its residents." To learn more about geotourism, visit National Geographic's Center for Sustainable Destinations at *www.nationalgeographic.com/travel/sustainable*.

NATIONAL GEOGRAPHIC
TRAVELER

prague & the czech republic

ABOUT THE AUTHORS

Stephen Brook first visited Prague in the mid-1980s, and it was one of the central European cities featured in his book *The Double Eagle* (1988). When he returned in 1991, the days of communist rule were over, and the city was enjoying a new lease on life, as reflected in his next book about the city, *Prague* (1992).

Brook grew up in London, studied at Cambridge, and worked as a publisher's editor in the United States and in London before becoming a full-time writer in 1982. Since then he has written 30 books on a wide range of subjects including travel, wine, opera, dreams, and infidelity. He has also contributed numerous articles to *Vogue, The Times, Cigar Aficionado, Condé Nast Traveller, Decanter,* and other publications.

Now living in London with his wife, Brook takes every opportunity to travel and explore the world. He retains a special affection for Prague, where some of his forebears lived, as there are few other cities that combine such dramatic beauty with such a vigorous cultural life.

Prague resident and editor **Will Tizard** updated and wrote new features for the 2010 edition. Tizard is a former California crime reporter who emigrated to Bohemia in 1994 in pursuit of novel characters and documentary ideas. A former managing editor of *The Prague Post* and a correspondent for *Variety, Time Out, The Guardian,* and *Global Post,* he is currently developing film projects that explore health, environmental, and geopolitical issues for AskFilm.

Charting Your Trip

The Czech Republic—less than 20 years old—combines the fairy-tale world of Old Europe with a palpable sense of history in the making, mixing modernity and tradition in uniquely Bohemian ways. With playwright Václav Havel as a founder of the Velvet Revolution, it's fitting that in Prague you can wander cobblestones in the shadow of Gothic spires en route to an international bookstore's poetry slam.

Getting Around

Maneuvering around Prague is a snap, thanks to the clean, fast, and cheap public transit system. Riding the metro and trams with the locals is both safe and efficient. The No. 22 tram steals the show with a grand tour of the heart of historic Prague, including New Town, the border of Old Town, the Vltava riverfront, Lesser Town, and Prague Castle. Be forewarned that when the metro closes at midnight, you risk getting stuck on overcrowded night trams full of raucous drinking parties.

Reputable taxi companies such as **AAA** *(tel 14014, www.aaaradiotaxi.cz)* or **City Taxi** *(tel 257 257 257, www.citytaxi.cz)* charge 28 crowns ($1.50) per kilometer, are a handy option if your destination is a bit farther out—or if one of Prague's unpredictable cold or wet fronts has suddenly moved in. Just note that if you're bound for Old Town, the Lesser Quarter, or the Castle district during rush hour, a tram may be faster and cheaper.

Outside the city, popular destinations such as those listed below are all served by trains and the quicker, more comfortable bus services—a hit new one is **Student Agency** (see p. 294), which is by no means just for students.

If you're going a bit more off the beaten path, driving is often the best way. While rental rates are competitive, especially with a Czech company such as **Alimex** *(www.alimex.cz)*, fuel prices are higher than in the United States and traffic has become as bad as in any Western country in recent years—perhaps worse. As in the rest of Europe, you also share narrow roads with slow-moving trucks and sometimes aggressive passenger cars weaving between lanes. This, combined with confusing destination signs and entrance and exit ramps in various forms, does not make for relaxing motoring and can seriously add time to what should be a two- or three-hour drive.

Astronomical Clock, Old Town Square

Trains provide a more scenic and calming experience, but often involve at least one change; timetables and platform markings can also be confusing, even for Czechs. (See p. 295 for information on Prague train stations.) Helpful websites such as *www.idos.cz* clearly show the bus and train schedules and transfers but offer scant English. Thus, it's best to have your route well planned in advance; you also may want to show it to your hotel clerk to be sure the departure times haven't changed due to some local bank holiday.

Prague

The Czech capital, with its ancient heart of Old Town and vibrant and evolving arts, dining, and nightlife scenes, has plenty to keep a visitor interested for a week. Its main sights are within walkable distance—one of Prague's many charms.

Prague's center is divided into five parts, divided by the River Vltava and surrounded by hills. A first-time visitor should start at **Prague Castle,** the seat of Czech culture for the last millennium, and consider spending the morning touring its several galleries, chapels, palaces, and royal halls. It stands atop the **Castle District,** known in Czech as Hradčany, which overlooks the city's left bank. From here, a walk downhill to the east and south delivers you to the **Lesser Quarter,** a charming warren of storied palaces, embassies, cafés, and gardens (some of the best are walled, so don't miss the gates). Across the Charles Bridge to the east lies **Old Town,** home to the city's other main sights and attractions, including the Astronomical Clock on **Old Town Square,** and, within the micro-district of **Josefov,** the Old Jewish Cemetery and Jewish Museum buildings, a must-see.

To the south of Old Town lies **New Town,** intersected by bustling **Wenceslas Square,** where modern, commercial Prague is all too evident—and where Communism was brought down in 1989. To the north of Old Town across the Vltava is the up-and-coming **Holešovice** district, home to the National Gallery's modern art collection, the

---

NOT TO BE MISSED:

Viewing Prague Castle's most modern exhibit, The Story of Prague Castle **70**

The unique architecture of the capital **94–97**

Visiting Prague's Old Jewish Cemetery and the Jewish Museum's collection of synagogues **102–105**

The palace rooms in the Rožmburk castle in Český Krumlov **167**

A tour of the historic Pilsner Urquell brewery in Plzeň, West Bohemia **187**

Visiting a *skansen,* or historic peasant village, in Bohemia or Moravia **282–283**

Tasting Moravia's wine **268–269**

Visitor Information

Prague Information Service
www.prague-info.cz, **tel 221 714 444**
Three main visitor centers:
- Starotaroměstská radnice (Old Town Hall)
- Na Príkope 20
- Hlavní nádraží (Main railway station)

Czech Tourism
www.czechtourism.com
United States: 1109 Madison Avenue, New York, NY; tel 212 288 0830
Canada: 12 Bloor Street West, Toronto, Ontario; tel 416 363 9928
Great Britain: 13 Harley St. London, UK; tel 207 631 04 27

Tourist Safety

Prague is, by and large, a remarkably safe city, where people feel comfortable walking at just about any hour, even on its sometimes dimly lit streets. As in any touristed destination, pickpockets target areas where tourist congregate, so be mindful and don't keep valuables in an accessible place. Most accommodations above the level of hostel have room safes. In the event of trouble, local police can be reached by dialing 112 and are required to bring in a translator if needed—but most robbery victims find they don't help much and almost never recover stolen goods.

trade fairgrounds, and rambling parks. East of Old Town, the districts of **Vinohrady** and **Žižkov** are lined with 18th- and 19th- century apartment houses and a thriving club and dining scene.

The city has plenty to occupy a visitor for four or five days, including dozens of museums of all kinds and several theaters and opera houses, where you can experience the spectacle that has run in the Czech blood for centuries: *divadlo* (or theater to Westerners).

If you're in town for a week, visit some of the country's smaller towns as day trips or overnights, such as the characterful former silver mining boomtown **Kutná Hora,** situated a half-hour's drive east of Prague. The lovely spa towns of **Karlovy Vary** and **Marianské Lázne** hold appeal two hours west of Prague, while the hilltop castle town of **Cesky Krumlov,** three hours by bus to the south, is worth the trek for its quaint storybook nature.

Beyond Prague

If you have two weeks, consider spending one driving through the country to take in the slower pace and friendlier faces of life outside Prague. You'll have the chance to step back centuries in former medieval fortress towns such as you'll find in the pristine, forested **Šumava** mountains, located a two-hour drive south and west of Prague along the Austrian and German borders. The region also features peat bogs where Czech fishermen still haul in massive carp catches for winter holidays, in addition to protected national parks.

The spa towns of **West Bohemia,** such as **Karlovy Vary,** 80 miles (130 km) west of Prague, also make for a memorable experience, especially when enjoying the town's promenades between visits to thermal baths. This region is also where the historic city

How to Call Home

Phone booths have become rare in Prague, as most people own more than one mobile phone. A cellular phone call is bound to be cheaper than a hotel call. For cheaper local calls, buy a sim card and credits in a phone shop (T-Mobile and Verizon shops are common in the city center) if your phone is unblocked, meaning it can work on the local network. Be sure to arrange for roaming with your provider before you

leave home if you're willing to pay the extra rates for the convenience. Many travelers also set up their cell phones to work with Skype (*www.skype.com*) so they can call home at little or no cost. Whatever phone you call from, dial the country code first (1 for the United States), followed by area code and local number. Most areas of the Czech Republic have a strong mobile phone signal nowadays.

Strolling past brightly painted shops on Prague Castle's Golden Lane

of **Plzeň** sits, appreciated for its lovely architecture, famous old breweries, and memorials to Patton's Third Army, which liberated this area in World War II.

A drive two-and-a-half-hours north of the capital will deliver you to the country's favorite winter holiday grounds, the **Krkonoše** mountains, where ski resorts offer attractive deals and local character. The **Český Raj** region, just to the east, rewards visitors in warmer months with lakes, forest hikes, and dramatic castles jutting from rocky outcrops.

The Czech Republic's eastern province, **Moravia,** has the cultured capital of **Brno,** two hours southeast of Prague, complete with stunning churches, palaces, crypts, and a thriving arts scene. This region also features the forested **Jeseníky** mountains to the north—remote but popular with hikers and skiers. The university town of **Olomouc,** an hour farther east, shows off Communist-era civic pride on its main square, while, in the southeast of the Czech Republic, some five hours' drive from Prague, lies the former shoe boom town of **Zlín,** where Utopia-minded industrialist Tomas Bat'a created a modernist marvel for his workers.

Rural Moravia has no shortage of natural landscapes and enchanting characters, especially around the wine-producing centers near the Austrian border to the south such as **Mikulov, Znojmo,** and **Pavlov,** where the earliest known fired ceramic figurines have been found. ∎

Tipping Etiquette

The days of simply rounding up to the nearest 10 Czech crowns are over, at least in modern Prague restaurants, where service has improved over the years—but so has the expectation of receiving a 10–15 percent tip. Rather than leaving money on the table, at bill time state the amount you'd like to pay, factoring in the tip. If credit cards are taken, most servers still prefer a tip in cash. At cheaper pubs, servers still don't expect tips to factor into their salary in a major way, so rounding up a few crowns is fine.

Tour guides often get an optional small tip at the end of the journey— 50 crowns will usually do fine.

Only at upper-end places do hotel staff expect tips; again, 50 crowns is plenty unless it's the lap of luxury.

History & Culture

An irreverent statue of St. Wenceslas mimics the more traditional one in Prague's Wenceslas Square.
Opposite: Local women celebrate the Festival of St. Wenceslas in Southern Moravia.

Prague & the Czech Republic Today

At Europe's heart, where diverse cultures have collided for centuries, the City of a Thousand Spires has endured dynastic, religious, political, and racial conflict. The fairy-tale city has collected artistic styles from far and wide, so visitors may sip beer in a Romanesque cellar, gaze at baroque and Gothic church spires, admire grand baroque and rococo palaces, and view art nouveau and cubist architecture.

The "New" Czech Republic

Bohemia and Moravia have been through so many transformations over the past century that their inhabitants could be forgiven for feeling perplexed about their

Venerable bridges and spires provide a graceful backdrop for Prague at twilight.

identity. More than two decades have passed since the fall of communism kicked off a new era. Now firmly ensconced within democratic Europe, the country is still weighed down to some extent by the consequences of more than four decades under a totalitarian regime. Essentially Slav in language and culture, its gaze is nonetheless set firmly westward, and the Czechs have enjoyed European Union membership since 2004. Despite the country's newly regained independence, there is a bit of unease among the Czechs, some of whom see their republic as freshly colonized by external investors on the one hand and by criminal fraternities on the other.

Amid all the trappings of progress ... the Czech Republic has not abandoned its traditions.

The Czech Republic has adapted swiftly to its liberation from Communist rule in 1989. Yet that adaptation has been uneven, and any visitor is bound to notice the discrepancies. Cities such as Prague and Brno have become dynamic business centers, with bright new office buildings, hotels, and supermarkets. The Trabants and Ladas of old, consigned

to the country lanes, have been replaced by new-model Škodas (built by Volkswagen) and Audis. Czechs who have invested wisely or benefited from the burgeoning tourist industry or latched on to the right high-tech industry at the right moment have done very well for themselves. Foreign investment, most notably from Germany and Austria, has focused on the cities, where high-tech industries are sprouting, and a sophisticated cultural and gastronomic way of life thrive.

Prague in particular has become a truly cosmopolitan city once again. A large expatriate community, drawn by both business and professional opportunities and by a low cost of living, has enlivened the city. There are Internet cafés, bagel emporia, restaurants offering eclectic cuisines, foreign language bookshops, and all the other support services that help prop up an international population while also offering new prospects to the indigenous population.

Traditions

Amid all the trappings of progress, though, the Czech Republic has not abandoned its traditions. The quality of its glassware and semiprecious jewelry, especially that with garnets, has been lauded for centuries. You can still find beautiful handcrafted

Visitors walking along Prague's Charles Bridge admire its statuary and enjoy the street musicians.

pieces as well as a huge range of glassware. You can buy such items in major towns throughout the country, but be sure to shop around, as quality and prices may vary greatly.

Western Bohemia is rich in spa towns, whose health resorts are beloved by overindulged Europeans. Originally founded to offer treatments involving bathing in or drinking the supposedly healthful mineral waters bubbling from springs, they quickly became social centers, offering smart hotels with casinos, restaurants, coffeehouses, and tea shops. The two biggest ones in the Czech Republic are Karlovy Vary and Mariánské Lázně, which used to be better known by their German names of Karlsbad and Marienbad. Although the spas became run-down during the Communist era, they since have been revived and restored and now are extremely popular with visitors, some of whom come for treatments, though many come as tourists to enjoy the scenery and walks, the coffeehouses and restaurants.

In the past it was not easy to get to know the locals. During Communist rule, contacts with foreign visitors were more or less forbidden, so attempts at conversation often led nowhere. Even today, the older generation of Czechs can seem reserved to visitors, but you'll find the younger generation far more open and inviting. In the past German was often the second language, but today many people are eager to study English and welcome an opportunity to practice their skills.

The Countryside

While Prague is the Czech Republic's heartbeat, the countryside possesses abundant charms of its own. Vast tracts of land remain relatively undeveloped, places that are rich in natural beauty and cultural interest as well.

Nearly every town of any size in the Czech Republic has something to offer the visitor. Most are laid out with a large central square, often used as a marketplace, overlooked by the main church and the often brightly decorated town hall. Away from the main square, lanes lead to other churches and, often, to a castle that once guarded the valleys and the vast trade routes.

The Czech Republic is very conscious of its rich cultural heritage. Almost all of its fortresses, castles, and country mansions are open to the public and contain historical exhibits and, sometimes, art collections as well. Even a small town may have a little museum full of local—sometimes dusty—artifacts.

The landscape is varied. In the north, mountains rise above the landscape, covered in pretty woods and spangled with resorts beloved by hikers and skiers, depending on the season. In the southern parts of Bohemia and Moravia, the terrain is gentler: There are hilly regions, but also flatter areas dotted with lakes that have for centuries been used to farm fish. Here, too, you'll find the country's best vineyards.

The Bohemian countryside in particular is a hiker's paradise. National parks and nature reserves, such as the Český ráj and the Šumava mountains, are crisscrossed by trails. These parks are filled with rare and bizarre geological formations, ruined castles, fast-moving rivers, deep gorges, and stands of primeval forest. The Czechs are enthusiastic when it comes to outdoor recreation, so activities such as mountain biking, hiking, and canoeing are all readily available. In winter, the focus turns to skiing, skating, and snowboarding. ∎

City of Views

Prague has been called City of a Thousand Spires, and with that comes a thousand different views. Here are some of the best:

St. Vitus's Cathedral: Climb the tower's 287 stairs for rooftop views of the city (Castle District, see pp. 64–64; free).

Petřín Hill Observation Tower: On a clear day, look for the republic's highest peak, Snezka, from atop this Eiffel Tower lookalike (Lesser Town, see p. 86; $$).

Lesser Town Tower Bridge: More fantastic views of the Charles Bridge and river, from the west side (Lesser Town; $).

St. Nicholas Church: From the tower await 360-degree views of Lesser Town, the river, and Old Town beyond (Lesser Town, see p. 93; $).

Old Town Bridge Tower: On the east end of Charles Bridge, take in the heart of Prague, and, of course, the antlike walkers on the bridge (Old Town, see p. 100; $).

Old Town Hall Tower: Fabulous views of Old Town and Old Town Square. A trumpeter here blows his horn on the hour after the Astrological Clock has performed (Old Town, see pp. 92–93; $).

Powder Gate: Views of Old Town (New Town, see pp. 119–120; $).

Jindřišská Tower: From the 10th floor, views of Wenceslas Square and beyond; a restaurant on the 7th to 9th floors has good views, too (New Town; $).

Astronomical Tower at the Klementinum: 360-degree views of Prague (see pp. 94–95; $$$).

Food & Drink

Czechs have hearty appetites. Rich soups, large portions of meat and dumplings, and heavy desserts are mainstays of their diet, all washed down with what many consider to be the world's best beer. Nourishing and full-flavored, Czech cuisine is heavily meat based, with beef and, above all, pork taking center stage.

Prague's oldest and largest pub, U Fleků boasts seating for 1,200 in its many rooms.

Polévky (soups)—hearty and satisfying—can always be recommended, especially at lunchtime. Smoked meat, such as *uzený* (pork) and *šunka* (boiled Prague ham), or *vejce* (eggs) are often used as appetizers. The principal types of fish *(ryby)* are *pstruh* (trout) and *kapr* (carp), which can be excellent—it is advisable to order them only in specialist restaurants or at lakeside inns, where they are likely to be fresh.

Main courses are usually served with *knedlíky* (dumplings) or some kind of filling potato dish. Dumplings are much maligned by those who find them dull and heavy on the stomach. Made from flour, bread, or potatoes, they are served in slices hacked off a large dumpling roll. Their main function is to mop up the rich sauces ladled over most dishes, and this they do admirably.

Svíčková, a Bohemian specialty, consists of thin slices of beef served with dumplings to absorb an abundant white creamy sauce. In winter look for game dishes such as *husa* (goose) and *bažant* (pheasant). When in doubt, choose *vepřové* (pork), which is usually reliable; *vepřový řízek* (schnitzel) is universally available. *Kuře* (chicken) and *kachna* (duck) are also popular meats.

Traditionally, Czechs didn't bother too much about vegetables, except for *zelí* (cabbage) and *žampiony* (mushrooms). Main courses are usually garnished with *obloha*, a small pile of pickled cabbage, carrot, beets, and lettuce.

For vegetarians, a useful, if somewhat stodgy, standby is *smažený sýr* (fried cheese). In recent years, pizza parlors and vegetarian restaurants have made life a little easier for those who prefer a meat-free diet.

In cities many places feature international menus, though the dishes may not be very accomplished. (These establishments may also offer vegetarian options.) Of course, in Prague and Brno you will find sophisticated restaurants with a standard of cooking as high as most European cities, with prices to match.

Desserts

Desserts tend to be filling but often lack variety. *Palačinky* (pancakes) are a good bet. They are usually filled with chocolate sauce, ice cream, or fruit, then topped with whipped cream. *Kompot* (stewed fruits) can be good, too, and fruit dumplings, usually stuffed with plums, apricots, strawberries, or blueberries, are delicious if filling. *Sýr* (cheese) will seem tasteless to visitors more used to French or Italian varieties. The best places to satisfy a sweet tooth are streetside stands, which sell *zmrzlina* (ice cream), or a *cukrárna*, the Czech equivalent of the German or Austrian *konditorei*, where you can usually find excellent *presso* (espresso) and delicious pastries and cakes.

Drink

The best drink to accompany rich Czech food is undoubtedly *pivo* (beer; see pp. 186–187). Bohemia has been famous since medieval times for the quality of its hops, and almost every town in the republic has its own brewery. The local brew is usually well worth trying; otherwise, stick to major brands, such as Budvar, Pilsner, and Staropramen.

Wine (see pp. 268–269) can be very good. Only in wine regions and in top restaurants, however, will you be offered any information about what is poured in your glass other than the variety of grape. Opinions are mixed on *Becherovka*, a liqueur made from a secret formula blending 20 different herbs. Fruit brandies such as *slivovice* (plum) can be delicious.

Markets

During times of shortages under Communism, Czechs got by quite well with supplements of carrots, cabbage, beets, squash, fruit, and walnuts from their own gardens. Despite an ongoing crisis for some sectors of agriculture, which have not been able to compete with Western European farms (often better subsidized ones), local open-air markets, even in downtown Prague, are a mainstay for those seeking freshness at affordable prices. Although Prague's Havelská street market in Old Town tends to fill its stalls with tourist-targeted wares, such as puppets, handmade jewelry, and questionable paintings in the afternoons, the early risers will find it full of fresh, nutritious produce, just as it has been for centuries.

Counterparts to this market exist in just about every small town and village. In addition, at Christmas and Easter central squares are taken over by holiday markets filled with sellers of homemade candles, honey, baked goods, woolens, and ceramics.

Land & Landscape

The Czech landscape is a gentle one for the most part—rolling hills, often extensive forested plains, with, on the northern borders, some fairly serious mountains. The landlocked Czech Republic encompasses an area of 30,449 square miles (78,703 sq km) and straddles central Europe, poking deep into Germany to the west and meeting Slovakia to the east.

The Czech Republic also shares borders with Austria and Poland. The Carpathian Mountains rise to the north and east of the country. The development of coal mines, steelworks, and other heavy industries has led to conurbations in various parts of the republic, but most notably along the northern border with Poland and Germany. The population is dispersed, partly as a consequence of the placing of new industries and workshops throughout the former Czechoslovakia during the Communist years, in effect transforming hitherto rural areas into industrial centers. Prague is easily the largest city, with a population of 1.2 million, followed by Brno in Moravia.

Rivers

The Vltava is the best known of Bohemia's rivers and, thanks to its musical and artistic associations, it has a special place in the hearts of the people. The region's main river, the Labe (better known in Germany as the Elbe), has its source in the Krkonoše (Giant Mountains), then flows south, west, and north through Bohemia. Many important towns were founded on its banks, and close to the German

View from the ruins of Trosky Castle to the verdant green fields of Northern Bohemia

Deforestation Debate

Under the surface of the outwardly quiet forests of South Bohemia, a battle is raging over sustainability and the long-term health of the region's natural bounty. An infestation of European spruce bark beetle (Ips typographus) in Šumava National Park has sparked debate for years on how—or whether—to respond. One camp has argued that the beetles, if left alone, will eat themselves out of house and home while the forest will develop natural resistance, eventually causing the tree parasites to crash.

Another camp, including local officials who argue for cutting down and removing infested trees, has been accused

of secretly profiting from sales of the resulting lumber. The bark beetles don't damage the timber itself and some 5,000 acres (2,000 ha) of forest have already been clear-cut—with no significant effect on the beetle population.

Yet one local governor recently urged that a state of emergency be declared, calling the situation "a bark beetle pandemic that requires a prompt action."

The Czech Ministry of the Environment and the directors of Šumava National Park reject any such emergency. At stake is the largest natural park in the Czech Republic—one that is 80 percent covered with trees.

border inland ports such as Ústí nad Labem and Děčín edge its shores. From here barges and boats carry cargo downriver through Germany toward the port of Hamburg on the North Sea.

The Vltava begins in the Šumava mountains of southern Bohemia. Many picturesque castles are perched above its banks as it winds northward toward Prague, but the Vltava Valley is not especially fertile. Stretches of the river have been dammed and converted into artificial lakes for recreational purposes. These include the Lipno and, closer to Prague, Slapy reservoirs. From the capital, the Vltava continues to flow north until it joins the Labe at Mělník. The rivers Jizera and Ohře are tributaries of the mighty Labe, and the Sázava, which winds through castle-strewn country southeast of Prague, is a tributary of the Vltava. Another important river, the Morava, a tributary of the Danube to the south, rises in the Jizera mountains to flow south through Olomouc and eastern Moravia.

The republic is richly supplied with medicinal springs credited with great benefits to health. Some of these springs were prized by the Celtic tribes that once inhabited the region, but they were developed commercially only in the 18th and 19th centuries. This led to the creation of many spas, notably Karlovy Vary and Mariánské Lázně, which became fashionable social and medical centers.

Mountains & Karst

Much of Bohemia's wealth derived from the extraction of minerals from the Krušné hory (Ore Mountains), which straddle the German border northwest of Prague. The area was settled by Saxon miners in medieval times, but after a few centuries the mines were exhausted. Uranium was once mined at Jáchymov, which is now better known for its radioactive medicinal springs.

The other important mountain range within Bohemia is the Krkonoše (Giant Mountains), which is shared with Poland along the border northeast of Prague. These mountains form a region of alpine pastures and extensive forests, and industrial towns were established lower in the glacial valleys that descend toward the south. The less dramatic Jizerské hory (Jizera Mountains) adjoin the Krkonoše to the west; to the southeast, within Moravia, the Jizera range reaches 4,892 feet (1,491 m).

Many Bohemian hills feature strange rock formations, including freestanding pillars, labyrinths, and natural arches.

Riding above the Moravian-Silesian Beskids mountains at the Pustevny Ski Resort

In southern Bohemia, the rolling Šumava (Bohemian Forest) encompasses a large nature reserve of great beauty. Many Bohemian hills feature strange rock formations, including freestanding pillars, labyrinths, and natural arches. These are found in the crag country, known as the Adršpach–Teplice rocks, and in the Český ráj (Bohemian Paradise), which is famous for its "rock towns," a series of bizarre formations created principally by erosion.

Within Moravia, the most fascinating geologic feature is undoubtedly the Moravský kras (Moravian Karst; see pp. 265–266), a Devonian limestone region of ravines and gullies northeast of Brno. It is celebrated for its caves, chasms, grottoes, and underground rivers, some of which have only recently been explored for the first time. ■

History of Prague & the Czech Republic

The Czech Republic's early history is exceedingly complicated. Mammoth hunters inhabited the region in Paleolithic times. Bronze Age burial sites have revealed that Celtic peoples settled the more fertile river valleys. One such tribe, the Boii, arrived about 400 B.C. from present-day Germany and gave its name to Bohemia.

Early History

Around 100 B.C., the Celts were driven out by German tribes, notably the Marcomanni, who also drove the Romans away many years later. Germanic tribes held sway over the area for centuries, but by the sixth century A.D., Slav tribes began to invade

Prague in 1750—already centuries old—was a flourishing capital city.

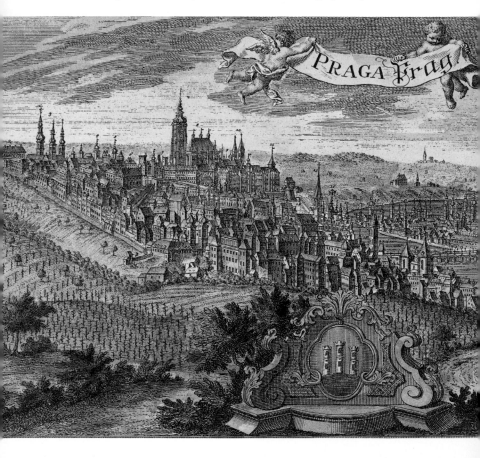

the region that is now the Czech Republic. Toward the century's end, the Slavs were in effective control of Bohemia and Moravia. One of these tribes was the Czechs, named after their legendary ancestor Čech. The Slavs were dominated by the Avars, an Asiatic people who controlled what is now Hungary and required tribute from their neighbors. At the end of the eighth and beginning of the ninth centuries, Charlemagne, the first Holy Roman Emperor, made inroads into Bohemia, even converting a few nobles to Christianity; his forces helped expel the Avars from the region.

In 846 Mojmír was succeeded by his nephew Rastislav, who converted to Christianity.

At about the same time, Mojmír I established what later became known as the Great Moravian Empire, which lived up to its grandiose name by pushing east and conquering parts of Slovakia and Hungary. (Excavations from this time can be visited at Uherské Hradiště in southern Moravia; see p. 274.)

In 846 Mojmír was succeeded by his nephew Rastislav, who converted to Christianity. He requested the Byzantine emperor Michael III to authorize a religious mission to Moravia. Accordingly, the emperor dispatched two Greek brothers, Cyril and Methodius, to Moravia in 863. Here they converted some of the populace, although pagan elements remained for centuries, and Methodius became the first archbishop of Greater Moravia. The Great Moravian Empire was short-lived. Rastislav was deposed by his pro-Germanic nephew Svatopluk in 870, and in 907 Moravian troops were overcome by the Magyar tribes, who had settled in what is present-day Hungary.

The Přemyslid Dynasty

Meanwhile, Bohemia, with its forests and pastures and kinder climate, was prospering. According to legend, Prague was founded in the early ninth century, when Princess Libuše stood at Vyšehrad and foresaw the greatness of the city that would arise here. She married a plowman named Přemysl, heralding the beginning of the Přemyslid dynasty. Two Slav fortresses were built on either side of the River Vltava, at Vyšehrad and Hradčany. Prague was the Přemyslid capital, and its castle became the seat of a bishopric in 973. Bohemia's first monastery was founded nearby at Břevnov in 993. The city expanded swiftly into

EXPERIENCE: Celtic Roots

The first recorded settlers in what is now known as Bohemia were members of the Celtic tribe called the Boii, from which the word Bohemia is derived. Iron Age remains of their oppidium, or fortified settlement, south of the city of Pardubice, have been studied for decades but little is really known about the lives of its residents.

Several sites have helped fire a Czech passion for all things Celtic (Highland games are still played regularly in some towns). Above the hamlet of Nasavrky, an organization also called **Boii** *(tel 469 677 566)* operates a tour, "The CelticTrail to

Železné hory." Visitors walk to the ancient settlement, highlighted by the oppidium in Hradiště. The hike passes through the forested hills of a protected area of these eastern Bohemian mountains.

The route offers panoramic views of the Krkonoše, Orlické hory (Eagle Mountains), the massive Kralický Sněžník, and the Jizera mountains. The ruins lie on an outcropping above the Chrudimka River, whose steep slopes protected it. The site is believed to have been a link in a chain of settlements in central Bohemia and their counterparts in Moravia.

what is now Old Town (Staré Město), and Vyšehrad's importance faded in favor of the Hradčany area surrounding Prague Castle.

The Přemyslid dynasty had a tense relationship with the German rulers who held sway over much of central Europe. Prince Václav I was pro-German, but he paid for his alliance with his life when he was murdered in 935 by his brother Boleslav I. Much revered, Václav I was the "Good King Wenceslas" known to every carol singer; he was also declared the patron saint of Bohemia. Vratislav II became the first Bohemian king in 1085 and was crowned with the blessing of the German Holy Roman Emperor Henry IV. Henceforth, Bohemia was part of the Holy Roman Empire, a vast confederation of European nations.

Přemysl Otakar I (r. 1197–1230) invited German settlers, principally from Saxony, to Bohemia and Moravia to establish towns that soon became important mining or trading centers. Art and architecture flourished under the patronage of a wealthy merchant class.

Přemysl Otakar II (r. 1253–1278), backed by the wealth derived from mining, extended the Bohemian domains from Silesia to Austria, what is today Slovenia, and the shores of the Adriatic. He created the Little Quarter (Malá Strana) on the slopes beneath Prague Castle in 1257. Unfortunately, the German-based Habsburg dynasty was consolidating its power, and Otakar was unable to prevent encroachment. At the Battle of Moravské pole (Moravian Field) in 1278, Otakar was killed. He was succeeded by his son Václav II (r. 1283–1305), who conquered parts of Poland. The Přemyslid dynasty came to a sudden end in 1306, when Václav III (r. 1305–1306) made an abortive attempt to seize the crown of Poland and was murdered.

Charles IV

There followed a period of chaos and hostility between Czechs and Germans. In 1311 an arranged marriage between John of Luxembourg (r. 1310–1346), the son of the Holy Roman Emperor, and Václav II's daughter Eliška brought a measure of stability, and John reigned until his death in battle. John was succeeded by Charles IV (r. 1346–1378), who was subsequently elected Holy Roman Emperor. Charles made Bohemia a mighty European power and developed Prague into a major capital city.

Few rulers have left so lasting a mark on a single city as Charles IV did on Prague. Born in the city on May 14, 1316, he was educated at the court of France and the University of Paris, which may account for his cosmopolitan outlook. Although christened Václav, he changed his name to Charles after his uncle, Charles IV of France. Intelligent and competent, Charles was not on good terms with his father, King John of Luxembourg. As a result, he spent part of his youth in Italy until he was appointed governor of Moravia in 1334 and co-governor of Bohemia seven years later in 1341.

At the young age of 13, Charles married the sister of the future King Philippe VI of France, Blanche of Valois, but three more wives were to follow. He became king of Bohemia in 1346, and was elected Holy Roman Emperor in 1355. This, and his four dynastic marriages, helped him to consolidate his domains, adding parts of modern-day Germany and Poland. Legal and constitutional reforms made Bohemia one of the most advanced medieval states in Europe. Despite his international vision and aspirations, Charles did not neglect his capital, and Prague soon became the intellectual and cultural center of his empire. On his initiative St. Vitus's Cathedral (Chrám sv. Víta) and Charles Bridge (Karlův most) were constructed, and the castle, which had been severely damaged by fire in 1304, was renovated. In 1348 Charles IV added a fourth district to the city, the carefully planned New Town (Nové Město). Such remarkable churches as the Karlov and St. Mary of the Snows (Kostel Panny Maria Sněžná) were begun at his command, as was the glittering castle at Karlštejn, outside Prague. The Vltava and Labe Rivers were cleared to make them fully navigable, and vineyards were established on the outskirts of the city.

Charles won the support of Pope Clement VI, his former tutor in Paris, to elevate Prague from a bishopric to an archbishopric in 1344, which in effect put the Bohemian church under his control. Charles also founded Prague University, the first in central Europe. Scholars and artists from Germany, France, Italy, and elsewhere were invited to Prague and contributed to its cultural splendor.

Charles elevated Bohemia to one of the most sophisticated of European states, but the country's flourishing proved short-lived. After his death from pneumonia on November 29, 1378, the domains were divided among his three sons, and Bohemia's most glorious period was over. Charles's true memorial, however, is Prague. Despite all later additions and changes, the city retains the major monuments and urban structure he imposed on it.

The dissolute Václav IV (r. 1378–1419) succeeded Charles. Václav unwittingly created a martyr by having a priest, John of Nepomuk, murdered for refusing to reveal a secret told to him in the confessional. John was canonized in

Emperor Charles IV transformed medieval Prague into one of Europe's most important cities.

1729; statues of the saint appear all over Bohemia. Václav enjoyed a long reign, but eventually the nobility wearied of him, and he was deposed.

The Hussites

By the time of Václav's departure resentment had grown about Church's abuses. This led to the rise of the reformist Hussite movement: Influenced by the English preacher John Wycliffe, it had a political as well as religious agenda, seeking to diminish the Catholic nobility's control over the country. The movement was named after the preacher and university rector Jan Hus (ca 1372–1415). He was excommunicated in 1410 and expelled from the university with his followers a year later. In 1414 he was summoned to the Council of Constance to defend his heretical views, but although assured of safe conduct, he was arrested en route, tried for heresy, condemned, and burned at the stake.

Václav IV's anti-Hussite line led to the First Defenestration in 1419, when populist preacher Jan Želivský marched on the New Town Hall. There Želivský's followers threw Catholic officials to their deaths from the windows, starting a Prague tradition in dealing with one's opponents. Václav himself died two weeks later and chaos broke out. His brother Sigismund had himself crowned in 1420, but few accepted his legitimacy. Hussite warrior Jan Žižka took up arms against the German and Catholic forces, and his troops conducted a violent anticlerical campaign across the length and breadth of the land.

By 1423 the Hussites had split into two factions: the moderate Utraquists and the more radical Taborites, who were already warring among themselves. Žižka led the Taborites to victory over the Utraquists twice in 1423 and again in 1424. He subdued them, but after his death from the plague in 1424 the divisions led to further fighting. A settlement was finally negotiated by the Catholic Church with the Utraquists in 1433 at Basel in Switzerland, but the rebellious Taborites fought on for a year until they were soundly defeated by the Utraquists at Lipany, east of Prague. The Hussite wars were finally over, but the poor, who had been championed by the Taborites, remained destitute and the radicals' ideals remained unrealized. Nonetheless the Hussites, backed by the lesser nobility and the burghers, had won considerable gains, although the aristocratic landowners, some of whom were also Hussites, remained in overall control.

Castle Lore

The Czech Republic is, despite a passion for modernity, a land of castles. Invariably, these edifices have legends of dark deeds—and usually ghosts. A favorite is the Bilá Paní, or White Lady tale, in which the soul of a long-suffering woman, cruelly treated during her life, lives on, finally free to spread kindness. Dozens of castles, including Charles IV's summer retreat, Karlštejn, claim a lady in white (and variations on the tale occur throughout Europe and New England). The best known is Perchta of Rožmberk castle, unhappily married off by a tyrannical father, as documented in 32 surviving letters in her hand. Křivoklát castle, where Emperor Rudolf II sent would-be alchemist Edward Kelley after he failed to deliver the gold, also has colorful tales attached to it.

Utraquists & Jagiellons

The Utraquists took over, led by Jiříz Poděbřad (George of Poděbrady; r. 1458–1471); he was elected to the throne in 1458 after many years as regent to the heir to the Bohemian throne, Ladislav. The rise to power of this gifted and tolerant ruler proved unacceptable to the pope, who persuaded the Hungarian king and ruler of Moravia, Matthias Corvinus, to attack Bohemia. George averted this potential threat, but died in 1471. Numerous claimants to the Bohemian throne pressed their case. The successful candidate, elected king by the Bohemian Estates (in effect the Czech parliament), was Prince Vladislav Jagiellon (Vladislav II; r. 1471–1516), the son of King Casimir IV of Poland and descended on his maternal side from the Přemyslid dynasty.

He immediately found himself engaged in a power struggle with Matthias Corvinus. In 1490 Matthias died, and Vladislav inherited the crown of Hungary. The following year the Catholic Vladislav, whose daughter Anne had married into the Habsburg family, agreed that the succession to Bohemia and Hungary would pass to the Austrian rulers. There was still no stability in the kingdom: Religious strife between Hussite reformers and traditional Catholics continued unabated, if less bloodily than before. The Czech lands, already enfeebled by decades of war, stagnated under the rule of Vladislav and his son Ludvík.

The Habsburgs

After the death of the childless Ludvík in 1526, his brother-in-law Ferdinand of Habsburg claimed the throne of Bohemia. Although Ferdinand (r. 1526–1564) was no more Czech than the Jagiellons had been, he was a firm ruler, with the powerful backing of his brother Emperor Charles V. When Ferdinand invited the Jesuits to Bohemia in 1556, he initiated a new era of Catholic power, but did his best not to alienate the Protestants, who then constituted 85 percent of the population. Ferdinand was succeeded in 1564 by the toler-ant Maximilian II (r. 1564–1576), who accepted the Bohemian Confession of 1575, which guar-anteed religious freedom—in theory at least.

Refusing to recant his radical views, theologian Jan Hus was led to the Catholic stronghold of Constance in 1415 and burned alive.

In 1576 Rudolf II (r. 1576–1611) came to the throne and made Prague his principal resi-dence. Following his election as Holy Roman Emperor, Prague became an imperial capital and a center of intellectual life and culture. Scientists such as Danish astronomer Tycho Brahe, as well as less reputable alchemists like Edward Kelley, were welcome at his court.

All the while conflict between Catholic and Protestant was growing, as the Catholic establishment consolidated its grip on power. Rudolf himself was more interested in intellectual and mystical matters than affairs of state. Other members of the Habsburg dynasty were well aware of this and were keen to oust him. He tried to shore up his sup-port by wooing the Bohemian nobility. Their price for support was a declaration known as the Letter of Majesty of 1609, which guaranteed religious freedom and imposed limits on his powers as a ruler. As a strategy for survival it didn't work, and in 1611 Rudolf, who was increasingly ill, was forced to abdicate. His brother Matthias (r. 1611–1619) succeeded him.

Emperor Ferdinand ordered the murder of his too-powerful top general, Wallenstein, in Cheb in 1634.

Tension has to be diffused or something snaps. In the case of Bohemia, it snapped. In May 1618, Protestant nobles gathered in Prague to form a Diet (or parliament) to express their views. On May 23, a mob, convinced that the regime was ignoring the Letter of Majesty, threw three court officials from the castle windows (they were unharmed but humiliated), an act commemorated as the Second Defenestration. This proved to be the starting signal for the Thirty Years' War. The Protestant forces took up arms against the Habsburgs and initially scored a number of successes, including the capture of Plzeň.

Matthias died in 1619 and was succeeded by Ferdinand II (r. 1619–1637). He was soon deposed by the Bohemian Estates, who felt entitled to elect Bohemia's king and chose Frederick V, ruler of the Palatinate in Germany, and brother-in-law of the future Charles I of England. Amiable Frederick proved ineffectual, though, against the clever Ferdinand, who persuaded the Catholic Bavarians to work with the Habsburgs. At the Battle of White Mountain on November 8, 1620, the Protestants were routed in hours. Frederick slipped

away and Ferdinand returned to Prague in triumph and resumed control of the Czech lands. He persecuted the Protestant nobility, confiscating their estates and executing their leaders. As the Counter-Reformation strengthened, 30,000 Protestant families fled. Their lands were appropriated by foreign nobles or by Ferdinand's supporters, such as the imperial commander Albrecht z Valdštejn (Wallenstein). Bohemia and Moravia were now, in effect, dependencies of the Habsburg Empire.

Wallenstein

Wallenstein sowed the seeds of his own demise by succeeding so brilliantly as a soldier that he seemed to pose a threat to the emperor. Indeed, for a few decades, a large part of northern Bohemia was run virtually as a separate country under Wallenstein's rule. An aristocrat, he was born in eastern Bohemia in 1583. In 1606 he converted to Catholicism and supported the imperial cause before and during the Battle of White Mountain. Emperor Ferdinand II made Wallenstein a count in 1617 after a successful campaign against the Venetian Republic. Wallenstein prospered, and his wealth grew by marriage to the very rich Isabella von Harrach.

After the Battle of White Mountain, Wallenstein rapidly acquired estates such as Frýdlant and Jičín, many of them expropriated from Protestant noblemen who had backed the wrong side. Before long he owned 24 estates and castles, plus a colossal château in Malá Strana. The grateful emperor made him Duke of Frýdlant in 1625.

Because his estates included mines and other sources of wealth, Wallenstein became ever richer and more powerful. By putting his own troops at the disposal of Ferdinand II as mercenaries, he became indispensable to the emperor and was appointed supreme commander of the imperial forces in 1625. However, political pressure against the ambitious general led to his dismissal in 1630, but two years later he was reappointed. He soon justified the emperor's confidence in him by defeating and slaying King Gustavus Adolphus II of Sweden at the Battle of Lutzen, in November 1632.

The Second Defenestration [mob action against court officials in May 1618] ... proved to be the starting signal for the Thirty Years' War.

Unfortunately for Wallenstein, Emperor Ferdinand felt increasingly threatened by his commander's independence and by his negotiations with the Swedes. Wallenstein had raised his own armies, which served the emperor but also made him uneasy. When Wallenstein demanded that his officers swear an oath of personal loyalty to him, the emperor suspected treachery. On February 22, 1634, Ferdinand denounced Wallenstein as a traitor and ordered him captured dead or alive. Three days later, Wallenstein and some of his generals were assassinated by officers loyal to the emperor in Cheb in western Bohemia. His estates were soon distributed, projects such as the planned university at Jičín never came to pass, and the duchy of Frýdlant was no more. To this day it remains unclear whether Wallenstein's negotiations with the enemy were a sincere attempt to bring peace to the war-wracked Habsburg domains, or whether he really was conspiring against the emperor hoping to enrich himself further and even perhaps seize the Bohemian throne.

Habsburgs Triumphant

The repeated Swedish invasions of Bohemia and Moravia caused tremendous devastation; not even Prague was immune. The Thirty Years' War dragged on, causing unspeakable misery to the civilian population, until in 1648 the Peace of Westphalia was negotiated. Ferdinand died in 1637 and was succeeded by Ferdinand III (r. 1637–1657). Reactionary Habsburg rule was imposed with a vengeance in an unholy alliance between the Counter-Reformation and Germanization. What is more, the peace treaty insisted that Bohemians who had fought on the Swedish side should not be allowed to return to their country. One of those exiled was the leading intellectual and educationalist Jan Komenský (Comenius; 1592–1670), whose name is still revered in the Czech lands today.

The Habsburgs ruled from afar, oppressing the impoverished Czech peasantry with punishing taxation. Outbreaks of plague swept towns already devastated by war, adding to the suffering of the people. It was not until the mid-18th century that a measure of prosperity and economic development began to return to these exhausted and depopulated lands. The Czech language, which had flowered under the Hussites, was in danger of becoming no more than a peasant dialect.

> The Thirty Years' War dragged on, causing unspeakable misery to the civilian population, until in 1648 the Peace of Westphalia was negotiated.

Maria Theresa & Joseph II

Under Empress Maria Theresa (r. 1740–1780) and her son Joseph II (r. 1780–1790), Bohemia and Moravia were divided into two separate provinces that gained in importance after the Habsburgs lost Silesia in 1745. All political control was exercised from Vienna, and Czech national aspirations were ignored or suppressed, although the empress created a royal residence at Prague castle. Mines, glassworks, and other factories were beginning to bring prosperity to Bohemia and Moravia, and the population was increasing steadily. Conflict returned to Bohemia in 1756 when Frederick II of Prussia waged war against Maria Theresa. The Prussian troops reached Prague itself in 1757 but were defeated at the Battle of Kolín.

Emperor Joseph introduced religious tolerance and allowed Czech culture to develop, though he confirmed his Habsburg credentials by making German the official language.

Serfdom was abolished in 1781. A Czech grammar book, compiled by Josef Dobrovský, was published in 1809. Joseph's sensible reforms may have been what kept the Czechs relatively loyal to the Habsburgs and far less troublesome than the more volatile Hungarians.

The Nineteenth Century

Those great upheavals of the early 19th century, the Napoleonic wars, had little impact on Bohemia and Moravia, even though the major Battle of Austerlitz was fought close to Brno. Napoleon inflicted a severe defeat on the combined armies of Russia and Austria. Throughout the 19th century Bohemia and Moravia became increasingly industrialized, especially in the north.

Hrad Kralštejin, built to safeguard the royal treasures, was last restored in the late l800s.

Lip service was paid to national aspirations by the Habsburgs after the revolutionary movements of 1848, but little would change without the Czechs themselves taking the initiative. Compared with the turbulence in Vienna in 1848, which led to the flight of the emperor to Moravia, the Bohemia uprisings were mild and easily repressed, partly due to the lack of common ground between the German and Czech elements in the population. Some German speakers favored merging with German states.

Political assertion, as well as cultural expression, became increasingly divided along linguistic lines, with Czech and Slovak newspapers and theaters coexisting alongside their German and Hungarian counterparts; even Charles University was split in this way in 1882. Composers such as Dvořák and Smetana captured the spirit of Czech culture, especially folk culture, in their music.

An 1880 engraving catches the lively street life in the heart of Prague's Jewish quarter.

Political movements, predominantly liberal as well as nationalistic, made slow progress against the stately inertia of the Habsburgs. The establishment of the dual monarchy of Austria and Hungary in 1867, a concession to the national aspirations of the Magyars, only accelerated the pace of Magyarization in the Slovak provinces. It did not lead to comparable concessions to the Czechs, who felt sidelined by the compact between Austria and Hungary. Czech deputies, representing the region at the assembly in Vienna, were increasingly divided into two factions, of which the more radical were known as the Young Czechs. Compared with the Hungarians, their tangible successes were few; nonetheless, the Czechs benefited from reforms such as universal suffrage, which was granted by the Habsburgs in 1907 (women were not enfranchised until 1919).

End of the Habsburgs

When war broke out in 1914, the Czechs were required to fight alongside their Austrian oppressors, but about 100,000 defected and joined the Czechoslovak Legions on the Eastern Front, in France, and in Italy. Defeat in World War I led to the swift collapse of the Habsburg empire. The architects of the Czechoslovak state were Tomáš Garrigue Masaryk (1850–1937), Edvard Beneš (1884–1948), and Milan Ratislav Štěfánik, who had formed the Czechoslovak National Council in 1917. Masaryk and Beneš later became president and foreign minister, respectively, in the new government established after the Czechoslovak republic was declared on October 28, 1918. The new republic was composed not only of Bohemia, Moravia, and Slovakia, but also Ruthenia. It was a formula that helped to dismember the Austro-Hungarian Empire, and one that led to grave problems later in the century.

The Road to Independence

Tomáš Garrigue Masaryk was born in Hodonín in southern Moravia in 1850; his father was an ill-educated Slovak coachman, his mother a German-Moravian. At first Masaryk seemed destined to be a village craftsman, but his quest for education led

EXPERIENCE: Czech Trains

Rail lines have formed this country's life-lines since the 1880s, when Czech engineers were keen to adopt the latest technology, so it's probably no coincidence that the first Academy Award for a Czech film (in 1968) went to a movie called *Ostře sledované vlaky*, or *Closely Watched Trains*. These days, they're still cheaper, quieter, and cleaner—and often faster—than cars, though their routes are sometimes frustratingly indirect, depending on how popular your destination is.

Most Czechs, perhaps because car ownership is still considered a mark of status,

prefer to drive, but that just means more seats are available for those who prefer to take in the views while relaxing, traffic-free, all the way to their destination.

Czech trains would hardly be called a lap-of-luxury experience (though if you catch the Italian-made Pendolino, you can indeed count on comfort and Wi-Fi). There's a definite charm to the often overheated, sometimes creaking rides, though.

Timetables and destinations are all online at *www.idos.cz* and the ticket clerks at Prague's Hlavní nádraží, or Main Station, are generally helpful and English speaking.

World War II Ghosts

The legacy of World War II still resonates in the Czech Republic, where every year films and books probe difficult questions raised by the trauma. As many were celebrating the first 20 years of freedom in 2009 (the Communist regime itself having been the saviors after World War II and the Soviets' liberation of Prague), many were also thinking of another anniversary: 1939.

By that year, when war was declared, Czechs were under the Nazi occupation depicted in Marek Najbert's 2009 film, *Protektor.* Their nightmare began in 1938, with the Munich conference at which Britain's Prime Minister Neville Chamberlain, along with France's Prime Minister Edouard Daladier, agreed to raise no objection to Germany annexing the northern and western provinces of what was then free Czechoslovakia. *Protektor* examines the slippery moral ground of collaborators whose intentions are to protect those they love. Its stylish and sinister mood of paranoia made it one of the year's strongest premieres—but it was just one of half a dozen recent films to reconsider the role of morality during wartime.

One book that promises to make for another fascinating film is *Le Fantôme de Munich (The Ghost of Munich)* by French author Georges-Marc Benamou, which recounts the notorious 1938 pact itself. The book is being adapted by Václav Havel and is to be directed by Miloš Forman, who these days is spending more time than ever on projects in his native country.

As any visitor to Prague's many military and historical museums can tell you, the subject is a rich mine that continues to haunt the popular Czech imagination.

him in very different directions. The German School at Brno was followed by university studies in Vienna. He then spent a year studying for a doctorate in Leipzig, where he met his future wife, American music student Charlotte Garrigue. After their marriage in New York in 1878, he added her name to his. Masaryk became a classic liberal political leader; in 1882 he was appointed a philosophy professor at Charles University. In 1891 he was elected a member of the Reichsrat assembly based in Vienna.

His many academic works of cultural and political history developed his vision of the kind of state the new Czech nation should be. Although his views were strongly anticlerical, Masaryk was a nationalist in the broadest sense. He began by envisaging Czech nationhood as existing within the prevailing Habsburg monarchy rather than as a breakaway movement. However, the unflagging imperialism of the Austro-Hungarian Empire, especially in the Balkans, angered him deeply, and he turned increasingly toward the idea of Czech independence without embracing Slav nationalism.

At the beginning of World War I, Masaryk moved abroad and initiated the negotiations that would result four years later in the founding of Czechoslovakia. In Paris he, Beneš, and Štěfánik established the Czechoslovak National Council. The Czechoslovak Legions, a fighting force composed of former prisoners and emigrés who fought with Allied troops against Germany and Austria, ensured Allied support for Czech nationalist ambitions.

The Forming of Czechoslovakia

In May 1918 Masaryk negotiated the Pittsburgh Agreement, which laid the foundations for the merging of Bohemia, Moravia, and Slovakia into a single state. This arrangement was accepted by the Allied powers. A provisional government was established in October 1918, and a month later the National Assembly elected

Masaryk as the first president of Czechoslovakia. He was repeatedly reelected until he retired in 1935. As president of the fledgling republic, Masaryk was able to put his liberal ideas into practice, making Czechoslovakia one of Europe's most democratic and secular nations. Remaining aloof from the excitements of party politics, he was perceived as the dignified symbol of the nation and guardian of its integrity. He died at the château of Lány in 1937.

New nations are often founded in unpromising circumstances after decades of colonial exploitation, but the new state of Czechoslovakia got off to a good start. It had not suffered excessively during World War I, and there had been no prolonged struggle against its former masters, the Habsburgs of Austria-Hungary. Moreover, Bohemia in particular was strongly industrialized and had excellent natural resources on which a modern prosperous state could be based.

The only stumbling block was the reluctance of the German-speaking corners of the new nation to remain within its borders. President Masaryk had established the borders along historical rather than ethnic principles—essentially they incorporated the country's heavy industry and manufacturing bases—and his guidelines were accepted at the postwar peace conferences.

The German, Hungarian, and Ruthenian minorities who remained within the borders were not pleased at all, but it was the German population—about three million in number—who complained the loudest. Dissatisfied with the Czech nationalist agenda, Konrad Henlein (1898–1948) spearheaded a movement to initiate change under the banner of the Sudeten German Party. Urged on by Hitler, Henlein made more and more vociferous demands for German autonomy and attracted overwhelming support from Sudeten Germans in elections held in May 1938. Thereafter the demands changed: The Germans now wished to be incorporated within Hitler's Third Reich, a proposal the Czechs understandably found threatening as well as unacceptable.

German Invasion

Hitler stepped up the pressure and, due to the prevailing policy of appeasement, secured the support of the British and French governments. The Czech authorities were adamant in opposing the change. On October 1, 1938, German troops invaded the Sudetenland, the entire external border of Bohemia and Moravia, with the exception of a small part of northern Moravia that was occupied by Poland. Czechoslovakia had lost its industrial heartland. Four days later, Beneš resigned.

On March 15, 1939, Hitler invaded Bohemia and Moravia, which were designated a "protectorate" of the German Reich.

On March 15, 1939, Hitler invaded Bohemia and Moravia, which were designated a "protectorate" of the German Reich. For the next few years, the Nazis exploited Czech industrial strength to bolster their war effort. German oppression was constant. The Jews were persecuted, forced to live in ghettos or deported to camps; intellectuals, artists, Gypsies (Roma), and other "undesirable elements" were also imprisoned or murdered. Universities were closed. On May 27, 1942, Czech agents assassinated the brutal Nazi official Reinhard Heydrich. The consequences were fearsome: The village of Lidice, just outside Prague, was destroyed and its population either murdered or deported. This war crime only increased Czech antagonism to German occupation.

Soviet Invasion

On May 5, 1945, a bloody uprising in Prague spelled the end of German occupation, and four days later Soviet troops entered the city. The end of the war brought bitter consequences for the nearly three million Sudeten Germans—they began to be expelled from their homes during 1945, and some were sent to internment camps. Beneš returned to Prague as president of the republic.

Sharing a common Slavic culture as well as a hatred of fascism, the liberated population was well disposed to the Soviets and their ideology. In 1946 the Communist Party won more votes than any other. Although it was not a clear majority, it nevertheless led to the appointment of the Communist leader Klement Gottwald (1896–1953) as prime minister. The Communists consolidated their hold on power in 1948, and 12 non-Communist ministers resigned their posts, not all of which were filled by Communists. Foreign Minister Jan Masaryk (1886–1948), the son of the former president, did not resign; he was found dead two weeks later, on March 10, in his ministry's courtyard. It was long suspected that he had been murdered by defenestration in the traditional Prague fashion, but this theory is increasingly regarded as doubtful. President Beneš also resigned and was replaced by Gottwald. Rigged elections then secured an overwhelming majority for the Communists.

The Communist Years

Czechoslovakia was swiftly transformed into a Stalinist state, and all opposition, even that from within the ranks of the Communists, was crushed. Show trials were held, leading to more than 200 executions in the early 1950s. Just ten years after most of the Czech and Slovak Jews had been deported to death camps, anti-Semitism again became a feature of Czechoslovak ideology and propaganda, and a disproportionate number of those executed following the trials were Jewish. The government embarked on a policy of further industrialization, introducing heavy industry into rural Slovakia and elsewhere, with, in some places, disastrous long-term effects on the environment.

Gottwald died just nine days after Stalin in 1953. By the 1960s the Stalinist grip on the country had softened slightly, and a reformist group within the party was able to assert itself, egged on by many of the country's writers and intellectuals. In 1968 the leader of this faction, Slovak Alexander Dubček (1921–1992), became party leader, and the movement was popularly dubbed "socialism with a human face." The Prague Spring (see pp. 122) was

Soviet Scars

The most obvious traces of life as a Soviet satellite are, fortunately, gone in Prague, but it's common in the Czech Republic's smaller towns to find a Soviet soldier statue or a Communist-era concrete memorial on the main square.

In Prague, the most prominent surviving shrine to the old days is in the Žižkov district, where the National Memorial, also known as Vítkov, still towers and glowers from a hilltop. This mausoleum, actually built during the First Republic between the World Wars, was thoroughly co-opted by the Soviets. They not only covered it in worker hero bas-reliefs, but they entombed one of their best hard-liners here: Klement Gottwald, leader of the 1948 coup that made his country a satellite.

The other great Prague legacy from Moscow is considerably more useful. The city's underground metro—still a model of clean, affordable efficiency—has been extended considerably since Russian planners created it. The core lines and stops were built during the "normalization" period following the Prague Spring crackdown of 1968.

Adolf Hitler, who annexed part of the country in 1938, triumphantly entered Prague in March 1939.

enormously popular with the Czech and Slovak people, as the regime not only implemented economic reforms but permitted greater personal liberty and lifted much of the repressive censorship. The arts and intellectual life flourished after decades of suppression.

The Prague Spring would prove short-lived, however. Fearing that the movement ultimately would lead to secession from the Soviet bloc, the Soviets and their Warsaw Pact allies launched an invasion of Czechoslovakia in August. There was much heroic resistance in the streets of Prague, and in January 1969 a student named Jan Palach set fire to himself in Wenceslas Square (Václavské náměstí) in protest. (His grave, never identified during the Communist years, is now a place of pilgrimage at the Olšany cemetery in Vinohrady district.)

Homemade Czech weaponry and sacrificial gestures were no match for Soviet tanks, however, and might prevailed. Reforms were annulled, and a new hard-line leader, Gustáv Husák, was installed in power, even though he had initially supported the Prague Spring. The new regime was less murderous than Gottwald's, but dissent was stamped upon.

The Czechs, refusing to give up their quest for liberty, were heartened by the Helsinki Declaration on Human Rights. In 1977 a few thousand intellectuals, artists, journalists, academics, priests, and others from all walks of life signed Charter 77, which affirmed the values of the declaration and argued for the dismantling of the totalitarian state in Czechoslovakia. Not surprisingly, the Communist regime took exception to Charter 77 and persecuted many of its signatories, who lost their jobs, were forced into exile, or were even imprisoned on trumped-up charges. For the Communists, any reminder of human liberties was anathema. The historical museums of Czechoslovakia made only fleeting references to Tomáš Garrigue Masaryk, without whom there probably would have been no Czechoslovakia; while the statues and monuments honoring him in nearly every village and town were torn down.

Velvet Revolution

While Mikhail Gorbachev instigated his drastic economic, political, and social changes of *perestroika* in the Soviet Union, loyalists and dissidents alike in Czechoslovakia, with their anti-Soviet feelings, looked on with skepticism. As Soviet dogmatism shifted more and more, however, it became clear that the Czech government would have to introduce some modest reforms. The dissident movement took heart and gathered strength, and it was further bolstered by the demolition of the Berlin Wall on November 9, 1989. Street demonstrations became larger and more vocal, as religious groups joined the supporters of Charter 77. The violent suppression of a demonstration on November 17 marked the beginning of the end for the increasingly discredited regime, which had lost what little moral authority it ever had.

On November 20 a vast crowd, estimated at 200,000, gathered to demand the government's dissolution. Dissident groups formed the Civic Forum coalition, demanding

People crammed Old Town Square in a Communist-style celebration in 1978.

the resignation of the Communist leadership and an amnesty for political prisoners. Another, even larger demonstration took place on November 24 in Wenceslas Square, when the crowds were addressed not only by the playwright and political theorist Václav Havel but by Alexander Dubček, who had languished in obscurity after being deposed by the Soviets.

The Communists began making concessions, but it was too late. The Civic Forum stood firm, and the government fell from power a few weeks later. The old regime, which had long lost any vestige of credibility, succumbed to its own inertia; there was not a person in the land, party members included, who was not aware that the regime was living a lie.

> On November 20, [1989], a vast crowd, estimated at 200,000, gathered to demand the government's dissolution.

On December 29 an event took place that would have been dismissed as fantasy six months earlier: Havel, the most prominent and internationally renowned of the Chartists, was elected unanimously as the new head of state. Dissident

intellectuals, who under the Communists had been forced to eke out a living as window cleaners or stokers, suddenly found themselves running ministries or embassies. Elections were organized for the following June, and reformist parties, including Civic Forum and the Slovak party People Against Violence, received the most votes. Alexander Dubček became speaker of the new parliament. The Velvet Revolution, so-called at the time because little blood was spilled during the transition to democracy, was complete.

For some years after the Velvet Revolution, it was possible to see, daubed on the walls of Prague, the fading words HAVEL NA HRAD: Havel to the Castle. This was the battle cry for the entire nation in the final weeks of 1989.

Václav Havel

To many it seemed incongruous that this scruffy, chain-smoking, quiet-mannered writer and intellectual should be elevated to the highest office in the land. Václav Havel, however, had for at least two decades been deeply immersed in political and moral issues. His writings and petitions had earned him the constant attention of the secret police and numerous spells in prison, but none of this deterred him from his pursuit of the truth. After the Soviet invasion, Havel's officially sanctioned career as an artist ended; he was obliged to pursue a new one as a brewery worker. Nothing could suppress his artistic integrity, fueled as it was by his profound understanding of the lies and deceptions on which the Communist state was founded. In underground publications, he expressed his revulsion at totalitarianism and appealed to the nation's leaders to pursue more truthful and liberating policies.

Havel's Legacy

For many Czechs, Václav Havel is a far more complex figure than his image abroad would suggest. A surprising number of his countrymen and -women respect him but do not necessarily think of him as the nation's conscience, as he's been referred to more than once in foreign publications.

In interviews in 2009, he was asked to look at his nation's progress in view of what the Velvet Revolution leaders had hoped to achieve back in 1989. In many ways, their dream has come true, he has said. But petty party politics has also proven nastier than anyone ever expected—and such fractious power struggles have, in his view, held back the return of civil society.

The former playwright-dissident's return to writing, which was put on hold for the 13 years he held the office of president, may help fuel the cause. Aside from the quirky, insightful, and candid account in his biography, *To the Castle and Back*, he has penned a play, *Leaving*, which ironically parodies the vanity of elected officials in central Europe. Fans are also looking forward to Miloš Forman's upcoming film based on Havel's screen adaptation of Georges-Marc Benamou's book *The Ghost of Munich* (see sidebar p. 36)

Such appeals not only fell on deaf ears but also led to frequent imprisonment. In 1977 Havel co-founded Charter 77 and was subsequently incarcerated for four years.

When it became clear in the autumn of 1989 that the old Communist regime was about to crumble, it was natural for freedom-loving Czechs to turn to Havel. He was a leading figure in Civic Forum, where he demonstrated political savoir faire as well as the moral authority that emanated from his essays and letters, many of which had been written to his wife from his prison cell.

The New Czech Republic

The esteem in which Havel was held remained constant, despite the initial confusions that characterized Czechoslovakia's return to democracy. Finance Minister Václav Klaus, who would ascend the ranks to become prime minister of the newly formed Czech Republic in 1993, steered through monetarist policies based on those pursued by Britain's Prime Minister Margaret Thatcher. Czechoslovakia rapidly developed a full-fledged market economy based on the privatization of state resources, and it benefited from proximity to Germany, a country that began to invest heavily in Czech enterprises. Some Sudeten Germans expelled after the war began to press for the return of their former property, but Havel and the government showed no sympathy for their cases. In 1997, amid revelations of corruption within the Civic Democratic Party (ODS), Klaus resigned as prime minister. He staged a comeback in 2003, however, when Havel's term as president ended and Klaus, facing enormous opposition, won the seat in an extremely close, unexpected victory.

Social divisions, bigotry, nationalism, and racism had been suppressed under the Communists, but the restoration of liberty allowed the fears and prejudices to be expressed. The Vietnamese and Roma minorities suffered from attacks and discrimination. Crime, never a serious problem (apart from corruption) under the Communists, increased. Grave social and economic problems affecting the whole population seemed no nearer solution.

Nationalism also revived and culminated in demands for independence by Slovak politicians. Following the slim victory of the leading nationalist party under Vladimír Mečiar in the June 1992 elections, the country divided in two in January 1993. To many Czechs this seemed senseless, since Slovakia had always benefited from the industrial prosperity of the Czech lands from which it was now separated. The Czech Republic joined the European Union in 2004, and held the Presidency of the Council of the European Union from January 1 to June 30, 2009.

There is little reason for concern about the country's long-term future. Its economy has weathered the global financial crisis well and, even if unemployment has risen to new levels, its market base is strong and the standard of living is high. ■

In 1990 Soviet forces long stationed in the old Czechoslovakia finally left the country for good.

The Arts

After 40 years of Communist rule, the "new" Prague is experiencing a revival in the arts and theater, as young playwrights, musicians, writers, and artists flourish at their work. But Czech artistry dates far back into the country's past—indeed, few countries are as richly endowed with such a great legacy of art and architecture.

For most visitors, the earliest examples of artistry will be the three rotunda churches found beneath street level in Prague, dating from the 11th and 12th centuries, followed by Gothic buildings from the mid-13th century, among them St. Vitus's Cathedral of and St. Agnes Convent. Yet palaces and churches abound throughout the Czech Republic from every period following—Renaissance, baroque, art nouveau, and cubist foremost among them. Painting and sculpture thrived in these same periods, starring such artists as Karel Skreta and Cosmas Asam. In the 19th century, literature and music took front stage, culminating in perhaps the country's best known prodigy—Franz Kafka. As the 20th century progressed, Czechs quickly adopted new art forms such as film and mime.

Architecture & Art

Romanesque (11th–13th centuries): Little in the way of ancient artifacts exists, other than the scant remains from the Great Moravian Empire at Uherské Hradiště. Some of the earliest buildings still standing were constructed in the Romanesque style between the 11th and early 13th centuries. This style, which spread throughout Europe in the 11th century, was characterized by sturdy columns topped with rounded arches:

Prague's most eccentric modern building, Frank Gehry's "Fred and Ginger" house

Keep an Eye on ...

It didn't take long for the first democratically elected Parliament since World War II to encounter a scandal over freedom of expression, thanks to artist/prankster David Černý, who in 1991 famously coated a Soviet tank—still standing as a memorial—bright pink. More recently he stirred things up at the European Commission, where he installed "Entropa," a symbolic representation of each member country using such images as squat toilets from Bulgaria and packs of Ikea-like furniture from Sweden. Černý and other progressive artists are showcased these days at Prague's new DOX center for the arts (www.doxprague.org).

Pop and jazz music are Czech strong suits, and leading vanguards include JAR, Monkey Business, the Robert Balzar Trio, and sax man František Kop. Check out the **Lucerna Music Bar** (www.musicbar.cz), jazz club **U Méleho Glena** (www.malyglen.cz), or the **Jazz Boat** (www.jazzboat.cz).

In terms of literature, Twisted Spoon (www.twistedspoon.com), an international press based in Prague and founded by New Yorker Howard Sidenberg, is a good resource. It produces limited print runs of lovingly printed and illustrated translations of classic and contemporary Czech authors, from Kafka to Eva Švankmajerová.

a robust, imposing style of great nobility. The round churches and St. George's Basil-ica (Bazilika sv. Jiří) in Prague belong to this period, but more impressive survivals are found in Olomouc, and at Porta Coeli abbey and Třebíč, both in southern Moravia.

Gothic (14th–15th centuries): The Gothic style arrived from France in the early 14th century. The invention of new vaulting techniques allowed the weight of large buildings such as cathedrals to be more evenly distributed. This meant that the solid masonry characteristic of Romanesque architecture was replaced by a lighter, more exalted style with large traceried windows and lofty vaulted aisles and naves. Charles IV brought French architects such as Matthew of Arras to embellish Prague with the new style, notably St. Vitus's Cathedral (Chrám sv. Víta). Swabian architect Peter Parler (1332–1399), associated with continuing work on the cathedral, also built superb churches in other parts of Bohemia. Prague's Old and New Towns are filled with Gothic churches, mostly commissioned by Charles IV, and many other towns boast stately Gothic churches, sometimes enriched with glorious altarpieces, tabernacles, and paintings. Many castles were also built, at least partially, in a Gothic style. Karlštejn is one of the best known examples, but there are many other medi-eval fortresses with substantial Gothic elements, including Loket, Pernštejn, and Zvíkov. A few outstanding Gothic bridges also survive: The Charles Bridge (Karlův most) in Prague is the best known, but the one at Písek is even older.

The Ruckl factory in Nižbor turns out priceless glass pieces that go into collections worldwide.

EXPERIENCE: Glassblowing

Bohemian glass has been a hallmark of status for kings and kingmakers for centuries and, though many Czech glass factories are struggling to keep the doors open these days because of the intensive skilled labor required, nearly 200 operations are still turning out stunning work. One of the most successful glassworks, **Bohemian Crystal Factory,** a 45-minute drive outside Prague, offers visitors the chance to see up close this quintessential Czech art and craft.

The Prague Experience organization (*www.pragueexperience.com*) organizes half-day visits to the factory, showing off the best work of local glassblowers and cutters, along with the history of the profession and the industry in the Czech lands. Visitors can also try out glassblowing for themselves before deciding on whether to acquire a crystal collection or set of snifters.

The visit, via bus, includes hotel pickup or transport to and from a meeting point near Wenceslas Square—and the chance to escape the many tourist-targeted crystal shops lining it for a more in-depth experience in a far more authentic setting.

At the end of the 15th century, Bohemian architect Benedikt Ried developed a style marked by complex and daring vaulting. The most spectacular example is the Vladislav Hall in Prague Castle, but the church of St. Barbara at Kutná Hora is almost as impressive. Much Bohemian Gothic painting has survived. Though it varies in accomplishment, the best examples bear comparison with contemporary works from Italy and Germany. Very little is known about the identity of the painters, but one, who at least had a name of sorts—Master Theodoric—adorned the Holy Cross Chapel at Karlštejn Castle with enormous paintings commissioned by Charles IV. Many masterpieces of Gothic art from Bohemia and Moravia are gathered in St. Agnes Convent (Anežský klášter) in Prague.

Renaissance (16th–17th centuries): Renaissance architecture—a rebirth of the ancient classical style, replete with forms and ornaments such as columns, round arches, tunnel vaults, and domes—came from Italy but soon took on a distinctly Czech flavor, best demonstrated by the many castles with gabled battlements and three-tiered courtyards. Litomyšl in eastern Bohemia is an outstanding example. It is decorated, like so many similar edifices, with lofty gables and sgraffito decoration—a technique of removing an outer layer of plaster to outline the black mortar below. Many mansions were constructed, or reconstructed, in this style, notably the Schwarzenberg Palace (Schwarzenberský palác) in Prague. Two of the loveliest Renaissance buildings in the Czech Republic are the Belvedere, close to Prague Castle (Pražský hrad), and Star Castle (Letohrádek hvězda) on White Mountain, both built in Italianate style in the 1550s.

Baroque (17th–18th centuries): Artistic development ground to a halt after the civil disorder initiated by the Battle of White Mountain in 1620. The Thirty Years' War (1618–1648) allowed no time or leisure for such matters. Indeed, as during the period of the Hussite wars in the 15th century (see pp. 28–29), a substantial portion of the architectural and artistic heritage of the Czech lands was destroyed. Once the dust had settled after the war, though, the Catholic victors had the wealth and the confidence to construct town houses and vast country mansions in a full-blown baroque style. This was the style adopted throughout the Habsburg empire, and leading Austrian architects such as Johann Bernard Fischer von Erlach (1656–1723) were also employed in Bohemia and elsewhere.

Far removed from the harmonious and balanced proportions of the Renaissance, the baroque style was theatrical, delighting in tricks of perspective and light. Walls were not required to be flat: They could be concave or convex, bulging assertively or retreating modestly, according to the whim of the architect. All the resources of the visual arts were employed, providing work for battalions of sculptors, painters, and plasterers. The Wallenstein Palace (Valdštejnský palác) in Prague is probably the earliest substantial example.

Baroque art in Bohemia and Moravia is not confined to museums. Most major churches are decorated with altarpieces by ... masters.

The building boom encouraged architects, sculptors, and painters to descend on Bohemia. Nor were commissions lacking. Many of the masters of the baroque were French (Jean-Baptiste Mathey) and Italian (Francesco Caratti, Carlo Lurago). A distinctive Bohemian style developed in the 18th century thanks to the genius of Christoph Dientzenhofer and his son Kilián Ignác.

Christoph Dientzenhofer (1655–1722) grew up in Upper Bavaria and together with his four brothers came to Prague to study architecture with Carlo Lurago. Christoph stayed on in Prague and spent his life building churches and other edifices all over Bohemia. Major commissions include the abbey at Teplá in western Bohemia and the church at Břevnov Monastery (Břevnovský klášter) on the outskirts of Prague. But his masterpiece is the Church of St. Nicholas (Kostel sv. Mikuláše) on Prague's Malá Strana Square (Malostranské náměstí), with its broad nave, lofty dome, mighty pillars, and grandiose statuary.

In this project Christoph was aided by his son Kilián Ignác (1689–1751), who designed the dome and choir. Kilián was arguably even more gifted than his father. His dense designs radiate a tremendous power and mastery of space. Among his superlative buildings in Prague are the twin-towered Church of St. John on the Rock (Kostel sv. Jana na Skalce), the facade of the Loreto (Loreta), Church of St. Thomas (Kostel sv. Tomáše) in Malá Strana, the elegant Palace of Sylva-Taroucca (Palác Sylva-Taroucca) on Na Příkopě, and the Vila Amerika, now the Dvořák Museum (Muzeum A. Dvořáka). His works in other parts of Bohemia include the oval Church of St. Mary Magdalene (Kostel sv. Máří Magdalény) in Karlovy Vary and the elegant Ursuline convent (Voršilský klášter) in Kutná Hora.

Baroque architects worked hand in hand with painters and sculptors, whose works decorated the many churches and palaces. From the workshops of artists such as Karel Škréta (1610–1674) and Petr Brandl (1668–1735) came huge numbers of altarpieces. Ferdinand Brokoff (1688–1731), Jan Bendl, and the great Matthias Braun (1684–1738) produced a wealth of dramatic sculpture; much of it is in Prague, but splendid examples are at Kuks in eastern Bohemia. Baroque painting is perhaps harder to appreciate. Gifted artists such as Škréta and Brandl were prolific, and there is inevitably a certain uniformity to their works. The same is true of famed fresco painters, including Václav Reiner and Austrian Franz Anton Maulbertsch.

Baroque art in Bohemia and Moravia is not confined to museums. Most major churches are decorated with altarpieces by baroque masters, and facades are often rich in carvings by the likes of Brokoff and Braun. Plague columns, a feature of central European town squares, were erected to give thanks for the end of an epidemic; these, too, are often richly decorated by the most famous baroque sculptors.

Vernacular: A vernacular tradition that probably originated in medieval times also continued, especially in the isolated rural areas in northeastern Moravia. Wooden farmhouses with distinctive decoration, as well as lovely wooden churches found in eastern Moravia, were built in a solid yet unchanging style. Many structures,

A characteristic Alfons Mucha design for the stained glass in St. Vitus's Cathedral in Prague

from churches to huts and schoolhouses, are now in *skansens,* open-air museums, of which the largest is at Rožnov pod Radhoštěm in northern Moravia (see p. 282).

Rococo: The grandeur of baroque gradually gave way in the mid-18th century to the charm and delicacy of rococo, with its swooping, curvaceous lines and playful elegance. Prague's Goltz-Kinský Palace (Goltz-Kinských palác) is a stylish example. Early in the 19th century neoclassicism was briefly in vogue, and a few country mansions, notably Kačina, were built in this grand but slightly monotonous style, which is marked by regular colonnades and pavilions. However, rather than employ a faded neoclassical style, most 19th-century architects in Bohemia and Moravia, as elsewhere in Europe, opted for eclecticism, selecting elements from a variety of styles. This gave rise to a proliferation of pseudo-baroque mansions and neo-medieval castles such as Bouzov. Typical of this reaching for grandeur are institutional buildings—the National Museum and National Theater in Prague are examples. Painters, too, adopted eclectic styles, and the works of Josef Mánes (1820–1871) and Karel Purkyně (1834–1868) are stylistically wide ranging. Josef Navrátil (1798–1865) was among the most versatile and gifted of the 19th-century painters. The best of their work can be seen to good advantage in the Trade Fair Palace (Veletržní palác) in Prague, in itself a constructivist masterpiece of the 1920s.

The genius of Franz Kafka was unrecognized during his own lifetime (1883–1924).

Secession & Cubism: At the turn of the 20th century, the branch of art nouveau known as secession, marked by exuberant surface decoration and inventive ironwork, made its way to Bohemia from Vienna. You can see examples in Josefov in Prague and in many smaller towns, such as Pardubice in eastern Bohemia and Karlovy Vary.

Another modern design movement, cubism, also caught on in Bohemia, and some striking structures, notably Josef Gočár's House of the Black Madonna (Dům U černé Matky Boží) on Celetná in Prague and now a museum of Czech cubist art, were built in this style.

The architectural regeneration of the early 20th century had its counterpart in the fine arts, especially in the paintings of art nouveau artists such as Alfons Mucha (1860–1939). Innovative painters, including Emil Filla, Bohumil Kubišta, and František Kupka, showed both originality and energy working in cubist, expressionist, and other styles. Mucha's most internationally celebrated works, his posters, were done in Paris, and after his return to Bohemia in 1910, he found himself caught up in Slav nationalism with his stirring "Slav Epic" cycle of the 1920s (see p. 273) and other pieces.

Communist Times: The Communist years, with a dreary insistence on socialist realism as the only acceptable style, were dark ones for architecture and art, despite a brief flowering in the 1960s. Grimly functional buildings, often erected with no sensitivity for their urban context, scarred town centers. Since the Velvet Revolution, the works of modern Czech and Slovak artists, whose paintings could not be shown under the previous regime, are being rediscovered and exhibited. Perhaps the best known is artist and poet Jiří Kolář (1914–2002), who specialized in collages.

Many new buildings are going up in major cities, most notably Prague, but it is too soon to say whether modern architecture will find a distinctive Czech tone. So far the office blocks and hotels could have been airlifted in from Frankfurt or Vienna, and only Prague's most characterful modern building—a joint venture between the Californian architect Frank Gehry and the Yugoslav Vlado Milunić—known as the Dancing House or "Fred and Ginger" building, stands out as truly original.

Literature

Czech developed as a written language only in the 13th century. Before then the languages used were German, Latin, and Old Slavonic, a church dialect brought to the Czech lands by Bishops Cyril and Methodius in 863 (see p. 25). The earliest known works are biographies of saints and historical chronicles.

Even in medieval times, there was a tension between the Czech and German cultures, a tension that by the mid-19th century led to separate cultural institutions for the Czech- and German-speaking populations. Nonetheless, medieval Bohemia and Moravia were essentially bilingual. The religious reformer Jan Hus (see p. 28), who gave his name to the Hussite movement founded after his death, preached only in the vernacular, and thus transformed Czech into a language of literary importance. Hus himself reformed Czech orthography to make this possible. The Czech language continued to be employed principally for theological and philosophical works in the centuries after his death. Protestant teacher and preacher Comenius (Jan Komenský; 1592–1670) became one of the most revered figures in Czech literary history. His writings brought him renown as an advocate of universal education for children and of greater unity within the Christian faith.

Under the Habsburgs the Czech language was eclipsed by German. The revival of Czech took place at the prompting of Josef Dobrovský (1753–1829), who wrote a definitive history of the Czech language and compiled a German-Czech dictionary. As Czech speakers gained confidence during the 19th century, combining nationalist, artistic, and political aspirations, so their literary outpourings gained in sophistication and influence. Poets such as Karel Hynek Mácha (1810–1836) and playwrights such as Josef Kajetán Tyl (1808–1859) and Václav Klicpera (1792–1852) proved popular and influential. Easily the best known Czech writer of the 19th century was Jan Neruda (1834–1891), who achieved rapid fame in a variety of literary forms, including essays, vignettes, and short stories, mostly set in Prague (see p. 127).

> **Jan Hus ... preached only in the vernacular, and thus transformed Czech into a language of literary importance.**

Despite the resurgence in the Czech language, much important literature continued to be written in German. For many ambitious writers, Bohemia and Moravia constituted too small an arena, and they moved abroad where they hoped to make a greater impact. This was true of the poet, playwright, and novelist Franz Werfel (1890–1945) and of the poet Rainer Maria Rilke (1875–1926), who was a native of Prague.

Yet many writers remained in Prague. The most famous was novelist Franz Kafka (1883–1924), whose bleak fables include *The Trial*. Hard-hitting journalist Egon Erwin Kisch (1885–1948) traveled the world but returned to his native Prague in 1945.

The declaration of the republic in 1918 gave a new burst of energy to the literary scene. Dramatist Karel Čapek (1890–1938) entertained the Czechs with his satirical plays and travel books, many of which conveyed his underlying message that humankind's wish to dominate and control nature could be destructive to humanity itself. His best known plays are *R.U.R.* (1920), which introduced the word "robot" to the world and was widely translated, and *The Macropoulos Case* (1922), later set as an opera by Leoš Janáček.

EXPERIENCE: Marionette Making

In a country with a long history of foreign occupation, the arts sometimes take on special meaning. Thus, for centuries, Czech marionettes have been able to parody the vanity of kings and despots in a way that no living person could have managed—at least if they wanted to keep their head attached.

For centuries marionettes have been a popular art form.

What's more, if time won't permit a session in the studio workshop, you can take home a marionette "Do it Yourself" kit, with complete instructions and a hint book of dozens of possible characters—all ready and willing to parody the most pompous of kings and presidents. But, don't forget the marionette theater.

Performances

The creations have well established performance chops, as it turns out. In the early 1990s Truhlář launched the local puppet theater group The **Kampa Amateur,** running one-man shows in pubs and cafés, delighting both adults and children with his ironic takes on popular Czech fairy tales. Live music was melded into the performances in an avant-garde style that proved a hit, resulting in shows such as "The Sailors," "The Musicians," and "The 13 Clocks."

The Bohemian craftsmen who perfected puppet theater during the baroque era were celebrated throughout Europe for the mastery of their figures, movement, and effects. In those times puppetry was an itinerant art, but today it is a sophisticated form employing satire, fantasy, music, and humor. Prague's National Marionette Theater remains a prominent institution.

Making Marionettes

Marionettes come in all shapes and styles. They can be built of wood, plastic, plaster, et cetera, but many puppets sold on the main streets of Prague are a poor imitation of the whimsical, sinister, or majestic creations of old. Fortunately, a handful of old-style craftspeople still practice the art of puppetmaking and abhor mass production. Marionette maker Pavel Truhlář and his wife, Karolina, create and sell fully functional wooden or plaster puppets and relish passing on their skills.

The couple holds afternoon courses for up to eight people, including children from age six, at their Lesser Quarter workshop (*U lužického semináre 5*) for 1,500 Czech crowns. All materials are provided, plus expert instruction. They'll set you up with ready-made starter components created from linden wood, plus the needed fittings.

The longest-running puppet theater shows in recent Prague history continue today. For information, check *www.marionety.com.* Dozens of puppet companies are scattered across the republic, and at Chrudim there is a museum and festival of puppetry (see p. 242).

The country's most famous modern poet was Jaroslav Seifert (1901–1986), probably best known for his poems about Prague during the Nazi occupation. He was a signatory of Charter 77 (see p. 39) in 1977, and was awarded the Nobel Prize for literature in 1984. By far the most popular writer in the Czech language of the interwar period, however, was Jaroslav Hašek (1883–1923), who managed, despite a penchant for the bottle, to produce a classic novel that has been translated into numerous languages, *The Good Soldier Švejk*.

Important Jewish writers who left searing accounts of life under Nazi occupation and persecution were Jiří Weil (1900–1959), most famous for his *Life With a Star,* and Arnošt Lustig (1926–), a filmmaker and novelist who settled in the United States. Most of Lustig's fiction is set during World War II, a period he spent in Nazi death camps.

Soviet Rule: Literature was no more likely to flourish under the Communists than under the Germans. The Nazis had murdered many intellectuals and literary figures, while the Communists tried to compel them to write works of "Socialist Realism" extolling the class struggle. Until the 1960s Czechoslovakia was a literary desert. Only a few publishing houses were authorized, and the state-controlled Czechoslovak Writers' Association defined the limits of acceptability. The years leading up to the Prague Spring (see p. 122) were more liberating, and a number of authors made their reputations during this period, among them Arnošt Lustig, Josef Škvorecký, Milan Kundera, and Ivan Klíma.

After 1968 serious literature went underground, and writers who remained in Czechoslovakia were either silent or published clandestinely, circulating photocopied editions within a small circle of subscribers. A handful of writers avoided sensitive or controversial topics and published their works despite censorship. They include Miroslav Holub (1923–1998) and Bohumil Hrabal (1914–1997). Hrabal wrote the delightful and touching *Closely Observed Trains* (1965) and the fantastical comic novel *I Served the King of England.*

Among the many writers who left the country was Josef Škvorecký (1924–), who was raised in Náchod and set some of his novels, such as *The Cowards,* in this Silesian region. He immigrated to Canada in 1968, where he founded 68 Publishers, a publishing house that kept the Czech literary flame alive. Much contemporary Czech fiction is serious, but Škvorecký writes with a light and often bawdy touch.

> **After 1968 ... writers who remained in Czechoslovakia were either silent or published clandestinely.**

The most famous novelist who went into exile is Milan Kundera (1929–), who left for France in 1975 to teach in Rennes and was subsequently stripped of his citizenship by the Czechoslovak government. His sophisticated, occasionally arch novels have met with great international success; among his best known works are *The Book of Laughter and Forgetting* and *The Unbearable Lightness of Being.* His earliest novels include *The Joke,* originally published in Prague in 1967, which probes the absurdities of life under communism.

Among the writers who stayed in Czechoslovakia were Ludvík Vaculík, author of *A Cup of Coffee With My Interrogator,* and Václav Havel (see pp. 41–42), whose plays, such as *The Garden Party* and *Audience,* were more frequently performed in London or Paris than in his native Prague. Havel, as a supporter of Charter 77, was repeatedly arrested in the 1970s and '80s. He wrote many of his eloquent essays in prison; one of his best known books collects letters to his then wife, Olga. Another writer with a well-deserved international reputation is Ivan Klíma (1931–), who published in secret before the Velvet Revolution. His work explores his childhood in Terezín (see pp. 210–213) and the perplexities of love in a Communist state. *Love and Garbage* and *Judge on Trial* are among his finest novels.

A new generation of Czech writers—Michal Ajvaz (1949–), Jáchym Topol (1962–), and the science-fiction author Eva Hauserová (1954–)—are carving reputations for themselves inside the Czech Republic, but they are as yet little known in other countries.

Music

Bohemia and Moravia have a powerful musical tradition, but were late to join the mainstream of European classical music. Musical giants such as Bedřich Smetana (1824–1884) and Antonín Dvořák (1841–1904) brought folk music into the more formal embrace of chamber and orchestral music. But from the early Middle Ages

A chamber music ensemble performs at the Dvořák Museum in Prague.

there was a tradition of church music, set to Slavic texts, and Czech Hussite hymns emphasized congregational singing; these undoubtedly influenced the Lutheran chorales that became so important in Germany. A more sophisticated strand of baroque music flourished in Bohemia. Musical education formed part of the school curriculum, and many country houses had their own orchestras. This native tradition of baroque composition did not establish deep roots. The most successful Czech composers—violin virtuoso František Benda (1709–1786), Johann Stamitz (1717–1757), and Jan Ladislav Dusík (1760–1812)—all preferred to work either in Germany or Vienna, where the profusion of courts offered musicians ample employment.

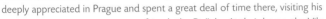

Antonín Dvořák often ... [used] folk melodies of great beauty and singularity within his compositions.

Mozart, Smetana, & Dvořák: Wolfgang Amadeus Mozart (see p. 101) was deeply appreciated in Prague and spent a great deal of time there, visiting his friends the Dušeks. At their home, the Vila Bertramka, he completed *Don Giovanni*—first performed in Prague in 1787.

Smetana (see pp. 230–231) was the first Czech composer who clearly identified himself with the national aspirations of his people. He is best known for his six-part symphonic poem *Má vlast,* celebrating the natural beauties of Bohemia, and every child in the Czech Republic can whistle the principal theme of the movement that depicts the River Vltava.

Dvořák, who played the viola in orchestras under Smetana's baton, was an ardent admirer of the elder composer's work, but by the end of the 19th century his international reputation had eclipsed that of his mentor. Although Dvořák composed 11 operas, he is better known as a symphonic and chamber music composer, often using folk melodies of great beauty and singularity within his compositions.

Other Czech composers include Dvořák's son-in-law Josef Suk (1874–1935), who adopted a rich romantic style. Gustav Mahler (1860–1911), a great conductor and symphonic composer, is not often considered to be Czech, but he was Moravian by birth, from the town of Jihlava.

Leoš Janáček (1854–1928) delved deeply into the country's earlier musical traditions, incorporating them into his own work. Born in Hukvaldy, he studied in Prague and spent most of his working life in Brno. His late works—the operas *Katja Kabanova, The Cunning Little Vixen,* and *Jenůfa*—now have a permanent place in the established repertoire, but pieces such as the remarkable *Glagolitic Mass* allude most obviously to the traditions of Czech music.

Bohuslav Martinů (1890–1959) was very prolific, and during his life completed more than 400 works, including operas, ballets, and chamber works of varying quality. The country has produced many performers of exceptional talent, including sopranos Ema Destinnová and Eva Randová. The Czech Philharmonic Orchestra, under its conductors Karel Ančerl and Václav Neumann, is one of Europe's outstanding orchestras. Josef Suk is one of the leading violin virtuosos with an international reputation.

The Czechs have long been devoted to jazz, which attracted enormous disapproval from the Communist authorities. In the 1970s and 1980s young Czechs fervently embraced the punk movement—the leading band was Plastic People of the Universe. Punk has since been displaced by many other strands of popular music and rock.

Theater & Mime

Czech theater, mainly a vehicle for national aspirations in the 19th century, was given a new lease on life by Karel Čapek and the avant-garde director E. F. Burian in the interwar years. In the 1920s the Liberated Theater (Osvobozené divadlo) in Prague became a major European center for the presentation of surrealist plays by the likes of André Breton (1896–1966) and Jean Cocteau (1889–1963). After World War II there was another revival, and in the 1960s a number of excellent small theater companies sprang up in Prague, Brno, and other towns. Some of these, including the Theater on the Balustrade (Divadlo Na Zábradlí) in Prague, had a high quality of direction and performance. They showcased the most talented of the new Czech writers and the fashionable avant-garde playwrights, among them Samuel Beckett.

Alfred Radok invented the Laterna Magika Theater, now part of the National Theater (Národní divadlo), in 1958, a deft marriage of cinema and theater. This technical device—once considered brilliant—combines song, ballet and mime, film projections, movable walls, and drama. Mime is a long-standing Czech tradition, and its supreme exponents were Ladislav Fialka (1931–1991) and Bolek Polívka (1949–).

> In the 1970s and 1980s young Czechs fervently embraced the punk movement ... [It has] since been displaced by many other strands of popular music and rock.

Film

Filmmaking has been at the heart of central and Eastern European culture since movie cameras were first rolled out in the 1930s. Directors such as Martin Frič (1902–1968) produced films that gained the republic an international reputation for the medium. Zlín, in Moravia, was rebuilt as an avant-garde company town by shoe manufacturer Tomáš Bat'a and became a center for film animation under his patronage. Director Karel Zeman (1910–1989) made his reputation here.

The war years and the early years of Stalinist rule virtually froze cinematic development, but after 1956 there was a gradual thaw. Earlier films, such as Jiří Weiss's (1913–2004) *The Last Shot* (1950), had already adopted novel ideas, including the use of amateurs. There was a revival in the 1960s, but works like Jan Němec's political parable

Report on the Party and the Guests (1966), with its play on the word "party" in its two senses of political organization and festivity, were soon banned. Other outstanding directors were Miloš Forman (1932–), whose best known works include the comedies *A Blonde in Love* (1965) and *The Firemen's Ball* (1967)—both set in provincial Czech towns—and Jiří Menzel (1938–), who made an exquisite version of Hrabal's *Closely Observed Trains* (1966).

Czech cinema struggled to recovered the verve of its accomplishment following the Velvet Revolution. These days, however, a renaissance is flowering, thanks to new, affordable technologies and dozens of organizations and ministries dedicated to reviving movie mastery. There's plenty to engage today's film buffs, with their proud heritage that spans pioneering art films (including the first nude scene widely distributed in cinemas, Hedy Lamarr's swim in Gustav Machatý's 1933 melodrama, *Ekstase*), through the 1960s to Marek Najbrt's World War II drama, *Protektor*—the 2009 Czech hit.

The Czech film scene also has benefited from foreign capital infusions, thanks to its A-list status as a location for big-budget action films such as *Wanted, GI Joe: The Rise of Cobra,* and the James Bond flick *Casino Royale*. These mega-productions shoot at Barrandov, the vast studio complex built before World War II by the Havel family, but Czechs tend to shoot in much more humble environs—and at a fraction of the cost.

The country produces 20 to 25 feature films each year, often focused on family drama or coping with fast-changing post–Velvet Revolution life. Films such as Jan Hřebejk's *U me dobrý (I'm All Good)* have made it to arthouse theaters in North America, while documentaries such as Helena Třeštíková's *René,* the tale of a career criminal/ novelist, have swept awards around the world. ∎

Czech director Jan Hřebejk poses next to the poster for his Oscar-nominated film.

prague

Prague, one of Europe's best preserved baroque cities, with a spectacular castle and cathedral, plus unrivaled palaces and gardens

Castle District & Little Quarter

One of the many statues of St. John of Nepomuk found throughout Prague
Opposite: Chapel of St. Wenceslas, Prague Castle
Pages 58–59: Týn Church and Old Town Square from Old Town Square Tower

Castle District & Little Quarter

When a fortified castle *(hrad)* was built high above the River Vltava in the ninth century, settlements soon began to grow up around it. The area surrounding and next to this—the first Prague Castle—became known as Hradčany (Castle district), whereas the district between the castle and the river was called Malá Strana (Little Quarter).

By the 12th century a bridge linked the two sides of the river, and churches and houses were built close to both banks. Malá Strana formally became a town in 1257. During the 14th century it was enclosed by fortifications, but these provided little protection during the Hussite wars of the 15th century, which inflicted grave damage on the area. Malá Strana was rebuilt, only to be ravaged by a great fire in 1541. It then enjoyed a new period of prosperity, as aristocrats hired Italian architects to construct their mansions and palaces.

Building accelerated after the Battle of White Mountain in 1620, when the Habsburg nobility consolidated its presence in Prague. By the beginning of the 19th century, New Town (Nové Město) and other districts across the river began to gain in importance. Malá Strana became something of a backwater, helping to conserve

Area of map detail

NOT TO BE MISSED:

its unique character. Few European cities have retained so many centuries-old palaces and mansions, as well as their baroque gardens.

Although commercialism has invaded the main squares and streets of both Malá Strana and Hradčany, it is surprising how many tranquil streets and gardens remain. Tour guides tend to lead their groups along the main routes and up to the castle and down again, ignoring entire tracts of this ancient quarter. But the details are what make this side of the city so exquisite:

the ancient house signs, the terraced gardens climbing the slopes, the pubs tucked away in narrow cobbled lanes. It can be explored only on foot; the steepness of the streets can make this a tiring, yet always rewarding, experience. With few permanent residents compared with the bustling districts across the river and the suburbs, Malá Strana is particularly enchanting at night, when the visitors have gone and there is nothing in the townscape to spoil the illusion that you have stepped back three centuries. ∎

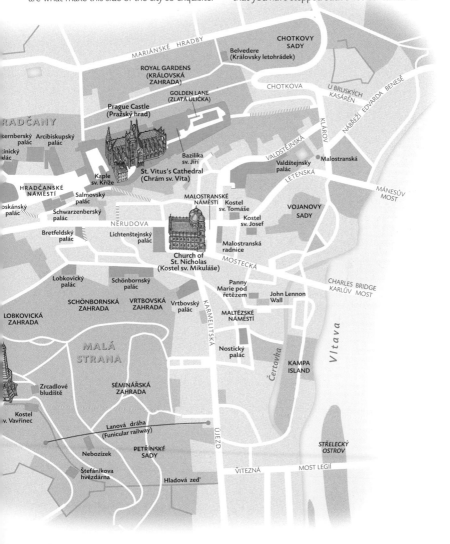

Prague Castle

From below, Prague Castle (Pražský hrad) looks monolithic and forbidding, but within the castle gates you find yourself in a town within a town. Scattered among the precinct's courtyards and picturesque lanes are the royal palace and the cathedral, plus many other palaces, a Romanesque basilica, and the fortifications. Allow plenty of time here, as many of the buildings are museums, and both the cathedral and the royal palace are among the highlights of any visit to Prague.

The Changing of the Guards at Prague Castle takes place every hour on the hour.

Prague Castle

🅰 63

✉ Hradčanské náměstí

💲 $–$$$$ depends on tour options

☎ 224 373 368

🚃 Tram: 12, 22, 23 (Malostranské náměstí); 22, 23 (Pražský hrad); 1, 2, 8, 18 (Prašný most). Metro: Malostranská, Hradčanská

Cathedral of St. Vitus's

One of the great Gothic cathedrals of Europe, St. Vitus's (Chrám sv. Víta) occupies a magnificent perch high above the River Vltava. It stands in the third courtyard of Prague Castle on the site of a rotunda church of 929. When Prague became an archbishopric in 1344, King John of Luxembourg (r. 1310–1346) decided to build a larger church worthy of the city, but it took

600 years to complete.

Charles IV (r. 1346–1378) continued with these ambitious schemes, calling on the services of the French architect Matthew of Arras. When Matthew died in 1352, only parts of the choir and its radiating chapels and the ambulatory had been completed. He was succeeded in 1356 by the Swabian architect Peter Parler, who built the superb choir and the glorious south porch known as the Golden Gate. The tower was added by Parler's sons after his death in 1399.

The Hussite wars in the 15th century halted construction, but work was resumed in the mid-16th century. Bonifác Wohlmut is credited with topping the unfinished **Great Tower,** which was further capped by a cupola designed by Nikolaus Pacassi in 1770. The total height of the tower is 317 feet (96.5 m). Work continued on the west front in the 1870s, but the cathedral was not finally completed until 1929. Despite having such a protracted history, the neo-Gothic west end blends well with the original Gothic structure, and the interior manages to be thoroughly French in its elegance.

Interior: Before the west front was built, the **Golden Gate** (Zlatá brána) was the main entrance into the cathedral. This radiant expression of imperial pride portrays Charles IV and Elisabeth of Pomerania kneeling beneath Christ in Majesty in glass mosaics, which consist of more than a million colored pieces. On either side is a Last Judgment. The huge window above the gate was added in 1908, but it blends in well enough with the Gothic structure. The Parlers' choir is equally masterly, an exuberant jungle of flying buttresses and gargoyles.

As you enter the cathedral, the first impression of the interior is one of harmony, which is surprising given its prolonged construction history. Look up and along the gallery above the nave. You may just be able to glimpse a series of busts of the royal family and other dignitaries, carved by the Parler workshop, but you will need binoculars to see them properly.

In the center of the choir is the immense **imperial mausoleum,** completed in 1589 for the tombs of Ferdinand I, his wife, Anna Jagiellon, and their son Maximilian II. It is surrounded by a beautiful, wrought-iron grille by J. Schmidthammer. The tombs were created by the Dutch sculptor Alexander Collin between 1571 and 1589. Three effigies lie in repose on top of the tombs.

Side chapels: Return to the west end of the cathedral to look at the numerous side chapels. The first ones on the north side contain late Gothic altarpieces and paintings, as well as monumental heraldic tomb slabs. In the third chapel there is brightly colored stained glass by Alfons Mucha (1860–1939).

Cathedral of St. Vitus's

 63

✉ Pražský hrad

🕐 Choir & steeple closed Mon.

🚌 Bus: 22, 23. Metro: Malostranská

PRAGUE CATHEDRAL TOUR OPTIONS
The **long tour** includes Old Royal Palace, St. George's Basilica, Convent of St. George, Golden Lane with Daliborka Tower, Prague Castle Picture Gallery, and Powder Tower ($$$$$).

The **short tour** covers the Old Royal Palace, St. George's Basilica, and Golden Lane with Daliborka Tower ($$$).

English language audio guides are available for an extra fee.

Czech Phrases

Promiň	Excuse me
Děkuje	Thank you
Kde je...	Where is...
Vpravo	Right
Vlevo	Left
Rovno	Straight
Kolík to stoje?	How much does it cost?
Zaplatím	I'd like to pay
Dve pivo, prosím	Two beers, please
Pokoj pro dva, prosím	A room for two, please
Pomoc!	Help!
Potřebujeme doktor	We need a doctor

St. Vitus's Cathedral

Renaissance Bell Tower

Twin West Towers

West Front

Main Entrance

Triforium

Nave

Old Provost's House

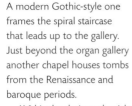

Chapel of St. Wenceslas

Great Tower

A modern Gothic-style one frames the spiral staircase that leads up to the gallery. Just beyond the organ gallery another chapel houses tombs from the Renaissance and baroque periods.

Within the choir, on the right, you come to the first of a series of wooden reliefs carved in 1623 by Caspar Bechteller, including a vivid depiction of the flight of Frederick V of the Palatinate after the Battle of White Mountain. Others give a vivid impression of Prague just before the baroque period. Note that Charles Bridge (Karlův most) has been carved without its statues. Close by is a far more modern work, the bronze statue of Cardinal Bedřich Schwarzenberg at prayer by Josef Myslbek (1895).

Tombs: Several chapels in the north ambulatory contain tombs of the 11th- and 12th-century Přemyslid kings, produced by the Parler workshop in the 1370s. In the reliquary chapel, these include tombs for Otakar I and Otakar II. Between the Virgin Mary Chapel and the high altar is the tomb of St. Vitus, a surprisingly modest 19th-century repository for his relics.

The medieval royal tombs in the side chapels and the Habsburg tombs in the burial vaults are overshadowed by the glorious **tomb of St. John of Nepomuk.** Wenceslas (Václav) IV ordered John to be thrown into the Vltava in 1393, and in doing so created a Czech martyr (see pp. 27–28). After John was murdered, his body was recovered, and a cult

developed around him, resulting in his canonization in 1729. Johann Bernhard Fischer von Erlach's son Joseph Emanuelhis designed the spectacular tomb in 1736, using two tons of silver in the process. The saint kneels on his canopied tomb, which is supported by angels and enclosed within a marble balustrade.

Neighboring chapels are filled with riches: four silver half figures of saints in **St. Adalbert's Chapel,** dating from the late 1690s; a monumental tomb slab in the **Waldstein Chapel** bearing the features of Peter Parler; and, facing

INSIDER TIP:

Follow the side aisle around the church and behind the apse you will find the huge silver tomb of St. John of Nepomuk, who was martyred by being tossed from the Charles Bridge.

—ROZ HOAGLAND
Guide, Hoagland Art Travel

the chapel, another carved panel by Bechteller depicting the destruction of the Cathedral of Sts. Vitus's, Václav, and Adalbert by the Hussites on December 21, 1619. Next to the Waldstein Chapel is the rather grotesque **Vladislav Oratory,** created by Benedikt Ried in 1493 with tracery in the form of twigs and branches. Look for the polychrome figure portraying a miner leaping forward and bearing a lamp; it's by Matthias Braun.

Vault: The entrance to the royal burial vault is in the next chapel, the **Holy Cross Chapel,** where you will find a silver altar and a faded 14th-century fresco of the patron saints of Bohemia. The passage down to the vault leads through some of the Romanesque remains of the rotunda. Many of Bohemia's rulers—Charles IV, George of Poděbrady, Václav IV, and Rudolf II—are buried here, though most rest in modern tombs from the 1930s.

As you emerge from the vault, return to the ambulatory. To the right of the Holy Cross Chapel is the **Martinitz Chapel** with its Renaissance tombs. Jaroslav von Martinitz was a fanatical Catholic who survived the Second Defenestration of 1618 (see p. 30) and lived on for more than 30 years. Opposite the chapel is a finely carved monument to the distinguished military commander Count Schlick created by Joseph Emanuel Fischer von Erlach and František Kaňka.

Chapel of St. Wenceslas:

The last chapel in the ambulatory is the most splendid: the Chapel of St. Wenceslas (Kaple sv. Václava), built by Peter Parler between 1362 and 1367 above the saint's burial place. The shrine, from the early the 20th century, is embellished with a silver bust of the saint. Some 1,300 semiprecious stones—jasper, amethyst, and chrysoprase—are embedded in the walls, which are painted with fresco cycles from the 1370s. The lower cycle shows scenes from the Passion, executed by Prague's Master Oswald, court painter to Charles IV. The upper cycle is by one of Bohemia's great medieval painters, the Master of Litoměřice; illustrating scenes from the life of Wenceslas, these date from the 1500s. A panel to the right of the 14th-century statue of Wenceslas, by Jíndřich Parler, depicts the moment when the saint was murdered. With so much decoration it is easy to overlook the powerful bronze candelabrum of 1532 by Hans Vischer of Nuremberg.

Before leaving the cathedral, take a look at the modern stained glass. In addition to the work of Alfons Mucha, there is the rose window in the west front by Josef Klasak, based on 1920s designs by

---

St. Wenceslas & the Door Knocker

St. Wenceslas (Václav) was cut down by assassins as he was reaching for a church door knocker in 929 or 935—the victim of a power struggle with his brother Boleslav. According to legend, Wenceslas remained standing even after he had been killed. This explains why the knocker in the chapel is attached to the door near the ambulatory. The knocker, however, dates from the 14th century.

František Kysela. In the south transept, an immense window by Max Švabinský, completed in 1934, depicts the Last Judgment.

Beyond the Cathedral

Founded in the ninth century as a Přemysl fortress, Prague Castle has often been the seat of political power in the Czech lands. There were extensive building programs during the reigns of Charles IV (r. 1346–1378) and Vladislav Jagiellon II (r. 1471–1516), and again under the Habsburgs. Since 1918 the castle has been the official residence of the nation's president, and guards dressed in uniforms created by Theodor Pištěk—the Oscar-winning costume designer for the 1984 film *Amadeus*–parade in the First Courtyard (První nádvoří) to protect the state rooms.

Second Courtyard: Within the Druhé nádvoří, entered through the impressive baroque Matthias Gate (Matyášova brána) of 1614, is the boxy **Holy Cross Chapel** (Kaple sv. Křiže), with its charming gilt and frescoed interior. Access is from the *bureau de change* (exchange office) that occupies part of the building. The chapel, designed by Nikolaus Pacassidates, dates from the mid-18th century. In the opposite corner of this courtyard is the entrance to the **Castle Gallery** (Obrazárna Pražského hradu), located in the former stables. Although the contents are based on Emperor Rudolf II's collection, they have

Towering stained-glass windows adorn the nave of St. Vitus's.

been expanded–paintings by Titian, Veronese, Tintoretto, and Rubens, and Czech baroque masters such as Petr Brandl. Near the gallery is the entrance to the immense **Spanish Hall** (Španělský sál), built in the early 17th century *(closed to the public)*.

Arched passageways lead from the Second Courtyard to the square beside the cathedral Tucked against the west end is the **Old Provost's House** (Staré Proboštsví), a dignified 17th-century building on the site of the former

Old Royal Palace
🕐 Closed Mon.

Prague Castle

bishop's palace. Just beyond the house, right in the middle of the courtyard, stands a rare copy of a Gothic, 14th-century equestrian sculpture of St. George and the Dragon by the brothers Jiří and Martin of Cluj.

Old Royal Palace: Straight ahead is the entrance to the 12th-century Old Royal Palace (Starý královský palác), which is built on multiple levels. It contains the castle's newest exhibit, "The Story of Prague Castle." Just beyond the entrance hall is the large **Vladislav Hall** (Vladislavský sál), designed by Benedikt Ried in the late 15th century. Lit by enormous Renaissance windows, this hall has brilliant vaulting, one of Ried's hallmarks. A passage on

the right leads to the **Bohemian Chancellery** (Česká kancelář), another Renaissance chamber; it was from here that Prague's Second Defenestration took place in 1618 (see p. 30). Protestant nobles, indignant at the loss of privileges under Matthias, confronted two Catholic governors and their secretary and ejected them from the windows (they survived).

Various rooms can be reached from the Vladislav Hall: **Diet Hall,** the former throne

Prague Castle

Labels: St. Vitus's Cathedral · Powder Tower · Castle Gallery · Third Courtyard · Second Courtyard · First Courtyard · Matthias Gate · Bastion Garden · Castle Gates · Holy Cross Chapel · Old Provost's House

room, saw the deliberations of the Bohemian nobility; a spiral staircase leads to the New Appeal Court of 1558 and its adjoining repository of land rolls, which documented the property rights of the Bohemian Estates. In these rooms, the ceilings are beautifully decorated with colored crests. A doorway from Vladislav Hall leads to Ried's astonishing staircase, with its knotty rib vaults; the staircase is broad enough to accommodate mounted horsemen riding to participate in the tournaments that were held in the hall.

Powder Tower
🕐 Closed Mon.

Basilica & Convent of St. George
🕐 Closed Mon.

Convent of St. George

Golden Lane

White Tower

Black Tower

Lobkowicz Palace

Basilica of St. George

Old Royal Palace

Ramparts Gardens

Steps leading to the Little Quarter

St. George's Square: The staircase leads down to Jiřské náměstí, which is close to both the Basilica of St. George and the Convent of St. George. Vikářská, a lane alongside the cathedral choir, leads to one of the castle towers on the right, the Mihulka or **Powder Tower** of 1494, rebuilt in the 16th century. During Emperor Rudolf II's time, it was an alchemist's workshop, and later it served as a gunpowder storehouse. The tower currently has a display on the Castle Guards.

During its restoration, the **Basilica of St. George** (Bazilika sv. Jiří) was stripped of most of its

EXPERIENCE: Prague Castle Music & Art

Czech President Václav Klaus has a knack for creating international headlines that may trouble Czechs, usually when he worries that the European Union will be the death of independence. But there's no questioning his taste in music, at least. The **Jazz at the Castle** series *(www .jazznahrade.cz)*, begun after he took over from predecessor Václav Havel in 2003, regularly attracts top international talent for performances in historic halls that are a treat in themselves. Past guest stars such as Israeli bass artist Avishai Cohen, pianist Hank Jones, and guitar master Rudy Linka have made for unforgettable evenings in the grand Bohemian tradition.

Summer plays and well curated gallery shows also draw audiences to the castle, including Shakespeare classics performed in Czech. The **Culture at the Castle** series *(www.kulturanahrade.cz)* organizes exhibitions such as prewar paintings by Josef Čapek, documentary photography, and diverse performances from Gregorian choirs to historical collections from key moments in Czech history.

It's all a far cry from the usual guided architecture and chapel tours.

INSIDER TIP:

The audio tour of Lobkowicz Palace, narrated in Prince Lobkowicz's own voice, is sprinkled with family stories that add a friendly touch.

—BARBARA NOE
National Geographic Books editor

baroque encrustations and returned to its pristine Romanesque form. A church has stood on this spot since around 920, making it older than St. Vitus's, although the present basilica dates from 1142; the somber facade was constructed in the 1670s. In front of the choir are the painted wooden tomb of Vlatislav I, who died in 921, and a tomb slab, possibly belong to Duke Boleslav II, who died in 999. Ludmila, the wife of the ninth-century ruler Duke Bořivoj, is buried in the basilica, too; she is venerated as the first female Czech martyr and saint.

Adjacent to the basilica is the **Convent of St. George** (Klášter sv. Jiří). During the reign of Joseph II (1780–1790), the convent was secularized and used as a barracks. In the 1950s the buildings were renovated and converted into the present gallery. For many years it housed the republic's finest medieval art, now located in St. Agnes convent (Anežský klášter; see pp. 108–111). St. George's has retained its collections of mannerist and baroque art. Whereas medieval art is comparatively rare, 17th-century paintings and altarpieces are encountered everywhere. St. George's has many dark canvases by Karel Škréta (1610–1674) and Jan Kryštof Liška (1650–1712), along with striking canvases such as the self-portrait by Jan Kupecký (1667–1740). His many portraits of old men show Petr Brandl to be a great painter; included is his study of one of the Apostles. Also worthwhile are the baroque sculptures by such masters as Ferdinand Brokoff and Matthias Braun.

Continue past the basilica along Jiřská. On the left is **Golden Lane** (see p 74), a street of artisans' cottages in sharp contrast to the palatial splendors. The tower at the end of the lane is the **Dalibor Tower** (Daliborka), named after a violin-playing knight who was imprisoned here; his story was the subject of an opera by Smetana.

Lobkowicz Palace: Returning from Golden Lane to Jiřská, you come to an imposing mansion, the Lobkowicz Palace (Lobkovický palác). Originally built in the 16th century, in 1952 it was confiscated from Prince Maximilian Lobkowicz by the Communists. Returned to the family in 2003 under restitution laws, the gorgeous building now houses the Princely Collections. Through beautifully reconstructed galleries filled with world-famous paintings, decorative arts, and musical instruments, you'll discover 700 years of family history, which parallels the history of central Europe itself. You'll come across such marvelous treasures as Pieter Brueghel the Elder's "Haymaking" (Gallery H); an original score of Beethoven's Symphony (Gallery G), with corrections made in the master composer's own hand; and one of central Europe's important collections of firearms. The palace hosts occasional concerts; the café with its panoramic view is an ideal spot to take rest; and the museum shop stocks quality items.

Opposite the palace is the 16th-century **Burgrave's House** (Nejvyšší purkrabství), which in communist times was converted into one of the world's largest toy museums and a children's center. At the far end of Jiřská stands the grim **Black Tower** (Černá věž), the castle's eastern gate, built in the 12th century and rebuilt during Renaissance times. Inside you'll find a display of gruesome torture devices from the Middle Ages. From here the Old Castle Steps lead to the Malostranská metro. ∎

Lobkowicz Palace
🕐 Closed Mon.
💲 $$$

During the restoration of the Basilica of St. George in 1670, the Romanesque front was replaced with a baroque one.

Golden Lane

Tucked against the castle walls, Golden Lane (Zlatá ulička) is framed by the White Tower (Bílá věž) and Dalibor Tower (Daliborka). This now charming little street, with its brightly painted cottages, was the haunt of alchemists during the reign of Rudolf II (1576–1611). The lane was originally inhabited by members of the imperial entourage.

Emperor Rudolf was greatly interested in alchemy, and in the 16th century English pseudo-scientists such as Edward Kelley and John Dee found a welcome at the Bohemian court, where the emperor became a devotee of the mystical arts. Rudolf, a troubled man given to spells of insanity, was fascinated by the theories of alchemists and other quasi-scientists who claimed the keys to the secrets of the universe. Alchemy was essentially the application of scientific principles, as then understood, to magic. Its principal goals were to find the elixir of eternal life and to transform base metals into gold, but there was a strong mystical component in its experiments. Although many alchemists were quacks, the subject was taken seriously, and in the 17th century mathematician Sir Isaac Newton conducted alchemical investigations.

Golden Lane actually took its name not from the alchemists, but from the goldsmiths who lived here in the late 17th century. It was greatly improved when Empress Maria Theresa (r. 1740–1780) required that the shabby wooden houses be rebuilt from more solid materials such as brick. The street became fashionable as an artists' quarter in the late 19th century. Franz Kafka and his sister lived at No. 22 for a short while in 1917. Nobel Prize–winning poet Jaroslav Seifert was a resident a decade later, but his house no longer exists.

In the 1950s, the residents were moved out and the present-day color scheme was devised. Thus over the centuries a slum was converted into a picturesque lane dedicated to selling souvenirs. The somewhat folksy appearance of Golden Lane offers a stark contrasts to the two towers—used as prisons until the 18th century.

Colorfully painted shops adorn the much restored Golden Lane.

Around Prague Castle

Hradčany (Castle district), an area alongside the castle, occupies a spur above Malá Strana. It was originally a residential neighborhood for the employees of the castle. Some of the streets around Nový Svět retain that artisanal atmosphere, but much of Hradčany is today occupied by immense palaces and gardens.

The old castle steps wind up to the castle from Malá Strana.

The Royal Gardens

For his wife, Anna, Ferdinand I commissioned Paolo della Stella of Genoa and Bonifác Wohlmut in the 16th century to design **Belvedere** (Královsky letohrádek), the exquisite Renaissance pleasure palace set within the **Royal Gardens** (Královská zahrada). Stately arcades transform the first floor into a shady loggia, and the copper roof resembles an inverted ship's hull.

In front of the building is the Singing Fountain of 1568, though it requires considerable imagination to discern the song created by the water falling into the bronze bowl. Since the Belvedere is now used as an art gallery, you can visit it only when special exhibitions are held.

Also in the Royal Gardens is Wohlmut's **Ball Game Hall** (Míčovna), built in 1569. Since the original structure was destroyed

Castle District

⚑ 63

Schwarzenberg Palace

✉ Hradčanské náměstí 233

☎ 233 081 716

www.ngprague.cz

during World War II, what you see today, including the sgraffito decoration, is a modern reconstruction. Once a tennis court, the building was converted into a stable block in 1723. The former baroque **Riding School** (Jrdzárna), designed by Jean-Baptiste Mathey, now houses an exhibition gallery.

Near Hradčany Square

Hradčany Square (Hradčanské náměstí), with Ferdinand Brokoff's plague column of 1726, faces the entrance to the castle. On the left is the 19th-century

Salm Palace (Salmovsky palác) and the Renaissance bulk of the gabled **Schwarzenberg Palace** (Schwarzenberský palác), its surfaces entirely covered with the best sgraffito designs in Prague. Originally built for the Lobkowicz family (see p. 73), it was bought by the Schwarzenbergs in 1719. It now contains the National Gallery's (Národní galerie) most impressive collection of baroque painting and sculpture.

Across the square stands the elegant **Archbishop's Palace** (Arcibiskupský palác), with its delightful rococo facade. The palace was designed by Wohlmut for Ferdinand I, who wanted a suitably impressive headquarters for a Catholic archbishop. It has been much altered and renovated, but the final outcome is very satisfying. The stucco decoration on the facade dates from the 1760s.

A passage alongside the Archbishop's Palace leads to the **Sternberg Palace** (Šternberský palác), designed by Giovanni Alliprandi and since 1949 the home of the National Gallery's fine collection of European art. The collection was begun by Count František Josef Šternberk in 1796, and it was rapidly expanded by gifts from other families. It includes Byzantine icons and exceptional Renaissance bronzes. One of the finest medieval works is the eloquent "Lamentation of Christ" by Lorenzo Monaco (1408). Among the other highlights are the confident and complex "Feast of the Rosary" (1506) by Albrecht Dürer, part of Rudolf II's personal collection;

Nový Svět is Hradčany's most picturesque and tranquil lane.

Decorative Art & Design

Ever since at least the golden age of Bohemia in the 14th century under Charles IV, Prague has attracted some of the finest artisans in Europe, hundreds of whom were inspired to create intricate works that go far beyond traditional painting and sculpture. Indeed, decorative art, whether in the form of royal jewelry, ornamental glass, fabulous textiles, or refined woodwork and inlaid furniture, has gilded the lives of many of the city's wealthier denizens through the centuries.

The best of the country's immense collection can be seen at the fascinating **Museum of Decorative Arts** in Old Town *(17, Listopadu 2, tel 251 093 111, closed Mon., $$, Tram: 17, Metro: Staromestská; www.upm .cz).* It's also known as UmPrum, a word created from the Czech for Decorative Arts (as in Uměleckoprůmyslové muzeum, the full name). Founded in 1885, it lies opposite the Rudolfinum concert hall. Although its exhibits range from the Middle Ages to the 20th century and include superb clocks, porcelain, and furnishings, the main attraction is the magnificent collection of art nouveau and art deco objects.

So many thousands of fine pieces are in the state's collections, however, that the National Gallery's newest venue, the **Schwarzenberg Palace**, and its major modern art venue, **Veletržní Palace** (for both see *www.ngprague.cz*), also are needed to host works ranging from Alfons Mucha windows to intricate baroque gowns.

INSIDER TIP:

The view from the lookout point near Hradčany Square helps you understand why Prague is called the city of 1,000 spires.

—BARBARA NOE
National Geographic Books editor

the sensuous 1530s "Adam and Eve" by Lucas Cranach the Elder, as well as three other works by the same artist; the wonderfully sulky portrait of Eleanor of Toledo by Agnolo Bronzino; a luminous head of Christ by El Greco; a Rembrandt painting depicting a scholar in his study (1634); the rugged portrait of Don Miguel de Lardizábal by Goya; and works by Tintoretto, Hals, and Rubens. On the second floor is the Chinese Cabinet, a finely restored room with black lacquered walls where the Šternberks exhibited their Oriental porcelain collection.

At the square's far end, you will find the heavy Roman baroque **Tuscany Palace** (Toskánský palác), at one time the property of the Grand Dukes of Tuscany. Close to the palace, the Renaissance **Martinitz Palace** (Martinický palác), at No. 8, belonged to one of the imperial counselors defenestrated in 1618 (see p. 30). The house at No. 6 still belongs to the Mucha family. Once a museum created by Alfons's son Jiří, in the 1990s it was replaced by the Mucha Museum in the New Town (see p. 137).

Beyond the Tuscany Palace, Loretánská leads past the former town hall (Hradčanská radnice) of 1603 and some 18th-century *(continued on p. 82)*

Sternberg Palace

 Hradčanské náměstí 15

☎ 233 090 570

🕐 Closed Mon.

🚊 Tram: 22, 23 (Pražský hrad)

💲 $$$; free first Wed. of the month

www.ngprague.cz

A Walk Around Little Quarter

This walk will take you through all the main streets and lanes of Little Quarter (Malá Strana). Huddled around the castle are baroque palaces and mansions, while lower and closer to the river are more palaces as well as some of Prague's most lavish and interesting churches and squares.

The exquisite baroque Vrtba Gardens are concealed behind a house on Karmelitská.

Start this walk from **Malá Strana Square** (Malostranské náměstí), easily reached by tram 12 or 22. You will return here later so begin by walking up **Nerudova ❶**, one of the best preserved baroque streets in the city, to get a general feel of Malá Strana. At the top, Nerudova becomes Úvoz, a cobbled lane lined with charming baroque houses that leads to the **Strahov Monastery** (see pp. 83–84). Retracing your steps down Nerudova—named for poet Jan Neruda, who once lived at No. 47, note the glorious collection of facades and carved signs that identified the houses before numbering became the norm. Larger buildings include the 1765 **Bretfeld Palace** (Bretfeldský palác, No. 33), with its baroque railings. The 1720s **Thun-Hohenstein Palace** (Thun-Hohenštejnský palác, No. 20), now the Italian Embassy, has

NOT TO BE MISSED:

Church of St. Nicholas • Lobkowicz Palace • Vrtba Gardens • Kampa Island • Wallenstein Gardens

striking Renaissance gables at the rear and a principal doorway guarded by two eagles carved by Matthias Braun. **Number 12** has a charming sign in the form of three fiddles; a family of violinmakers, the Edlingers, once lived here. Number 5, the **Moržin Palace** (Moržinský palác), is adorned with stooped figures of Moors. At the foot of Nerudova you can quench your thirst at the excellent beer hall, U Kocoura (At the Cat), after tackling the hills of Hradčany.

Malá Strana Square

Now it's time to explore Malá Strana Square. In the center stands the **Church of St. Nicholas** (Kostel sv. Mikuláše) **❷**, and, facing it, at the top of the square, rise the majestic plague column of 1715 and the vast **Lichtenstein Palace** (Lichtenštejnský palác) of 1791 at No. 13. The church is one of the masterpieces by the Dientzenhofers, father and son. Its facade, completed in 1710, is curvaceous and eloquent; the interior's undulating galleries are richly painted and crowded with fine statues by Ignác Platzer the Elder. Admire the trompe l'oeil paintings in the dome, the green and pink marble piers, the four massive statues of the Church Fathers by Platzer beneath the dome, and the enormous pulpit by Richard and Peter Prachner. The gilt organ was played by Mozart during his 1787 visit.

Now walk to the bottom of the square. Number 21 is the former district **town hall** (Malostranská radnice), completed in 1622 in Renaissance style; today it holds a restaurant, snack bar, and music club. Facing the parking lot at No. 18 is the arcaded, turreted **Smirickych Palace** (Smiřický palác), built in the 17th century and modified a century later.

Sněmovní, the lane beside the palace, leads to more baroque palaces; some are now Czech parliament offices. After a short distance you reach Thunovská. Turn left and pass the British Embassy and then to the steps that lead up to Prague Castle. From Thunovská you can see the rear of some of the palaces along Nerudova, many of them Renaissance in origin. Zámecká lane brings you back to Malá Strana Square.

> ⊠   See area map pp. 62–63
> ►   Malá Strana Square
> ⊕   3 miles (5 km)
> ⬌   4 hours, plus time for lunch
> ►   Vojanovy Garden

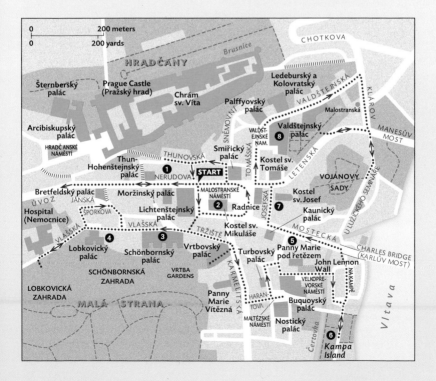

Tržiště & Vlašská Streets

From No. 12 at the top of the square, a passage leads to Tržiště and Vlašská. Today, many of the palaces along here are embassies. Turn right up Vlašská. On the left at No. 15, the **Schönborn Palace** (Schönbornský palác) ❸, with its carved wooden doors and splendid gardens, is the U.S. Embassy. Continue to the spectacularly pedimented **Lobkowicz Palace** (Lobkovický palác) ❹, the German Embassy. In late 1989 thousands invaded these gardens and began the exodus that led to the collapse of the communist regimes of Eastern Europe. Continue walking and opposite the hospital entrance on Vlašská is a gate on the left that leads to a park that overlooks Lobkowicz.

Backtrack to Lobkowicz Palace, where opposite Sporkova street leads to a small square; on the corner with Jánská is a charming sgraffitoed house. Cross the square and bear right until you reach Vlašská again. Back track toward the main square until you reach Karmelitská. On the corner of Karmelitská at No. 25 is the **Vrtba Palace** (Vrtbovský palác,) where artist Mikolás Ales once lived.

A passage beneath the palace leads to the terraced **Vrtba Gardens** (Vrtbovská zahrada; closed Nov.–March), a tranquil place to take a break. Walking past, you would never suspect

there are delightful baroque gardens on the slopes behind the palace. About 330 feet (100 m) down Karmelitská on the right you'll see the early baroque **Church of Our Lady Victorious** (Panny Marie Vítězná). This Carmelite church houses the venerated doll-like statue, "Infant Jesus of Prague" ("Pražské Jezulátko"). Visitors come from all over the world to pray to the statue and to leave gifts.

Toward the Vltava

From Karmelitská turn left down Harantova to Maltézské náměstí, a peaceful square dominated by the **Nostitz Palace** (Nostický palác) and Ferdinand Brokoff's statue of St. John the Baptist. At No. 6, the lovely rococo 18th-century **Turba Palace** (Turbovský palác) houses the Japanese Embassy. Behind the U Malířů restaurant is the **Church of St. Mary Under the Chain** (Panny Marie pod řetězem) ❺, the oldest church in Malá Strana, dating from 1169. Romanesque arcades and two squat Gothic towers survive; the interior is a baroque design by Carlo Lurago (1640).

To the left of the church are several baroque mansions, including the former hotel at No. 11 where Mozart and Beethoven once stayed. To the right, at No. 2, is the former palace of the Grand Priory (Velkopřevorský palác), and

---

EXPERIENCE: Sunday Jams at UMG

Prague's acclaimed jazz club is surprisingly unprepossessing—a well-worn bar at street level, and a submarine-size music one below that opens around 9 p.m. Nevertheless, **U Malého Glena** (Karmelitska 23, www.malyglen.cz) holds a special place in the memories of many; it's infused with an inclusive spirit and attracts colorful Bohemians, both local and international.

One great way to meet and bond with them is on the micro stage, where Sunday jazz jams have attracted scores of players and singers since the place opened in the mid-1990s. The last Sunday evening of each month is given over to the blues jam,

MC'd capably by the Chicago guitarist and crooner Rene Trossman.

For any jam, just show up a little before 9 p.m. and tell the bar staff collecting the entrance fee you're there to perform. The host will put you on the sign-up sheet and tell you when you're up after ascertaining what your specialty is, if any.

Crowds are relaxed, small, and forgiving, so there's no excuse to let the shy bug stop you. Letting loose in Little Glen's, as it's also known, is an experience to be remembered—and your adventures as an artist in Bohemia will make for a great tale to recount when you're back home.

INSIDER TIP:

If you are a Beatles fan, the John Lennon Wall, near Panny Marie pod řetězem, is a must. The graffiti wall pays homage to the singer; pause and write a personal message on the wall.

—WENDY YASCUR
National Geographic contributor

residence of the Grand Prior of the Knights of Malta. Around the corner, on peaceful Velkopřevorské náměstí, are the two Buquoy palaces, both belonging to the French Embassy, and from here it is a few paces to **Kampa Island ⑥**. The Čertovka stream divides the island from the main shore. Here, the largest of the three mills has been restored. Until the 16th century the island served as private gardens belonging to the palaces. The peaceful park was created in the 1940s. Depart in the direction of Charles Bridge (Karlův most) to reach the large square— and former pottery market—called Na Kampě.

To Mostecká & Around

Climb the steps to the bridge and turn left along bustling Mostecká. Despite the glittering shops here, don't ignore the older buildings above. The finest is the 1775 **Kaunicky Palace** (Kaunický palác), with its rococo facade. The street opposite is Josefská, which leads to the baroque **Church of St. Joseph** (Kostel sv. Josef) ⑦ on the right (with a simple domed interior and a painting of the Holy Family by Petr Brandl on the altar). The **Church of St. Thomas** (Kostel sv. Tomáše), straight ahead, is another masterpiece by Kilián Ignác Dientzenhofer. Frescoes in stucco frames adorn the ceiling and dome; the pews are richly carved. The church and its monastery are part of an unusual business enterprise. With its buildings in near ruin after the Soviet departure, the monastery partnered with Rocco Forte Collection, to convert seven

of the buildings into the luxury Augustine hotel (see Travelwise p. 302). Monks share the cloisters and live in separate quarters. Stop by the hotel's Brewery Bar, housed in St. Thomas's former brewery, where the signature beer has been brought back to life.

Return past the church to the square where Tomášská, yet another street with fine baroque houses, links Malá Strana Square with Wallenstein Square. A statue of St. Hubert and a stag adorn the portal at No. 4, a celebrated baroque house. At No. 14 is the large **Palffy Palace** (Palffyovský palác), partly the Prague conservatory, partly a restaurant.

Wallenstein Palace (Valdštejnský palác) ⑧, a magnificent early baroque residence of ambitious warrior Albrecht von Wallenstein (see pp. 31–32), dominates the square of the same name. Three gardens and 23 houses were destroyed to make room for this palace. In its heyday it employed 700 servants and had its own riding school and sumptuous gardens.

Unlike the palace, now used as the Czech Senate, the gardens are open to the public. Before visiting them, follow the curve of Valdštejnská, where two palaces—the **Ledebur Palace** (Ledeburský palác) at No. 3 opposite the Wallenstein Palace, and the **Kolowrat Palace** (Kolovratský palác) at Valdštejnská 10— have terraced gardens clambering up the slopes behind them. These gardens have been linked by staircases and passages to create a multi-level series of terraces, pavilions, and loggias (*$$*).

To reach the Wallenstein Palace's gorgeous **gardens,** bear right at the end of the street; cut through the metro station, and take a right on Letenská. The entrance, several doors down at No. 10, is marked but not numbered. The gardens—dominated by the impressive 1627 loggia known as the **Sala Terrena**—accommodate an aviary and a chestnut grove dotted with statuary. Another formal garden, the **Vojanovy Garden** (Vojanovy sady), along U lužického semináře, between here and Charles Bridge, is usually less crowded. From here you can return past Letenská on the left to the Malostranská metro.

Loreto Church

🏛 62

✉ Loretánské náměstí

🕐 Closed Mon.

💲 $$

www.loreta.cz

palaces. It then enters a square dominated by the enormous **Černín Palace** (Černínský palác), completed in 1697 for the imperial ambassador to Venice. Francesco Caratti was the principal architect, and the interior decorations are by František Kaňka. In 1851 the Černín family, who could no longer afford to maintain such a vast residence, sold it to the state. Since 1929 it has served as the Foreign Ministry. Though the palace is closed to visitors, concerts are sometimes held in its gardens.

Loreto Church

Facing the palace, a ramp leads down to the **Loreto Church (Loreta)** of 1626, with a facade from the 1720s by Kilián Ignác Dientzenhofer. This extraordinary pilgrimage complex was commissioned by Kateřina of Lobkowicz, who was obsessed by the Santa Casa of Loreto, Italy. This was supposedly the home of the Holy Family until it was transported to Italy by angels in the 13th century. Kateřina's Santa Casa was not the only reproduction to be built in Europe; in the Czech lands alone there were about 50, but this is by far the most important such edifice. Here the house is surrounded by elaborate frescoed cloisters. The Loreto has great baroque charm, if your taste extends to cherubs. The Santa Casa is a brick, barrel-vaulted structure in a boxlike Renaissance-style casing enriched with statuary. Piety apart, the main reason to come here is to see the extraordinary treasury. The most dazzling exhibit is the gilded silver sunburst monstrance studded with 6,222 diamonds. Other exhibits here are embellished with pearls and amethysts.

Continue down the ramp, past the modest Capuchin church of 1602, to reach a cobbled lane called **New World** (Nový Svět). With its modest houses, dating mostly from the 17th and 18th centuries, this

Anselmo Lurago's dignified gateway leads into the Strahov Monastery.

used to be the poorest quarter of Hradčany; it is in complete contrast to the palatial splendor of the rest of the district. The artisans and servants departed long ago, and today Nový Svět is the trendy location of galleries and restaurants, although it has lost none of its charm. Despite its new chic status, Nový Svět remains a relatively isolated and tranquil corner of the city. The lane leads to another fine Dientzenhofer church, **St. John of Nepomuk** (Kostel sv. Jan Nepomucký), completed in 1729. The interior is adorned with frescoes by Václav Reiner. From here you can follow Kanovnická back to Hradčany Square.

Strahov Monastery

You enter the Strahov monastery (Strahovský klašter) complex through a substantial baroque gateway designed by Anselmo Lurago in 1742; the statue on top depicts St. Norbert, the founder of the Premonstratensian order. Straight ahead is the entrance to the abbey church, dedicated to the **Church of the Assumption of Our Lady** (Kostel Nanebevzetí Panny Marie). On the left is the soaring former **Church of St. Roch** (Kostel sv. Rocha), built on the orders of Rudolf II in 1612; it is now used for art exhibitions. Within the spacious courtyard the monks, who returned here after 1989, run a restaurant and beer garden.

The facade of the abbey church is another of Lurago's designs, embellished with statues by Johann Anton Quittainer (1709–1765), who also carved the statues above the gateway. Step into the nave and you will be treated to the ravishing sight of this glorious—and wonderfully restored—church, with its symmetrical altarpieces marking the eye's passage toward the lofty, exuberant main altar.

INSIDER TIP:

Walk through the picturesque New World part of the Castle district, open the little gate leading to the upper part of Stag's Moat, walk on the footbridges to the green meadow, and picnic there (April–Oct.).

—MILOŠ ČUŘIK
Tour guide, Arts & Music Travel

Look up and admire the stunning rococo frescoed ceiling. The furnishings richly reconstructed in the 18th century—pulpit, pews, organ, railings—are dark and sumptuous. Mozart improvised on the organ in the west gallery when he visited in 1787; the monks transcribed his impromptu composition.

The former monastic buildings now house two of the most beautiful baroque libraries in Europe, though they are only visible from their doorways. The first one is the lofty, galleried **Philosophical Library** (Filosofický sál). Its magnificent bookcases and other wooden furnishings were brought

Strahov Monastery

🏛 62

✉ Strahovské nádvorí

☎ 233 107 722 (gallery); 233 107 711 (library)

🕓 Gallery: closed Mon.

🚋 Tram: 22, 23 (Pohořelec)

💲 $

www.strahovsky klaster.cz

here after the monastery at Louka in southern Moravia was dissolved in the 1780s. So important was the Louka library that the Strahov monks had no qualms about altering the dimensions of their own library to accommodate the Moravian furnishings and the collections from Louka.

The monks further embellished the library by commissioning the great Austrian artist Franz Anton Maulbertsch (1724–1796) to paint the ceiling; he chose the theme of Enlightenment, charting the progress of humankind to knowledge under divine guidance. The Roman busts on display are a recent contribution from a private collector in 1965.

Strahov's Garden

A door in the east wall of the monastery leads to Strahov's gardens and orchards (Strahovská zahrada), which stretch down the hill in the direction of Malá Strana. This part of the grounds offers excellent views.

A corridor leads to the **Theological Library** (Teologický sál), the older of the two libraries. It was built in 1671 by Giovanni Orsi and enlarged in the 1720s. The bookcases are older than the library itself. Its intimate atmosphere is enhanced by its low ceiling, with frescoes painted by the Strahov monk Siard Nosecký and placed in elaborate stucco frames. These paintings include a self-portrait and depictions of other

illustrious members of Nosecký's monastic order. Six antique globes and wooden lecterns help furnish the library.

Most of the collections in the libraries were donations, and it's hard to imagine a finer setting for about 3,000 manuscripts and more than 1,500 incunabula (rare volumes printed before 1500). The oldest manuscript is a ninth-century lectionary, the **Strahov Gospel,** with a richly bejeweled cover; a facsimile is on display near the entrance to the Theological Library. Other rare missals, miniature books, manuscripts—including a 9th-century manuscript with 10th-century illuminations of the Evangelists—and a 14th-century astronomical atlas are on display close to the bookshop.

The cloisters beyond the east end of the church used to house a museum of Czech literature, established here in the 1950s after the monastery was closed by the Communists. Now it has been replaced by a **gallery** exhibiting about one-tenth of the monastery's own art collection of a thousand items. Highlights include a magnificent anguished Crucifixion from Jihlava (1330s); panels by the Master of Litoměřice; works by Karel Škréta, Franz Palko, Václav Reiner, and Petr Brandl; and rococo panels by Maulbertsch. The gallery also displays some of the treasury of bejeweled crosses and monstrances. As in the National Gallery (Národní galerie; see pp. 76–77), Brandl is represented by a series of dark portraits of elderly saints, and a fine self-portrait. ∎

Petřín Hill

Adjacent to Hradčany and the Castle is a large open expanse of parkland, which is known as the Petřín Hill (Petřínské sady). Largely unspoiled and in places still quite wild, it is the largest green space within the city boundaries.

Massive Petřín Hill parkland with its own Eiffel Tower look-alike

In early medieval times, this area was part of the large forest fringing the town, and vineyards grew on the sheltered southern slopes. Over time gardens and orchards replaced most of the vineyards, and many fruit trees survive, creating an enchanting sight—especially in spring when they blossom. Not surprisingly, the meandering paths that criss-cross the hill are popular with courting couples; high-energy children love them too.

You can reach the hill from various spots. There are entrances from Úvoz and Vlašská in Malá Strana and from the Strahov Monastery. Closer to the river short streets connect the park to main thoroughfares such as Karmelitská and Újezd. (From Újezd, it's quite a climb to the top of the hill, which is 1,043 feet high / 318 m).

The easiest way to reach the summit is by the **Funicular Railway** (Lanová dráha), which leaves from near Újezd. It operates every ten minutes from 9:15 a.m. until 8:30 p.m. daily. The railway was built in 1891 and has two stops, the first of which leads to the

Petřín Tower

🅰 62

🕐 Closed Mon.–
Fri. Nov.–March

💲 $$

Mirror Maze

🕐 Closed Mon.–
Fri. Nov.–March

💲 $

Observatory

🕐 Closed Mon.

💲 $

expensive Nebozízek restaurant, named for the original vineyard.

The Tower

Once at the top, you can bear right toward the **Petřín Tower** (Petřínská rozhledna)—you can't miss it, this miniature version of the Eiffel Tower. Built just two years after the original was completed in Paris, for the 1891 Prague Exposition, it demonstrates the close cultural ties between the two capital cities in the late 19th century. It was moved to this spot on **Petřín Hill** in the 1930s. It's quite a steep climb to the viewing

INSIDER TIP:

In spring, wander among the flowering fruit trees that pack the Petřínské sady. Meandering paths offer many a tree to sit under with a book. In the fall, stop by for a free snack of apples and pears.

—TAYLOR KENNEDY
National Geographic photographer

platform—almost 300 steps—but you'll be rewarded with breathtaking views over the city and far beyond. There's a handy café at the foot of the tower.

Between the funicular station and the tower you'll pass the unusual **Mirror Maze** (Zrcadlové bludiště). This neo-Gothic castle-like structure, modeled on one of

the old gates at Vyšehrad, was built at the same time as the funicular, in 1891. The maze is a major draw for children in particular, who delight both in the maze itself as well as in the rooms filled with distorting mirrors.

Behind the tower and the maze you'll see the **Hunger Wall** (Hladová zed), the surviving part of the great fortifications constructed in the 1360s by Charles IV as a public works project for the starving unemployed. The remains are quite substantial: They stretch for nearly a mile (1,200 m) and are 23 feet high (8 m), linking Újezd to the Strahov Monastery. Indeed, there are many paths on the Petřín Hill that lead directly to the monastery.

Alongside the wall, just a few paces from the Mirror Maze, stands the **Church of St. Lawrence** (Kostel sv. Vavřinec), with its distinctive onion-shaped towers. The church, designed by Ignác Palliardi, was completed in the mid-1770s on the site of an earlier Romanesque chapel, for which it is named.

You can reach the **Observatory** (Štefánikova hvězdárna) in the park by taking the path in the opposite direction from the one that leads to the tower. It's open to the public, and you can try out some of the remarkably powerful telescopes. There's a small historical exhibition of astronomical devices, many of which, like the telescopes, are intended to excite the curiosity of children.

Close to the observatory is the **Rose Garden** (Růžový sad), where you can rest before descending back to the city. ■

Anchored by Old Town Square, a maze of medieval streets studded with palaces, squares, and churches, and home to the Jewish quarter

Old Town

A pair of horses pulls a carriage through Old Town Square.

Old Town

Old Town (Staré Město) has retained its medieval layout, centered on the Old Town Square (Staroměstské náměstí). All around the square, and along the lanes connecting it with the River Vltava, stand houses with foundations dating from the 11th and 12th centuries. The Old Town Hall (Staroměstská radnice) was founded as late as 1338.

Despite the rather small area of Old Town, it contains a huge amount of cultural, religious, and educational activity. Numerous churches, both medieval and baroque; the remains of the medieval university, the Karolinum, and its Jesuit successor, the Klementinum; and the major concert hall, the Rudolfinum, all are found here. In addition to the vast Old Town Square, there are more intimate squares and marketplaces such as Betlémské náměstí and Uhelný trh. Old Town features fewer aristocratic palaces than Malá Strana, as the nobility preferred to have their residences as close to the royal palace as possible; nonetheless, the Clam-Gallas and Goltz-Kinský Palaces are as impressive as anything found on the other side of the river.

Just north of Old Town Square is the former Jewish quarter of Josefov, best known for its ancient cemetery (Starý židovský hřbitov) crowded with thousands of gravestones. Its name honors Emperor Joseph II, who showed tolerance to the Jews in the late 18th century. In 1850 it became a municipal district of the city of Prague. Overcrowding and unsanitary conditions blighted the area, which was razed toward the end of the 19th century. Its tenements were replaced by imaginatively designed blocks with art nouveau flourishes. Today it houses not only the fascinating remnants of the Jewish quarter but some of the city's chicest shopping streets, with designer boutiques and upscale restaurants and bars.

On the northeast edge of Josefov you will find the Convent of St. Agnes (Anežský klášter), with its two churches now used for concerts. St. Agnes is also notable for its display of the National Gallery's medieval art. ■

Area of map detail

Charles Bridge (Karlův most)

Muzeum Bedřicha Smetany

Uměleckoprůmyslové muzeum

Rudolfinu

NÁMĚSTÍ JANA PALACHA

Staroměstská

Kostel sv. Františka z Assisi

KŘIŽOVNICKÉ NÁMĚSTÍ

Staroměstská mostecká věž

Kostel sv. Salvátor

Náprstko muzeu

Vltava

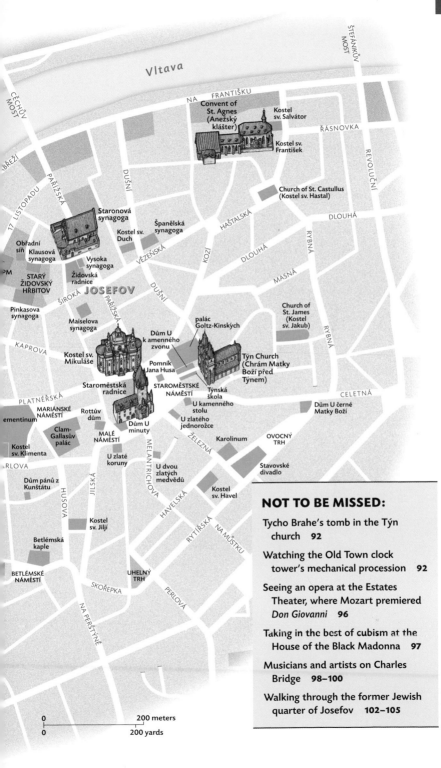

Vltava

ŠTEFÁNIKŮV MOST

ČECHŮV MOST

BŘEŽÍ

17 LISTOPADU

PARÍŽSKÁ

DUŠNÍ

NA FRANTIŠKU

Convent of St. Agnes (Anežský klášter)

Kostel sv. Salvátor

Kostel sv. František

ŘÁSNOVKA

REVOLUČNÍ

Church of St. Castullus (Kostel sv. Hastal)

DLOUHÁ

Staronová synagoga

Kostel sv. Duch

Španělská synagoga

HAŠTALSKÁ

KOŽÍ

DLOUHÁ

RYBNÁ

MÁSNÁ

Obřadní síň

Klausová synagoga

Vysoka synagoga

VĚZEŇSKÁ

PM

STARÝ ŽIDOVSKÝ HŘBITOV

Židovská radnice

ŠIROKÁ JOSEFOV

PARÍŽSKÁ

DUŠNÍ

Pinkasova synagoga

KAPROVA

Maiselova synagoga

Dům U kamenného zvonu

palác Goltz-Kinských

Church of St. James (Kostel sv. Jakub)

RYBNÁ

Kostel sv. Mikuláše

Pomník Jana Husa

Týn Church (Chrám Matky Boží před Týnem)

Staroměstská radnice

STAROMĚSTSKÉ NÁMĚSTÍ

Týnská škola

CELETNÁ

PLATNÉŘSKÁ

MARIÁNSKÉ NÁMĚSTÍ

ementinum

Rottův dům

Dům U minuty

U kamenného stolu

U zlatého jednorožce

Dům U černé Matky Boží

Clam-Gallasův palác

MALÉ NÁMĚSTÍ

ŽELEZNÁ

Karolinum

OVOCNÝ TRH

Kostel sv. Klimenta

RLOVA

U zlaté koruny

MELANTRICHOVA

U dvou zlatých medvědů

Kostel sv. Havel

Stavovské divadlo

Dům pánů z Kunštátu

HUSOVA

JILSKÁ

HAVELSKÁ

RYTÍŘSKÁ

NA MŮSTKU

Kostel sv. Jiljí

Betlémská kaple

BETLÉMSKÉ NÁMĚSTÍ

UHELNÝ TRH

SKOŘEPKA

PERLOVA

NA PERŠTÝNĚ

0   200 meters
0   200 yards

NOT TO BE MISSED:

Tycho Brahe's tomb in the Týn church 92

Watching the Old Town clock tower's mechanical procession 92

Seeing an opera at the Estates Theater, where Mozart premiered *Don Giovanni* 96

Taking in the best of cubism at the House of the Black Madonna 97

Musicians and artists on Charles Bridge 98–100

Walking through the former Jewish quarter of Josefov 102–105

Old Town Square

Immense Old Town Square is surrounded by mansions, palaces, and churches. The houses facing the square are often Romanesque in origin, but facades are mostly baroque. Since medieval times the square has been Prague's social core and home to the mightiest merchant families. It has witnessed executions and street battles, and in February 1948, Klement Gottwald proclaimed the establishment of the Communist state from the balcony of the rococo Goltz-Kinský Palace.

Restaurants and cafés now occupy many of the arcaded houses facing Old Town Square (Staroměstské náměstí).

The Goltz-Kinský Palace (palác Goltz-Kinský) faces the vast **Hus Monument** of 1915, designed by Ladislav Šaloun to commemorate the execution of the great radical reformer 500 years earlier. The monument is more than a statue; it's an impassioned drama: Hussite soldiers and Protestants are portrayed being driven into exile, while a young mother signifies national revival. The palace—once a grammar school attended by Franz Kafka—houses the National Gallery's (Národní galerie) collection of prints and drawings. Though it is not always open to the public, it is sometimes used for temporary art exhibitions.

To the right of the palace stands the Gothic **House at the Stone Bell** (Dům U kamenného zvonu). Until the 1980s this structure had a baroque facade. The restorers decided, controversially, to remove the baroque mask and reveal the original Gothic windows and tracery that adorned the 14th-century house; in doing so they created a charming pastel-tinted scene.

Týn School & Church

Next to the house, on the other side of Týnská lane, you will find the former Týn School (Týnská škola), which functioned from the 14th to 19th centuries. An early

Best of Guided Walks

Prague is one of Europe's great walking cities, with much of Old Town closed to vehicle traffic and narrow cobblestone lanes laid out in enticingly random curves, complete with arcaded passages and stunning ornamental facades on all sides.

At least a dozen guided walks vie for the attention of curious pedestrians eager to explore the city. The Communism Walk, as you'd expect, visits the places where the Velvet Revolution took hold, while Franz Kafka merits his own walk through the Josefov district of Old Town, his childhood home. Some of the more intriguing offerings focus on Prague's dark past and its countless legends of evil deeds and mysteries. Ghost Tour: Esoteric Mysterious Prague, led by night, naturally, is a hit with fans of the macabre, covering alchemy, the occult, and, purportedly, even Kafka's spiritual circumlocutions. **Prague Walks** (www.praguewalks.com) has entertained hundreds of ramblers with these three walks.

Walks of Prague (www.walksofprague .cz) focuses more on conventional approaches, including historic strolls through the Prague Castle grounds and important medieval sites throughout the city, among other routes.

Gothic, round-gabled structure, the windows suggest an Italianate makeover in the 16th century.

The distinctive twin towers of the **Týn Church** (Chrám Matky Boží před Týnem), a Prague landmark, loom over the square behind the school. You reach the entrance to the church through the arcades of the school. Building started on the church in 1365 and, despite much alteration since, the structure retains its Gothic atmosphere. Work began on the towers in 1402 but was interrupted by the Hussite wars; the spires were not completed until 1511.

The vaulting of the lofty interior is baroque, replacing the Gothic roof destroyed in a fire in 1679. However, the original arcades and aisle windows remain. So do various Gothic furnishings: a winged tabernacle depicting the Annunciation, Nativity, Baptism; the 1414 pewter font, the oldest in the city; an early 15th-century crucifix in the north aisle flanked by the figures of Mary and St. John; and a large seated Madonna and Child, also early 15th century. The baroque furnishings, notably the high altar of 1649, include paintings by Karel Škréta. Given the importance of this church, it is strange that access is limited to a few minutes before and after services.

INSIDER TIP:

During the Christmas holidays, enjoy the Christmas Market at Old Town Square. Sample traditional treats like gingerbread cookies and purchase a cup of warm mulled wine while wandering past the live nativity listening to carols.

—WENDY YASCUR
National Geographic contributor

Old Town Square
- 🅰 89
- 🚇 Metro: Staroměstská

Old Town Hall
- 🅰 89
- ☎ 724 911 556
- 💲 $

Just east of the pulpit you will find the church's most interesting monument, the **tomb** of the great Danish astronomer Tycho Brahe (1546–1601), who was invited to Prague by Rudolf II in 1599, but died two years later. Brahe was a remarkable figure, especially as an inventor of astronomical instruments. He formulated a theory

INSIDER TIP:

Buy a guidebook to the house signs painted, carved, or engraved over so many doorways in Old Town. Sightseeing with a "treasure hunt" is perfect for kids.

—CHARLES RECKNAGEL
Radio Free Europe, Prague

to appease the church that the planets revolved around the sun, yet died convinced the universe revolved around the Earth.

Around the Square

Return to the square to take a look at some of the houses here. On the south side, **No. 17** has a hefty 16th-century portal beneath a bay window, adorned with a contemporary carving of a ram. Next to it is No. 18, **At the Stone Table** (U kamenného stolu); this is a pretty baroque house with delicate stucco decoration. At No. 20, At the **Golden Unicorn** (U zlatého jednorožce), the composer Smetana ran a music school.

Near these Gothic arcades stands the **Dům U minuty,** with 17th-century sgraffito and a carving of a lion and shield. The house is now part of the **Old Town Hall** (Staroměstská radnice) complex, a jumble of buildings. The citizens of Old Town successfully petitioned to establish their own town hall in 1338. The main entrance is a splendid ogee-arched Gothic doorway carved by Matthias Rejsek. One Renaissance building has a beautiful gilt window surmounted by the Old Town coat of arms. The town hall's most famous feature is the **Astronomical Clock** (Orloj), designed by Mikuláš of Kadaň and constructed in 1410. It's the oldest of its kind in Europe and, not surprisingly, draws immense crowds when it strikes the hour; figures of the Twelve Apostles appear in procession and others portraying Human Vanity, Miserliness, Death, and a Turk begin their gesticulations. The clock has often been renovated, most recently after it was damaged by German troops in 1945, when the figures of the Apostles were replaced.

The interior of the town hall, entered through the tourist information office, is well worth visiting. The building is no longer an administrative center, but it is still used for ceremonial occasions. Art exhibitions are held here, and attractive doorways and painted ceiling beams enliven some rooms. Peter Parler built the chapel in the Old Town Hall in 1381, and the walls are decorated with heraldic frescoes; the glass was destroyed in 1945 and has been replaced with a modern equivalent. It is sometimes possible to visit the Romanesque basement of the town hall; the former prison was here, beneath the tower. You can climb up the Old Town Hall tower (or take an elevator most of the way) to see the astronomical clock's inner workings, and, from the top, fabulous views.

On the square between the town hall and the Týn School, you can see the **memorial** to the 27 Protestant noblemen executed here after the Battle of White Mountain (see pp. 30–31): 27 white crosses, dated June 21, 1621.

of the celebrated Matthias Braun. The church is essentially cruciform, topped by a squarish dome. Lavish stucco work by Bernardo Spinetti decorates the inside. The iron railings along the gallery are particularly attractive.

Return to Dům U minuty and follow the passageway into **Little Square** (Malé náměstí), once the city's fruit market. The square focuses on a Renaissance fountain, with an exquisite 1560 grille, and contains many delightful houses. Number 2, **At the White Lion**

Lights from the Christmas market decorations brighten Old Town Square in a profusion of colors. The festival runs daily through December in several locales.

Walk behind the town hall to the sumptuous **Church of St. Nicholas** (Kostel sv. Mikuláše), built by Kilián Ignác Dientzenhofer in the 1730s. In a city crammed with fine baroque church interiors, this must be one of the best, its broad facade decorated with statues and busts by Antonín Braun, nephew

(U bílého lva), is an engaging blend of Gothic and rococo. Number 13, **At the Golden Crown** (U zlaté koruny), houses a beautiful pharmacy with Empire-style furnishings. Number 3, the **Rott House** (Rottův dům) dates to Romanesque times, though the facade has 19th-century paintings by Mikuláš Aleš. ■

A Walk Around Old Town

This walk takes you through the twisting lanes of Old Town (Staré Město), more or less encircling Old Town Square (Staroměstské náměstí). It's a fascinating jumble of mansions, churches, palaces, and museums, as well as the old part of Charles University.

Begin at the Old Town end of **Charles Bridge** (Karlův most; see pp. 98–100). Bear right and continue through the covered shopping arcade until you come to a promenade that juts into the river. You'll pass the upscale Mlýnec restaurant and a pleasant wine bar, the Three Graces (Tři Grácie), before reaching the **Smetana Museum** (Muzeum Bedřicha Smetany) **❶** *(closed Tues., $)*. Founded in 1926, the museum houses a collection of original scores, as well as portraits, letters, and some of the composer's personal possessions. Smetana is revered by the Czechs both as a composer and as an

ardent nationalist (see pp. 230–231).

Return to the square and continue to the **Church of the Holy Savior** (Kostel sv. Salvátor) where there is an entrance to the bulky **Klementinum ❷**. The former Jesuit college was founded by the Habsburgs in 1556 to promote the Counter-Reformation and provide an alternative institution to Charles University. This is the city's largest building complex apart from the castle. As the Klementinum is now part of Charles University, some areas are closed to visitors, but you can gain access to the 170-foot-high (52 m) **Astronomical Tower** (Hvězdárenská věž; *closed Mon.–Fri., $$*),

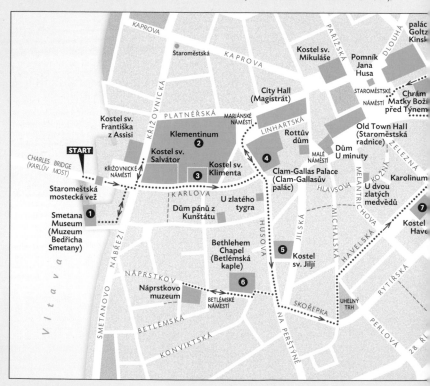

NOT TO BE MISSED:

Baroque Hall Library, Klementinum
• Celetná • Church of St. James
• Ungelt

the immense 17th-century reading room with
its stucco decorations, the sumptuous baroque
Hall Library of 1727, and the decorated and
gilt chapel known as the **Chapel of Mirrors**
(Zrcadlová kaple; *closed except for concerts, $*).
The hall, where Mozart played one of the
baroque organs, is now used for concerts
and exhibitions.

Karlova Street

The road linking the Charles Bridge with
Old Town Square is Karlova. **Number 2**

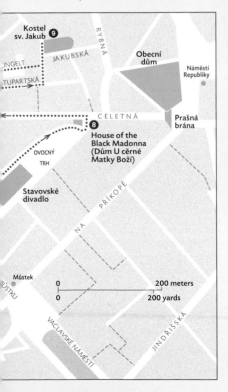

Town houses, such as At the Golden Well, were
often embellished with statuary, both as decoration and as a means of identification.

is the baroque Colloredo-Mansfeld Palace
(palác Colloredo-Mansfeldský); **No. 3,**
At the Golden Well (U zlaté studny), has
a fine baroque facade; and **No. 4** is the
house where the great German astronomer
Johannes Kepler lived from 1607 to 1612.
Note the baroque mansions with Romanesque foundations that line Karlova as well as
pubs, restaurants, a marionette museum, and
souvenir shops. In medieval times, this was
part of the royal route through town; today it
is the main thoroughfare used by thousands
of tourists passing from Charles Bridge to
Old Town Square. On the way you pass the

> ⚑ See area map pp. 88–89
> ► Old Town end of Charles Bridge
> ⟳ 2 miles (3.2 km)
> ⬏ About 4 hours
> ► Old Town Square

Church of St. Clement *(Kostel sv. Klimenta)* ❸; it has a ravishing interior filled with statuary by Matthias Braun, but it is rarely open to visitors. The best time to gain access is in the late afternoon just before services begin.

Continue down Karlova, then turn left onto Husova, to the huge **Clam-Gallas Palace** (Clam-Gallasův palác) ❹, now the city archives. The palace has one of the finest facades in Prague, designed in the early 18th century by the great Austrian architect Fischer von Erlach. Though it is closed to visitors, you can walk through the public areas; the magnificent stone staircase with

When the Town Hall's Astronomical Clock strikes the hour, figures are set in motion.

its frescoed ceiling is worth seeking out. On leaving the palace, turn right into Mariánské náměstí, where you can see the mass of the **City Hall** (Magistrát), designed in a secession style by Osvald Polívka in 1906–1911.

Return to Husova and continue down the street, which has some exceptionally pretty rococo facades on the left. Opposite the famous **U zlatého tygra** pub is Cream & Dream at **No. 12,** with its delicious Italian ice creams. On the left you will pass the Dominican **Church of St. Giles** (Kostel sv. Jiljí) ❺. Although the exterior dates from the early 14th century, the high interior was renovated in the baroque style and adorned with frescoes (1734) by Václav Reiner, who is buried in the nave.

Turn right onto Betlémské náměstí to see the **Bethlehem Chapel** (Betlémská kaple) ❻ *($)*, a somber hall church dating from the late 14th century and reconstructed in the 1950s. It was here that the reformer Jan Hus preached in Czech; he lived in the house to the right of the chapel. On the corner of Náprst-kova, an 18th-century house now contains the **Náprstek Museum** *(Náprstkovo muzeum; closed Mon., $)*. Founded by Vojtěch Náprstek (1826–1894), this ethnographic museum contains a major collection of 95,000 objects from all over the world, including masks, statues, and weaponry. Its greatest strength lies in the artifacts from early American civilizations.

The Markets & Beyond

Walk back toward Husova and continue on Skořepka to Uhelný trh. From this market square three parallel streets lead toward the Karolinum and Estates Theater. Walk along Havelská, its center crowded with market stalls, to the **Church of St. Gall** (Kostel sv. Havel) ❼, which was founded in 1280 but renovated in the 18th century by Giovanni Santini. Beyond is the green and cream bulk of the **Estates Theater** (Stavovské divadlo) and the **Karolinum,** original home of Prague University founded by Charles IV in 1348. Although few of the old buildings of the

EXPERIENCE: Coffeehouse Culture

It wasn't just the Velvet Revolution that was fomented in the *kavárna*, or typical coffeehouse, of Prague. During the 19th century, most of the principles of an independent Czech state, along with its greatest work in arts and letters, were first envisioned through clouds of cigarette smoke and steam from hot cups of java.

Just a handful of the Old Town's great coffeehouses, which once numbered in the dozens, have survived with their spirit intact. Long gone is the favorite of Kafka, the Arco, which gave rise to the group of writers and artists known as the Arconauts

(actually, a lackluster modern café opened in the space a few years back, but this hardly qualifies).

One great old space with its Mitteleuropa spirit still in evidence is the **Café Montmartre** at Řetězová 7 in Old Town. Here, worn Victorian-era sofas, mismatched wooden chairs, and a dim and comforting space still form a backdrop for long debates about theater, books, film, and arts gossip in general. It's hidden away on a quiet little lane but well worth scouting out—and don't neglect to try the *svarák*, or mulled wine, in cooler months.

INSIDER TIP:

Don't be afraid to get lost in the Old Town or Lesser Town. The streets can get packed, but most visitors stick to the main tourist trail. Instead, head off on your own and, after a block or two, you'll find yourself completely alone in this beautiful city.

—MARK BAKER
National Geographic Traveler *magazine writer*

Karolinum survive. It still forms part of the university. The 1781 theater has been much altered and renovated. It was here that two of Mozart's greatest operas, *Don Giovanni* and *La Clemenza di Tito,* were premiered.

Taking Ovocný trh between the Karolinum and the theater brings you to Celetná, a major thoroughfare. On the corner is the unmistakable **House of the Black Madonna** (Dům U černé Matky Boží) ❽ (*Ovocní trh 19, tel 224 211 746, www.ngprague.cz, closed Mon., $$, Metro: Náměstí Republiky*) an example of an only-in-Prague architectural form, cubism. Built by Josef Gočár in 1911–1912, this former department store, whose

café has been restored and reopened, hosts the National Gallery's best collection of cubist art, with paintings by Emil Filla, Josef Čapek, Antonín Procházka, Václav Spála and sculpture by Otto Gutfreund. Many of the facades along Celetná are baroque, but most of the houses are far older; others date back to early medieval times. Franz Kafka lived at **No. 3** from 1896 to 1907.

From the square retrace your footsteps and take the left fork along Štupartská, then the second left along Malá Štupartská to the **Church of St. James** (Kostel sv. Jakub) ❾. This late 17th-century church, with its immensely long nave and theatrical double-galleried choir, has some of the finest baroque ornamentation in Prague. In the left aisle is the tomb of Count Vratislav of Mitrovice, a masterwork of 1716 by Fischer von Erlach and Brokoff. Just inside the entrance on the right is a mummified arm said to belong to a thief who tried to steal the jewels from the statue of the Madonna on the altar four centuries ago; the Virgin seized his arm so hard, it had to be cut off in order to free the thief.

Opposite the church is the **Týn courtyard,** or Ungelt, a warehousing and merchants' center until the 18th century. Almost derelict in the 1980s, today it bustles with shops, cafés, and restaurants. Leave through the Týn Church arcade, which will take you back to Old Town Square.

Charles Bridge

Malá Strana is linked to Old Town by one of Europe's most spectacular bridges, a medieval masterpiece, the 1,700-foot-long (500 m), 16-arched Charles Bridge (Karlův most). Begun by Peter Parler on the orders of Charles IV in 1357, it was not completed until 1402. It replaced the nearby Judith Bridge, destroyed in the floods of 1342. For 500 years Karlův most, called simply the Prague bridge until the 19th century, was the only bridge uniting the two halves of the city.

The most famous medieval bridge in central Europe, the Charles Bridge has linked the two sides of the city since 1402.

But it's not just Charles Bridge itself that is enthralling; the views from the bridge are superb. Halfway along, looking in either direction, you can enjoy fabulous roofscapes of baroque domes, Gothic spires, medieval towers, Renaissance gables, and the broad expanses of the palaces of the nobility.

Close to the Malá Strana end is the famous old Three Ostriches (U tří pštrosů) inn. Its name comes from the fresco depicting ostriches, a reference to Jan Fux's feather business, a vital fashion accessory in Renaissance times. In 1714, it's thought, Prague's first coffeehouse opened its doors here.

Bohemian Statues

Charles Bridge's finest feature, sometimes obscured by the crowds of peddlers, entertainers, and tourists, is the series of baroque religious statues lining the balustrades; some of them, however, are 19th-century replacements of carvings damaged in floods, the originals of which can be seen in the Lapidarium of the National Museum. The statues are the work of such Bohemian masters as Ferdinand Brokoff and Matthias Braun. The marriage between the Gothic

Vltava Rowboats

It's been argued that the finest perspective on Matka Praha, or Mother Prague, is not from any street or castle, or even a riverbank. From the River Vltava itself, the city rises gracefully in a way that almost makes you suspect it was built with this view in mind.

From April through October, rowboats and paddlewheels for two can be rented for around 60 crowns per hour. You'll find them on Slovanský ostrov, the island just opposite the National Theater, or from the downstream end of the Lavka bar just upstream of the Charles Bridge on the Old Town side.

Gliding out onto the calm, cooling river is one of the great ways to pass an hour or two in warm weather, with the only traffic concern the occasional slow-moving pleasure boat—and even these tend to be in locks on this stretch of the Vltava.

Evening rowing is even more idyllic, with boats available in summer months until well after dark. Bring along a bottle of local white wine if you like—the boat companies don't mind a bit.

bridge and its baroque adornments works perfectly. Not all the statues have artistic merit, but the following are among the highlights, beginning at the Malá Strana end.

Brokoff designed two magnificent groups of statuary in 1714. One of them, the second group on the left, depicts **St. Vitus** atop a rocky peak, seemingly unfazed by the snakes and wild animals just beneath him; the other, directly opposite, shows the Saints John of Matha, Felix of Valois, and Ivo.

The next figure along, St. Adalbert, is a copy of a Brokoff statue. Opposite you will see the only marble statue, depicting St. Philip Benizi. The saint standing in front of a putti-encrusted obelisk is St. Cajetan, also by Brokoff. Opposite is another splendid group: the blind **St. Luitgarde** by Matthias Braun. Farther along on the right, Brokoff also contributed statues of Saints Vincent Ferrer and Procopius (1712), standing on a pedestal that shows the dead rising from their opened coffins.

INSIDER TIP:

Visit the Charles Bridge early in the morning, say around sunrise. Not only can you enjoy the bridge's ambience sans crowds, you may also experience the sun rising behind the Gothic towers of Prague's Old Town.

–SCOTT WARREN
National Geographic photographer

No group of Prague statuary would be complete without one of **St. John of Nepomuk,** who is represented toward the middle of the bridge on the left by a fine bronze by Matthias Rauchmüller and Jan Brokoff (1683); the pedestal shows the martyrdom of the saint as he was thrown into the Vltava.

Back on the right side of the bridge, Brokoff again indulged in exoticism with his statue of

representation of Saints Margaret, Elizabeth, and Barbara, also by Brokoff. The final pair on the bridge are copies: on the left, Jäckel's Virgin with St. Bernard (1709) and, opposite, the figure of St. Ivo (1711) by Matthias Braun.

Tower & Churches

After such an excess of baroque statuary, it's tempting to race under the Old Town Bridge Tower onto terra firma, but the tower is definitely worth a closer look. The best facade faces Old Town; the coats of arms depict the territories of the Holy Roman Empire during the reign of Charles IV, who is shown above, with Václav (Wenceslas) IV wearing an imperial crown. You can climb the tower and survey the city ($).

Two churches near the bridge end are worth a visit: on the left, the domed **Church of St. Francis** (Kostel sv. Františka z Assisi) and ahead, the **Church of St. Salvator** (Kostel sv. Salvátor). ∎

Visitors crossing the Charles Bridge enjoy the street musicians as much as the statuary.

St. Francis Xavier (a copy), who is accompanied by a pigtailed Chinese, a Turk, and an Indian chieftain, alluding to the saint's missionary activities. Farther along on the left, a fine 17th-century **Crucifixion** replaces a medieval cross that once stood here. Beyond, on the right, is a surprisingly staid

EXPERIENCE: Prague Marathon

First established in 1995, the Prague Marathon has grown from a humble foot race hoping to compete with the similar runs in New York and Berlin to a series of events that span from spring to autumn. They feature top runners and amateurs from around the globe, plus accompanying music, parties, and citywide celebrations.

Every May more than 5,000 people turn out for the full marathon (www.prague marathon.com) and in March some 5,800 scramble across Prague's cobblestones for the half marathon. The Grand Prix run, begun in 2003, has grown steadily

as well, now garnering more than 2,800 fleet-footed visitors every September. The Grand Prix is a series of 10K and 5K races, including such attention-getting specialty events as a bartender run and a race for embassy staffers.

Czechs have changed lifestyles radically since 1989, when coal dust choked the air and most diets included regular portions of smoked meats and dumplings. The next generation is already in training for longer lives, with more than 2,000 schools signing up annually for the Junior Marathon, held concurrently with the main event in May.

Mozart in Prague

Wolfgang Amadeus Mozart (1756–1791) first visited Prague in January 1787, when he came to conduct a performance of *The Marriage of Figaro*, which was received with great acclaim by the people of Prague. He was then commissioned to write a new opera that would be given its first performance here: *Don Giovanni*.

An engraving depicts mourners heading to the Church of St. Nicholas for Mozart's Requiem Mass.

Mozart returned to Prague in October to complete work on the new opera. At first he lodged at the Three Golden Lions (Dům U tří zlatých lvů) in Uhelný trh, which belonged to the composer and pianist František Dušek (1731–1799). Mozart had met Dušek and his wife, Josefina, a renowned singer, in Vienna and Salzburg, and they invited him to stay at their home, Vila Bertramka. This villa stood among the vineyards in Smíchov district. Their hospitality offered Mozart tranquility and congenial company, and here he completed *Don Giovanni,* writing the overture only the night before the premiere on October 29, 1787.

It is said that Josefina, anxious to have Mozart complete a concert aria for her, locked the composer in a pavilion until he had finished it. The result was one of his masterpieces in this form, *Bella Mia Fiamma.*

Mozart returned to Prague many times, usually staying with the Dušeks. He also played on some of the most renowned keyboards in the city—on an organ in the Chapel of Mirrors in the Klementinum and at the Church of St. Nicholas (Kostel sv. Mikuláše) in Malá Straná Square. And there's a story that he improvised a sonata on the organ in the church of the Strahov Monastery (see pp. 83–84).

His last visit was in 1791, when he was commissioned to write an opera to celebrate the coronation of Emperor Leopold II as king of Bohemia. He wrote it at astonishing speed. By this time Mozart was ill, and he was unable to remain in Prague to see the opera, *La Clemenza di Tito,* performed at the Estates Theater.

When he died three months later, he was remembered with a Requiem Mass sung by Josefina and attended by thousands of mourners at the Church of St. Nicholas.

Josefov

Like many Bohemian and Moravian towns, Prague had a Jewish community from the early Middle Ages onward. Although the Jews' presence was tolerated, their lives were often dogged by insecurity. They were tolerated because Bohemian rulers depended on their skills as money-lenders, but for that very reason they were also resented and often persecuted. The original Jewish quarter was near the castle, and it first spread across the river in the 12th century.

Josefov

🗺 89

Josefov was named after Joseph II, during whose reign laws restricting Jewish activities were relaxed. A walled ghetto until 1848, the Jewish quarter developed an invigorating mix of thriving business establishments, overcrowded tenements, and ancient synagogues. In 1850 Josefov was designated a separate district of Prague, but it remained a slum with a completely inadequate water supply. Wealthier Jews had already begun to move to more salubrious parts of the city. Finally, in 1892 Josefov's overcrowded and noisome lanes and tenements were torn down and replaced by art nouveau apartment blocks. Some splendid ones endure along Pařížská and Břehová.

The Jewish quarter is easily approached up Pařížská from Old Town Square. After a couple of blocks you will see on your left the gabled brick structure of the **Old-New Synagogue** (Staronová synagoga). This ancient building dates from about 1275 and resembles a medieval chapel; it's also the oldest synagogue in regular use in Europe. Originally known as the New School to differentiate it from an even older synagogue, it changed its name after other houses of worship sprang up in the district. The brick gables are part of the original medieval structure.

Because the street level has been raised since it was built, and the synagogue is partly underground, the interior is gloomy.

The Old Jewish Cemetery still contains thousands of tightly packed gravestones.

The dark rib-vaulted interior, with its 15th-century wrought-iron grille and ancient chandeliers and banners and pews, has remained unchanged for centuries.

The tall pew to the right of the Ark was the seat occupied by the famous Rabbi Judah Loew ben Bezalel (1520–1609). He was a leading figure in Jewish intellectual circles in the late 16th and early 17th centuries. The legend of the Golem (see pp. 106–107) is associated with him. The banner that hangs over the bima (the raised portion of the synagogue from which services are conducted) is that of the Jewish community, which was granted the right to its own flag by Charles IV in 1357. Damaged and renewed, the present banner dates from 1716.

On leaving the synagogue, bear left down Maiselova. On the left you will see the imposing **Jewish Town Hall** (Židovská radnice). It was established in 1541 but after a fire in 1764 was rebuilt. Its most remarkable feature is the clock whose hands move counterclockwise, reflecting the right-to-left movement of Hebrew script. The privilege of building a clock tower was granted to the community in recognition of the role played by Jewish residents in the defense of Charles Bridge against Swedish forces in 1648. The building still houses the Czech Jewish community's governing body.

Old Jewish Cemetery

Turn right onto Široká. On the right lies the entrance to the **Old Jewish Cemetery** (Starý židovský hřbitov). First you come

to the 16th-century **Pinkas Synagogue** (Pinkasova synagoga). Frequently rebuilt, it now serves as a poignant monument to the 77,297 Jewish victims of the Holocaust from Bohemia and Moravia. All the names of those who perished are individually recorded on the interior walls. As a crude anti-Israeli gesture, the Communist regime painted over them in 1975, but the names

INSIDER TIP:

The names of the Czech Jews sent to the Nazi camps have again been restored, following the damaging 2002 floods, making the Pinkas Synagogue a quiet, somber, and moving memorial.

—ROZ HOAGLAND
Guide, Hoagland Art Travel

were painstakingly restored. The names had to be restored again after flood damage in 2002.

For many visitors the old cemetery is the prime attraction in the area. The last burial here took place in 1787, after which Joseph II prohibited further internments within the city walls. Since then the walled compound seems scarcely to have been disturbed. Many of the ancient gravestones are leaning and worn, but that adds to the dignified calm. The oldest grave, that of **Avigdor Karo,** dates from 1439. A celebrated mayor of the

Old-New Synagogue

🕐 Closed Sat. & Jewish holidays

💲 $$$$

Jewish Museum

☒ Several locations;
   U Staré školy 1
☎ 221 711 511
🕑 Closed Sat. &
   Jewish holidays
💲 $$$$
🚇 Metro:
   Staroměstská
www.jewishmuseum
.cz

Jewish town, **Mordechai Maisel** (1528–1601) is buried between the Klaus Synagogue (Klausová synagoga) and the Museum of Decorative Arts (Uměleckoprůmslyové muzeum; see p. 77). Close to the museum wall is another unusually ornate tombstone, that of **Hendela Bassevi** (1628), whose husband was raised to the nobility. Over the centuries up to 100,000 bodies were buried here; a shortage of space meant that earth was piled on top of existing graves to permit fresh burials; explaining the cemetery's undulating terrain.

INSIDER TIP:

Piled within the Old Jewish Cemetery's walls are some 12,000 gravestones. To avoid noisy groups, try to visit at off-peak hours.

—SCOTT WARREN
National Geographic photographer

The old stones are covered with Hebrew inscriptions commemorating the dead and their virtues. They are often adorned with symbolic carvings of pine cones, pitchers, and grapes, which denote values such as fertility and the historic tribe of Israel to which the deceased belonged. Jewish visitors still observe the custom of placing pebbles on gravestones as a mark of respect. No tomb contains more stones than that of Rabbi Loew (see pp. 106–107), which lies close to the Museum of Decorative Arts.

Other Jewish Museum Sites

You emerge from the cemetery by a gate right next to the neo-Romanesque **Ceremonial Hall** (Obřadní sín). For many years this housed drawings and paintings produced by children incarcerated in the ghetto at Terezín in the early 1940s (see pp. 210–213), but these exhibits have now been appropriately removed to Terezín itself. Today the hall is a museum containing objects associated

Jewish Museum Highlights

Prague's Jewish Museum maintains a major role in education and spreading an understanding of history through art and culture. The museum's Robert Guttman gallery at U Staré školy 3, in the Josefov district of Old Town, has regular openings of compelling work, such as the recent show of Helga Hošková-Weissová.

One of the few living survivors of the Terezín prison camp north of Prague, this artist was on one of the first transports to the fortress town along with her family. There she sketched to pass the time and

to take her mind off the growing menace and separation from her father, who had been shipped farther east. Hošková-Weissová and her mother were also put on transports after three years at Terezín, but the girl was lucky enough to be liberated by the U.S. Army in 1945 at the Matheissen camp.

After a lifetime of art and graphic design in Prague, inspired by trips to Israel, Hošková-Weissová's art—including her Terezín sketches—is the kind of unique exhibit at which the Jewish Museum excels.

with Jewish rituals and customs.

The Ceremonial Hall is one of several buildings close to the cemetery that make up the Jewish Museum. Ironically, it was the Nazis who, by collecting Jewish artifacts from Czechoslovakia in order to demonstrate Jewish "degeneracy," inadvertently helped preserve their history. As you leave the hall, you will see the entrance to the 1694 **Klausová synagoga** to the right. It has an ornate barrel-vaulted interior and displays ancient Hebrew manuscripts and books reflecting the history of the Jewish printed book in Prague. Other exhibits are related to the Sabbath and Jewish festivals, and include embroidered Torah curtains and silver finials and shields used to decorate the scrolls of the law, as well as objects associated with Jewish rituals.

From here, return to the Jewish Town Hall and turn right down Maiselova. Cross Široká and, on the left at No. 10, you come to the **Maisel Synagogue** (Maiselova synagoga). It contains what is, from the artistic point of view, the most absorbing of all the exhibitions in the Jewish Museum: Jewish silverware from all over Bohemia and Moravia, manuscripts, and Torah mantles, some dating back to the 17th century. Other exhibits give an idea of daily life in the ghetto.

The last synagogue is the Spanish Synagogue. To reach it, turn right after emerging from the Maisel Synagogue, then right again on Široká. After a block and a half you come to the Church of the Holy Ghost (Kostel sv. Duch). Just beyond is the 1868 **Spanish Synagogue** (Španřlská synagoga),

Stalls near the Old Jewish Cemetery attract many of the visitors who stroll past.

which catered to the Sephardic community of Prague. The magnificent domed interior is patterned and painted in a neo-Moorish style. Closed for many years, it has been renovated and now serves as a hall illustrating the life of the city's Jewish community in the 19th century. The gallery houses fascinating old photos of Jewish life throughout Bohemia and Moravia; some give a vivid idea of how Josefov looked before its demolition. Documents and photographs illustrate the deportations of 1941–1945 that brought the once vibrant Jewish community of Prague to the point of extinction. ■

Rabbi Loew & the Golem

In the Old Jewish Cemetery in Prague is the gravestone of the revered Judah Loew ben Bezalel ben Chaim, Rabbi Loew (1520–1609), who persuaded Rudolf II in 1592 to offer greater protection to the city's Jews. The rabbi was also a friend of the famous astronomer Tycho Brahe. Loew was credited with fashioning a creature called the Golem from mud and clay but imbued by the rabbi with a life of its own.

It is not surprising that this fantastical legend emerged from Prague. In Renaissance times, under the patronage of Emperor Rudolf II, the city was the leading European center of alchemy and magic. Although Loew is credited with creating the Golem, such legends were not new. The word, meaning "unformed substance," appears in the Psalms. Medieval texts of the Jewish mystical writings known as the cabala describe a creature whose role was to act as a dependable servant and protector of the Jews. But Rabbi Loew, who had a reputation as an expert in the natural sciences as well as in the cabala, invested his Golem with an anarchic energy of its own.

The best known version of the legend tells how Loew, alerted to unspecified but terrible danger, raced to the banks of the Vltava with his acolytes. Their spells conjured the creature into existence from mud and clay, involving the four elements—earth, fire, air, and water. The Golem became a living creature, so the story goes, after Loew uttered the word "Shem," which is the unknown name of God. Other versions tell how the rabbi placed a piece of paper or stone with the holy word written upon it into the creature's mouth or walked around the Golem seven times counterclockwise. Once given life, the Golem became hard to control. In some tales the rabbi

The Golem has been the source of inspiration for many.

forgot to remove the paper from the Golem's mouth, so the creature went on the rampage, terrifying the ghetto's inhabitants.

Elaborations of the legend depict the Golem as a heroic creature whose adventures are part sinister, part playful, riding to the rescue when Jewish values or lives were under threat. In an age when Jews felt chronically insecure after centuries of persecution, exile, and false accusations, it must have been reassuring to think that a supernatural creature had the powers to defend the Jewish people. The only way to render the Golem lifeless was to remove the breath of life from it, whereupon it would return to its original state. Eventually, according to legend, the inert Golem was deposited out of harm's way beneath the Old-New Synagogue's roof.

The story of the Golem has been popularized by frequent retellings, most notably in a novel of the same name by Gustav Meyrink in the early 20th century. In 1920, the tale was the subject of a silent film by Paul Wegener, and sound versions followed. The legend is clearly related to the Frankenstein story, in which a man-made monster, initially benign, acts in ways beyond the control of its creator. The Golem also figures prominently in Michael Chabon's Pulitzer Prize–winning novel, *The Amazing Adventures of Kavalier and Clay* (2000).

Rabbi Loew was the immensely respected leader of the Jewish community in 16th-century Prague.

Convent of St. Agnes

The Convent of St. Agnes (Anežský klášter), on the northeast edge of Josefov, was founded in the 1230s by Agnes, the daughter of Otakar I, and construction continued until 1280. It fell into decay in the early 19th century, but today its two restored churches are used for concerts. The galleries in and near the cloisters are now the home of the superb collection of medieval art belonging to the National Gallery (Národní galerie).

The atmospheric medieval cloisters of the Convent of St. Agnes are often used for concerts.

The complex thrived until the Hussite wars (1419–1434) interrupted devotions. Various monastic orders occupied the convent until 1782, when it was secularized by Joseph II. The two churches—**Church of the Holy Savior** (Kostel sv. Salvátor) and **Church of St. Francis of Assisi** (Kostel sv. František)—were semi-ruinous after years of misuse as storehouses, but they have been well restored, the cloisters have been rebuilt, and excavations have unearthed the tombs of Václav and other Přemyslid rulers. The choirs of the two mid-13th century churches lie side by side. In 1986 the Church of St. Francis was adapted as a concert hall; much of the rest of the convent is now an art gallery.

Medieval Art

For many years the medieval collections of the National Gallery were housed in the Convent of St. George within Prague Castle. Reorganization of the collections has moved the medieval section to the Convent of St. Agnes, where it is beautifully displayed. This is one of the great collections of medieval central

Europe: panel paintings, carved Madonnas, winged altarpieces, and entire cycles of paintings. Although their styles are very distinctive, the identities of many of the medieval painters represented here are unknown, and they are simply referred to as Masters of the towns where they worked, such as Vyšší Brod and Třeboň.

The collections: The first room contains enthroned Madonnas from the 12th and 13th centuries, and the influence of French art is evident. There is a painted Madonna and Child from Vyšehrad Church (1350s); an unusual silver-gilt *herma*, a covering that encased the skull of St. Ludmila, the grandmother of St. Wenceslas; and Madonnas by the Master of Vyšší Brod.

In the second room a cycle of nine paintings depicts scenes from the life of Christ by the same artist, commissioned in the 1350s. These are devotional panels of considerable charm, but not of outstanding quality, as the artist seems to have had difficulty matching the heads he painted with the bodies to which they were attached. However, the panels showing the Nativity, Christ on the Mount of Olives, the Crucifixion, and the Resurrection are of much better quality. It's unclear whether the Master painted all the panels; some were likely by his assistants.

The third room displays works by the painter known only as **Master Theodoric.** He is best known for the 128 paintings he produced for the Chapel of the Holy Cross (see p. 143) at Karlštejn

Castle (Hrad Karlštejn) in the 1350s and 1360s. Six of them are here, and whether you share the Bohemian admiration for these works is a subjective matter. They are painted in what became known as the "soft style," a self-explanatory term once you see the overly fleshy portrayals.

The next room delivers a blow to the senses with a Crucifixion, graphic in its immediacy and realism, that once belonged to the Emmaus Monastery (Klášter na Slovanech; see p. 125). There are also rare stained-glass panels from Kolín, 22 miles (35 km) east of Prague, and elegant carvings of the Madonna and Child, plus a moving carved Pietà from Lásenice.

Convent of St. Agnes

▲ 89
✉ U Milosrdných 17
☎ 224 810 628
⏱ Closed Mon.
$ $$$, free first Wed. of month
🚊 Tram: 5, 8, 26 (Dlouhá). Metro: Náměstí Republiky

INSIDER TIP:

Don't miss Prague Spring—a month of renowned music from classical to experimental style. The international music festival *(www.festival.cz)* dates back to 1946.

—ANDREA LIŠKOVÁ
CzechTourism USA

The following room contains one of the collection's highlights: panels by the **Master of Třeboň,** all that remains from a winged altarpiece painted about 1380. These are wonderful works, showing the precision and restrained emotion that are so lacking from the Vyšší Brod panels. There is also a moving Crucifixion by the same artist. One of his masterworks is the "Madonna of Roudnice" from the 1380s, a tender depiction of the familiar scene.

Bear right into the next hall, with its succession of Madonnas, painted and carved, and the early 15th-century "Capuchin Cycle," consisting of 14 vivid portrait panels. In the same room you will see a resplendent monstrance of about 1400 from Sedlec near Kutná Hora. Highlights of the following room are the early 15th-century "Roudnice Altarpiece" and a Gothic masterpiece: a variant of the carved "Madonna of Český Krumlov."

Retrace your steps past the "Capuchin Cycle" to descend into a large hall. Here the displays include six very decorative panels by the **Master of Rajhrad** and his workshop from Moravia (ca 1430). There is an exceptionally vivid and grimly realistic triptych known as the "Reininghaus Altarpiece," gory, dense, and high in emotion; a tender "Assumption" from Deštná, highly formal and beautifully detailed; and the "St. George Altarpiece," realistic and accomplished, with beautifully rendered draperies. From Austria comes the "Virgin Mary with the Garlands," an elegant work from the 1480s. The impeccably preserved winged "Velhartice Altarpiece" is a complex work in painted reliefs flanking a statue of the Madonna and Child. There are more panels, beautifully colored, from the workshop of the **Master of Litoměřice,** and the Master's exceptionally dignified triptych of the Holy Trinity.

The next room holds a sumptuous reliquary bust of St. Adalbert (ca 1490), while the following room houses some superb wooden carvings by the I. P. monogrammist (1520–1540), an anonymous artist identified only by his initials, which, with clear influence from Dürer (1471–1528) and Mantegna (1431–1506), are more international in style than some of the earlier sculptures in the collection. Paintings by Lucas Cranach the Elder and his workshop signal the end of the medieval period and of the collections. An admirable feature of the gallery is that developments in Czech medieval art are placed in a European context. ■

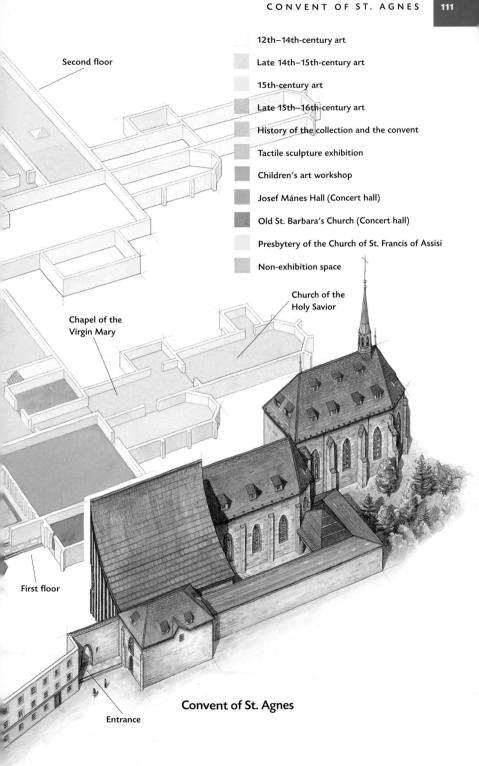

Second floor

12th–14th-century art

Late 14th–15th-century art

15th-century art

Late 15th–16th-century art

History of the collection and the convent

Tactile sculpture exhibition

Children's art workshop

Josef Mánes Hall (Concert hall)

Old St. Barbara's Church (Concert hall)

Presbytery of the Church of St. Francis of Assisi

Non-exhibition space

Church of the Holy Savior

Chapel of the Virgin Mary

First floor

Convent of St. Agnes

Entrance

More Places to Visit in Old Town

At the Two Golden Bears

The fine Renaissance house called At the Two Golden Bears (U dvou zlatých medvědů) stands along Melantrichova, the lane opposite the entrance to the Old Town Hall (Staroměstská radnice), on the corner with Kožná. The carved stone doorway of 1590 was created by Bonifác Wohlmut and is topped, as its name suggests, by carvings of two bears. If the house's door is open when you visit, you can walk through to the beautiful courtyard with its Renaissance loggia.

Ⓜ 89 ✉ Kožná 1 Ⓜ Metro: Staroměstská

Church of St. Castullus

Located in a small square, close to the Convent of St. Agnes, is the fine Gothic Church of St. Castullus (Kostel sv. Haštal). Originally built in the 1230s, the present building dates from the late 14th century. The sacristy contains the remnants of Gothic frescoes depicting the Apostles, and there is a notable Calvary sculpture here by Ferdinand Brokoff.

Ⓜ 89 ✉ Haštalské náměstí

Rotunda

The tiny 11th-century rotunda church (Kostel sv. Kříž), one of three surviving Romanesque round churches in Prague, stands on the corner of Konviktská and Karoliny Světlé. Inside are fragments of 14th-century wall paintings, but it's rarely open to the public.

Ⓜ 88 ✉ Karoliny Světlé Ⓜ Tram: 17. Metro: Národní třída

Rudolfinum

Near the Old Town end of Charles Bridge the neo-Renaissance Rudolfinum, named after Crown Prince Rupert of Austria, spreads along the riverbank. It is the home of the Czech Philharmonic Orchestra and also the headquarters of the annual spring music festival known as Prague Spring, which runs from May 12 (Smetana's birthday) to June 3. Tickets go on sale one month before the festival opens.

Ⓜ 88 ✉ Alšovo nábřeží 12 ☎ 224 893 238 (box office), 227 059 227 (gallery) Ⓜ Tram: 17. Metro: Staroměstská **Prague Spring box office** www.festival.cz ☎ 257 312 205

Art at NoD Gallery

One of Prague's most progressive centers for contemporary art, Old Town's NoD gallery (Dlouhá 33, http://nod.roxy.cz), is part of the youthful nonprofit program organized by the Linhart foundation, which also runs the attached "experimental space" known as the Roxy club. The former prewar movie theater is itself a magnet for all manner of international culture, ranging from Balkan wedding music to British masters of dub mixing.

But it's in the upstairs NoD gallery that emerging artists can express themselves fully in a venue that doubles as an Internet café. In addition to hosting art exhibits such as Peter Beste: Houston Rap Culture or a show by U.S.-based Czech performance artist Milan Kohout, the space has recently expanded its programming to include theater. It has launched a theater series called teatroNoD. These popular events (if probably not for everyone) range from the stage clowning of the Czech-Finnish Krepsko company to local avant-garde musicals.

But visitors are just as likely to come across bizarre graphic art at NoD, such as during the recent KomiksFest, which showed off the best illustrations found in underground 'zines.

Prague's popular gathering place, Wenceslas Square (Václavské náměstí), among New Town's medieval churches and squares

New Town & the Suburbs

Troja Castle manor house

New Town & the Suburbs

One of Prague's charms is the fact that most of its sights concentrate within a small area. Because of this, it's tempting to ignore the many attractions elsewhere in the city. The New Town and the suburbs, however, contain a good number of sights worth seeking out; all of them are easily accessible by the city's efficient public transportation system.

The quirky gables of the New Town Hall overlook Charles Square.

New Town (Nové Město) is simply an extension of Old Town (Staré Město) that became necessary as the city grew. It was established by Charles IV in 1348 and designed on an ambitious scale in a remarkable and forward-looking feat of town planning. Charles created large open spaces as marketplaces and constructed broad thoroughfares, all in complete contrast to the tortuous lanes, irregular squares, and confined spaces of both Malá Strana and Old Town. The centerpieces of the project were three enormous squares, two of which survive in much their original form: Wenceslas Square (Václavské náměstí) and Charles Square (Karlovo náměstí). Larger in area than Old Town, New Town was protected by fortifications some 2.5 miles (4 km) in length.

As a district, Nové Město has far less character than Malá Strana or Staré Město. Not as compact as the older parts of town, it was easier to rebuild and develop in the 19th and 20th centuries. But among the apartment blocks, hospitals, schools, office developments, and other large buildings, there are some gems. These include the Vila Amerika, now a museum devoted to the life and work of Antonín Dvořák; the Karlov church, another legacy of Charles IV; and, at the other end of the historical band, the Dancing House, designed by the modern architect Frank Gehry. Its unusual sculptural form is suggestive of two dancers, and it is affectionately known as the "Fred and Ginger" building.

This chapter includes Vyšehrad and other districts of Prague that don't belong to any of the ancient townships within the city. It takes you to remarkable sites on the city's outskirts, including the magnificent castle of Troja, the fascinating technical museum, and the ancient monastic foundation at Břevnov. ■

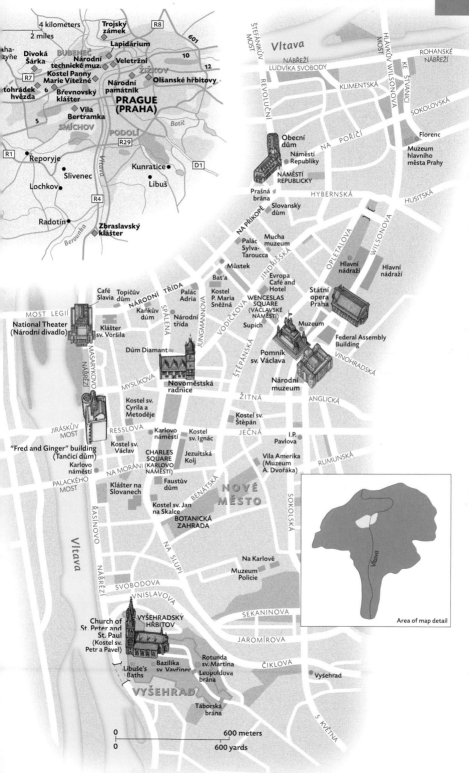

4 kilometers
2 miles

Trojský
zámek

R8

601

Lapidárium

10

12

aha-
zyně

Divoká
Šárka

BUBENEČ

Národní
technické muz.

Veletržní

ŽIŽKOV

Olšanské hřbitovy

R7

Kostel Panny
Marie Vítězné

6

Břevnovský
klášter

Národní
památník

tohrádek
hvězda

PRAGUE
(PRAHA)

Vila
Bertramka

Botič

5

SMÍCHOV

PODOLÍ

R29

R1

Reporyje

Slivenec

Kunratice

D1

Lochkov

Libuš

R4

Radotín

Zbraslavský
klášter

Berounka

Vltava

Vltava

ŠTEFÁNIKŮV
MOST

NÁBŘEŽÍ
LUDVÍKA SVOBODY

REVOLUČNÍ

HLÁVKŮV
MOST

KE ŠTVANICI

ROHANSKÉ
NÁBŘEŽÍ

KLIMENTSKÁ

SOKOLOVSKÁ

Obecní
dům

Náměstí
Republiky

NA POŘÍČÍ

WILSONOVA

Florenc

Muzeum
hlavního
města Prahy

NÁMĚSTÍ
REPUBLIKY

Prašná
brána

Slovanský
dům

HYBERNSKÁ

HUSITSKÁ

NA PŘÍKOPĚ

Palác
Sylva-
Taroucca

Mucha
muzeum

JINDŘIŠSKÁ

OPLETALOVA

WILSONOVA

Můstek

Baťa

Hlavní
nádraží

Hlavní
nádraží

Café
Slavia

Topičův
dům

NÁRODNÍ TŘÍDA

Palác
Adria

Kostel
P. Maria
Sněžná

Evropa
Café and
Hotel

WENCESLAS
SQUARE
(VÁCLAVSKÉ
NÁMĚSTÍ)

Státní
opera
Praha

SPALENA

Kaňkův
dům

Národní
třída

JUNGMANNOVA

VODIČKOVA

Supich

Muzeum

MOST LEGIÍ

National Theater
(Národní divadlo)

Klášter
sv. Voršila

Dům Diamant

ŠTEPÁNSKÁ

Pomník
sv. Václava

Federal Assembly
Building

VINOHRADSKÁ

MASARYKOVO
NÁBŘEŽÍ

MYSLÍKOVA

Novoměstská
radnice

ŽITNÁ

Národní
muzeum

ANGLICKÁ

JIRÁSKŮV
MOST

RESSLOVA

Kostel sv.
Cyrila a
Metoděje

Kostel sv.
Štěpán

JEČNÁ

I.P.
Pavlova

RUMUNSKÁ

"Fred and Ginger" building
(Tančicí dům)

Kostel sv.
Václav

Karlovo
náměstí

Kostel
sv. Ignác

Jezuitská
Kolj

Vila Amerika
(Muzeum
A. Dvořáka)

Karlovo
náměstí

CHARLES
SQUARE
(KARLOVO
NÁMĚSTÍ)

Faustův
dům

BENÁTSKÁ

NOVÉ
MĚSTO

SOKOLSKÁ

PALACKÉHO
MOST

Klášter na
Slovanech

NA MORÁNI

Kostel sv. Jan
na Skalce

BOTANICKÁ
ZAHRADA

RAŠÍNOVO
NÁBŘEŽÍ

NA SLUPI

Na Karlově

Muzeum
Policie

Vltava

SVOBODOVA

VNISLAVOVA

SEKANINOVA

Church of
St Peter and
St. Paul
(Kostel sv.
Petr a Pavel)

VYŠEHRADSKÝ
HŘBITOV

JAROMÍROVA

Libuše's
Baths

Bazilika
sv. Vavřinec

Rotunda
sv. Martina

Leopoldova
brána

ČIKLOVA

Vyšehrad

VYŠEHRAD

Táborská
brána

S KVĚTNA

Vltava

Area of map detail

0   600 meters

0   600 yards

Wenceslas Square

Seen from the Můstek plaza, Wenceslas Square (Václavské náměstí) unfurls before you in a long sweep, barred at the far end by the portico and domes of the National Museum (Národní muzeum). This is the commercial and political heart of the city, the place everyone flocks to in times of national jubilation or dismay.

The steps of the National Museum offer one view of the expanse of Wenceslas Square.

Wenceslas Square
🗺 115

Originally a horse market established by Charles IV in the late 1340s, the square assumed greater importance in the mid-19th century, when houses, apartment blocks, and commercial buildings were erected. Then in 1885 the Horses' Gate, part of the city fortifications at the far end of the square, was replaced by the National Museum. The museum has

become a city landmark, thanks to its imposing cupola.

Wenceslas Monument

The square's most celebrated monument, the statue of St. Wenceslas (Pomník sv. Václava), stands in front of the National Museum. There had been a statue of the patron saint in the square since the 17th century, but it was moved to

Vyšehrad in 1879. The Czech sculptor Josef Václav Myslbek was commissioned to design a replacement, and the work was finally completed in 1924. The monument is surrounded by statues of four other patron saints of Bohemia: Ludmila, Procopius, Vojtěch, and Agnes.

The statue soon became the focal point for patriotic demonstrations, which often spilled over into the entire square. In 1918 the Czechs clamored here for their independence from the defunct Austro-Hungarian Empire, and in 1968 thousands came here to protest against the Soviet invasion of the country (see pp. 39 & 122). Nearby, on January 16, 1969, student Jan Palach set fire to himself in protest against this invasion. Inevitably, when the Velvet Revolution began in 1989, Wenceslas Square again attracted huge crowds, who were addressed by Václav Havel and the hero of the Prague Spring, Alexander Dubček.

The Buildings

The buildings lining the square mostly lack architectural merit, but there are notable exceptions. The best known is the art nouveau extravaganza of the **Evropa Café and Hotel,** built in 1906. Close to No. 6 is the **Baťa Building,** with its plate glass windows, still untarnished and stylish after more than 80 years. Next door, at No. 8, is the Adam Pharmacy (Adamova lékárna), tall and narrow, with figures over the entrance portraying Adam and Eve, each draped with a snake. Number 12 is a good example of

Prague secession style. On the corner of Štěpánská stands the **Supich Building** (Nos. 38–40), constructed between 1913 and 1916 by Matěj Blecha in a brutal secessionist style.

National Museum: The vast National Museum (Národní muzeum) was built in the 1880s at the top of Wenceslas Square to house the museum that had been established in 1818. There was a nationalist as well as scientific motive behind its founding, a purpose furthered by its prominent position.

Palach Memorials

In front of the Wenceslas Monument is a small shrine dedicated to Jan Palach— the 21-year-old student who set himself on fire on the square in August 1968 to protest the Soviet invasion—and to other "victims of communism."

Red Army Square in Old Town was renamed Náměstí Jana Palacha after the Velvet Revolution of 1989. On the facade of the philosophy building where he was a student, on the east side of the square, is a small bronze death mask of Jan Palach by Olbran Zoubek.

The interior is an impressive example of monumental design. From the lobby you climb the massive staircase beneath its glass roof, your path lit by globe lamps on brass candelabra. It leads up to

National Museum

✉ Václavské náměstí 68

☎ 224 497 111

🕐 Closed first Tues. of month

💲 $$$; free entry first Mon. of month

🚊 Tram: 3, 9, 14, 24. Metro: Můstek, Muzeum

Prague State Opera (Státní opera Praha)
- ✉ Legerova 75
- ☎ 224-227-266
- 💲 $$–$$$$
- Ⓜ Metro: Můstek, Muzeum
- www.opera.cz

a square galleried hall beneath a cupola known as the **Pantheon.** This hall commemorates major figures of Czech intellectual and scientific achievement.

One half of the first floor houses a comprehensive series of prehistory displays; national medals, mostly 19th century; and theater costumes. The other half contains the mineralogy collections. On the second floor you'll

INSIDER TIP:

The Prague State Opera, a city gem, offers year-round performances of Verdi, Puccini, Mozart, and local favorite Dvořák for around $30 a ticket.

—PHILIP HEIJMANS
Writer & photographer,
The Prague Post

find the zoological collections. Though the captions on both floors are in Czech only, most visitors find much here to appreciate.

Other buildings: To the left of the main museum building on Wilsonova is the former **Federal Assembly Building,** which housed Radio Free Europe from 1995 to 2009, when it became part of the museum. The original 1930s building is surmounted by a modern stone-and-glass structure by Karel Prager. Farther along Wilsonova you come to the **Prague State Opera (Státní opera Praha).** This handsome building with a grand neoclassical portico is now the city's principal opera house. Though its charming red and gold interior was modeled on the Vienna State Opera, its scale is considerably smaller. ∎

Secrets of Wenceslas Square

Prague's best-known promenade is, sadly, ill-suited to promenading these days. As you look out on the area's adult clubs, casinos, and garish crystal shops, it can be hard to raise the memories of the crowds of students gathered here in November 1989, shaking their keys in unison to protest Communist control.

But this is the place, all right. Hundreds of thousands who had finally had enough indeed stood shoulder to shoulder on this street and demanded their freedoms. It was far from clear that they would be heeded, let alone allowed to peacefully protest without injury or arrest. A turning point in the crowd's morale was reached

after several days, however, when then dissident playwright Václav Havel, standing next to former First Secretary Alexander Dubček, appeared on the balcony of the Melantrich building (No. 36) to inspire the masses. Dubček, who had seen his own efforts at "socialism with a human face" crushed by the Warsaw Pact invasion of 1968, seemed to be symbolically passing the mantle to Havel.

In fact, at the top of Wenceslas Square, on the sides of the National Museum, you can still see the places where bricks were replaced after the Russian invaders fired on the building during that earlier, failed reform effort.

Na Příkopě & Národní Třída

The city's best-known commercial and shopping districts run in a more or less straight line from Republic Square (Náměstí Republiky), along Na Příkopě, past Můstek at the bottom of Wenceslas Square, and then along Národní třída to the River Vltava. The Czech and German populations divided the area between them in the 19th century, with the Germans preferring Na Příkopě and the Czechs congregating along Národní třída farther south.

Starting from Republic Square, you can scarcely miss the huge **Municipal House** (Obecní dům), built in the first decade of the 20th century as a cultural center and concert hall. This prestigious project was thrown open to competition, and the winners were Antonín Balšánek, who designed the exterior, and Osvald Polívka, who was responsible for the essentially art nouveau interior. But all the leading artists of the day contributed to the decor, including Alfons Mucha, who added striking murals. The main concert hall is the glass-domed **Smetana Hall**. Guided tours are sometimes offered; you also can enjoy the opulent decor by visiting the coffeehouse on the left of the lobby. If you are feeling extravagant, lunch at the Francouzská restaurant here.

The art nouveau Municipal House is a showcase of early 20th-century design and decoration.

Na Příkopě

To the left of Obecní dům rises the **Powder Gate** (Prašná brána), a former city gate and gunpowder store constructed and reconstructed from the 15th to the 19th centuries. The gate marks the beginning of Celetná street, but pass it by to reach the broad street of Na Příkopě. Originally a moat alongside the ramparts of Old Town, it was filled in during the 1760s. By the middle of the 19th century Na Příkopě had become a fashionable street, lined with restaurants, hotels, and mansions; it was also home to many of the city's banks.

At No. 22 is the **Slav House** (Slovanský dům), of baroque and neoclassical origin; today it is filled with upscale stores and offices. **Number 20** is the former Commerce and Craft Industry Bank

**Na Příkopě &
Národní třída**

 115

🚇 Metro: Můstek,
Náměstí
Republiky,
Národní třída

Summer Movie Screening

The Vltava island known as Střelecký ostrov, accessed from the Most legií, or Legionnaire's Bridge, has long been a favorite gathering spot for music lovers. Concerts are held when it's warm enough. Evening movies *(www.strelak.cz)* appeal to an even bigger crowd. The trees around the clearing at the downstream end make a natural amphitheater and provide decent acoustics for the eclectic selection of current and classic films screened here almost nightly from April through October.

Czech feature films that would be hard to find outside this country are often shown with English subtitles (such as 1968's *A Case for a Young Hangman* by Pavel Juráček), while arthouse films from Western Europe or American indie cinema are also on the schedule. Beer tents, snacks, and plastic chairs make the evening even more relaxing, but it never hurts to bring along an extra layer or a blanket in case the unpredictable Czech summer climate decides to add some suspense.

(Živnostenská banka), a heavy-handed structure linked by bridges to another bank building at **No. 18.** Yet another turn-of-the-20th-century bank is the State Bank, at **Nos. 3–5,** topped by Babylonian-style copper reliefs and statuary.

A few older buildings survive, of which the finest is No. 10, the **Sylva-Taroucca palace** (Palác Sylva-Taroucca), built in the 1740s by Kilián Ignác Dientzenhofer. The facade is essentially rococo, but the building houses restaurants and a theater.

Celetná opens on to Můstek, at the head of Wenceslas Square. Můstek, which means "little bridge," refers to the bridge that crossed the moat here in medieval times; some of its spans can be seen behind a glass wall in the metro station.

Walking from Můstek toward Národní třída, you pass on your left the **Church of Our Lady of the Snows** (Kostel Panny Maria Sněžná), founded by Charles IV in 1347 as his coronation church. Only the very tall chancel, soaring to 108 feet (33 m), was finished; the Hussite wars of the early 15th century

interrupted work on the ambitious project. Near the tympanum-topped entrance gate *(closed)* to the churchyard is a strange-looking column—a 1912 lamppost in the cubist style.

Národní Třída

The square (Jungmannovo náměstí) at the Národní end of the churchyard is named for Josef Jungmann (1773–1847), the linguist who helped establish the historical foundations of the Czech language; there's a monument to him here. Beyond the square, Národní třída stretches toward the river; like Na Příkopě, it was built in the 1760s when the moat dividing Old Town and New Town was filled in.

The enormous top-heavy building straight ahead on Národní třída is the **Adria palace** (Palác Adria) by Pavel Janák and Joseph Zasche. Originally the home of the Laterna Magicka (see p. 56), it was named after an Italian insurance company that was located here. Today it houses offices, restaurants, and the Divadlo Bez zábradlí theater. On the right, at No. 37, is the neoclassical Platyz, with a large shop-filled courtyard behind it. Just beyond the supermarket is the famous Reduta jazz club, where President Bill Clinton played his saxophone in January 1994. Farther along, beneath the arcades of the **Kaňka House** (Kaňkův dům) at No. 16, you'll find a plaque commemorating a large demonstration held nearby on November 17, 1989. Much of the next block is filled by the **Ursuline convent** (Klášter sv. Voršila), designed by Marc Antonio Canevale in 1704, and its wine bar and restaurant, the Klášterní vinárna. Across the street are two remarkable secession designs. At No. 7 is the former Praha Insurance Company building, and at No. 9 is the **Topic House** (Topičův dům). Both date from 1903–1906.

National Theater: The convent adjoins the National Theater (Národní divadlo), a place of great cultural importance to the Czechs, who were keen to present plays and operas in their own language. Josef Zítek (1832–1909), who designed the Rudolfinum (see p. 112), was the architect, but the theater was open only briefly before it burned down in 1881. It was replaced in 1883 by a massive structure designed by Josef Schulz (1840–1917) and decorated in part by Mikoláš Aleš. The main entrance and portico lie along Národní třída, but the bulk of the structure faces the river. The operas of Smetana and Janáček were often first performed here and remain in the repertoire alongside those of Dvořák. The relatively small interior is exuberantly decorated with gilt and statuary.

The theater is now part of a complex that offers theater, opera, and ballet, and it remains the flagship of Czech performing arts. The 1983 New Theater (Nová scéna) is a glass structure by Karel Prager. The Laterna Magika theater is also based here. Opposite the theater is **Café Slavia,** one of the city's best-known coffeehouses. Smetana lived in the apartments above it. ∎

Švandovo

✉ Stefanikova 57
☎ 234 651 111
🚋 Tram: tram No. 6, 9, 12 or 20 to Švandovo Divadlo
www.svandovodiva dlo.cz

Archa

✉ Na Poříčí 26
☎ 221 716 333
www.archatheatre.cz

EXPERIENCE: Theater

It's no coincidence that the first president of a free postwar Czechoslovakia was a playwright. Theater runs deeply through Czech history. The country's greatest monument to nation-building in the 19th century was the National Theater, which laid its cornerstone—funded by public subscription—in 1868, and opened its doors with a poem to Slavic myths, *Libuše*.

This rich world, in which Czech Oscar winners Jiří Menzel and Miloš Forman have worked, is increasingly open to non-Czech speakers through the advent of surtitles,

the translations of dialogue projected over the stage. One of the city's most progressive theaters (*divadlo* in Czech) is the **Švandovo** in the Smíchov district. Here international audiences can take in such productions as Václav Havel's own *The Beggar's Opera.*

The **Archa** theater is another leading light of the Prague stage. Many productions offer English printed text; others are based on movement or nonverbal theater that's universally accessible and of high artistic quality.

Prague Spring

The Prague Spring describes the springlike sense of renewal that seemed to launch Czechoslovakia into a freer era in 1968.

In January 1968, hard-liner Antonín Novotný was replaced as First Secretary of the Communist Party by Slovak Alexander Dubček. Though he was known to be a reformist, his radical ideas must have shocked the Soviets. Dubček had risen through the party ranks like his predecessors, so it was astonishing that his ideas came close to suggesting that Czechoslovakia evolve into a social-democratic state incorporating such liberal ideas as freedom of assembly and the abolition of censorship. He even proposed democratizing parliament.

A cartoonist's sardonic comment on the 1968 Soviet invasion

Despite huge popular support for this new policy of "socialism with a human face," it was not going to go down well with the hard-liners, whether within his own party or in Moscow. The Czechs and Slovaks responded quickly to his unexpected loosening of the shackles; the arts flourished, ideas circulated, and anti-Soviet articles, previously a sure path to imprisonment, were published in newspapers. The party leadership often attacked such dangerous ideas but did not prevent them from being raised. The sweet air of freedom was actually wafting through the country, and in the heady atmosphere of the 1960s no one believed it would end.

But it did. By August the Soviet regime had had enough. Challenging party rule in Czechoslovakia was not only undesirable in itself, but it was setting a deplorable precedent for other countries within the Eastern bloc. On August 21, 1968, the Soviets invaded Czechoslovakia, supported by 500,000 troops from other Warsaw Pact nations (except Romania). Tanks took up positions in Wenceslas Square (Václavské náměstí). Courageous men and women confronted the invading forces directly; others occupied the steps of the St. Wenceslas statue, which once again became a symbol of national independence.

There was considerable bloodshed. Dubček and other members of his leadership team protested against the invasion but were flown off to Moscow, where they were browbeaten into submission before returning home. Dubček remained nominally in charge of the Czechoslovak government, but power lay elsewhere. Protests continued, and, on January 16, 1969, the resistance to Soviet occupation reached new levels of intensity and despair when a student named Jan Palach set fire to himself in front of the Wenceslas statue (see p. 117). He died three days later from his burns.

Finally, in April 1969, the broken Dubček was replaced by Gustáv Husák, who had supported the Prague Spring until he saw which way the wind from Moscow was blowing. With his appointment, spring turned to winter. Many Czech artists and intellectuals were among the 150,000 who emigrated before the borders were sealed; the country soon lost such talents as Miloš Forman, Milan Kundera, and Josef Škvorecký.

Husák purged the party, reasserted centralized control, and boosted the secret police's powers. Czechs and Slovaks were urged to make the following pact: If they conformed to the new regime's neo-Stalinist orthodoxies, they would be guaranteed a decent standard of living. It worked for 20 years; in 1989, the regime collapsed as the Velvet Revolution got under way (see pp. 40–42).

Charles Square

New Town has largely lost its medieval character, but it retains the spacious Charles Square (Karlovo náměstí) and many fine churches as planned by Charles IV in 1348. The New Town gradually developed into Prague's commercial center. In the mid-19th century the gardens in Charles Square were laid out, offering welcome shade and tranquility in this busy part of town.

The imposing church of St. Ignatius and the Jesuit College dominate the east side of Charles Square.

On the north side, the proud tower of the **New Town Hall** (Novoměstská radnice) overlooks the square. Originally built in the 1360s, it was the setting for the First Defenestration in 1419 (see p. 28). Today the hall is used for cultural events and weddings.

Fans of Czech cubist architecture should be sure to walk behind the town hall to **Diamond House** (Dům Diamant), completed in 1912. Its texture—pebble against concrete—is raw, but its decorative forms are bold and angular.

Between the square and the River Vltava, along Resslova, is Kilián Ignác Dientzenhofer's baroque **Church of St. Cyril and St. Methodius** (Kostel sv. Cyrila a Metoděje), the spiritual home of the Czech Orthodox Church in Prague since 1935. In May 1942 the Nazi governor

Charles Square

🚇 115

🚊 Tram: 4, 6, 10, 16, 18, 22, 23. Metro: Karlovo náměstí

The roof of the Emmaus Monastery was added in 1967.

Church of St. Cyril & St. Methodius

✉ Resslova 9

Church of St. Wenceslas

✉ Resslova & Dittrichova

of Bohemia and Moravia Reinhard Heydrich was assassinated by Czech paratroopers, who took refuge here. They died when their hiding place was betrayed to the Nazis. A memorial plaque on the church's facade commemorates these events; the walls are still pockmarked with bullet holes from German machine guns.

Opposite is the small Gothic **Church of St. Wenceslas** (Kostel sv. Václav), containing fragmentary Gothic frescoes. On Resslova, by the river, is the celebrated **"Fred and Ginger" building** (Tančící dům; see p. 136).

Along the square's east side stands the large Jesuit **Church of St. Ignatius** (Kostel sv. Ignác), which was mostly completed by 1671. The nobly proportioned interior has sumptuous baroque decor and furnishings. Your eye is drawn down the tall pink-and-white barrel-vaulted nave to the dramatic, pillared high altar. Beside the church, the immense **Jesuit College** (Jezuitská Kolj) fills the entire side of the square between Ječná and U Nemocnice Streets. The college later became a teaching hospital.

At the foot of the square you will find **Faust House** (Faustův dům), once thought of as the residence of Dr. Faustus. It is more certain that it was the home of Edward Kelley, the Elizabethan

---

EXPERIENCE: Studying Czech

There's no better way to gain a sense of Czech culture—or to make inroads with the locals—than to learn the language. Dozens of schools offer short, intensive courses, but many International companies send their staff to the **Akcent International House** (www.akcent.cz), where three-week classes will have you conjugating verbs, getting around on your own, and asking for what you need in any village.

The long-established **Caledonian School** (www.caledonianschool.com) offers Czech classes monthly and teaches all

levels. It may take more than a short course before you're able to read *Good Soldier Švejk* in the original, but learning the language actually is not all that difficult. Czech has no silent letters, a simple past tense and relatively few irregular verbs. The genders and declensions (verbs change endings depending on how they're used and even who is using them) take more practice, but keep practicing.

And there's nothing like seeing the smile that breaks out when a local hears you uttering their mother tongue.

Underground Prague: The Eco-Technical Museum

Perhaps under the spell of such cinematic greats as Carol Reed's *Third Man*, which has spawned a cottage industry of movie fan tours in Vienna since its 1949 opening, Prague officials have been pushing to open the city's sewers, hoping to cash in. But, just as in the climax of the noirish thriller starring Orson Welles, which unfolds in the smelly labyrinth that runs under Vienna's streets, the Czech tourism business has found success elusive.

Various official plans are announced and deadlines set for opening sections of Prague's sewers, usually with pomp and professional presentation and press conferences, often featuring Prague's youthful mayor espousing the advent of experiential tourism and fresh ideas. But so far the only real access to the vast subterranean passages beneath the Czech capital is via the Eco-Technical Museum (*www.ekotechnickemuseum.cz*). In fact, the museum takes some work to find, requiring visitors to take bus 131 from the Hradčanská metro station to the Nádraží Bubeneč stop. After that, they must hunt down the museum by walking under the railway bridge to Papírenská 6. If that sounds like something out of a spy novel already, then perhaps it's a suitable warm-up for the museum itself.

Commemorating the grand Czech tradition of civil engineering, the Eco-Technical Museum shows off the best of the one hundred-year-old designs created with Prague's first modern sewer system. The trek to the entrance is worthwhile: Inside lie vast chambers, long passages, and elegant, soaring brickwork worthy of a Gothic cathedral, and an engine room straight out of a Jules Verne novel.

When built, the system was not just one of the most advanced of its kind in Europe—it was also the answer to a growing public health and sanitation problem. Like many cities at the time, Prague was using its main river, the Vltava, as an open sewer. As the population grew with industrialization, so did the problems.

The sewer works rose to the challenge magnificently, helping to raise the city's status to one of Europe's finest. The city chose a dual-level design by Englishman William Heerlein Lindley; its nine-year construction began in 1896 and operations started a year later. Today Prague sewers run to 2,175 miles (3,500 km).

The Eco-Technical Museum is open on weekends from April through October. At times, it also hosts concerts and can be rented out for parties. And why not? After all, the sewer biz seems to be going great guns in Paris, Brussels, Rome...

adventurer who convinced Rudolf II that he could create the "philosopher's stone" and turn lead and other base metals into gold (see p. 74). Kelley made such slow progress that the exasperated emperor had him imprisoned.

Go south on Vyšehradská and you'll come to the **Emmaus Monastery** (Klášter na Slovanech) on the right. Charles IV founded the Klášter in 1347 in an attempt to bridge the Eastern and Western branches of Christianity. In 1880 German Benedictines rebuilt much of the structure in neo-Gothic style. In 1967 František Černý created the striking twin spires, replacing a roof which was damaged during World War II. Gothic frescoes survive, although in poor condition, in the cloisters. Otherwise the monastery is beautifully restoration. ∎

Emmaus Monastery

☒ Vyšehradská 49

Vyšehrad

It was long believed that Vyšehrad was the original fortress of what would become the future capital of Bohemia, but recent archaeological research suggests the castle at Hradčany was established earlier. In any case, Vyšehrad existed by the mid-tenth century, situated on a crag high above the Vltava. The site was large enough for a sprawling fortress and relatively easy to defend.

Vyšehrad

🗺 115

🚇 Metro: Vyšehrad

Legend recounts how Vyšehrad was founded. Libuše was a Czech princess, a daughter of chieftain Krok. When he died, she needed a husband in order to legitimize her rule. She chose a plowman called Přemysl, thus creating the Přemyslid dynasty, and promptly founded first Vyšehrad and then Prague Castle at Hradčany. This story has a tenacious hold on the Czech imagination and folkloric tradition. Although Vyšehrad

The rugged cliffs of Vyšehrad offer a fine view of the city and the River Vltava.

later became the royal residence of Vratislav II, it gradually lost influence to Hradčany castle on the other side of the river, and by 1140 had been supplanted by it.

Vyšehrad's location, protected by craggy cliffs, is best appreciated from the other side of the Vltava. Under Charles IV its defenses were improved, linking them to other walls around the city. Charles also decreed that the coronation route for Bohemian rulers would begin at Vyšehrad and terminate at Hradčany. The Hussites occupied the fortress for some years in the 15th century, making their own additions. The only significant alterations occurred in the 17th century, when further fortifications were added. By the 19th century Vyšehrad had outlived its usefulness; many of the buildings were dismantled, although the gates and some walls were left intact.

Despite all these changes, there are some genuinely ancient corners of Vyšehrad. Inside the fortress the **Rotunda of St. Martin** (Rotunda sv. Martina), a Romanesque round church from the late 11th century, is one of three such churches still in existence in Prague. Some of Charles IV's fortifications also survive. Excavations are continuing to ascertain the archaeological history and legacy of the site. The gateways into the fortress, the **Tábor**

Gate (Táborská brána) and the **Leopold Gate** (Leopoldova brána), both date from the mid-17th century. The Tábor Gate was the main entrance to the fortress, but to enter the citadel you must also pass through the impressively rusticated baroque Leopold Gate. Its pediment is topped by battered stone lions and an eagle; the mighty brick walls of the 1740s stand on either side.

Just beyond the rotunda, turn left on K Rotundě. The lane leads to the remains of the **Basilica of St. Lawrence** (Bazilika sv. Vavřinec; *closed Tues. & Fri. p.m.*), then continues to an esplanade high above the walls from which there's an impressive river view. Bear right and follow the path to other viewpoints. From these you can see the Gothic ruins on a crag called **Libuše's Bath,** and over to the castle and Petřín Hill.

You are now close to the **Church of St. Peter and St. Paul** (Kostel sv. Petr a Pavel). The original church was a Romanesque structure, but today it's essentially neo-Gothic. This handsome building, with its two tall spires built in 1902, is visible for miles. The lane near the west front of the church offers excellent and unusual views of the city. Nearby is a copy of Jan Jiří Bendl's statue of St. Wenceslas, and a restaurant opposite the church entrance has a pleasant terrace. The park south of the church contains four enormous statues by Josef Myslbek (1848–1922).

Vyšehrad is also the site of Prague's most revered cemetery, **Vyšehradský hřbitov.** An existing burial ground was expanded in 1875 and Renaissance-style

arcades were added. It became a resting ground for the major figures of the Czech national revival, including composers Dvořák and Smetana, opera singer Ema Destinnová, poet Jan Neruda (see above), writer Karel Čapek, and artists Mikoláš Aleš, Josef Myslbek, and Alfons Mucha. Competitive zeal among the bereaved has resulted in an abundance of extravagant tombstones with busts and portrait reliefs. Dvořák's gilt-lettered tomb is one of the grandest, topped with a conventional bust of the composer. Nearby is the brightly gilt secession monument to one Josefina Brdlíková, and at the end of the cemetery is the grandiose Slavín monument, a memorial to 53 famous Czech artists. ∎

Jan Neruda

A tobacconist's son, Jan Neruda (1834–1891) was born in Malá Strana and spent much of his life in the house known as The Two Suns *(Nerudova 47).* After a spell as a teacher, in 1865 he began work as an essayist—expressing radical views on social problems— and critic for Prague's leading daily newspaper. He was best known for his poems and short stories, notably *Tales of the Malá Strana* (1878), and earned an international reputation. The Nobel Prize–winning Chilean poet Pablo Neruda adopted Jan Neruda's name as a pseudonym out of admiration for his work and his politics.

Church of St. Peter and St. Paul

🕐 Closed Tues. & Fri. p.m.

Trade Fair Palace

Near the Stromovka Park, the striking Trade Fair Palace (Veletržní palác) was built in the 1920s as an exhibition hall for Czech industry, but after a fire in 1974 it was virtually abandoned. In the 1990s reconstruction turned it into a showcase for 2,000 items from the National Gallery's (Národní galerie) collections of modern and contemporary art. It is also the new home for the modern art collection formerly in the Sternberg Palace (Šternberský palác).

Modern and contemporary arts are displayed in the Trade Fair Palace's functionalism-style building.

The conversion of the building has been brilliantly executed. The principal galleries are laid out on the main floors, with subsidiary exhibits in the galleries around the main atrium. The result is spacious and airy, and the clean lines of the building never distract from the exhibits themselves, which are informatively displayed. If you want to visit the galleries in chronological order, start on the fourth floor and work your way downward.

Fourth Floor

The earliest exhibits are the collections of 19th-century art. Josef Myslbek, whose grandiose sculptures adorn much of the city, is represented by various busts. The paintings are varied.

Antonín Machek (1775–1849) was an accomplished portraitist, as were Josef Manes (1820–1871) and Karel Purkyne (1834–1868), but you may be more intrigued by the Prague interiors of Ludvik Kohl (1746–1821). There are gentle landscapes by F. X. Procházka (1746–1815) and Josef Navrátil (1798–1865), as well as inflated historical and genre paintings by the revered Mikoláš Aleš (1852–1913). Aleš's work is found all over Prague; he decorated the Storch house in Old Town Square and contributed murals to the National Theater. His work is revered by the Czechs, but it may seem too highly colored and overblown to less partisan observers. A painting by Gabriel Max (1840–1915) depicting the crucifixion of St. Julia caused a stir in 1865, when the saint was portrayed as a buxom peasant girl. There are symbolic wood carvings by František Bílek (1872–1941) and a few fine works by Austrians Gustav Klimt (1862–1918) and Egon Schiele (1890–1918). Galleries devoted to applied arts supplement this core collection, a pattern repeated on the other floors.

Third Floor

The third floor focuses on the years from 1900 to 1930. There are garish paintings, including some boisterous nudes, by František Kupka (1871–1957), and later, purely abstract work. Fine Czech cubist paintings confirm the stature of artists such as Emil Filla (1883–1953), Antonín

Procházka (1882–1945), and Bohumil Kubišta (1884–1918). Watch for the cubist furniture, too: It looks uncomfortable, but the design is remarkably original. A fine collection of modern art has come here from the Sternberg Palace (see p. 76). This includes a substantial array of paintings by Delacroix and Daumie, busts by Rodin, a rare self-portrait (1890) by Henri Rousseau, and Impressionist and Post-Impressionist works by van Gogh and others. The Picasso collection is exceptional in its quality and quantity.

INSIDER TIP:

Check out Dox *(www .doxprague.org)*, the Center for Contemporary Art, in a newly renovated factory. This hip, minimalist gallery offers an amazing art experience.

—ANDREA LIŠKOVÁ
CzechTourism USA

Second Floor

Here you will find eclectic examples of Czech art from 1930 onward. Some are derivative—Daliesque paintings by František Janoušek (1890–1943), Bonnard-influenced Václav Bartovský (1903–1961)—while others are typical of various art movements, from abstraction to modish installations. The lower floors are used for temporary exhibits. ∎

Trade Fair Palace
- 🅰 Inset p. 115
- ✉ Dukelských hrdinů 47
- ☎ 224 301 111
- 🕐 Closed Mon.
- 💲 $$$. Free first Fri. of the month
- 🚊 Tram: 5, 12, 17. Metro: Nádraží Holešovice
- **www.ngprague.cz**

Dox
- ✉ Poupětova1
- ☎ 224 301 111
- 🕐 Closed Tues.

Prague Pubs

With a history dating back to medieval times, Bohemian beer is more of a social glue than a beverage to Czechs. Prague pubs, which remain ubiquitous, unpretentious, and smoky, have cleaned up somewhat in recent years but are still cheap and full of locals.

Prague's pubs are a good place to enjoy a hearty lunch, washed down with mugs of beer.

Easily identified by the word *pivnice* or *hospoda*, pubs tend to offer limited menus mainly consisting of snacks such as pickled cheese or smoked herring. They will offer variety at the taps, however, with 10-degree and 12-degree brews (the latter being stronger), light (*světlé*), dark (*černé*), and mixed (*řezané*) beer.

Prague's pubs are not always consistent in quality—but new technologies are rescuing flavor and body. Many beerhalls are now outfitted with tanks that allow them to serve beer that's fuller in flavor because it has not been pasteurized, a heating process that kills microbes but also taste. Such pubs, designated as *tankovna*, get their raw beer in sealed sacks that go into the tanks, which has proven a hit with Czech aficionados in a growing trend. For a sample, try U Pinkasů and U Medvídků in Old Town (see below).

Many, like Pivovarský dům, have also improved their menus substantially, with hearty duck dishes and revived classics such as dumplings stuffed with smoked meat and savory soups.

The best known of all Prague pubs is **U Fleků** at Křemencova 11 *(tel 224 934 019)*, between the New Town Hall and the river. This enormous pub, named for the Flek family, has wood-paneled halls and a large courtyard, moderately priced Czech food, and strong dark beer, brewed on the premises since 1499 and known as Flekovský ležák. It's on the tourist circuit, though, and mysterious extra charges sometimes appear at bill time.

Almost as well known is **U kalicha** (At the Chalice) at Na bojišti 14 *(tel 296 189 600)* in New Town, near the Vila Amerika. It's the setting of much of Jaroslav Hašek's novel *The Good Soldier Švejk* (see p. 53, since the hero is a committed beer drinker. Inevitably it has become a mecca for tourists, even those who have no familiarity with the novel. These days it's more of a restaurant than a pub.

New Town

Two microbreweries in New Town (Nové Město) serve excellent beer. The first is the **Novoměstský pivovar** *(Vodickova 20, tel 224 237 552)*, a basement warren off Wenceslas Square. This busy place also serves standard but flavorful Czech dishes. The other is the airier **Pivovarský dům** *(tel 296 216 666)* on the corner of Ječná and Lípová, near Charles Square. The beers are delicious, especially the regular beers and the wheat beer. Both also produce coffee, banana, and sour cherry varieties. The food is simple Czech fare.

Little Quarter

There are few authentic pubs in the exclusive Little Quarter (Malá Strana) district, but the following are all worth a visit:

U Hrocha (At the Hippo): This is the genuine article, located beneath the castle *(Thunovská 10)*. The interior has plain wooden tables and chairs—and good beer.

U Kocoura (At the Cat): Quench your thirst here after tackling the hills of Hradčany *(Nerudova 2)*. Try the inexpensive dumplings with red cabbage or the cold food platters to accompany the Pilsen or dark Regent beers.

U Glaubiců: This grand old baroque hall hosts one of the Little Quarters's last mainstays for locals, the seven-century-old pub serving Pilsner and hearty Czech traditional grub *(Malostranské náměstí 5)*. Gruff but friendly waiters hoist lagers for guests from all over the world who sit at wooden benches in the many halls and cellars of this venerated cultural gem.

Old Town

Many pubs have disappeared from Old Town (Staré Město) to make way for boutiques and restaurants. But some searching will unearth several unequivocally authentic examples.

U Medvídků: The pedigree of Old Town's most favoured Budvar pub dates to 1466 and U medvídků *(Na Perštýne 7)* still serves up the classics in old-fashioned style, with vested waiters laying out pork knuckle and beer-basted beef goulash to go with the beer. The house special, the heady Oldgott, is well worth a try.

U Pinkasů: One of the city's most venerated pubs, this labyrinth of rooms covering three floors is a homey classic, with a menu rich on Czech game dishes and savory sauces, plus the full complement of beer sops, such as potato pancakes and pickled sausage with onion. The beer's the star, of course, with the freshest tasting Pilsner Urquell in town. Since 1943, this pub's been the hub of downtown life and a guarded treasure to Praguers.

INSIDER TIP:

Enjoy the famous Czech beers— Pilsner Urquell and Budvar— with some traditional Czech cuisine like dumplings with marinated beef sirloin.

—MAX MUNSON
Prague publican

U Rotundy (At the Rotunda): If you are feeling intrepid and want to try the real thing, this rough pub with its battered sign is just across from the rotunda church *(Karoliný Světlé)*. The interior is classic: thick with cigarette smoke and frequented by men in overalls.

U Zlatého Tygra (At the Golden Tiger): This crowded literary pub, where the novelist Bohumil Hrabal held court until his death in 1997, still boasts a loyal local clientele. It remains authentic despite its proximity to touristy Karlova *(Husova 17)*.

Around Prague

On the edges of Prague are a number of churches and châteaus well worth visiting. Most of them are easy to reach by public transportation. The Star Castle is quite unlike any other castle in Bohemia, and Břevnov Monastery is an excellent example of a moribund institution given a new lease on life when the monks returned here after the Velvet Revolution.

Břevnov Monastery

🅰 See map inset p. 115

✉ Markétská 1

☎ 220 406 111

🕐 Closed Mon.–Fri.

💲 $

🚋 Tram: 8, 22. Metro: Malostranská

www.brevnov.cz

Břevnov Monastery

In 993 Prince Boleslav II and St. Adalbert, bishop of Prague, founded the Břevnov Monastery (Břevnovský klášter), the very first monastic institution in Bohemia. In the 18th century, the Dientzenhofers (see p. 48) built a baroque complex. The grandest is the slightly austere **Church of St. Margaret** (Kostel sv. Markéta),

The strange and aptly named Star Castle stands in parkland on the fringes of Prague.

which comes into view as you enter the monastery gateway. Despite its size, the interior has no aisles and is, compared with most of Prague's other baroque churches, restrained in its decor. There's a fine organ gallery with white putti, choir stalls, and altarpieces by Petr Brandl (1668–1735). In the crypt you can see remains of the 11th-century church, excavated in the 1960s. Gradual restoration of the other sumptuous buildings is under way. The Benedictine monks returned to the monastery in 1990, just three years before its millennial anniversary.

Church of Our Lady of Victory at White Mountain

Soon after the decisive battle of 1620 (see pp. 30–31) a chapel dedicated to St. Wenceslas was built here. A few years later, Ferdinand II ordered that it be replaced by a monastery and chapel. The arcades around the Church of Our Lady of Victory at White Mountain (Kostel Panny Marie Vítězné) are reminiscent of those at the Loreto Church in Hradčany (see pp. 82–83); the interior is richly frescoed. The church is near the Bílá Hora tram terminus.

Star Castle

The remarkable Star Castle (Letohrádek hvězda), built in the shape of a six-pointed star, stands within a former game reserve founded in 1530 by Ferdinand I. A number of avenues traverse the park, all leading to the castle on the top of White Mountain. It was built in the 1550s as a hunting lodge for the son of Ferdinand I, Archduke Ferdinand of Tyrol. Used as a barracks and military store until 1874, the castle was not properly restored until the 1950s. The interior's most exciting features are the exquisite Renaissance stucco decorations, depicting mythological scenes, as well as medallions and purely ornamental plasterwork. Today the castle is a museum dedicated to the lives and works of writer Alois Jirásek (1851–1930) and artist Mikoláš Aleš (1852–1913). In the basement is an exhibit about the Battle of White Mountain (see pp. 30–31).

Troja Castle

Count Václav Vojtěch Šternberk built Troja Castle (Trojský zámek) as a summer residence, easily accessible from Hradčany, in the 1680s. The first building was designed by Gian Domenico Orsi, but the handsome if boxlike building you see today, with whitewashed walls and rust-red stonework, is Jean-Baptiste Mathey's Bohemian version of a Roman villa. Boldly gesticulating statues of deities adorn its grand exterior double staircase. The most imposing room is the lavishly frescoed banqueting hall; the murals mostly portray the Habsburgs' achievements and Leopold I's victories over the Ottoman Turks in the 17th century. An exhibit of Czech

INSIDER TIP:

Take subway line A to Divoká (terminal), switch to bus 119, and get off at Divoká Šárka resort. What other European metropolis has rock formations you can climb?

—MILOS ČUŘIK
Tour guide, Arts & Music Travel

paintings from the late 19th and early 20th centuries, notably works by Václav Brožík, is displayed in the villa. The terraced gardens were laid out in the early 18th century.

Zbraslav Monastery

Zbraslav Monastery (Zbraslavský klášter) was founded 8 miles (12 km) south of the city in 1292 as a burial place for the Bohemian kings, though only Václav II and Václav IV were actually laid to rest here. Subsequent wars left the monastery in ruins, until it was rebuilt as a château in the early 18th century. Since 1998 the interior has housed the National Gallery's fine collection of Asian and Islamic art. First-floor exhibits, mostly devoted to Japanese art, include enamelware, Buddhist sculpture, and lively figurative paintings. Upstairs, the first Chinese room is filled with bronze ritual objects up to 3,200 years old, as well as funerary figurines, ceramics, and examples of Buddhist art. Smaller collections of Tibetan, Indian, and Islamic art are on the same floor. ∎

Church of Our Lady of Victory at White Mountain

 See map inset p. 115

✉ Zbečenská

🚋 Tram: 25

Star Castle

 See map inset p. 115

☎ 220 516 695

🕐 Closed Mon.

💲 $

🚇 Metro: Hradcanská, then tram 1 or 18 to the terminus

Troja Castle

 See map inset p. 115

✉ U Trojského zámku 1

☎ 283 851 614

🕐 Closed Mon. April–Oct., & Mon.–Fri. Nov.– March

💲 $$$

🚇 Metro to Nádraží Holešovice, then bus 112 to end of line

Zbraslav Monastery

 See map inset p. 115

✉ Bartoňova 2, Prague 5 Zbraslav

☎ 257 921 638

🕐 Closed Mon.

💲 $$

🚇 Metro: Smíchovské nádraží, then bus 243 to Zbraslavské náměstí

EXPERIENCE: Czech Cooking

Czech cuisine does not generally win accolades for its refinement or creativity, but it's a hearty, filling, warming kind of comfort food with solid working-class credentials. Smoked meats (*uzený*), steamed dumplings (*knedlíky*), and sauerkraut (*zelí*) are mainstays. Almost invariably, they're accompanied by cold (but never frosty) lager, not wine.

Meat serves as the centerpiece of many traditional Czech meals.

For younger Czechs, the Velvet Revolution was as much about the freedom to travel and experience other cultures as it was about human rights—of course. Predictably, a fascination for East Asian, Indian, and Mexican cuisine, to say nothing of great seafood, has resulted from all their travels during the past two decades, which is certainly good news for all diners in the Czech Republic.

At the same time, the classics, many of which are contained in the seminal cookbook of Magdalena Dobromila Rettigová, a 19th-century romantic writer and maven for all things domestic, are seeing a resurgence.

The ambitious gentry figure's 1826 volume, *A Household Cookery Book or A Treatise on Meat and Fasting Dishes for Bohemian and Moravian Lasses*, was one of the best-selling Bohemian books of all time. Today, it can still be found in Prague bookshops.

Modern conceptions of these traditions, naturally, place new emphasis on fresh, quality ingredients, spices, technique, and presentation. (Many places have even invested heavily in retraining Prague's famously gruff and unconcerned waiters.)

There's still some distance to go, it seems. Even local food critics decry the sameness of menus so often seen at restaurants—they may offer something wrapped in a tortilla or a red curry fish filet, but feel compelled to include at least one goulash or schnitzel offering for customers who fear change.

One organization leading the charge for great cuisine, **Ola Kala** (*www.olakala.cz*), is happy to show you the ropes. This self-described "culinary atelier" runs a cooking course covering both traditional Czech dishes and international ones, ranging from the central European classic filet in cream sauce, known as *svíčková*, to potato pancakes with sour cream and smoked salmon.

Michal Nikodem, Ola Kala's chef, takes care of all necessary shopping. His well-kitted-out kitchen offers French copper pots and ample work areas. Participants learn the methods and tricks that result in the savory sensations that the company provides to many local companies through its catering side. Tasting is encouraged throughout the cooking process, to help students get a grasp on the evolution of taste and mouthfeel. Just be prepared to cart home your creations—or give up eating out entirely for a day after you complete the course.

More Places to Visit in New Town & the Suburbs

Botanical Gardens

The hilly open spaces that comprise Prague's Botanical Gardens (Botanická zahrada) are welcome in a district crowded with institutions and apartment buildings. Originally located in Smíchov, south of Malá Strana, the gardens were moved here in 1897. The giant water lily is the most popular attraction.

🅰 115 ✉ Na Slupi 16 ☎ 221 951 879 💲 $ 🚋 Tram: 18, 24 Metro: Karlovo náměstí

Church of St. John on the Rock

The delightful Church of St. John on the Rock (Kostel sv. Jan na Skalce), designed in the 1730s by Kilián Ignác Dientzenhofer, is remarkable for its magnificent exterior staircase, which was designed later by another architect, Anton Schmidt. The church is dramatically located on top of a crag above street level, facing the Emmaus Monastery along Vyšehradská; its towers are set at a jaunty angle on either side of the facade. St. John is open only during Mass, via the entrance on Charles Square (Karlovo náměstí).

🅰 113 🚋 Tram: 18, 24. Metro: Karlovo náměstí

Church of St. Stephen

Tucked between Žitná and Ječná, the Gothic Church of St. Stephen (Kostel sv. Štěpán) houses the tomb of Matthias Braun, one of Bohemia's greatest and most prolific baroque sculptors (see p. 48). It contains a fine 15th-century pulpit and paintings by baroque masters such as Karel Škréta, as well as a Gothic painting of the Madonna (1472).

🅰 115 ✉ Štěpánská 🚋 Tram: 4, 6, 10, 16, 22, 23. Metro: Karlovo náměstí, I. P. Pavlova

Divoká Šárka

A sylvan oasis just a 12-minute tram ride from the Dejvická metro, this vast Prague park rambles through a small valley formed by hikeable crags. In summer, its real appeal

---

Hockey Fervor

Czechs don't really get passionately exercised about many subjects, but there's one event that stirs souls even beyond the revelry of Bohemian beer. Major hockey victories get locals out into the streets cheering and waving tricolor Czech flags with fervor. When a Czech team defeats one from a rival country such as Russia, it's advisable to stay indoors or invest in earplugs.

To get some sense of the excitement, consider the small investment of tickets to a hockey game. The storied HC Slavia Praha team, which often makes headlines with its wins in the Czech Extraliga—the country's highest level league—will not disappoint. The team displays finesse and firepower befitting its hundred-year-plus history. Its home base is the comfortable **O2 Arena** (www.o2arena.cz), the city's biggest new indoor stadium. Tickets for games can be booked online, starting at 150 Czech crowns.

From September through February, the Slavia takes center stage at O2, garnering more fans and cheers than the rock concerts that also play at this 18,000-seat venue. Book early for an intense match (those against cross-town rival HC Sparta Praha often sell out fast).

EXPERIENCE: Globe Readings

Any country that elects an absurdist playwright as its first post–Cold War president should not be surprised to witness an invasion international writers. Thus, it seemed only natural that the **Globe Bookstore and Café** *(Pstrossova 6, tel 224-934 203, www.globebookstore.cz)* was founded in 1993 in Prague to cater to their needs. Though the storied literary heart of expat Prague has since changed locations and now resides in New Town, it still stocks thousands of volumes, new and used, covering everything imaginable, from film history to *samizdat*–self published, often political–literature.

The Globe also still features author readings, continuing a long tradition that has included prominent writers such as Allen Ginsberg, Richard Ford, and Amy Tan reciting from their work.

These days, it's more likely you'll hear emerging talents–poets and sometimes musicians–sharing their visions with patrons sipping coffee or cheap red wine. The full calendar is kept updated on the Globe's website, but you shouldn't be too surprised to hear an unscheduled scribe taking up the mic on an evening when you're sitting in the storied bookshop, leafing through pages.

---

is the swimming pond at the east end and the twin pools fed by chilly creek water at the west, both with popular beer stands and sunbathing.

🅰 Inset 115 ✉ Divoká Šárka 🕐 Open May–Oct. daily 💲 $ 🚇 Metro: Dejvická then tram 20

"Fred and Ginger" Building

It comes as a welcome surprise in historic Prague to see this funky, jazzy building by the brilliant, if quirky, Californian architect Frank Gehry. It is affectionately called the Dancing House (Tančící dům) for its resemblance to two dancers. The new office building sprang up along the riverbank next to a building owned by Václav Havel's family. The playwrite played a large part in encouraging an unconventional approach to this prime site. Its most striking feature is the curvaceous glass tower, which is topped by the Céleste Restaurant.

🅰 115 ✉ Corner of Resslova & Rašínovo nábřeží 🚇 Tram: 3, 7, 16, 17, 21. Metro: Karlovo náměstí

Karlov Church

Although slightly off the beaten track,

Karlov Church (Na Karlově) is one of the most remarkable buildings established by Charles IV, in 1350. Its highly unusual octagonal design is an architectural tribute to Charlemagne's imperial chapel in Aachen in Germany. The church was modified in 1575 by Bonifác Wohlmut, who built the extraordinary vaulting and cupola. Architect František Kaňka helped renovate the church during the 1730s and is largely responsible for the interior's appearance. This must be one of the most theatrical baroque churches in the republic, with polychrome figures portraying the Visitation, flanked by sculptured onlookers leaning out of windows to see what is going on.

🅰 115 ✉ Ke Karlovu/Horská 🕐 Open Sun. & holidays p.m. 🚇 Metro: I. P. Pavlova

Lapidárium

Stromovka Park is filled with exhibition buildings, and the pavilion on the right is the Lapidárium of the National Museum, a resting place for often fragile and weathered original stone statues dating from the 11th to the 19th centuries. The Lapidárium was established in 1905 and is a treasure house of sculptural art. Among the highlights are

many of the original carvings from the Old
Town Bridge Tower, the Charles Bridge,
the Loreto Church and the beautiful Krocín
fountain that stood in Old Town Square
until 1864.
 Inset 115   ✉ Výstaviště   🕐 Closed Mon.
💲 $ 🚇 Metro: Nádraží Holešovice, then
tram 5, 12, or 17 to Stromovka Park

Mucha Museum

This museum, dedicated to the work of one
of Bohemia's best known art nouveau artists,
is housed in the 18th-century Kaunicky palác,
which opened in 1998. Exhibits include
paintings, charcoal drawings, and sculptures,
as well as memorabilia of Alfons Mucha
(1860–1939). His posters have become
familiar images—fey girls with swirling draperies, all in art nouveau borders with stylish
floral embellishments. After Mucha's return
from Paris in 1910, his work became more
nationalistic, with poses reminiscent
of socialist realism.
www.mucha.cz   113   ✉ Panská 7   ☎ 224
215 409   💲 $$$ 🚇 Tram: 3, 9, 14, 24.
Metro: Můstek

National Technical Museum

For those interested in the history of
technology and industry, few museums in
Europe match Prague's National Techni-
cal Museum (Národní technické muzeum).
Founded in 1908, it houses exhibits related
to architecture, photography, timekeep-
ing, and transportation—an excuse to
assemble a huge collection of locomotives,
old motorcars, biplanes, penny farthings,
motorcycles, cameras, and a hot-air balloon.
In the basement is a realistic mock-up of
a coal mine that can be visited only on a
guided tour (45 minutes). After extensive
renovations, the museum is slated to reopen
in autumn 2010.
www.ntm.cz   Inset 115   ✉ Kostelní 42
☎ 220 399 111,   🕐 Closed Mon.   💲 $$
🚇 Metro: Vltavská, then tram 1, 8, 25, or 26

Olšany Cemetery

Since 1784 Olšany Cemetery (Olšanské
hřbitovy), the large burial ground along
Vinohradská, has been the city's main cemetery. It is divided into a number of sections.
Many visitors come to the Jewish cemetery,
on the other side of Jana Želivského street,
to visit the grave of Franz Kafka (clearly
indicated). This melancholy cemetery is a
reminder of the size of Prague's Jewish community before World War II. Just inside the
gates of the main Christian cemetery on the
right is the grave of Jan Palach (see p. 117).
His body was removed by the authorities in
1973, but in 1990 his coffin was returned to
its original grave.
 Inset 115   ✉ Vinohradská 153   🚇 Tram:
5, 10, 11, 16 Metro: Flora (Christian
cemetery), Želivského (Jewish cemetery)

**Alfons Mucha is best known for his art nouveau
posters, including the "Salon des Cent" of 1896.**

Police Museum

The Police Museum (Muzeum Policie) can be found in the former cloisters adjoining the Karlov church (see p. 136). The present-day museum ignores the distasteful role of the police before 1989 and focuses on uniforms, weaponry, and equipment. There are rooms devoted to road safety, showing videos of spectacular car accidents, and the crime and detection exhibits have some very gruesome photographs. For light relief there is a section on safe-breaking.

🅜 115 ✉ Ke Karlovu 453/1 ☎ 224 923 619 🕐 Closed Mon. 🚇 $ 🚌 Bus: 291. Metro: I. P. Pavlova

Prague Municipal Museum

A few yards from the Florenc metro station, the Prague Municipal Museum (Muzeum hlavního města Prahy) tells the story of the city and exhibits paintings, furniture, and sculptures from Prague's towers and churches. The most popular exhibit is the model of the city constructed from wood and paper by Antonín Langweil in the 1830s. This laborious work depicts 2,000 buildings. It provides firm evidence of the appearance of Kampa Island before it became a park and of the Jewish ghetto before its demolition.

🅜 115 ✉ Na Poříčí 52 ☎ 221 012 911 🕐 Closed Mon. 🚇 $ 🚌 Tram: 8, 25. Metro: Florenc

Vila Amerika

This exquisite, if boxlike, villa was built by the ubiquitous Kilián Ignác Dientzenhofer as a summer residence for Count Michna in 1720. The house became dilapidated during the 19th century, but it was saved from ruin and is now the Dvořák Museum. The displays, which include a small collection of the great composer's scores and musical instruments, document his career and life. Concerts take place between April and October in the small frescoed recital hall.

🅜 115 ✉ Ke Karlovu 20 ☎ 224 918 013 🕐 Closed Mon. 🚇 $ 🚌 Metro: I. P. Pavlova

Žižkov

The hilltop suburb of Žižkov is named after the Hussite hero Jan Žižka (ca 1360–1424). On top of the hill—site of a great Hussite victory in 1420—stands a vast monument (1929–1932) known as the National Memorial (Národní památník). Frescoes illustrate triumphant moments in Bohemia's history, and the colossal 1950s equestrian statue of the general by Bohumil Kafka is, according to UNESCO, the world's largest bronze equestrian statue. Rising above it all is Prague's tallest structure, the Žižkov television tower, completed in 1992 and later adorned with crawling babies by artist David Černý.

🅜 Inset 115 🚌 Metro: Florenc

Shrove Tuesday

For a nation that's officially made up of the largest proportion of agnostics in the world, Czechs are surprisingly dedicated to old religious rituals. The holiday known as Carnival to much of the Catholic world is also celebrated as *Masopust* by Czechs. The Shrove Tuesday festival calls for the slaughter of pigs, feasts, dancing in the streets, music, and imbibing worthy of New Orleans at Mardi Gras.

Dating back at least to Roman times, when citizens indulged before the lean days of Lent with costumes and masks, the celebration of Bacchus and Venus is seen in Prague mainly in the Žižkov district, always known for Bohemian living and bar-hopping. The **Akropolis club** (*www.palacakropolis.cz*) tends to be the hub of the festivities, intended to drive away winter—but only if revelers truly indulge.

A number of fascinating castles and interesting towns surrounding Prague—the highlight, Charles IV's summer castle of Karlštejn

Day Trips from Prague

The chapel at Karlštejn Castle sparkles with precious jewels.

Day Trips from Prague

Unlike most European capitals, Prague remains a small city. Heading out of the city, before long you will find yourself in open countryside. The country around Prague contains a surprising number of castles and châteaus, nearly all well worth visiting.

The best known castle is Karlštejn, the summer residence of Charles IV. It is also the most visited one in the country, apart from Prague Castle. But there are other medieval castles to see, such as Český Šternberk, Kokořín, and Křivoklát. Another popular excursion is to the château of Konopiště, which was rebuilt by Archduke Franz Ferdinand in the 1890s and is still packed with family memorabilia.

Two châteaus belonging to the Lobkowiczs, one of many Bohemian families who built up their fortunes under the Habsburgs, are open to the public. One is at Mělník, the best known of Bohemia's wine regions; the other is at Nelahozeves, the village where Antonín Dvořák was born. The château here is filled with some of the Lobkowicz family's art treasures.

Of the many small towns within easy reach of Prague, the most absorbing is Kutná Hora, a former rich mining town that is lavishly endowed with magnificent buildings. Nearby you will find one of Europe's largest charnel houses. Kolín has a mighty medieval church, Mladá Boleslav is home to the Škoda Museum, which motoring enthusiasts will find enthralling, and Poděbrady is famed for its spas.

Although none of these is very far from the capital, some are quite hard to reach without a car. Prague's ring road is still developing, so driving from one town to the next can require some time; plan your excursions to take this into account. ■

NOT TO BE MISSED

Viewing Master Theodoric's earliest Gothic art at Karlštejn **142–143**

A stroll under the flying buttresses at Cathedral of St. Barbara in Kutná Hora **145**

The charnel house, Sedlec's human skeleton collection **146**

Hiking the fairy-tale valley of Kokořín **148**

Checking out local crafts at Křivoklát Castle **149**

The grounds of Konopiště, home to Archduke Franz Ferdinand **149**

Touring the Lobkowicz palace and wine cellar in Mělník **150**

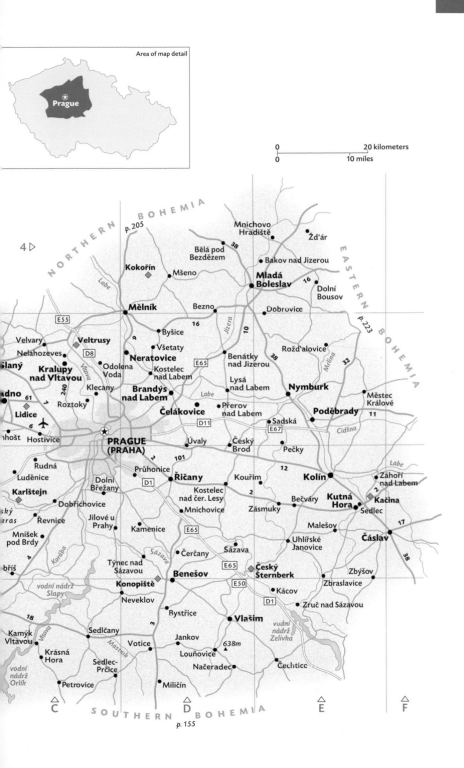

Area of map detail

Prague

0 _____ 20 kilometers
0 _____ 10 miles

NORTHERN BOHEMIA

4 ▷

p. 205

Kokořín   Mšeno
Bělá pod
Bezdězem   38

Mnichovo
Hradiště   Žd'ár

Bakov nad Jizerou

Mladá
Boleslav   16   Dolní
Bousov

EASTERN BOHEMIA   p. 223

Labe

Mělník   Bezno   Dobrovice

E55   Byšice   16

Velvary   Veltrusy   Všetaty   Rožďalovice

Nelahozeves   D8   Neratovice   Benátky
nad Jizerou   38

Slaný   Kralupy
nad Vltavou   Odolena
Voda   Kostelec
nad Labem   E65   Lysá
nad Labem   Nymburk   Městec
Králové

dno   61   Klecany   Brandýs
nad Labem   Labe   Přerov
nad Labem   Poděbrady   11

Roztoky   Čelákovice   Sadská   Cidlina

Lidice   D11   E67

nhošt   Hostivice   PRAGUE
(PRAHA)   Úvaly   Český
Brod   Pečky

Rudná   101   Průhonice   12   Labe

Luděnice   Dolní
Břežany   D1   Říčany   Kouřim   Kolín   Záhoří
nad Labem

Karlštejn   Kostelec
nad čer. Lesy   2   Bečváry   Kutná
Hora   Kačina

ský   Dobřichovice   Mnichovice   Zásmuky   Sedlec

ras   Řevnice   Jilové u
Prahy   E65   Malešov   17

Mníšek
pod Brdy   Kamenice   Uhlířské
Janovice   Čáslav

Korába   Sázava   Čerčany   Sázava   38

bříš   Týnec nad
Sázavou   E65   Český
Šternberk   Zbýšov

Konopiště   Benešov   E50   Zbraslavice

vodní nádrž
Slapy   Neveklov   Kácov

D1   Zruč nad Sázavou

18   Bystřice

Kamýk
Vltavou   Sedlčany   Jankov   Vlašim   vodní
nádrž
Zelivka

Votice   638m

Krásná
Hora   Sedlec-
Prčice   Loňovice   Načeradec   Čechtice

vodní
nádrž
Orlík   Petrovice   Miličín

C   SOUTHERN BOHEMIA   D   E   F

p. 155

Karlštejn

The walled fortress of Karlštejn, set amid the Český kras region, sprawls up a steep hillside above the Berounka River. Frenchman Matthias of Arras, who also worked on the Cathedral of St. Vitus, built it as a royal castle for Charles IV. Work began in 1348 to create a summer palace for the king that also would function as a safe place for his art treasures and the crown jewels. One of the peculiarities of Charles's tenure was his refusal to allow women to enter Karlštejn.

Karlštejn was both a fortress and a summer residence of Charles IV.

Despite partial reconstruction during the Renaissance and heavy-handed restoration in the late 19th century, Karlštejn's impregnable walls and towers —especially the 88-foot-high (27 m) keep, or Great Tower— remain an impressive sight. The interior, although bare, is worth a visit. Here you can see the emperor's apartments, including his bedroom, and two chapels. The first is the **Chapel of St. Mary** (Mariánská kaple), decorated with faded 14th-century frescoes depicting the castle's founding. Of more interest is the **Chapel of St. Catherine** (Kaple sv. Kateřiny), the emperor's private place of prayer. Decorated with medieval frescoes and plaques of semiprecious gems set into the wall, it includes a portrait of Charles IV with his third consort, Anne of Svídnik. The heart of the castle is the **keep tower**, where the most precious jewels and relics were housed. Inside, the astonishing **Chapel of the Holy Cross** (Kaple sv. Kříže), is gilded and richly embellished with 2,200 precious gems and a huge 14th-century cycle of paintings depicting the saints by Master Theodoric of Prague. This chapel was built to house irreplaceable religious relics as well as the Habsburg imperial jewels and insignia now displayed in Vienna and Prague. Until recently it was closed to visitors to preserve its artistic treasures, although some of Theodoric's panels can be seen in the Convent of St. Agnes (Anežský klášter) in Prague (see pp. 108–111). A tour that includes the chapel is offered part of the year. Limited to 15 people, it costs twice as much as the other tour, but is well worth it. This tour must be pre-booked.

Karlštejn is popular with tourists, so the approach to the castle is lined with souvenir stalls and snack bars. Arrive early, before it is overrun with bus tours. Trains leave Prague's Smíchov station hourly for Karlštejn. It's then a 15-minute hike to the castle entrance. In summer carriages will haul you most of the way there, for a price. ∎

Karlštejn

⚑ 141 C2

✉ 17 miles (28 km) SW of Prague

☎ 274 008 154 (to book tours)

🕐 Closed Mon.

💲 $$$–$$$$ Tours: $$$$

🚆 Train from Prague's Smíchov station

www.hradkarl stejn.cz

INSIDER TIP:

Be sure to check out Karlštejn village. Talented painters have shops that line the road; you will find more than kitschy souvenirs.

—EMILY THOMPSON
Special Sections editor,
The Prague Post

EXPERIENCE: Berry Picking

Czechs are deeply attached to their forests and meadows. Locals empty the streets of Prague on summer weekends, when they take off for their family cottages.

Long walks through the trees, with regular stops for wild strawberries, blueberries, and mushrooms, are a sacred ritual. Just about every Czech child learns early on which wild "forest fruit" is safe to eat. Most people have a favorite (usually secret) patch they return to every year.

Foraging yields key ingredients for traditional soups, cakes, and pickling jars.

On Sunday evenings, the train stations fill with returning students and retirees who are loaded down with the rewards of their weekend wanderings.

To try berry picking yourself, it's best to have a local guide—but many Czechs you meet will happily invite you along if asked. If you'd like to try solo, sticking to blueberries and strawberries is a safe bet, as long as you know what to look for. July and August are the best months and the woods outside any small Czech town will offer surprising yields.

Kutná Hora & Around

In the Middle Ages, Kutná Hora was one of central Europe's most important towns; in Bohemia, only Prague was larger. Silver mining, using German settlers as the main workforce, was the basis of its prosperity. About 1300, the royal mint was established, employing Italian workers. After three centuries the mines were exhausted and the town declined. A destructive fire in 1770 continued the ravages of the 15th-century Hussite wars and 17th-century Thirty Years' War.

Superb vaults at the Cathedral of St. Barbara in Kutná Hora

Husova street mounts the long ridge on which Kutná Hora is built and leads onto a small square set around the plague column dating from 1715. A lane called Lierova, on the right, brings you to **Stone House** (Kamenný dům), a lively Gothic house, inventively carved, and now a local museum. Farther up Husova is the lovely 1750 baroque facade of the **Church of St. John of Nepomuk** (kostel sv. Jana Nepomuckého) by František Kaňka. Husova emerges onto Náměstí Rejskovo, whose massive 1495 Gothic fountain dominates the center.

To the left lies Náměstí Narodního odboje, a larger and more tranquil grassy square. The massive 17th-century **Jesuit College** (Jezuitská kolej) designed by Domenico Orsi stands at the far end. By following the side of the college to the end and then bearing right, you can enjoy the wonderful approach to the fabulous **Cathedral of St. Barbara** (Chrám sv. Barbory), heralded by 13 large baroque statues opposite the facade of the college. From the balustrade there are fine views onto the Vrchlice Valley.

St. Barbara is the patron saint of miners, and it was the town's miners who financed the

Cathedral of St. Barbara

Tent roofs

Flying buttresses

West entrance

Ambulatory

Silver Mines

Although the silver mine in the city of Kutná Hora definitely dates from medieval times, it lay dormant and undocumented for centuries until a geohydrology team discovered it by accident in 1967. Archaeologists determined it dated from the days of mining by hand with a hammer and chisel, as evidenced by markings on its narrow walls.

The silver lode in Kutná Hora made the royal purse in Prague rich indeed during the reign of Charles IV, who expanded the empire and his fortunes thanks to the labors of hundreds who toiled in the dank subterranean passages. As you visit today, you'll notice the claustrophobic feeling of what's now called the "gallery," a 275-yard (250 m) section of mine that's been opened to visitors. Its walls and ceiling still contain quartz and gneiss nuggets, part of the rich conglomerate worked by men and horses pulling medieval mining engines. Small stalactites—sediments containing calcite—hang down in places, the result of the slow leaching of minerals. However, this process is much more visible in the Moravian karst caves in the Czech Republic's eastern province.

Kutná Hora

 141 E2

✉ 40 miles (65 km) E of Prague

🚆 Trains from Nádraží Hlavní via Sedlec. Bus from Florenc in Prague

www.kutnahora.cz

Visitor Information

✉ Palackého náměstí 377

☎ 327 512 378

Stone House

✉ Václavské náměstí 183

🕐 Closed Mon.

💲 $

Cathedral of St. Barbara

🕐 Closed Mon.

💲 $

Italian Court

✉ Havlickovo náměstí

💲 $

construction of the cathedral. It resembles a great ship, its flying buttresses like a galleon's oars, its roof like wind-puffed sails. Begun in 1388 by Peter Parler and his son Jan, it was continued by Benedikt Ried and Matthias Rejsek. They devised the marvelous geometric rib vaulting inside in the late 15th and early 16th centuries, but the cathedral was not completed until the 19th century. Remarkable 15th-century frescoes in the chapels of the south aisle and the choir depict miners at work.

Just south of Palackého náměstí, the main square, the tall tower of the Gothic **Church of St. James** (Kostel sv. Jakuba) looms up. This is Kutná Hora's oldest church, and its elegant interior has paintings by Petr Brandl, who is buried in the town, and Karel Škréta. Next to it is the **Italian Court** (Vlašský dvůr), the former mint until it was closed in 1726; it was also used as a royal residence by Václav IV in the early 14th century. The medieval oriel window

INSIDER TIP:

A short day trip outside of Prague, Kutná Hora is a must to view, roam around, and discover the old myths about the bones. To see the churches, travel during the warmer months.

—WENDY YASCUR
National Geographic contributor

of the chapel survives, adding a graceful note to the otherwise coarsely restored courtyard. Inside you can see a display of some of the silver coins minted here until production ceased in 1547. Between the Italian court and the cathedral is the Hrádek, or **Small fort,** a 15th-century building that now houses a museum of minting and coinage. Visit an abandoned medieval mine beneath its foundations on a guided tour.

North of the main square, on Jiřiho z Poděbrad, you come to the **Ursuline convent** (Voršilský klášter), designed by Kilián Ignác Dientzenhofer. This palatial convent would be hugely admired elsewhere, but in this architecturally rich town it is easily overlooked.

Sedlec

The village of Sedlec is situated 2 miles (3.2 km) northeast of Kutná Hora (reached by buses 1 or 4). This sleepy spot boasts a remarkable early church by Giovanni Santini, **Church of the Assumption of the Virgin Mary** (Kostel Nanebevzetí Pann Marie), with highly original stucco vaulting *($)*. Next to the church, the former Cistercian monastery is now, incongruously, a tobacco factory.

Across the road, signs lead to the monastery cemetery, where, in the Gothic chapel's crypt, you'll find an extraordinary **charnel house.** The cemetery was the fashionable burying place of the Bohemian nobility, but it was soon overcrowded. In 1870 František Rint was commissioned to use the bones for artistic purposes. He had the bizarre idea of fashioning bells, chalices, candelabra, and even a coat of arms out of them.

Kačina

At Kačina, 4 miles (7 km) northeast of Kutná Hora, is a magnificent neoclassical route-pedimented château linked to pavilions by elegant colonnades. This languorous cream-colored expanse of building, begun in 1802, rejoices in a large park laid out in English style. ∎

Small Fort
- ⊠ Barborská 28
- ☎ 327 512 159
- 🕑 Closed Mon. & Nov.–March
- 💲 $$$

Charnel House
- ⊠ Zámecká, Sedlec
- ☎ 327 561 143
- 💲 $
- **www.kostelnice.cz**

The charnel house at Sedlec presents a surprisingly artistic assembly of bones and skulls.

More Day Trips from Prague

Český Šternberk

The terrain around Prague is mostly flat, but to the southeast the Sázava Valley cuts the surrounding hills. High above it one of Bohemia's most sinister-looking castles, Český Šternberk, spreads along a crag; one side overlooks the village, the other the Sázava River. A medieval castle once stood here, but Český Šternberk has been often rebuilt and added to, so it now has a scruffy Renaissance style. It was in the hands of the Šternberk family, apart from a few decades, from the 13th century until 1948. Confiscated by the Communists, the castle was restored to the family in the 1990s.

141 D2   28 miles (45 km) SE of Prague via route E50 from Prague, direction Brno   317 855 101   Closed Mon. May–Sept. & all Nov.–March $–$$$

Kokořín

Northeast of Mělník is a picturesque region of wooded hills and dells called the Kokořínsko. It is a popular destination for day-trippers from Prague, because the pretty valleys and unusual rock formations make this attractive and relatively undemanding hiking country. The village of Kokořín is the dramatic setting for a 14th-century castle. The exterior is fun to explore, though the interior has little to offer.

141 D4   12 miles (20 km) NE of Mělník (see p. 150) via route 273

Kolín

Kolín is an old industrial town on the banks of the Labe. In the main square stands the richly sgraffitoed and gabled town hall, brilliantly decorated in 1887. Up the slope is the great 13th-century **Church of St. Bartholomew** (Kostel sv. Bartoloměje), with the belfry of 1504 attached by an arch to the church's towers. Built from coarse stone, the church is austere, though the sheer height of the choir and its flying buttresses, added to the existing church by Peter Parler, give it tremendous flair. In the

The Šternberk family has owned Český Šternberk for more than 700 years.

Nelahozeves

On a hill overlooking Nelahozeves village, just north of Prague, stands a massive late Renaissance château *(277 Nelahozeves 51, tel 315 798 111, closed Mon., $$, www .lobkowiczevents.cz, train from Masarykovo station in Prague)*, owned by the Lobkowicz family since 1623 (excluding its confiscation by the Communists, 1948–1993). The country castle's somewhat plain walls have been brightened by splendid 16th-century sgraffito. Inside, its lavish rooms are decorated in period style—using paintings, decorative arts, furniture, and memorabilia from the family's private collections—depicting the lives and times of the princes and princesses who resided here over a period of five centuries.

Famous composer Antonín Dvořák was born in 1841 in this same village (his father wanted him to be a butcher!). His house is now a modest museum *(Nelahozeves 12, tel 315 785 099, closed Mon.–Fri.).*

---

interior the elegance of the choir contrasts with the robust simplicity of the nave.

🅽 141 E2 ✉ 38 miles (58 km) E of Prague on route 12 🚆 Train from Hlavní nádraží Prague

Konopiště

The château of Konopiště, set in a splendid park with a famous rose garden, belonged to Habsburg Archduke Franz Ferdinand d'Este from 1887 until his assassination in Sarajevo in 1914. In the 1890s he rebuilt the castle, retaining its medieval towers and a baroque gateway by František Kaňka. Three tours are needed to see the entire interior. The first tours the state rooms, the second the Este family's arms and armor collection, and the third (eight-person limit) the apartments of the archduke and his family. The many hunting trophies reflect Franz Ferdinand's passion.
www.zamek-konopiste.cz 🅽 141 D1 ✉ 25 miles (40 km) S of Prague via route E50, then S on route 3 ☎ 274 008 154; fax: 274 008 152, 🕐 Closed Mon.–Fri. Nov. & all Dec.–March 🛇 $$–$$$$$ 🚆 Train from Hlavní nádraží Prague to Benešov. Bus from Florenc terminal in Prague

Křivoklát Castle

Křivoklát Castle (Zámek Křivoklát) overlooks the Křivoklátsko nature reserve, a forested craggy region. The castle was built in the 13th century as a hunting lodge for the Přemyslid kings. It was subsequently the childhood home of the future Charles IV. In the 1650s the Habsburgs sold Křivoklát, and from 1685 the Fürstenberg family, the new owners, reconstructed it. The 80-minute guided tour includes the elegant Gothic chapel and the Knights' Hall, with late Gothic sculpture.
www.krivoklat.cz 🅽 138 B2 ✉ 28 miles (45 km) W of Prague via route 6, and 201 ☎ 313 559 165, 🕐 Closed Mon. Nov.–March 🛇 $$–$$$ 🚆 Train from Hlavní nádraží Prague; change at Beroun for Křivoklát

Lány

The château of Lány, dating from the 14th century, was the summer residence of the presidents of Czechoslovakia. It remains the summer residence of the Czech president. Only the gardens and deer park are open to the public. Czechs visit Lány to pay homage to the founder of Czech democracy, President Masaryk, who is buried here.
🅽 138 B3 ✉ 25 miles (40 km) W of Prague on route 7, then left on route 236 🕐 Closed Mon.–Tues. April–Oct. & all Nov.–Dec.

Lidice

Few sites match the stark horror of Lidice, just northwest of Prague. On June 4, 1942, Nazi

Reichsrotektor Reinhard Heydrich was assassinated in Prague. Six days later, the Germans took their revenge. Every male inhabitant of the mining village was shot, and the women and children were deported to concentration camps. Then Lidice, which had been selected at random, was razed. After the war a new village was built nearby. These dreadful events are commemorated in a series of stone reliefs beneath concrete arcades. Next to this impressive monument is a small **new memorial** that narrates the barbaric events of that terrible day, which were filmed by the perpetrators. To the right of the museum, a large park contains more monuments to the dead of Lidice.

🅰 141 C3 ✉ 20 miles (32 km) NW of Prague via route 7, then left on route 61 toward Kladno   **Museum** www.lidice-memo rial.cz ✉ 10 června 1942, 🆂 $ 🚌 Bus from Dejvická metro station

EXPERIENCE:
Mělník Wine Tasting

The Lobkowicz palace in Mělník *(www .lobkowicz-melnik.cz)* still owns the same vineyards where Charles IV introduced French varieties to Bohemia, so a wine cellar tour is just about obligatory when visiting this sleepy town. The château, which lends its name to the Château Mělník label, bottles Pinot Noir, St. Laurent, Zweigeltrebe, and Blauer Portugieser reds and Pinot Blanc, Pinot Gris, Riesling, Traminer, Chardonnay Moravian Muscat, and Müller-Thurgau whites. With some vines up to 40 years old and wine fermented in giant casks of barrique oak, the estate attracts a steady flow of oenophiles. Less fancy blends, under the Ludmila and Lobko wicz labels, present bargains that still offer a satisfying dry but fruity wine. Tastings are held daily from 10 a.m.– 5 p.m. for 90–220 Czech crowns *($–$$$)*.

Mělník

Mělník is the principal town of the Bohemian vineyards. Despite its bucolic associations, it is easy to forget it is mainly industrial when standing on the castle terrace looking onto the plains, where the Labe and Vltava Rivers meet. The slopes were first planted with vines imported from Burgundy by Charles IV in 1365. Mostly destroyed by Swedish forces during the Thirty Years' War the **castle** has been largely rebuilt. Acquired by the Lobkowicz family in 1753, it was returned to them after 1989, following confiscation by the Communists. The courtyard boasts medieval elements and sgraffitoed galleries. The restored rooms are filled with baroque furnishings and Czech baroque paintings. Visit the wine cellars to taste the wines produced here, or drink them at the wine bar or restaurant *($$$)*. Next to the castle is a Gothic church; in the crypt a macabre **charnel house** is stacked with the bones of plague victims. Beside the town hall is a small viticultural **museum.**

🅰 141 D4 ✉ 20 miles (32 km) N of Prague on route 608, then on route 9 🚌 Train from Hlavní nádraží Prague to Všetaty, change for Mělník. Bus from Florenc or Holešovice nádraží Prague   **Castle** 🆂 $; Cellar tour: $$–$$$ **Charnel house** 🕐 Closed Mon. 🆂 $ **Museum** ✉ Náměstí Míru 11 ☎ 315 630 922 🕐 Closed Mon.

Mladá Boleslav

In an attempt to brighten up this town long dedicated to car production, the art nouveau post office is painted in lilac and blue, and the Renaissance town hall has been sgraffitoed. Just north of town center on Václava Klementa is the **Škoda Museum,** where old cars and motorcycles are displayed. Elegant motorcycles from the turn of the 20th century are especially interesting, as fetching in their way as the grander saloon cars in their bright red and yellow colors.

🅰 141 D4 ✉ 31 miles (50 km) NE of Prague on E65 🚌 Train from Hlavní nádraží Prague

Škoda Museum *www.skoda-auto.cz* ✉ Václava Klementa 294 ☎ 326 831 134, 🛈 $

Mnichovo Hradiště

Mnichovo Hradiště is the burial place of Albrecht von Wallenstein (Valdštejn). His descendants owned the E-shaped **château** here until 1945. Three tours are offered. The first takes in the elegantly furnished salons and library, the second showcases the château's still functioning theater, and the third visits Wallenstein's tomb within the grounds. The general was murdered in Cheb in 1634 and buried near Jičín; a century went by before his remains were brought back here. ⓜ 141 E4 ✉ 31 miles (50 km) NW of Jičín **Château** 🕐 Closed Mon. & Tues.–Fri. April & Oct. 🛈 $–$$

Poděbrady

Poděbrady is a glassmaking town on the Labe River, developed as a spa in the early 20th century due to mineral springs. Its main square is dominated not by its sturdy plague column but by the equestrian statue of the first Hussite king, George of Poděbrady, believed to have been born here in 1420. Behind the statue rises the formerly moated Renaissance **castle,** now part of Charles University. ⓜ 141 E3 ✉ 25 miles (40 km) E of Prague on route E67 🚆 Train from Hlavní nádraží Prague **Visitor information** ✉ Jiřího náměstí 20, 29031 ☎ 325 600 211 **Castle** 🕐 Closed Mon. & all Nov.–April

Přerov nad Labem

Přerov nad Labem is home to a small *skansen* (open-air museum of vernacular buildings). Founded in 1895, it was the first such museum in central Europe. Come see these partly timbered buildings if you are not going as far as the bigger skansens (see pp. 282–283). ⓜ 141 E3 ✉ 18 miles (30 km) E of Prague via E67 then N on route 272 🕐 Closed Mon. May–Sept.; Mon.–Fri. April & Oct.; & all Nov.– March 🛈 $ 🚆 Train from Hlavní nádraží

Prague to Čelakovice; change to local bus. Bus from Palmovka station in Prague

Příbram

Příbram is an unprepossessing mining town, but on the eastern outskirts is the Marian shrine **Holy Mountain** (Svatá Hora), a 17th-century Jesuit creation. A covered stairway leads to the vast shrine from Dlouhá street. The **Mining Museum** (Hornické muzeum) shows a miner's cottage, machine room with steam engine, and mineral collections. The main attraction is visiting the former coal face.

INSIDER TIP:

In Mělník, the Kavárna ve Věži, a coffeehouse situated atop the town clock tower, makes for a memorable Quasimodo retreat, with dozens of fresh brewed teas and Wi-Fi.

—WILL TIZARD
National Geographic contributor

ⓜ 141 B1 ✉ 35 miles (56 km) SW of Prague via route 4 🚌 Bus from Na Knížecí bus station Prague **Mining Museum** ✉ Náměstí Hynka Kličky 293, Příbram IV–Březové Hory ☎ 318 626 307 🕐 Closed Mon. April–Oct., & Sat.–Mon. Nov.–March 🛈 $$

Veltrusy

Veltrusy is a russet-colored, early 18th-century château. It has a highly original star shape with a huge dome at the center, and it sits in a large English-style park, packed with decorative follies. Many rooms are decorated in rococo style and filled with porcelain and fine furniture. ⓜ 141 C3 ✉ 15 miles (25 km) N of Prague via route E55, then N on 608 🕐 Closed Mon. May–Sept.; Mon.–Fri. March–April & Oct.–Nov.; & all Dec.–Feb. 🛈 $–$$$ 🚆 Train from Masarykovo nádraží Prague to Kralupy, then bus

czech republic

Medieval castles, baroque châteaus, charming towns like Český Krumlov and Písek, and the wilds of the Šumava

Southern Bohemia

Main door detail, Hluboká nad Vltavou castle
Opposite: Šumava National Park
Pages 152–153: Lednice château, Southern Moravia

Southern Bohemia

Southern Bohemia, largely free of the social and economic problems that blight parts of northern and eastern Bohemia, is a land of castles, handsome towns, and a variety of landscapes. The Šumava mountains offer ample outdoor opportunities, while farther east, Třeboňsko is a delightful watery region of fishponds that were established in the Middle Ages and still raise a large crop of Bohemia's favorite fish, carp, each year.

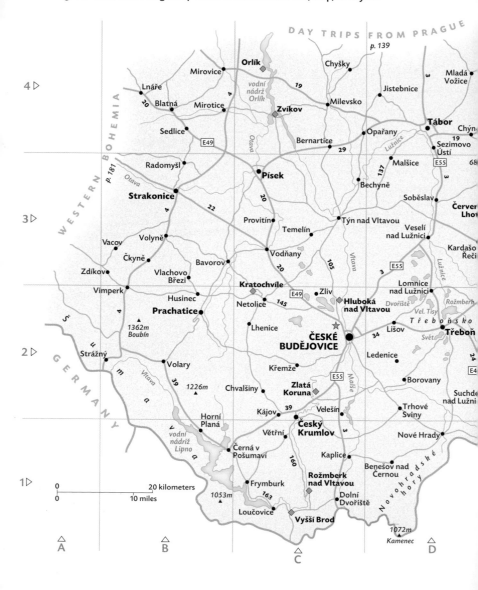

České Budějovice is the principal town of the region, and the home of Budvar beer. The town center is imposing and attractive, though there is little, other than sampling the local brew, to detain most visitors for more than a day or so. The ideal base for excursions has to be the medieval town of Český Krumlov, both fascinating and beautiful in itself, and perfectly located for visiting the many other towns and churches and castles of the region. Southern Bohemia is probably the best locale in the republic to sample the varied landscape and rich cultural heritage. It is also filled with castles and mansions. The castles drive links some of the country's most impressive castles, ranging in style from gauntly medieval to lavish 19th-century pastiche. Many of them overlook the River Vltava, which flows right through the region. Bohemia's northern stretches are popular with people from Prague looking for rural relaxation during warm weekends.

The eastern part of the region, beyond Třeboň, is less picturesque than the Vltava Valley and the Šumava mountains and lakes, but there are interesting towns and castles to visit, such as Jindřichův Hradec and Pelhřimov. Tábor is particularly worthwhile, especially if you have some interest in Bohemia's culture and history—it was a leading Hussite stronghold and retains many vestiges and reminders from that period. ■

NOT TO BE MISSED:

Exploring the castle interiors in Český Krumlov **158–159**

Having a fresh local Budvar in České Budějovice **163**

Seeing morning mist over the ponds in Třeboňsko **168–169**

The Jindřichův Hradec castle reflection in Lake Vajgar **170**

The view of Tábor from the town tower **172–173**

Crossing Pisek's ancient bridge **178**

Taking in Šumava's rolling green hills **176–177**

Strolling the historic town square in Pisek **178–179**

Český Krumlov

The fascinating medieval town of Český Krumlov is dominated in a spectacular way by its colossal castle, spread along a series of crags above a steep loop in the fast-flowing Vltava. So irregular is the rock formation here that one spur pierces the very underbelly of the main castle. From 1302 until 1602 the castle was owned by the Rožmberk family, who extended the fortress into the second largest castle in Bohemia; since 1717 it has been in the hands of the Schwarzenbergs.

Preparing to paddle along the twists of the River Vltava in Český Krumlov

Český Krumlov

156 C2

100 miles (160 km) S of Prague via E65, exit S onto route 3, then right on route 39

Train from Prague via České Budějovice. Bus from Prague

The Castle

Bridges link the castle *(hrad)* with the main part of the Old Town, and galleried houses loom out over the fast-flowing river. A short climb from the town brings you to the castle entrance, reached across a small bridge that crosses over a bear moat. The gorgeously colored castle tower, painted in 1590, overlooks the entrance, which leads to a series of sgraffitoed and frescoed courtyards. A three-tiered viaduct connects the castle from one crag to another, while above the viaduct are three more tiers of corridors.

To visit the castle, you must sign up for one or both of two tours. Most of the interiors are in a baroque or rococo style, and the collections displayed in some of the castle's 300 rooms include Chinese porcelain and rare tapestries. The ballroom, or Hall of Masks, is painted with charming trompe l'oeil carnival scenes completed in 1748 by Josef Lederer (Tour 1 only).

Walk across a long covered bridge to reach the terraced gardens and exquisite rococo **Castle Theater** (Zámecké divadlo), built in 1767. It retains much of its original scenery and costumes, and its refinement is a considerable relief after the primeval terrors of the castle's labyrinthine cellars.

Old Town

The old town has become very commercialized, and dozens of glass and porcelain shops, as well as tackier souvenir and clothes shops, cafés and restaurants, cater to the streams of mostly Austrian and German tourists. But the town is well organized, and guided tours are available from the town hall in the main square, Náměstí Svornosti. The **town hall** (radnice) itself has superb Gothic arcades and

a rustic cornice. Behind the square is the early 15th-century **Church of St. Vitus** (Kostel sv. Víta), with contemporary frescoes in the north aisle, lofty vaults, and the tomb of William of Rožmberk.

Nearby along Horní street is the **Jesuit College** of 1588 (now converted into a luxury hotel), with its beautifully sgraffitoed and painted eaves. The Austrian expressionist painter Egon Schiele (1890–1918) came to live in Český Krumlov in 1911, where he resided in a chilly hovel, churning out dozens of striking, haunting works. In the 1990s a former medieval

INSIDER TIP:

Rent a raft near Český Krumlov and ride it down the River Vltava as it flows through this perfectly preserved Renaissance-era town.

—CHARLES RECKNAGEL
Radio Free Europe, Prague

Visitor Information

✉ Náměstí Svornosti 2, 38101 Český Krumlov

 380 704 622

www.ckrumlov.cz

Castle & Gardens

☎ 380 704 721

🕐 Closed Mon. & Nov.–March

💲 Tours: $$–$$$ each Theater: $$–$$$

www.castle.ckrumlov .cz

Egon Schiele Art Centrum

✉ Široká 71

☎ 380 704 011

🕐 Closed Mon.

💲 $$

www.schieleart centrum.cz

Egon Schiele Art Centrum

The quiet, respectable folk in Český Krumlov were hardly ready for avant-garde art in the early 20th century—especially if it involved nude adolescent girls. That's just what the town got, however, in the work of the tormented Austrian painter Egon Schiele, whose sometimes grotesque gouaches created here are now considered the town's treasure. The collections on show at the

Egon Schiele Art Centrum reveal insights into his brief residence in Bohemia. He only managed a year of living in sin with former Gustav Klimt model Wally Neuzil before locals ran him out of town in 1911. But the local art center named for him carries on his spirit of boldness, bringing a surprising range of visiting exhibitions to its halls, whether Russian video art or Czech text processing.

Český Krumlov Castle

Passage to
5th courtyard

Picture Gallery

Hall of Masks

Cloak Bridge

Chinese Salon

Bedroom

Baldaquin Salon

Great Dining Hall

brewery on Široká was converted into **Egon Schiele Art Centrum,** a gallery with a permanent exhibition of his work (see sidebar p. 159). It is a more stimulating place to visit than the **Regional Museum** (Okresní muzeum) on Horní, whose displays relate to the town's history, weaponry, and furniture. Back on Náměstí Svornosti, the main square, is a

Museum of Torture *($$)*, a sad indication of the village's decline into commercialism.

In summer the town becomes even more crowded than usual during several festivals. The Five-Petaled Rose Festival in June is a two-day jamboree with medieval parades, fireworks, and street fairs. Also held are a chamber music festival in early summer, an early music festival in July, and an international music festival in August *(www.festivalkrumlov.cz)*. ■

Regional Museum

✉ Horní 152
☎ 380 711 674
⊕ Closed Mon. Oct.–April
💲 $

Courtyard

Bear Moat

Castle Tower

St. George's Chapel

České Budějovice

České Budějovice, regional capital of southern Bohemia, is located at the point where the Malše and Vltava Rivers meet. Beer lovers around the world are more familiar with the town's German name, Budweis. This is the home of Budvar, or Budweiser, and you can sample the mild golden brew in countless beer halls.

No town square in the Republic can match that of České Budějovice when it comes to sheer size.

České Budějovice

🅼 156 C2

✉ 88 miles (147 km) S of Prague via E65 then S on 3

🚆 Train from Prague

www.c-budejovice.cz

Close to the Austrian border, České Budějovice has a distinct air of prosperity. The town originally acquired its wealth from the salt trade and later from silver mining. Přemysl Otakar II gave it its charter in 1265. Although always a staunchly Catholic town, České Budějovice was spared attack during the Hussite wars. It also benefited from Habsburg patronage after the Thirty Years' War. A devastating fire in 1641 destroyed much of the town,

and decades went by before it regained the level of prosperity it enjoyed in the 16th century. In 1832 the first horse-drawn railway in Europe linked the town with Linz in Austria.

Rivers and canals encircle the city, and in the middle of its medieval grid plan is the immense main square, **Náměstí Přemysla Otakara II,** the largest in the Czech Republic. The arcaded square is a great urban ensemble, rather than a collection of buildings of individual quality, and many of its buildings date from the 18th and 19th centuries. Josef Dietrich's grandiose balustraded Samson fountain of 1727 gushes like a geyser in the center of the square.

The fine **town hall** (*radnice*), with its baroque steeples, was rebuilt by Antonio Martinelli in 1730. In the opposite corner of the square stands the imposing 16th-century **Black Tower** (Cerná věž), which rises 235 feet (72 m) and can be climbed by anyone with sufficient stamina to reveal a bird's-eye view of the town. In clear weather you can see Třeboň, 12 miles (19 km) to the east. The tower adjoins the cathedral, which was rebuilt in the baroque style in the 1640s and subsequently over-restored. As a result the interior is somewhat lacking in atmosphere.

Krajinská leads to the former 16th-century butchers' stalls (Masné krámy) on the left, long ago converted into a beer hall and the ideal place to sample Budvar. From this corner of the square, Piaristická goes to the medieval Dominican monastery, unimaginatively made

over in baroque. Next to the church the gabled **salt store** (*solnice*) of 1513 is a rare example of a Renaissance warehouse.

From the town hall, Biskupská takes you past the peach-and-white former bishop's palace in the direction of the Malše River, where some of the medieval fortifications survive, including the prison tower. The **Museum of South Bohemia** (Jihoceské muzeum), close to the river, has extensive historical and natural history collections as well as paintings and special exhibitions.

The **Budvar Brewery,** just north of the city center off the road to Prague, has been modernized. For beer aficionados the one-hour tour is essential. The tour explains why traditional Czech beer—Budweiser— has nothing in common with the American Budweiser. Attempts by the powerful American company to take over the Czech original have, up until now, been successfully resisted. Those who learn more than they bargained for can console themselves afterward in the brewery's beer hall and restaurant. ■

Visitor Information

✉ Náměstí Přemysla Otakara II

☎ 386 801 413

Black Tower

🕑 Closed Mon. & Nov.–March

💲 $

Museum of South Bohemia

✉ Dukelská 1

☎ 386 356 447

🕑 Closed Mon.

💲 $

Budvar Brewery

✉ Karoliny Světlé 4

☎ 387 705 341

🕑 Closed Sun. & Mon. Jan.–March

💲 $$, book in advance

http://budweiser-budvar.cz

EXPERIENCE: Canoeing on the Vltava

The River Vltava, although mighty enough to have wrought millions in damage when it flooded Prague in 2002. It is, near its source in south Bohemia, a far more calm waterway. Although it rolls over many weirs, offering occasional whitewater, the Vltava is generally a gentle, natural, and clean forebear of its downstream self.

Rafting, canoeing, and kayaking on the upper river are among the most refreshing and rewarding summer sports. In **Český Krumlov** (see pp. 158–161) alone, several companies offer rental boats and guides at

reasonable rates. One popular one, **Surfsport Rent a Boat** (www.surfsport.cz) offers four- to six-person rafts or canoes for two, including shuttling passengers and boats to and from launch and landing points, plus life jackets and waterproof bags.

For those who'd prefer to leave the piloting to someone else, **Český Krum Love** (www.ceskykrumlov-info.cz) offers rides for up to 12 from a pier in the historic center of Český Krumlov on an old-style wooden raft operated by a colorful two-man team.

Land of Castles Drive

Castles in all shapes and sizes scatter across southern Bohemia: strongholds guarding small towns; fortresses buried in the countryside watching over crucial trade routes; rural aristocratic retreats. Follow this drive to some of the most interesting and beautiful examples.

The Schwarzenberg family transformed a medieval fortress at Hluboká nad Vltavou into a neo-Gothic castle, using what they imagined to be a Victorian style.

Five miles (8 km) north of České Budějovice on route 105 you come to one of southern Bohemia's most popular attractions: the lofty castle of **Hluboká nad Vltavou** ❶. Standing on a broad crag above the River Vltava, it is one of the Schwarzenberg family's neo-Gothic fantasies *(closed Nov.–March, $$$)*. Originally a medieval royal fortress, it was acquired by the family in 1662, and two centuries later, having decided that Hluboká should be their principal Bohemian residence, they spent a fortune revamping the castle. The Schwarzenbergs also laid out its handsome park, which is open even when

NOT TO BE MISSED:

Hluboká nad Vltavou • Zvíkov
• Rožmberk nad Vltavou
• Červená Lhota

the castle itself is closed. This building is an enjoyable architectural romp, packed with crenellated towers and fearsome defenses to protect the family against no one in particular. The interior has exceptional woodwork and is sumptuously furnished, containing an armory, a library, tapestries, and a collection of Bohemian paintings. Equally worthwhile is the art collection, in the former riding school (*jízdárna; closed Mon.*), culled from municipal collections throughout southern Bohemia. It ranges from medieval Bohemian panels to 20th-century Czech paintings. There are two guided tours of the castle: One is comprehensive; the other, shorter and less interesting, focuses on the armory.

Along the Vltava

From here continue north for 15 miles (24 km) on route 105 to Týn nad Vltavou, then bear left toward Písek. At Albrechtice nad Vltavou head north on minor roads to

Zvíkov ❷, a remote castle spread across a wooded promontory overlooking the green waters of the Vltava and Otava Rivers (*closed Mon. May–Sept., Mon.–Fri. April & Oct., & Nov.–March, $*). Built in the 13th century by the Přemysl rulers, Zvíkov became first a property of the Rožmberks, a powerful feudal family and, in the 17th century, another Schwarzenberg possession. Fortunately the

▲	See area map p. 156
➤	České Budějovice
◷	233 miles (375 km)
⬌	2–3 days
➤	Červená Lhota

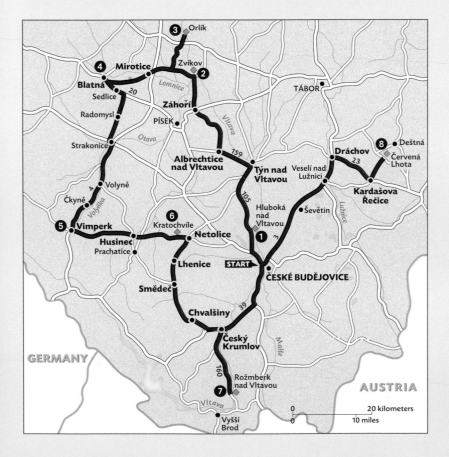

family resisted the temptation to improve this medieval and Renaissance structure, but after the castle was badly damaged during the Thirty Years' War, it had to be partly rebuilt. Zvíkov retains a formidable 13th-century round tower, Gothic cloisters, and lovely though heavily restored frescoes from about 1500 in the chapel and bridal chamber.

Take the road northward along the Vltava, to **Orlík ❸**, owned by the Schwarzenbergs since 1719; it was confiscated by the Communists in the 1940s but reclaimed by the family in 1992. The castle *(closed Mon. April–May & Sept.–Oct., & Nov.–March, $–$$$)* was founded in the 13th century and largely rebuilt in the second half of the 19th century as a somewhat preposterous neo-Gothic fantasy. The interior is furnished in empire style, with weaponry and porcelain, as well as displays chronicling the history of the owners. Set beside a reservoir, it must have been even more impressive before

INSIDER TIP:

Have fun biking from Prague to Vienna through the country-side with open fields, wooded areas, small villages, and castles along rivers and lakes *(www .pragueviennagreenways.org)*.

—ANDREA LIŠKOVÁ
CzechTourism USA

the river was dammed in the 1950s when the castle soared high above the flowing waters.

Rose Country

Return south the way you came, then turn west through Mirotice to **Blatná ❹**, a small town best known for cultivating roses. Its splendid moated castle *(closed Mon. mid-May–mid-Sept., Mon.–Fri. April–mid-May &*

Encircled by a large moat, Blatná castle enjoys an idyllic location.

mid-Sept.–Oct., *& Nov.–March, $), along the* road to Plzeň, is entered beneath a large machicolated gate tower. The Gothic chapel, with its delicate oriel window, is all that survives from the 13th-century structure. The Renaissance wing, designed by Benedikt Ried in the 1520s, has curious tiers of windows set at an angle to the main arrow-heads. You can visit the interior on a lengthy guided tour; the most bizarre highlight is a set of furniture made from antlers.

hunting lodge by the Rožmberk family, it is now a museum dedicated to film animation.

From here head south to Český Krumlov and keep going to **Rožmberk nad Vltavou ⑦,** a village and **castle** *(closed Mon. May–Sept., Mon.–Fri. April & Oct., & Nov.–March, $–$$)* named for the Rožmberks. The sgraffitoed building, which overlooks the winding River Vltava, is more like a succession of fortresses built along a ridge. Inside, the finest room is the banqueting hall, covered in 16th-century Italianate frescoes.

Šumava Former Forbidden Zone

In the days before 1989, anyone caught walking in the Šumava mountains who was not a member of the Czech military was bound for serious trouble. Because this southwestern border region of green hills and lakes borders on Austria, it made a tempting route into the West for anyone wanting to escape the clutches of life in a Soviet satellite. Ironically, this meant that the verdant hills and wildlife, including numerous raptors, lynx, foxes, and chamois, were left more pristine than in other natural parks around the country.

These days, Czechs wanting to escape the go-go development that's taken over much of the rest of the republic with the new economy come to Šumava. Here they can hike, stroll, pick berries, and generally commune with nature. One useful guide to outdoor activities is Kudy z nudy, or Escape from Boredom (*www.kudyznudy .cz*). This helpful website includes lists of organizers of walks for all abilities, guides who speak multiple languages, and attractions such as the forest architecture park in Netolice and ancient hilltop ruins.

From Blatná head road south to Strakonice, and continue on route 4 to **Vimperk ⑤,** on the edge of the Šumava mountains. The village cowers beneath a crag on which the **castle** *(closed Mon. & Nov.–April)* perches. Reached by a steep path from the main square, it was built by Přemysl Otakar II in the 13th century; the castle was restyled over time by the Schwarzenbergs. The view is terrific; the interior, now the local museum, has a collection of glass objects.

Head east 22 miles (36 km) to the charming Renaissance château of **Kratochvíle ⑥** *(closed Mon. May–Sept., Mon.–Fri. April & Oct., & Nov.–March, $–$$$).* Designed and built by Italian architects in the 1580s, it is perfectly symmetrical and neatly surrounded by walls, pavilions, and formal gardens. Founded as a

Country Manor

Return to Český Krumlov and take route 39 northeast to **České Budejovice** (see pp. 162–163). Continue past on route 3 in the direction of Tábor. At Dráchov turn right toward Jindřichův Hradec; then turn north at Kardašova Řečice toward Deštná and watch for signs to **Červená Lhota ⑧.** The long drive is worth your time, as this **château** *(closed Mon. May–Sept., Mon.–Fri. April & Oct., & Nov.–March, $–$$),* buried in remote wooded countryside, is the most exquisite of them all. The rust-red 16th-century building—a manor house that replaced a castle on this site—sits on an islet reached by a cobbled causeway. Seen after some of the more pompous châteaus of Bohemia, this aristocratic retreat is a real gem.

Třeboňsko Region

Since the 14th century, Czechs have capitalized on the swampy, peat-mossy Třeboňsko region by building fishponds to raise carp, a popular dish especially during the Christmas holiday. Much of the area is now a nature reserve, as the bogs and other wetlands support a precious variety of wildlife—notably the white-tailed eagle.

Třeboň's typically Czech square boasts arcaded Renaissance houses and a baroque Marian column.

The powerful Rožmberk family turned carp farming into an industry in the 16th century. A system of canals had to be devised to link the numerous ponds and lakes and assist with their drainage. The Rožmberks constructed these conduits, hiring the best engineers of the time. Their successors at Třeboň, the Schwarzenbergs, continued to manage this important resource, which at one time contained 6,000 ponds.

Třeboň

The walled town of Třeboň retains some of its original gateways, which remain the sole access to its center. Close to the 16th-century Svinenská Gate is the **Regent Brewery**, functioning here since the town was founded by the Rožmberk family. The last of the line, Petr Vok, died here in 1611, after a lifetime of intellectual and hedonistic activity, notably the pursuit of alchemy, then wildly fashionable in Bohemia.

The **castle** dominates the little town. It was built by the Rožmberks soon after Třeboň was founded in the 1370s. In 1660, some years after Petr Vok's death, the castle became the property of the Schwarzenbergs, a Bavarian family that soon got into the habit of acquiring properties from extinct aristocratic Bohemian families. Before long they were the largest landowners in the country, and remained so until their expulsion in 1945.

Sprawling Renaissance buildings with sgraffitoed walls occupy much of the old town. There's even room in the courtyard for a pizzeria. Approaching from the main square, you pass through elaborate Renaissance portals into tranquil courtyards. The castle itself can be visited only by one of three guided tours. The first visits the Renaissance interiors; the second views the Schwarzenbergs' private apartments, furnished in the 19th century; and the third combines the two. Afterward it's pleasant to stroll in the English-style park.

From the castle, walk the short distance to the elongated **main square.** The arcaded Renaissance and baroque houses look onto a crisply carved Marian column (1780) and a fountain (1569). The town hall's sturdy 17th-century galleried tower can be climbed in summer. The houses are ornamented with a variety of gables, notably the crenellated ones of the 1544 house called the White

Pony (Bílý koníček), now a hotel. One block from the square, on Husova, is the 14th-century **Church of St. Giles** (Kostel sv. Jiljí). Frescoes from the 15th century survive in the elegant church interior.

Around Třeboň

Třeboň lies beside tree-fringed **Lake Svet** and the spa, where you can enjoy therapeutic mud baths, is set back from the shore. Across the lake, a 20-minute walk from the town, is the park called **U Hrobky,** where the Schwarzenbergs built their **mausoleum** in 1877. It's a thrusting neo-Gothic fantasy more appropriate to a Scottish estate than the Bohemian countryside. A guided tour takes you into the burial crypt.

INSIDER TIP:

Take an organized tour of the Třeboň Square church of St. Giles and Virgin Mary the Queen or enjoy an organ concert there.

—PHILIP HEIJMANS
Writer & photographer,
The Prague Post

A network of well-marked trails allows you to explore the Třeboňsko, linking some of the bigger ponds north of Třeboň. The largest, aptly named Lake Rožmberk, created in the 1580s, is nearby. A trail also traverses the peat bogs from Červené blato, 10 miles (15 km) south of town. The region is popular with bird-watchers. ∎

Třeboň

🗺 156 D2

✉ 90 miles (145 km) S of Prague via route 3, then route 24

🚌 Bus from České Budějovice. Most fast trains from Prague to Vienna stop here.

Visitor Information

✉ Masarykovo náměstí 103

☎ 384 721 169

www.trebon-mesto.cz

Castle

🕐 Closed Mon. April–Oct., & Nov.–March

💲 $–$$$

Schwarzenberg Mausoleum

🕐 Closed Mon. April–Oct., & Nov.–March

💲 $

Jindřichův Hradec

The little-visited town of Jindřichův Hradec is situated close to the Moravian border, east of České Budějovice. In medieval times the Rožmberk family were Lords of Hradec, one of two families who dominated southern Bohemia, and parts of Moravia. They built the first stronghold here in the early 13th century, and it was added to over the centuries. In the Middle Ages the town, situated on a major trading route, became prosperous.

The castle at Jindřichův Hradec is a showcase anthology of Bohemian architectural styles.

Jindřichův Hradec

🗺 157 E3

✉ 80 miles (128 km) SE of Prague via E65, then S on route 3

🚆 Train from Prague, change at Veselí

Over the years the town gradually lost its eminence; it's now a small textile-producing center. By the time the last member of the Rožmberk family died in 1611, the **castle**, set above Lake Vajgar, had become a hodgepodge of architectural styles. There's a stone-built round

keep from the 13th century, an assorted range of Renaissance buildings, and several tiered, arcaded courtyards. A legend tells that it is roamed by the White Lady, the ghost of Perchta of Rožmberk, an unhappy chatelaine of the 15th century (see p. 28). She was forced into a loveless marriage but when bidding farewell to the man she loved, Count Šternberk, the couple were caught by her husband and she suffered years of mistreatment thereafter.

Although much of the castle exterior is unappealing, the recently restored interior is a marvel. To see it all, you are obliged to take three separate 50-minute guided tours: Tour A covers the baroque rooms, Tour B takes in the medieval sections, and Tour C follows the Renaissance portions.

Perhaps the most arresting structure within the castle is the pink-and-white garden "Rondel," or rotunda, with its porthole windows and lovely gilt stucco decoration (the highlight of Tour C). It was designed, like much of the castle, by Italian architects. Baldassare Maggi was the most important, and he worked for the Rožmberks beginning in 1575. The most striking rooms are the austere Gothic chapel and the ceremonial hall, with 14th-century frescoes narrating the life of St. George (Tour B).

With its cobbled lanes and sober but attractive houses, this is an interesting town to explore on foot. Follow the lane that leads from the castle to the main square, **Náměstí Míru,** where an 18th-century Marian column tapers up to a resplendent sunburst. Stuccoed merchants' houses and the town hall surround the square; there are two fine Gothic churches. The **Church of St. John the Baptist** (Kostel sv. Jana Krtitele), unfortunately, is closed to the public. Behind the town hall, the **Church of the Assumption of Our Lady** (Kostel Nanebevzetí Panny Marie) has some uninspiring 17th-century frescoes.

The **District Museum** is on Komenského in the former 17th-century Jesuit seminary. A big draw is the mechanical nativity scene, peopled with over a thousand figurines fashioned by Tomáš Krýza (1838–1918), after half a century of toil. It is said to be the largest such scene in the world. Another room is devoted to the composer Bedřich Smetana, who lived near the castle from 1831 to 1835. ∎

Visitor Information

✉ Panská 136

☎ 384 363 546

www.jh.cz

Castle

☎ 384 321 279

🕐 Closed Mon. & Nov.–March

💲 Tours: $$–$$$ each; all three $$$–$$$$$

District Museum

✉ Balbínovo náměstí 19

☎ 384 363 661

🕐 Closed Mon. April–May & Oct.; & Nov.–March

💲 $

www.mjh.cz

Bohemian Cuisine to Seek Out

Without even trying, visitors to the Czech Republic invariably encounter a handful of ubiquitous, if tasty, dishes, done with varying degrees of delicateness: goulash, smoked meat platters, and schnitzel, or *řízek*. But for the connoisseur, it's worth seeking out masterful forms of the more rewarding classics, from Bohemian duck with white and purple sauerkraut, or *zelí*, to warming comfort foods such as the Slovak gnocchi, or *halušky*, best with sour cream and cracklings.

Soups are a particular Czech forte, and the potato and thyme version, known as *bramboračka,* is virtually the law of the land at most eateries, while the garlic soup, or *česnečka,* is a beloved curative for winter viruses. *Kulajda*, or egg and dill soup, is better for warmer weather.

And don't forget the classic dessert, the apple strudel known as *závin*, almost invariably fresh, warm, topped with whipped cream, and spiced with raisins and cinnamon.

Tábor

An extreme wing of the Hussites founded Tábor in 1420 to establish a stronghold in southern Bohemia near where Jan Hus had retired six years earlier. The settlement was named for Palestine's Mount Tabor; the name then became associated with these radical religious and social reformers—henceforth known as the Taborites (see p. 174). Proclaiming the equality of all peoples, and holding all possessions in common, the Taborites created an early form of commune.

The River Lužnice glides far below the old town of Tábor, once a Hussite stronghold.

The Lužnice River flows below the town, while to the west is Lake Jordán, Bohemia's oldest artificial lake, created in 1492 by damming the Tismenicky River. The old city is a compact maze of narrow streets, hemmed in by the fortifications, some of which survive. Of the medieval castles that stood here before the Hussites came, only the Kotnov tower remains.

The town's splendid main square, **Žižkovo náměstí**, is named after the Hussite general Jan Žižka, whose statue stands here. A Renaissance fountain of 1567 sits in the center of the square. The proudly gabled old town hall, originally built in 1440 but since rebuilt in an essentially Renaissance style, now contains a splendid vaulted council chamber of 1515 and the **Hussite Museum** (Husitské muzeum). Its most intriguing exhibit is a cart fortified by Žižka with cannon, a formidable weapon in its day.

A series of tunnels radiate out from beneath the town hall, some for 9 miles (14 km). Initially said to have been used to store beer kegs, they were probably intended shelter from both attack and the fires that frequently raged through the town. A half-mile (0.8 km) stretch of these catacombs can be visited (tours leave from the museum).

EXPERIENCE: Volunteering

The rise of nonprofit organizations in a land where the state was once expected to provide cradle-to-grave care for every citizen has been a mixed bag. Czech President Václav Klaus has shocked many Westerners with his frequent comments expressing suspicion of NGOs, or nongovernmental organizations, as they are known in central Europe. His notion that bodies "elected by no one" should be mistrusted, despite the great works they do, is quite hard to fathom—especially in light of the many gaps in state programs they help fill.

Nevertheless, international volunteers have poured into the Czech Republic since 1989 although those who don't speak Czech will find their possibilities limited. One international organization, **Hestia** (*www.hest.cz*), is a useful resource for English speakers and has a long tradition of running programs such as a local version of Big Brothers (to Czechs it's known as Pět P, lest its name evoke an Orwellian ring). Volunteers are trained by child counselors and psychologists to discuss issues such as drugs and emotional problems that youth may be struggling with.

Hestia also works with the website *www.volunteer.cz* to help match up givers with those in need in both large and small towns countrywide.

On the north side of the main square is the **Church of the Transfiguration** (Kostel Proměnění Páně), built in a late Gothic style during the second half of the 15th century, although the generous gables are clearly Renaissance additions. The rib-vaulted interior is a curious blend of baroque and neo-Gothic. Its very tall **tower** can usually be climbed for a fine view of the town (*$*). A lane next to the church, Svatošova, leads to the Augustinian priory, with its curvaceous baroque facade. Also leading into the square is the main shopping street **Pražská**, which has more attractive Renaissance houses than the square itself; some of the sgraffito decoration remains in good condition.

From the town hall, Mariánská and then Klokotská lead from the square to the remains of the round medieval **Kotnov Castle** (hrad Kotnov), a section of which has been used as a brewery since 1611.

INSIDER TIP:

Stroll down Pražská to dům Albrechta pekaře (House of Albert the Baker), where a cannonball from the Thirty Years' War is lodged in the facade.

—EMILY THOMPSON
Special Section editor,
The Prague Post

Next to the castle is the 15th-century **Bechyně Gate** (Bechyňská brána). The gateway is now a small well-organized museum about medieval society. Exhibits include weapons, armor, and farming implements. It gives access to the castle tower, which can be climbed for views over the town. Half a mile (1 km) west of the old town you'll find the baroque church of Klokoty with its onion domes. ∎

Tábor

- 🅰 156 D4
- ✉ 52 miles (84 km) S of Prague via E65, then route 3
- 🚆 Train and bus from Prague

Visitor Information

- ✉ Infocentrum, Žižkovo náměstí 2
- ☎ 381 486 230
- **www.tabor.cz**

Hussite Museum

- 🕐 Closed Mon. Sept.–May
- 💲 Museum: $ Catacombs: $

Bechyně Gate

- 🕐 Closed Mon. Nov.–April
- 💲 Museum: $ Tower: $

Jan Hus & the Hussites

Jan Hus, the Czech people's first national hero, was born about 1370 in Husinec in southern Bohemia. He studied at Prague University and was influenced by the radical social and theological doctrines of Oxford theologian John Wycliffe (ca 1330–1384). In 1400 Hus joined the priesthood; in 1402, he became a professor of philosophy at Prague University.

A 16th-century portrayal of the death at the stake of Jan Hus in 1415

Adapting Wycliffe's ideas and preaching in Czech rather than in Latin, Hus gave a reformist and nationalist message to the congregations who came to hear him at Prague's Bethlehem Chapel (Betlémská kaple). He opposed indulgences, the self-enrichment of the clergy, and other abuses of church power, and he attacked the often miserable conditions in which the peasantry were compelled to live.

Hus's espousal of the Czech language and literature proved divisive. German-speaking teachers and students, who formed the majority at the university, left Prague to found a new university in Leipzig in 1409. Church authorities soon lost patience with him; in 1410 he was excommunicated and forbidden to preach. Initially he enjoyed the support of King Václav IV, but by 1413 his condemnation of the sale of indulgences to fund papal wars alarmed the king, who benefited from the practice. Hus prudently took refuge in southern Bohemia; here he wrote theological works and spread his ideas throughout the countryside. Arrested on the way to the Council of Constance under a safe-conduct assurance, Hus was burned at the stake on July 6, 1415.

Some of the doctrines most closely associated with Hus were spread only after his death. The central tenet of Hussitism was the need to take communion *sub utraque specie* (in both kinds), when the congregation would be given both bread and wine, unlike the Catholic practice of the time of giving wine only to the clergy. King Václav allowed Hussite opponents to return to their parishes in 1419, but rioting broke out and ended in the First Defenestration (see p. 28). A few weeks later the pope initiated a crusade against the Hussites.

The Hussite movement was not a united force. The more moderate supporters, known as Utraquists, were essentially religious reformers. The radical Taborites, who linked religious reform with social reform, favored the abolition of class differences. The Taborites leveled violent attacks against Catholic property and clergy, as well as the powerful German merchant classes. At first they enjoyed remarkable success. Under their charismatic leader, Jan Žižka, the Taborites had huge support from the impoverished peasantry of Bohemia and Moravia. The Taborites easily defeated Catholic forces. In 1433 the Vatican agreed with the Utraquists at the Council of Basel to permit communion "in both kinds," but this alone was not acceptable to the Taborites. They fought on, but they could not withstand the combined forces of the Utraquists and the Catholics, and were finally defeated at the Battle of Lipany in 1434.

The modern Hussite Church, formed in 1920, advocates the ordination of women and the right of priests to marry.

No one is sure whether this 16th-century portrait is a true likeness of the great reformer.

Šumava

The gentle rolling Šumava mountains unfurl along the border with Austria and Germany, becoming more rugged and sparsely inhabited as you move northwest along the ridges. At the range's southern end a resort area has been created on the northern shores of Lake Lipno, a narrow reservoir some 25 miles (40 km) in length. The low-key developments appeal to families in search of a tranquil, inexpensive vacation, and the low forested hills offer peaceful, undemanding hiking.

A lonely scene near Kristanov in the Šumava mountains

Šumava

📍 156 A2, B1, B2

🚌 Bus from Prague to Prachatice. Train from České Budějovice to Volary

A few hotels are located at **Loučovice,** not far from Vyšší Brod (see p. 180). If touring, not boating, is your aim, then best stay in **Prachatice,** a former hilltop salt-trading post and a highlight of the region. Although of medieval origin, with some surviving fortifications, most of the compact little town was rebuilt under the Rožmberk family in the 16th century; the beautifully vaulted Gothic **Church of St. James** (Kostel sv. Jakuba) has been retained. Many houses on the main square and the narrow streets of the old town are

sgraffitoed, both with geometrical and vivid battle scenes. The town is at its liveliest in mid-June, when a medieval festival, the Gold Trail, with parades, fireworks, and sports contests, takes place.

For a lakeside stay, try **Frymburk** at the end of a peninsula jutting into the lake. From the jetty a ferry links the town to the southern shore, which used to be off-limits as a military zone. The village of **Černá v Pošumaví** is more spread out, with many guesthouses, cottages, and campsites. The lake's main resort, **Horní Planá,** was the birthplace of the poet and painter

Adalbert Stifter (1805–1868), whose house is now a **museum** containing the artist's memorabilia.

Northwest of here in the Bohemian Forest section of the Šumava the landscape changes. The name Šumava derives from *šumět*, which means "to murmur" or "to rustle," as the rustling of trees was the only sound that disturbed the scattering of people, mostly German foresters, who from medieval times inhabited and traveled across the mountains. (The German-speaking population was expelled after World War II; see p. 38.) These days, well-developed roads run through the forests and plateaus, attracting motorcycle clubs.

Volary is one of the most convenient towns for exploring the region. Although not exceptional, it retains a handful of alpine-style houses that survived a fire in the mid-19th century; this was an architectural fashion imported in the 16th century by Tyrolean and Styrian settlers. The town of **Vimperk,** with its castle (see p. 167), is an increasingly popular year-round resort.

The absence of industrialization means there is little pollution; in 1991 much of the region was designated a national park to preserve its unspoiled character. Not least because of its proximity to the German border, Šumava has become popular with vacationers, hikers, and cyclists; so it's a good idea to book well ahead. Although the highest peak has an elevation of only 4,776 feet (1,456 m), the Šumava is surprisingly wild and austere, its forested and stony plateaus punctuated by mountain lakes and treacherous peat bogs such as the Modrava moors. With luck, visitors may even spot a lynx or an otter.

Today marked trails guide the hiker through the terrain, but in the past secret paths through the bogs were used by smugglers. The slopes of Boubín (4,468 feet/1,362 m) are easily accessible from Volary or Vimperk and covered with a primeval forest—a nature reserve since 1858. Glimpses of ruined hilltop fortresses are a constant reminder that the Šumava was always a natural frontier between the Germanic west and the Slav east. ∎

Stifter Museum

 Palackého 21, Horní Planá

 380 738 473

🕐 Closed Mon. March–June & Sept.–Oct., Sun.–Mon. Nov.–mid-Dec.

$ $

EXPERIENCE: Horseback Riding in Šumava

Czechs have a long history of equine mastery and horse farms, and riding schools are common as you travel the Bohemian countryside. If some of the graceful stallions you see cantering along look familiar, it's entirely possible that's because they've had roles in some of the many historical films shot in the Czech Republic. In fact, the breed most favored in central Europe, the Shagya-Arabian, has a particularly elegant gait that's much sought after by filmmakers.

In southern Bohemia, the **Slupenec Horse Riding Club** *(www.jk-slupenec.cz)* outside Český Krumlov (see pp. 158–161) is one option, with one-to-four-hour rides through the hills and forests. Like most local riding schools, they use English saddles and riding style, but the helpful staff offer tips and training if you're not an experienced rider or are more accustomed to Western riding. The school and stables feature a pub, serving barbecue and homemade baked goods in warmer months.

More Places to Visit in Southern Bohemia

Bechyně

Bechyně is a small spa town on the edge of a gorge above the Lužnice River. The Rožmberks' castle here is not open to the public, but the town's other medieval stronghold is now used for local history and art exhibitions. The former Franciscan church has a stunning 16th-century vault; however, the monastery has become a school, and access to it is tricky except during Sunday services. The town's former synagogue on Široká houses the **Museum of Firefighting** (Hasičké muzeum; closed Mon. & Nov.–April, $).

📫 156 C3 ✉ 12 miles (22 km) SW of Tábor on route 137, then W at Sudomerice on route 135 🚂 Train from Tábor; bus from Tábor and České Budějovice **Visitor information,** www.mestobechyne.cz ✉ Náměstí T. G. Masaryka 9 ☎ 381 213 822

Husinec

North of Prachatice, on the road to Vimperk, is Husinec, the birthplace of Jan Hus. The unpretentious house in which he was born is now the **Hus Museum** (closed Mon. & Oct.–April, $). A festival commemorates his life and achievements every July 5 and 6.

📫 156 B2 ✉ 25 miles (40 km) NW of České Budějovice on route 20, then W at Cesnovice on 145 🚂 Bus from Prachatice

Kámen

The 17th-century **château** at Kámen squats above the village on top of a large rock outcrop. It houses, of all things, a **Museum of Motorcycling.** Between the wars, Czechoslovakia built impressive motorbikes, and aficionados should enjoy this large display.

📫 157 E4 ✉ 15 miles (24 km) E of Tábor on route 19 🚂 Bus from Pelhřimov and Tábor **Museum** 🕐 Closed Mon. May–Sept., Mon.–Fri. April & Oct, & Nov.–March 💲 $

Pelhřimov

The old walled town of Pelhřimov has two surviving gateways, a Gothic church, and gabled Renaissance and baroque houses in its cobbled main square. The **town museum** (closed Mon., $) is also here; its most interesting feature is the frescoed music room. Pelhřimov comes to life in June for a beer festival, which coincides with Czechs attempting to set new records of bizarre feats. A special museum, the **Muzeum rekordů a kuriozit** (Museum of Records and Curiosities; closed Mon. June–Aug.; & Sept.–May, $), located in the Jihlava Gate (Jihlavská brána), features, among other things, a wooden bicycle, a large painting made from pasta, and the world's longest paper chain.

📫 157 E4 ✉ 22 miles (39 km) E of Tábor on route 19 🚂 Bus from Prague and Brno

Písek

Písek straddles the Otava River, which deposited the gold-bearing sand that brought the town prosperity in the Middle Ages. The town boasts the oldest stone bridge (built in the mid-13th century) in the Czech Republic—now pedestrian-only. The scant remains of the medieval **castle** (closed Mon., $), which was burned down in 1510, can be seen within the courtyard of the mustard-colored baroque town hall. The surviving wing of the castle contains the town museum (Prácheňské muzeum) and is worth seeing for the Knights' Hall, frescoed in the 1470s, and some gold exhibits. There are also displays relating to the concentration camp at nearby **Lety,** where a quarter of the Gypsies (Roma; see pp. 286–287) who were sent there in 1942 and 1943 died. Within the main square and the neighboring streets are fine Renaissance houses, the delightful **Church of the Holy Cross** (Kostel Povýšení sv. Kříže), and the Gothic **Church of the**

The stone bridge at Písek, built in the mid-13th century, is the oldest such structure in the Republic.

Birth of the Virgin Mary (Kostel Narození Panny Marie).
156 C3   28 miles (46 km) W of Tábor via route 19   Train and bus from Prague; train from České Budějovice   **Visitor information**, *www.icpisek.cz* Heydukova 97   382 213 592   Closed Sat.–Sun. Sept.–June

Slavonice

Founded in the 13th century, Slavonice, situated close to the border with Moravia and Austria, prospered because of its proximity to Vienna. After the Thirty Years' War in the 17th century that renown may have faded, but the architectural glories remain. Slavonice has been nominated a UNESCO World Heritage site thanks to its numerous Renaissance houses, many of them sgraffitoed, grouped around two squares,

Náměstí Míru and **Horní náměstí**. The Gothic **church,** with its lofty bell tower of 1549, is especially worth seeing.
157 F2   20 miles (32 km) SE of Jindřichův Hradec. E on route 164, then 151, right on 409   Bus from Prague via Dačice

Strakonice

The inhabitants of Strakonice are an enterprising people, as this little town manages to produce fezzes, motorcycles, and even a local version of bagpipes, known as *dudy*. It is the venue for an annual bagpipe festival.

Near the town center is an eclectic **castle,** the headquarters of the powerful chivalric order of Knights Hospitaller of St. John until 1694. The outer windows of the castle make its 13th-century origins clear, although the overall aspect is Renaissance. Inside the courtyard you can see the elegant Gothic choir of the chapel and the medieval round keep. The castle now houses a museum of bagpipes and motorbikes. It's a bit ramshackle, but for enthusiasts of either passion it is worth a visit.

🅰 156 B3 ✉ 34 miles (57 km) NW of České Budějovice via route 20 to Vodňany, right on route 22 🚆 Train from České Budějovice **Castle** 🕐 Closed Mon. & Nov.–April 💲 $

Vyšší Brod

South of Český Krumlov in the Vltava Valley is the white Cistercian **monastery** of Vyšší Brod *(closed Mon. & Oct.–April, $–$$)*, founded in 1259 by the Rožmberk family. It took a century to complete. Protected by its walled compound, the monastery managed to deter Hussite attacks, but the buildings were damaged in a fire in 1536 and again during the Thirty Years' War (1618–1638). The Communists closed the monastery in 1950, but in 1990 the Cistercians returned.

After the demise of the Rožmberk dynasty in 1611, Vyšší Brod came under the patronage of the Schwarzenbergs. The cloisters and 13th-century chapterhouse, its vaults supported on a single central pillar, are impressive. The dark Gothic church itself, despite drastic restoration and alteration, is also worth visiting. But to see the great medieval cycle of paintings by the Master of Vyšší Brod, visit the Convent of St. Agnes (Anežský klášter) in Prague (see pp. 108–111). The surviving monastic buildings contain a fabulous 70,000-volume rococo library with fantastical carved bookcases, painted ceiling, and a **postal museum** *(closed Nov.–March, $)*.

🅰 156 C1 ✉ 19 miles (31 km) S of Český Krumlov on route 160, then W on 163 🚌 Bus from Český Krumlov

Zlatá Koruna

The walled Cistercian monastery of Zlatá Koruna was founded in 1263 by Přemysl Otakar II. Badly damaged during the Hussite wars, it was later restored. The 13th-century **chapterhouse** is impressively vaulted, and the Gothic **church** is very fine, despite baroque additions. The library is a much later addition, dating from the 1770s, and contains an unmissable confection of gilt and stucco.

🅰 156 C2 ✉ 4 miles (6.5 km) NE of Český Krumlov via route 39 🚌 Bus from Český Krumlov 🕐 Closed Mon. & Nov.–March 💲 Guided tour: $$

Temelín Nuclear Tension

One of the hottest international debates to arise since the end of Communist rule is whether the Soviet-designed Temelín nuclear power plant, which stands just 19 miles (30 km) from the Austrian border in southern Bohemia, should have been allowed to go online in 2000.

Skeptics point to technical mishaps that have plagued Temelín and argue that its old design should have prompted a decision to abandon plans for it after 1989. However, the plant's two reactors, comprising a third of those running in the Czech Republic, are expected to be expanded into four with the help of one of three rivals for the job: U.S. energy giant Westinghouse, the French-German group Areva, and the Russian consortium AtomStroyExport.

It may be that geopolitics have trumped all the concerns over nuclear safety in the end. Russia has twice moved to cut off oil and natural gas supplies to Europe in recent years, making energy self-reliance a high priority for even green-minded Czechs. Many now consider nuclear power a lesser evil than oil, gas, or the other Czech natural energy resource, coal.

In the meantime, Temelín continues running, and with more than 100 billion Czech crowns invested so far, its keepers say it's as safe and sound as any of the dozens of other plants operating in Europe.

Home to the republic's famed spas, most notably Karlovy Vary, with Plzeň drawing beer fans

Western Bohemia

Ghost on the gate, Mariánské Lázně

Western Bohemia

Since western Bohemia borders Germany, it is hardly surprising that the German influence on the region has always been strong. Even today, more than six decades since the German population was expelled after its enthusiastic embrace of Hitler's Third Reich (see pp. 37–38), the famous spa towns of western Bohemia are still better known under their old German names of Karlsbad (Karlovy Vary) and Marienbad (Mariánské Lázně).

The Chotěšov cloister, located near Plzeň, was founded in the 13th century.

Germans and Bohemians lived side by side for centuries, though not always in harmony. These days the German half of this old equation is missing, however, leaving the region as a whole somewhat depleted. Now that the borders are no longer an obstacle, German tourists are returning to the spa towns, which are reverting to their former glory. Karlovy Vary has become a highly commercialized tourist center, though its grandeur and charm remain unimpaired. And the regional capital of Plzeň has certainly retained its importance, since it is the home of major industries like engineering and brewing. Laid out on a grand scale, Plzeň is one of the noblest towns in Bohemia and well worth visiting.

A less welcome feature of the easing of travel restrictions between Germany and former Eastern Europe is the burgeoning of prostitution close to the borders. The proliferation of street-walkers in towns such as Cheb and along the main highways has brought with it drug dealers and petty criminals. None of this should put you off, though, as such problems rarely impinge on tourists.

The old town center of Cheb is a delightful relic of German Bohemia, although it has become somewhat run-down. The Chodsko region is one of the few that has retained its folkloric traditions, best seen in the town of Domažlice. Western Bohemia doesn't have as many castles and monasteries as other parts of the Czech Republic, but places such as the Teplá monastery are of great interest. Also, there are quite a few charming old towns, such as Loket and Klatovy. ∎

5 ▷

Hranice

Aš

Luby

Kraslice

Ore (Krušné
Mts. hory)

Nejdek

Jáchymov

Ostrov E442 Ohře

Chodov

★ Karlovy Vary

Františkovy
Lázně E49

Kynšperk
nad Ohří

Sokolov

Loket E48

Bochov

Cheb

Horní
Slavkov

Becov nad Teplou

Žlutice

6

Teplá

21

Lázně
Kynžvart

940m ▲

Mariánské
Lázně

Toužim

Teplá

Žilhe

Manětín

Kralovice

20

Bezdružice

Plasy 27

Berounka

Planá

Kaznějov

DAY TRIPS FROM PRAGUE
p. 139

NORTHERN BOHEMIA
p. 205

Tachov

Černošín E49

Horní
Bříza

Radnice

Zbiroh

21

Mže

Stříbro

Třemošná

Chrást

Brasy E50

D5

Bohemian (Český

Kladruby

Nýřany E50

PLZEŇ

Rokycany

D5

Bor

Stod

Radbuza

Šťáhlavy

Mirošov

Bělá nad
Radbuzou

Úhlavka

Dobřany

27

19

les)

Staňkov

Holýšov

Přeštice

Blovice

Úslava

20

Horšovský Týn

Poběžovice

Kolovec

Úhlava

Nepomuk

GERMANY

Dراženov

Újezd

Domažlice 22

Kdyně

Švihov E53

Klatovy

Bradlava

1042m ▲
Čerchov

Chodsko

Janovice
nad Úhlavou

Plánice

22

Horažďovice

2 ▷

Nýrsko

Kolinec

27

Sušice Otava

SOUTHERN BOHEMIA
p. 155

Petrovice

1343m ▲

Kašperské
Hory

Šumava

B

Železná
Ruda

1 ▷

1370m

C

D

Area of map detail

★ Prague

0   20 kilometers
0   10 miles

Plzeň

To most people, Plzeň, at least in its German form of Pilsen, means beer. And rightly so. Pilsner Urquell, for many beer lovers, epitomizes lager-style beer. Some of the visitors who flock to Bohemia's second largest city do so to visit its churches and monuments, but it would be safe to say that the majority head straight for the brewery, a short distance from the city center.

A dazzling church-top view over part of the main square at Plzeň

Plzeň
🅰 183 C3
✉ 55 miles (88 km) SW of Prague on route E50

Visitor Information
✉ Náměstí Republiky 41, 30116
☎ 378 035 330
www.plzen.eu

Brewery Museum
✉ Veleslavínova 6
☎ 377 235 574 (for tours)
💲 $$
www.prazdroj.cz

You can't miss the famous gateway, the emblem that appears on every label of Plzeňský Prazdroj, to give Urquell its Czech name. After touring the brewery, you can visit the Prazdroj restaurant beside the entrance. Northeast of the main square, Náměstí Republiky, on Veleslavínova, is a charming old yellow house that is now the excellent **Brewery Museum** (Pivovarské muzeum), with its own beer hall, Na Parkánu.

But there is more to Plzeň than beer (see pp. 186–18/). The old town is built on a grand scale and encircled by wide boulevards that isolate it from the surrounding industrial city. Founded in 1295 by

King Václav II, the city's location at the confluence of four rivers (Mže, Radbuza, Úhlava, Úslava) helped it to prosper. After a period of decline following the Thirty Years' War in the 17th century, Plzeň grew quickly in the 19th century, when both the brewery (1842) and the Škoda armaments works (1859) were established. This accounts for the high proportion of turn-of-the-20th-century buildings, including ornate apartment houses and the railway station.

Similar houses in Náměstí Republiky tend to be overshadowed by gabled Renaissance and baroque houses, and by the lofty **Church of St. Bartholomew**

(Kostel sv. Bartoloměje). The bulk of this Gothic sandstone church obscures the fact that this is the largest city plaza in Bohemia. You can climb the 335-foot-high (102 m) steeple—the highest in the republic. Another tower, felled by lightning in 1525, was never rebuilt. The dignity of the church's interior is not enhanced by the lurid stained glass, but the high altar boasts an exquisite 14th-century Madonna.

North of the church is the 1686 plague column, topped by a gilt Madonna, and the dark sgraffitoed Renaissance town hall. The Franciscan friary just south of the square has a lovely Gothic interior despite its baroque facade. Behind it, the restored **Museum of Western Bohemia** (Západočeské muzeum) holds a comprehensive armory from the 14th century onward, among other exhibits. West of the square, down Prešovská, you can visit the huge quasi-Oriental **Great Synagogue** (Velká synagoga), one of Europe's largest, restored to use in 1998. Across the boulevard, the neoclassical **Tyl Theater** (Divadlo J. K. Tyla) would not look out of place along Vienna's Ringstrasse. ■

What's in a Name?

Plzeň never patented its name—a grave oversight, since all manner of insipid brews now parade as Pilsner or Pils. Similarly, the bland American Budweiser (fermented partly from rice) has little of the flavor of Bohemian Budvar or Budweiser. Budvar remains the only state-owned brewery, which has protected it from takeover by Western or American rivals.

Museum of Western Bohemia

⊠ Kopeckého sady 2

☎ 378 370 110

🕐 Closed Mon.

💲 $

www.zcm.cz

Great Synagogue

⊠ Sady Pětatřicátníků 11

🕐 Closed Sat., & mid-Oct.– March

💲 $$$

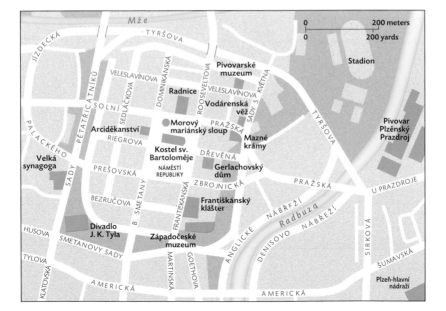

Pilsner Beer

If Bohemia is identified worldwide with one product, then it has to be beer. No village is without its *pivnice,* or pub, in which waiters wade through the crowds dispensing foaming glasses of delicious lager from loaded trays. The Czechs not only make excellent and inexpensive beer, they drink huge quantities of it, too, estimated at about one bottle per day for each member of the population, and that includes babies!

Beer production begins with hop cultivation and ends with a full mug in a pub.

It's not easy to pin down precisely why Bohemian beer has set the standard for the rest of the world, but the crucial element is probably the quality of the hops. These have been grown around Žatec in northern Bohemia since the ninth century; their quality is so outstanding that they are exported worldwide. Since water, as well as hops, is added to the malt before fermentation begins, the quality of the water is important, too. Plzeň's

water is especially soft; this quality, combined with the handpicked Žatec "Bohemian Red" hops and sweet top-quality barley, may well account for the rich flavor and texture of the beer brewed in the town.

It's impossible to say when brewing began in Bohemia, but by the 13th century the industry was established in Prague, Plzeň, and České Budějovice, which remain the principal Czech brewing centers. No one knows for certain

EXPERIENCE: Brewery Tours

To get a sense of the role beer has played in Czech history and society—and also experience the frisson of walking through a secret labyrinth under the Plzeň town square—the Brewery Museum (U Prazdroje 7, www.prazdroj.cz) is the place to start.

While awaiting a tour of the vast subterranean chambers that proved ideal for beer vat storage in the days before refrigeration, be sure to take in the museum's exhibits on the origins of malting, the complicated process itself, and the social standing of brewmasters in the Czech lands.

As the art and science of beermaking formed one of the great Bohemian fortes over the last 500 years, the beverage was adopted among virtually every segment of the nation's population. Interestingly, even in the days before zoning permits, the industry was once banished to locations outside Plzeň's former fortress walls. That's because oldtime breweries were prone to catch fire and because the brewing process once gave off powerfully unpleasant smells.

These days the beer tour results in a chance to both smell and taste a rare treat: unpasteurized *pivo*. Though perfectly safe to drink here, this organic form of Czech gold is illegal to import in most countries because it has not been deemed sterile enough. So don't miss the chance to use your free beer tokens from the museum to savor a cloudy mug of the stuff that Europeans of old prized dearly.

what medieval beers tasted like, but they were dark and often flavored with herbs and spices.

It was not until the 1840s that a new, cooler method of fermentation—known as bottom fermentation—permitted the production of a stable, translucent, golden lager beer, the style enjoyed today. The Plzeň Brewery was the first to adopt the new method after its foundation in 1842, and Pilsner Urquell remains the standard-bearer for this popular style of beer: bracing and hoppy in flavor, and topped with a thick creamy head.

The strength specified on the label refers to "original gravity" or density rather than alcoholic degree. You are most likely to encounter strengths of 10 degree (about 3.5 percent) and 12 degree (about 4.5 percent). Some special bottled beers are often dark in color (černé) and are considerably higher in alcohol. Higher strength beers are undoubtedly fuller, sweeter, and richer, but their power means that they are less well adapted to quenching thirst than their lighter counterparts.

Today there are dozens of breweries in the Czech Republic, and many local brews, rarely encountered outside their production area, can be extremely good. The best of the more celebrated brands include Urquell and Gambrinus from Plzeň, Staropramen and Braník from Prague, the milder Budvar from České Budějovice, Kozel from Velké Popovice, and the exceptionally hoppy Krušovice from Krušovice.

Bohemian beer has always been acclaimed for its purity of flavor, a quality to do not only with the excellent raw materials but also with the absence of chemicals and other additives. Although the beers remain pure, changes that are quite controversial include the growing use of pasteurization of bottled beers, which can diminish the aromas and flatten the flavor, and the injection of carbon dioxide, leading to a thinner, gassier brew.

Drinking Beer

In pubs, beer is served in half-liter mugs, but you can always ask for a *malé,* holding a third of a liter. Pubs tend to focus on one or two brands, so do not expect a wide range of products. On the other hand, there is no such thing as bad Bohemian beer.

Karlovy Vary

Karlovy Vary—Karlsbad—is the grandest of the Bohemian spas, known for the curative properties of its waters for at least a thousand years. It remains hugely popular with visitors partly
because of the grandeur of the spa buildings, and partly because of its dramatic location within
a narrow valley. Prettily decorated houses, many in an art nouveau style, line the steep lanes,
while the shopping streets close to the springs are always thronged with visitors.

The spa buildings and hotels of Karlovy Vary lie along the banks of the Teplá River.

The spa town was popularized
during the reign of Charles IV
and continued to enjoy royal
patronage. Peter the Great
visited at least twice (in 1711
and 1712). Earlier visitors came
here to bathe, though by the
late 18th century the fashion
changed to drinking the waters.

Very few old buildings survive
in Karlovy Vary despite its antiq-
uity. Most of the spa buildings,
hotels, sanatoria, and mansions
date from its boom years in the
late 19th and early 20th centuries.
Karlovy Vary follows the twists of
the Teplá River just before it joins
the Ohře, and the narrowness of

the forested valley means that the spa town is a very elongated place. Traffic is banned from the main streets and parking lots are provided at various locations. Many of the buildings in the secession style, the Austrian and Czech version of art nouveau, have undergone sparkling renovations. New hotels also have been replacing some of the more staid establishments in recent years. Serious cure-seekers, however, still opt to stay in the various hotel-sanatoria of the resort.

Several popular annual festivals add to Karlovy Vary's appeal. The film festival held each July attracts a large number of visitors. Others come in May for the jazz festival, in June for the music and opera festival, and in the autumn for the Dvořák festival. ∎

INSIDER TIP:

Becherovka, known as "the 14th spring," is an herbal liquor produced here. Visit the Jan Becher Museum (see p. 190) for a tour of the distillery and a sample.

–STEPHANIE ROBICHAUX
National Geographic contributor

Karlovy Vary

⊠ 183 B5

✉ 78 miles (133 km) W of Prague

Visitor Information

✉ Mlýnské nábřeží 5

☎ 353 321 171

www.karlovy-vary.cz

EXPERIENCE: The Curative Nature of Spas

Since Roman times, if not earlier, Europeans have recognized that waters from mineral springs can have therapeutic qualities. By the late 18th century certain spas, including many in the Czech Republic, had become not only renowned for their curative properties but also fashionable, particularly with the wealthy.

Spa-going is still very popular in the Czech Republic, especially in the Spa Triangle—Karlovy Vary, Mariánské Lázně, and Františkovy Lázně—and especially with Germans and central Europeans. Spa visitors stay in a hotel-like sanatorium and follow a medically prescribed program of treatments for some weeks, which could include mud baths and pool treatments as well as the imbibing of mineral waters. Different spas claim to have waters and treatments to ameliorate specific ailments.

The spa process itself can seem fairly clinical to those who imagine it as a series of relaxing hot tubs that go well with Chardonnay. The tradition is more along the lines of stern health care workers pushing you toward one water jet chamber after another, interspersed with tables where you get pounded or treated in other ways, depending on your options package.

One Karlovy Vary spa lays on the luxuries is the **Zámecký lázně**, or Castle Spa *(Mariánskolázeňská 23, tel 353 222 649, www.zamecke-lazne.cz)*, which features seven different kinds of saunas, from those aimed at improving breathing via ionized salt air to an anti-inflammatory herbal hot room to Russian and Finnish saunas. These cures go along with aromatherapy massage, oxygen therapy, and foot reflexology, among other treatments.

Another popular spot is the more established **Lázně III** *(Mlýnské nábřeži 5, tel 353 225 641-3, www.lazneiii.cz)*, where it's all business. The professionals here lay on balneological treatments, hydrotherapy, massage, mud packs, paraffin wraps, dry carbon dioxide packs, electrotherapy, magnetotherapy and even, should you require it, intestinal irrigations (colonics).

A Walk Around Karlovy Vary

In a few hours you can traverse the whole of Karlovy Vary. It's a very compact place, hemmed in by the steep hills on either side, and almost all the buildings are within a short distance of the springs strung out along the valley floor.

The mighty columns of the late 18th-century Mlýnská kolonáda reflect a time when this was the most fashionable spa area in all of Europe.

If you come by train or road from Prague, you will end up in the commercial part of the town, where you must leave your car. Head for the broad pedestrianized T. G. Masaryka, which is close to the railroad station. At the top of the street is the **Jan Becher muzeum ❶** *(T. G. Masaryka 57, $$),* dedicated to an herbal digestive tonic that you will either adore or loathe. The tonic, invented by Jan Becher at the end of the 18th century, has been produced here commercially since 1807. Continue down T. G. Masaryka to the banks of the Teplá and the Poštovní Bridge, where you can hire a horse-drawn carriage, if desired The grand impression made by the turn-of-the-20th-century buildings

NOT TO BE MISSED:

Mlýnská kolonáda • Vřídlo spring • Church of St. Mary Magdalene • Grandhotel Pupp

is marred by the modern Hotel Thermal, erected here in the 1970s. Behind it is a large open-air swimming pool.

The spa center consists essentially of two streets on either side of the Teplá River, with frequent bridges linking the two sides. Continuing southward you pass the 12 principal springs housed within five colonnades along the river. The first is on the far side of the genteel and flower-filled Dvořák Gardens (Dvořákovy sady), the cream-painted **Sadová kolonáda ❷,** designed by Viennese architects in 1882. The street called Sadová, heading away from the river to the right, climbs to the restored onion-domed **Russian Orthodox church** (Kostel sv. Petra a Pavla) of 1897. From the colonnade, Mlýnské leads to the splendid 1871 **Mlýnská kolonáda ❸,** the heart of the spa, resembling a Greek marketplace. Four very hot springs bubble beneath its columns. Facing the main portico is a timber-framed building called Petr, where Peter the Great is said to have lodged.

To sample the waters, stop at any of the street stalls and buy a small porcelain beaker shaped like a flattened teapot to keep the water from staining your teeth; alternatively, bring your own cup. Then help yourself from any of the warm springs at the various colonnades. Don't

smoke near the springs; the no-smoking police will make a firm approach in your direction.

Immediately after the Mlýnská kolonáda you come to one of the main streets of the spa, Lázeňská, with its secession buildings painted mustard and green, and decorated with ornate ironwork. A major draw is the **Moser glassware shop** at No. 28, a retail outlet for the Moser factory and glass museum *(www.moser-glass.com)* with more than 2,000 exhibits. Many visitors clearly are more interested in spending than curing, and Karlovy Vary is full of shops selling glassware, porcelain, jewelry, arts and crafts, and *oplatky* wafers (see pp. 198-199).

> 🅰 See area map p. 183
> ➤ T. G. Masaryka street
> 🕐 3 miles (4.5 km)
> ⟺ 3 hours
> ➤ Diana Lookout

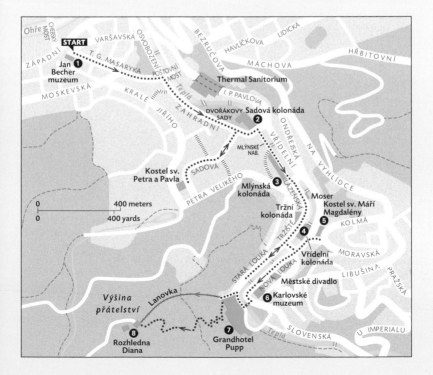

Lázeňská bends right past the dainty wooden **Tržní kolonáda** of 1883. Across from it is the principal spring, the **Vřídlo**, housed in the **Vřídelní kolonáda ❹**, which was constructed from glass and marble in 1975. The Vřídlo is the hottest and most vigorous spring in town, surging up with such force that it resembles a geyser.

Continuing south you come to the main shopping street, Stará Louka. Across the Teplá, on a slope overlooking the Vřídelní kolonáda, is the curvaceous blue-gray and white **Church of St. Mary Magdalene** (Kostel sv. Máří Magdalény) **❺**, built by Kilián Ignác Dientzenhofer in 1736. Its interior is sensational: a single galleried space beneath a broad dome adorned with richly gilt baroque altars.

On Nová Louka stands the primrose neobaroque theater (Městské divadlo), where the European premiere of Dvořák's *New World Symphony* was given in 1894; the frescoed interior and curtain were painted by leading secession artists, including Gustav Klimt.

At the end of this stretch of the river is the **Karlovy Vary Museum** (Karlovské muzeum) **❻** *(Nová Louka 23, closed Mon.–Tues., $$)*, featuring local ecology and history. At the bend of the river, the **Grandhotel Pupp ❼** sits among lovely gardens and pine woods; it has a

INSIDER TIP:

While on the hillside west of the Teplá River, check out the monument to Karl Marx, who visited the spa town in its 19th-century heyday.

—EMILY THOMPSON
Special Sections editor, The Prague Post

dynamic statue of Beethoven, who patronized the spa. The hotel was founded in the late 18th century, but it has been rebuilt and extended. (It served as setting for much of the action in the 2006 Queen Latifah film *Last Holiday.*) Today it is a club and casino as well as a luxurious hotel, and it's worth sneaking in to look at the lavish interiors, notably the concert hall.

The hotel is also the starting point for many walking trails. The most popular one leads up to a café and **Diana Lookout** (Rozhledna Diana) **❽**, which you can also reach by funicular *(Lanovka).* Especially keen walkers might be tempted by the trail that covers the 10.5-mile (17 km) distance from here to the charming town of Loket, southwest of Karlovy Vary, on the Ohře River (see pp. 203–204).

EXPERIENCE: Karlovy Vary Film Festival

The most star-studded event on the Czech film calendar is undoubtedly the Karlovy Vary International Film Festival *(www .kviff.com)*, which transforms this sleepy Western Bohemian spa town for nine days every summer. The likes of Sharon Stone, Robert Redford, and Robert De Niro roll in and more than 200 feature films and documentaries from around the world attract hordes of Czech backpackers.

The festival dates back to 1946, but, because it was co-opted by the Soviets and moved to Moscow on alternate years for a time, 2010 officially marks only the 45th edition. Movie tickets only go on sale the day before the screening but the schedule is all online and ticketing via the Web is being phased in. Note that hotel rooms are at a premium during the festival—but more options are opening every year, some quite reasonable.

The festival's East of the West section highlights the best in filmmaking from the former Eastern bloc. The gathering's documentary section presents such excellent fare as the 2008 winner *Man on Wire,* the story of Philippe Petit's 1974 act of unbelievable daring in running a cable between New York City's Twin Towers and walking across it—eight times.

Natural springs, with their bracing curative waters, are encountered all over Karlovy Vary.

Cheb

Modern Cheb is an industrial town, but the historic center is well worth exploring. With many half-timbered houses, it looks more like a small German town than a Czech one, which is not surprising, given its history. Cheb is situated just 3.5 miles (6 km) from the German border. Germans first settled here in the 11th century; the town quickly became an important trading post between Bavaria and Bohemia. Only in 1322 did it become part of the Czech domains.

Clock tower atop new Cheb's baroque town hall

Cheb's strategic border location meant that it suffered badly during the Thirty Years' War, when both sides used it as a base. Industrialization during the 19th century revived the fortunes of the town, however. Enjoying a good deal of political independence, Cheb, with its German population, fought hard against growing Czech nationalism in the 19th century. Much of the population was also sympathetic to the Nazi cause during World War II, which prompted the government to expel all such sympathizers after the German defeat. Cheb was known as Eger before World War II.

Cheb's arrow-shaped main square (Náměstí Krále Jiřího z Poděbrad) is fringed by unusually tall houses, most of them dating from the 17th century and more German than Bohemian in style. Neglected for many years, the square is now lively once again, with many cafés and restaurants. At the top end of the sloping square is the famous **Roland fountain,** and at the bottom is a medieval group of half-timbered houses known as **Špalícek,** once inhabited by Jewish merchants.

The streets across from Špalíček, notably Židovská, occupy the former ghetto; the Jewish

Border Town Prostitution

One definite scourge of the free market's sudden arrival in the Czech Republic has been the steady growth of prostitution—along with the associated issues of human trafficking. Because Czech law does not define the oldest profession as a crime, it's practiced openly. Unlike in Germany or Holland, however, no regulation of prostitution occurs, and there are no mandated health or safety checks.

Thus, visitors to border towns such as Cheb or Dubí are often taken aback to see highways lined with young women scantily clad in micro-miniskirts, even in the dead of winter. It's a grim life for the women in the trade, but very little has been done to deal with the issue other than for local mayors to announce occasional antiprostitution campaigns.

International human rights agencies have called for a more systematic approach to addressing prostitution. Yet it seems that Prague lawmakers are afraid to consider legalization for political reasons—and equally afraid to take on the well-financed mafia running the show.

community was expelled on many occasions and was exterminated during World War II. The baroque town hall, situated at the narrow end of the square, now houses a collection of modern Czech art and temporary exhibitions ($). Opposite the town hall, Jateční, a lane packed with fine baroque houses, leads to the former Franciscan friary. Here, admire the impressive 14th-century cloister and the 18th-century **Church of St. Clare** (Kostel sv. Kláry), which is attributed to Kilián Ignác Dientzenhofer.

Opposite Špalíček is a house with ostentatiously steep gables and a fine Gothic doorway, now a gallery. Next door stands the **Gabler House** (Gablerův dům), lavishly decorated with rococo stucco, where the German writer Johann Wolfgang von Goethe was a guest. The **Cheb Museum** (Chebské muzeum), also at this end of the square, was where General Albrecht von Wallenstein (Valdštejn) was murdered in 1634 (see p. 32). The museum contains a reconstruction of the room in which the general was assassinated on the order of Ferdinand II. Behind the museum, the **Church of St. Nicholas** (Kostel sv. Mikuláše) is of Romanesque origin but mostly neo-Gothic in style; only the towers of the original structure remain. Nearby is the baroque Dominican church.

Little is left of the town's riverside imperial castle, **Chebský hrad,** apart from its black keep constructed with volcanic stone. The Holy Roman Emperor Frederick Barbarossa had the castle built in the 12th century as both a stronghold and a royal palace. Climb the keep and enjoy the views of Cheb and the surrounding countryside. Then visit the remarkable two-storied chapel, with Romanesque capitals in the lower story, and more elegant Gothic capitals in the upper.

The nearby deconsecrated **Chapel of St. Bartholomew** (Kaple sv. Bartoloměje), with fine vaulting dating to 1414, displays Gothic statuary. ■

Cheb

- 🅰 183 A4
- ✉ 107 miles (180 km) W of Prague
- 🚆 Train or bus from Prague, Karlovy Vary, & Plzeň

Visitor Information

- ✉ Infocentrum, Náměstí Krále Jiřího z Poděbrad 33
- ☎ 354 440 302

www.mestocheb.cz

Cheb Museum

- ✉ Náměstí Krále Jiřího z Poděbrad 4
- ☎ 354 400 620
- 🕐 Closed Mon.
- 💲 $–$$

www.muzeumcheb.cz

Chebský hrad

- 🕐 Closed Mon. & Nov.–March
- 💲 $

Mariánské Lázně

Mariánské Lázně (Marienbad), the most charming of Bohemia's spa towns, is a relative newcomer among spas: It was developed only in the early 19th century by the abbot of the Teplá monastery, some 8 miles (12 km) to the east. Václav Skalník designed the landscaped gardens, and within a few decades this isolated spot in the Bohemian forest was a delightful ensemble of parks and pavilions, grouped around 40 therapeutic springs.

Below a mantle of white, Mariánské Lázně displays the charming elegance of a bygone period.

Mariánské Lázně

- 183 B4
- 117 miles (196 km) W of Prague. SW on route E50 past Plzeň, then N on route 21
- Train or bus from Prague, then take trolleybus 4 or 5 to the town center from the station

The great German writer Goethe was a prominent early visitor in the 1820s. Russian writer Nikolai Gogol wrote part of his novel *Dead Souls* while staying here, and Wagner composed *Lohengrin* at Marienbad in 1848. Surpassing these artistic seals of approval was the patronage of royalty—King Edward VII of England and Emperor Franz Josef of Austria were frequent and celebrated visitors. Today Mariánské Lázně is especially popular with German visitors.

The stately and sometimes pompous buildings have been well restored after decades of gentle decay. The ensemble is better than the individual components, and of all the Czech spas, this is probably the most harmonious and alluring.

The main street, Hlavní, which runs the length of the town, is an almost uninterrupted row of hotels, coffeehouses, and opulent turn-of-the-20th-century apartment houses. Here, too, you'll find a very small **museum** (Dům F. Chopina) dedicated to another famous visitor, Polish composer Frédéric Chopin (1810–1849). He came here in 1836 to pursue the young woman who was to become his fiancée; they never married because of his failing health. During the third week of August, the spa hosts a Chopin festival. All these buildings, many of with balconies, face onto the spa gardens and to the Slavkov hills. The buildings are splashy and

showy and excessively ornate, yet somehow they retain their dignity. Behind Hlavní, on Ruská, are the former **Anglican church** (Anglickánský kostelík), now an exhibition

INSIDER TIP:

Above town near the Hotel Krakonos is Park Boheminium (www.boheminium.cz) —a footpath with 41 significant miniatures, a functional model train, and a pond with a model steamboat.

–BARBORA TINTEROVÁ
*Tourist Information Centre,
Mariánské Lázně*

Visitor Information

✉ Infocentrum, Hlavní 47

☎ 354 622 474

www.marianske lazne.cz

Chopin Museum

✉ Hlavní 47

🕐 Closed Mon., Fri., & Sat.

$ $

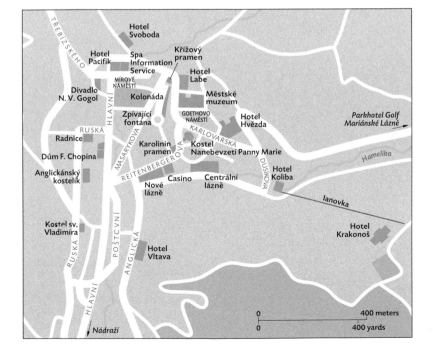

Municipal Museum

✉ Goethovo náměstí 11

⏱ Closed Mon.– Tues.

💲 $

Lázně Kynžvart Château

☎ 354 691 269

⏱ Closed Mon. May– Sept.; Mon.–Fri. April & Oct.; & all Nov.–March

💲 $$

hall, and the **Russian Orthodox church** (Kostel sv. Vladimíra) of 1902. It's worth going inside the Russian church to see the lavish iconostasis that is made of porcelain and often claimed to be the largest single piece of porcelain in the world.

Lázně Kynžvart

Five miles (8 km) northwest of Mariánské Lázně is Lázně Kynžvart, once the private spa of Klemens Metternich, the archconservative chancellor of Austria from 1821 to 1848. It is now a spa for children with respiratory ailments. The Metternichs' ancestral home, a baroque castle, was rebuilt in the 1830s as an empire-style château designed by Italian architect Pietro Nobile. The château and park are open to the public, and displays include Metternich memorabilia and the chancellor's library.

The Colonnade

Hlavní ends at the Hotel Pacifik, and to the right are the spa buildings, many of which are being overhauled. The core of the spa, the curving **Kolonáda,** or Colonnade, was built from wrought iron in 1889. Resembling a greenhouse or Victorian railroad station, it is a structure of great charm. People taking the cure at the various springs sheltered by the Kolonáda could also make a beeline for the

pastry shops and coffeehouses along Hlavní. The springs themselves have different chemical compositions, and the spa doctors prescribe doses from only those springs that will improve a specific condition. At the southern end of the Kolonáda is the **Singing Fountain** (Zpívající fontána), whose jets and spume are coordinated with classical music every two hours to entertain passersby. Continuing south from the fountain, you come to the casino, where a disco provides entertainment for younger visitors.

Behind the Kolonáda, in Goethovo náměstí, is the **Municipal Museum** (Městské muzeum), located in a building where Goethe used to stay. Captions are in Czech only, but there is an English-language video that gives a thorough historical overview of the town. Nearby is another of Goethe's residences, the former Hotel Weimar, the first choice of celebrities in the 19th century. The curious octagonal neo-Byzantine **Church of the Assumption of Our Lady** (Kostel Nanebevzetí Panny Marie), built in 1848 and as fanciful as everything else in the spa, faces the hotel across Goethovo náměstí. The atmosphere, as in all Bohemian spas, is very decorous: No smoking in the gardens, no cycling, and no dogs.

Waters, Wafers, & Walking

Spa towns generally are not given to gastronomic excesses, but Mariánské Lázně is famous for its widely available *oplatky* wafers. These light cookies

Mariánské Lázně is a winter skier's paradise. A five-minute walk from the Colonnade, next to the Kolibá Hotel, are slopes of varying challenge.

–BARBORA TINTEROVÁ
Tourist Information Centre,
Mariánské Lázně

come in a range of flavors. They are often eaten on their own to neutralize the strong flavor of the spring waters.

A further attraction of Marienbad is the ease with which you can hike into the pine woods around town, directly from the spa gardens. On the plateau above the town is an 18-hole golf course, one of the best in the country, and the luxurious adjoining Parkhotel Golf. A cable car operating from May to September connects the Hotel Koliba with the Hotel Krakonoš, an excellent base for hiking through the woods on marked trails.

Indeed, walking is one of the pleasures of visiting the spa, especially for those who have no wish to drink the waters or sign up for a "treatment." The air up here, at 1,896 feet (578 m), is fresh and clean. Miles of walking and hiking trails were laid out in the 19th century, many of them leading to the remoter springs.

To retain the unspoiled character of the little town, no cars are permitted in the center. There is, however, ample parking within easy walking distance of the spa. ■

The popular Singing Fountain at Mariánské Lázně

Domažlice & Chodsko

Domažlice is the main town of the Chodsko region. In the remote past many Slavic tribes inhabited the Czech lands and were absorbed into the Czech people and culture, but one exception is the once ferocious, axe-wielding Chod tribe. Their origins are obscure, but they rose to prominence when they were employed as frontier guards and escorts in the 11th century. Indeed, their name derives from the Czech word *chodit* (to walk).

The small town of Domažlice springs to life each August for an exuberant Chodsko folk festival.

Domažlice

🅰 183 B2

Visitor Information

✉ Náměstí Míru 51,

☎ 379 725 852

www.idomazlice.cz

In medieval times an essential trading route traversed the Chodsko region, which links Bohemia with the Bavarian city of Regensburg and beyond. In exchange for safeguarding this important line of communication for the benefit of the rulers of Bohemia, the Chods were granted extensive privileges in 1325, including freedom from serfdom. From then on, no outsiders could acquire lands within the Chodsko region, and their sole master was the king of Bohemia.

Their influence and independence waned once the Habsburgs resumed complete control over Bohemia after the Battle of White Mountain (see p. 30). The Chods had backed the losing side. Their part of the nation was put under the harsh rule of Wolf Maximillian Lammingen, a Habsburg general. These proud people rebelled in 1692, but the revolt was brutally crushed and the Chods' leader, Jan Sladký Kozina, was executed in Plzeň in November 1695. Nonetheless, they retained their cultural values and distinctive dialect, even in the face of ardent Germanization by the Habsburgs.

Domažlice was the location of the customshouse they once controlled, as well as the castle that served as their administrative headquarters and as their court. The town is set around its main square, Náměstí Míru, which is lined with unpretentious gabled and arcaded houses. Bohemia is not short of fine arcaded squares, but this is one of the best preserved and most charming. It is framed at one end by the turreted 13th-century **Lower Gate** (Dolní brána) and at the other by the 18th-century Augustinian church. Halfway along is Kilián Ignác Dientzenhofer's **Church of the Nativity of the Virgin** (Kostel Narození Panny Marie) of 1747, which incorporates a round medieval watchtower. Climb the tower's 200 or so steps for a view over the whole town (closed Oct.–March, $). The delightful church interior, decorated with baroque frescoes, has a lavish altarpiece.

A lane opposite the Augustinian church leads to what remains of the **Chod Castle** (Chodský hrad), in the form of another medieval round tower. Once the local courthouse, it is today a rather dusty **museum** that portrays the colorful history of the town and includes folkloric items typical of the region.

Domažlice maintains its folk traditions proudly, but it is becoming rare to glimpse townsfolk in typical Chod dress making their way to church on a Sunday morning. At the folk festivals held here the people have an excuse to wear their traditional costumes—the men in yellow pantaloons, white kneesocks, and broad-brimmed hats; the women in elaborate bodices and aprons—and to play the *dudy* (bagpipes). The most important festival takes place in August *(www.chodskeslavnosti.cz)*. You can see a good collection of costumes and other Chod folk art and cultural artifacts at the **Muzeum Jindřicha Jindřicha** beyond the Lower Gate. This collection of ceramics and costumes is displayed in a re-created cottage interior. Typical Chod-style ceramics are made by a local cooperative; find them at the shop on Husova, some 55 yards (50 m) beyond the Lower Gate.

Nearby, the villages of Újezd and Draženov still contain some traditional Chodsko log cabins. ■

Town Museum

⊠ Chodské náměstí 96

🕓 Closed Mon. mid-April–mid-Oct.; & Sat.–Sun. mid-Oct.–March

💲 $

Muzeum Jindřicha Jindřicha

⊠ Náměstí Svobody 61

🕓 Closed Sat.–Sun.

💲 $

EXPERIENCE:
Domažlice *Koláč*

While touring the festivals of Domažlice and Chodsko, it's inevitable that you'll encounter the tempting, calorie-rich cake, known as the *koláč*. This round, glazed treat is traditionally center-filled with cream cheese, fruit jam (plum and apricot are favored), or poppy seeds. These cakes, which are also a part of celebrations of Czech heritage from Texas to Iowa, are in just about every bakeshop in the Republic. But those seen in Domažlice reach epic size (some would overflow a record turntable) and are sold fresh and warm; the poppy variation is a particular point of local pride. Though you might expect any baked good to meet the fresh and warm criteria, Czechs are so fond of these cakes that they are often happy to buy any remaining in the shop, even if a few hours old and long since cold.

More Places to Visit in Western Bohemia

Františkovy Lázně

The most modest of the major western Bohemian spas, Františkovy Lázně was developed in 1793 and later renamed in honor of the Austrian emperor Franz I. Goethe and Beethoven were among its notable visitors. The town offers acres of gardens and parks but is surrounded by marshes rather than the hills of its better known rivals. Laid out on a strict grid plan, it gives an overall impression that is somewhat prim, and even the Colonnade of 1844 is rigid. With its gardens, outdoor cafés, and neoclassical buildings painted the mustard yellow called *kaisergelb*, it's pleasant enough. In recent years, the immense green-roofed casino has been reconstructed, bringing wealthier visitors from across the German border and giving the whole spa a new lease on life. The **Glauber Spring** (Glauberův pramen) is the most handsome spa building, but the main source is the **Francis Spring** (Františkův pramen) in a reconstructed rotunda. This is the best place to sample the sulfurous waters. The mud baths here have radioactive qualities, which some believe to be beneficial in the treatment of certain cardiac and rheumatic ailments.

🅜 183 A4   ✉ 4 miles (6 km) NW of Cheb on route 21   **Visitor information**
✉ Anglická 5   ☎ 354 543 162   🚍 Bus from Prague and Plzeň. Train from Prague, change at Cheb

Jáchymov

Jáchymov is one of Bohemia's more haunting spots. The town was founded in the 16th century when silver deposits were discovered here, and by the 1840s uranium was being mined and used to color glass and crystal. During the 1950s thousands of prisoners, mostly political detainees, were sent to work the mines, with dreadful consequences for their health. The mines were eventually closed in 1960, though at the upper and most shabby part of the town a pithead survives. Amazingly, this scruffy spa still attracts regular visitors who come here to take the treatments at the town's radioactive springs. One of the main centers is called Radium Palace.

🅜 183 B5   ✉ 10 miles (16 km) N of Karlovy Vary on route 25   🚍 Bus from Prague. Train from Karlovy Vary

The casino, as much as the springs, has become a major draw to visitors at Františkovy Lázně.

Former Sudetenland

The upheavals of the post-World War II years may be all but forgotten to most Europeans now. In the Czech lands, however, especially those that border on Germany and Austria, the sometimes violent expulsions of ethnic Germans still represent a troubling legacy.

In 2009, Czech President Václav Klaus held the attention of the entire European Union when he delayed signing the Lisbon Treaty, which was to create an EU constitution. His stated reason: worries that

German heirs might try to reclaim properties their families lost in 1945 and 1946.

That same year, a two-year Czech police investigation by inspector Pavel Karas wrapped up, solving a 64-year-old mystery by identifying the principal culprits of a massacre during the expulsions in which at least 763 people were killed. Though the perpetrators were not publicly named, the state promised justice. The ripples of what the Germans called the Sudetenland continue to spread.

Klatovy

This ancient walled town was founded in 1260 on the edge of the Šumava mountains (see pp. 176–177). In the top corner of its finely proportioned sloping main square, Náměstí Míru, is the immense rough-hewn **Black Tower** (Černá věž) of the 1550s with a splendid astronomical clock from 1759. It's pressed up against the 16th-century town hall, which is gabled and decorated with modern sgraffito in best Bohemian style. From the top of the tower you look out onto the Šumava mountains. Nearby is Kilián Ignác Dientzenhofer's superb **Jesuit church,** its broad white facade peopled with statuary in niches. The interior, with curvaceous galleries and stucco decoration, contains fine baroque furnishings and remarkable trompe l'oeil frescoes. The ghoulish **crypt** contains some 40 mummified corpses of town worthies exposed in their coffins. They include many Jesuit priests who died between 1676 and 1783. Near the church is a 17th-century pharmacy, since the mid-1960s, this beautifully preserved building, with its neoclassical facade and all the original rococo fittings, has been a **museum.** Take a stroll through the old town to visit what remains of the walls and bastions, passing a Gothic church and the Renaissance **White Tower** (Bílá věž) on the way. Today

Klatovy is best known for its cultivation of carnations after seeds were brought here from France in 1813.

🄰 183 C2 ✉ 25 miles (40 km) S of Plzeň on route 27 🚌 Bus from Prague or Plzeň **Visitor information** ✉ Náměstí Míru 63 ☎ 376 347 240 **Black Tower** 🕒 Closed M on. May–Sept.; Mon.–Fri. April & Oct.; & Nov.–March 🛇 $ **Crypt** 🕒 Closed Mon. April–Sept. & Oct.–March 🛇 $ **Pharmacy Museum** ☎ 376 313 109 🕒 Closed Mon. May–Oct. & Nov.–March 🛇 $$

Loket

The town of Loket stands on a loop of the Ohře River, beneath a 12th-century royal **castle** that seems to grow vertically from its irregular granite crag. Unlike many medieval castles in Bohemia, the original architectural style is almost intact, with towers, walls, and keeps huddled together. The three-year-old future Charles IV of Bohemia was imprisoned here by his father for some months in the late 1310s to forestall any possible uprising; it became a prison again between 1788 and 1947. The interior is not very interesting, but the watchtower offers attractive views. Much of the town is shabby but slowly being restored to its original charm. Loket, however, has a porcelain factory, and its shops sell fine contemporary examples.

One gate entrance into Loket castle

 183 B4 9 miles (13 km) SW of Karlovy Vary on route 6 Bus from Karlovy Vary **Castle** Closed Mon. $$

Plasy

This vast but dilapidated Cistercian monastery was originally constructed in the 12th century but rebuilt by Jean-Baptiste Mathey (1630–1696) and Giovanni Santini (1677–1723). The monastery's finest feature is the sumptuous cloister, with its frescoed side chapels, which can be visited on a guided tour. The rest of the buildings have been converted into a school and art gallery. In 1826 the recently secularized monastery became the property of the reactionary Austrian chancellor Metternich. The thick heavy structure exudes power rather than spirituality. Metternich had the church in the cemetery across the main road rebuilt as the family mausoleum in a neoclassical style.

183 C4 16 miles (26 km) N of Plzeň on route 27 Closed Mon. May–Sept.; Mon.–Fri. April & Oct.; & Nov.–March $ Bus or train from Plzeň

Švihov

South of Plzeň is the grim castle of Švihov, built in the late 15th century and completed in 1530 by the Rožmberk family as a fortress so formidable that the Habsburgs later demanded its fortifications be demolished. What remains is a somewhat emasculated fortress, an impression enhanced by the presence of sheep in the grassy forecourt and swans on the moat. The hall and Benedikt Ried's Gothic chapel can be visited on a guided tour.

183 C2 18 miles (29 km) S of Plzeň on route 27 Closed Mon. May–Sept.; Mon.–Fri. April & Oct.; & all Nov.–March $$ Train from Plzeň or Klatovy

Teplá

The once wealthy Premonstratensian abbey of Teplá, founded in the 1190s, is again in the hands of a monastic order, following its closure in 1950 by the Communists. In the 16th century the monks here were the proprietors of Mariánské Lázně and developed the spa in 1808. Following secularization Teplá was used first as a school and then as a barracks, but the returning monks have restored the abbey energetically, adding on a modern restaurant and hotel that blend in well with the mostly 18th-century buildings, designed by the Dientzenhofer family.

The facade of the church retains Romanesque features, but the interior is rich in baroque statuary, with a fine altarpiece. The pride and joy of the abbey is its galleried library: It is the second largest in the Czech Republic, stacked with 80,000 volumes, including many illuminated manuscripts and rare books from the 16th century onward. It was built in the early 20th century, but with all the swagger of neo-rococo opulence.

183 B4 8 miles (12 km) E of Mariánské Lázně. NE on route 230, then SE on route 210 or by signposted back roads Closed Mon. & Jan. $$ Train from Karlovy Vary and Mariánské Lázně

Lovely old towns and a hiker's paradise, home to both Czech
Switzerland national park and Jizerské hory

Northern Bohemia

Frýdlant medieval fortress

Northern Bohemia

Northern Bohemia is an absorbing corner of the country. Its cultural identity is German, and towns such as Děčín, Teplice, Liberec, and Ústí nad Labem were predominantly German speaking until 1945, when the Germanic population was expelled and, in some cases, murdered. The cultural vacuum left by their departure has never been filled.

The Czech Republic has always been a rich country, both under the Habsburgs and later as an independent nation. The source of that wealth was industry based on mineral resources. The industrial drawback was pollution. Changing economic fortunes, however, have done as much to stop the damage as has the rise of green consciousness in the country. Smokestacks and quarries remain, but much of the heavy industry has gone out of business, leaving mainly coal mining as the last great culprit. Still entire towns were abandoned or moved to make way for the bulldozers. The pollution has blighted the landscape, damaged the health of both Czechs and Germans, and destroyed much of the surrounding forests. Since 1989 protests from inside and outside the country have become more vocal, and some of the worst excesses have gradually been reduced.

Although much of the countryside is flat farming land, there are hillier stretches near the border and in places such as Klášterec in the Ohře Valley. Indeed, the region called České Švýcarsko (Czech Switzerland) is one of the most charming corners of hill country in the entire republic, and it has long been popular with ramblers.

Along the southern fringes of

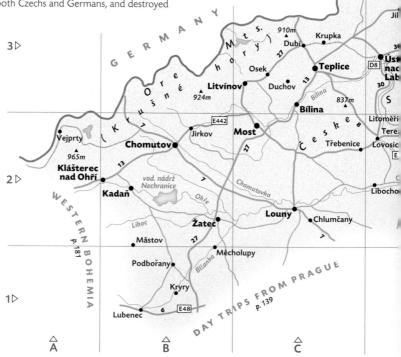

the region are delightful little towns, including Kadan, Žatec, Louny, and Litoměřice. The once German-speaking towns of Liberec and Jablonec nad Nisou may be shadows of their former selves, but they still retain some grandeur and civic pride.

Also worthy of a visit, but for very different reasons, is Terezín, which was a garrison town, fortress, and prison under the Habsburgs. It was later adopted by the Nazi occupiers as the ghetto of Theresienstadt, a staging post for most of its inhabitants on the way to the death camps of Poland. ∎

NOT TO BE MISSED:

The Master of Litoměřice's Renaissance panels   **209**

Paying respect at Terezín, the former concentration camp   **210–213**

Liberec's magnificent tapestries   **215**

Driving the forested lanes of České Švýcarsko   **216–218**

Gazing at Czech glass mastery in Jablonec nad Nisou   **219**

Area of map detail

0   20 kilometers
0   10 miles

Litoměřice

The beguiling town of Litoměřice lies in an exceptionally fertile agricultural region celebrated for its fruits and flowers. A former Slav fortress founded in the ninth century, it prospered following an influx of German merchants and became one of the richest towns in Bohemia.

Litoměřice's architectural styles span more than five centuries.

That period of prosperity came to an end when the town was wrecked during the Thirty Years' War. After the war, Ferdinand III (r. 1637–1657) ordered Litoměřice to be rebuilt. The reconstruction was undertaken by local architects, in particular Ottavio Broggio, who was born here in 1668. His stately baroque buildings line the slopes above the Labe River.

The main square, **Mírové náměstí**, has a plague column and fountains that are lost among its vast cobbled expanses. In one corner is Broggio's mostly rebuilt Gothic **Church of All Saints** (Kostel Všech svatých), which incorporates a tower from the medieval fortifications, and extraordinary witch's-hat turrets that line the ridge of the choir. Just down Jezuitská from here is another Broggio design, the **Jesuit church,** with its richly ornamented portal

INSIDER TIP:

Litoměřice is a perfect place to calm down and breathe again after visiting nearby Terezín. Relax in the market square with surrounding towers of several different eras.

—ROZ HOAGLAND
Guide, Hoagland Art Travel

Master of Litoměřice (ca 1500), who worked mostly as a court painter in Prague. His idiosyncratic, disproportionate style depicted heads that were too small and hands that were too large.

North of the square is the over-restored 14th-century **castle,** once a brewery but now a cultural center. At the end of Michalská, turn left. The second street on the right leads to the pink-and-gray **Church of St. Wenceslas** (Kostel sv. Václava) by Broggio. Straight on, you come to Náměstí Dómské, the cathedral square. The 11th-century **St. Stephen's Cathedral** (Chrám sv. Štěpána), rebuilt in 1654, contains paintings attributed to Cranach the Elder. ■

Litoměřice

 207 D2
✉ 46 miles (74 km) N of Prague via route E55
🚌 Bus from Florenc bus station in Prague

Visitor Information

✉ Mírové náměstí 15
☎ 416 732 440
🕐 Closed Sun. Oct.–April
www.litomerice.cz

North Bohemia Fine Arts Gallery

🕐 Closed Mon.
💲 $

and facade. The **Old Town Hall** (Staroměstské radnice) displays Gothic arcades and a Renaissance main building, topped by a profusion of gables. It now houses a museum *(closed Mon., $)* of art from nearby churches.

The most conspicuous house on the square is No. 15, **House at the Chalice** (Dům U Kalicha) from 1537, capped by an artichoke-shaped turret representing the Hussite symbol. Close to it, at No. 12, **House at the Black Eagle** (Dům U Černého orla), features chocolate-colored sgraffito.

At the far end of the square, at Michalská 7, is the **North Bohemia Fine Arts Gallery** (Severočeská galerie vytvarného umení), founded in 1874. The core of the collection is six panels from an altarpiece by the

Summer Retreat

Ottavio Broggio was not only a church architect. At Ploskovice, 4 miles (6 km) northeast of Litoměřice, is a fine country house he built in 1720. In the 1850s Emperor Ferdinand V and his family used this as a summer residence. They commissioned the sparkling neo-rococo interior decoration by Josef Navrátil. A guided tour takes you through the private rooms of the emperor and empress, and a splendid hall decorated with murals by Václav Reiner (1689–1743). Set in a walled park, this large white mansion is charmingly ornamented and has statues and urns adorning the top balustrades.

Terezín

A visit to Terezín will give you deep insight into some of World War II's darkest days. The Habsburgs built the town as a fortified garrison and prison in the 1780s, which was dreadful enough. But more atrocious years came with the Nazis, who expelled the residents and converted the town into a ghetto camp. Thousands of Jews from all over Europe were brought here; many died of hunger and disease, many more were shipped to death camps (also see pp. 212–213).

The tranquil main square of Terezín gives no hint of its sobering history.

The town was designed on a formal grid plan surrounded by a double set of immense brick fortifications 2.5 miles long (4 km), linked by underground tunnels, which are still intact. The Small Fortress had long been a state jail for political prisoners. The assassin of Archduke Franz Ferdinand, Gavrilo Princep, was held here until his death in 1918. In June 1940, the German SS took over the Small Fortress. It became a frequent destination for Resistance and political opponents, many of whom were executed here. Tours of the fortress are a vivid reminder of Nazi criminality, but greater imagination is needed to visualize the streets of the town itself as the vast ghetto it became.

Ghetto Museum

The starting point for any visit should be the Ghetto Museum (Muzeum ghetta), founded in 1991 and established in the center of the town on Komenského. It incorporates a memorial to the thousands of children who died here. The drawings made by them are movingly displayed. A video contrasts segments of the Nazi propaganda films that reversed the truth about Terezín with contemporary drawings portraying the reality of the camp. You can buy a ticket that gives you admission to all the sites, and pick up useful maps that will show you their location.

Magdeburg Barracks

One of these sites is the Magdeburg Barracks (Magdeburská kasárna), a few blocks to the south on Tyršova, in the building where the self-governing council of the ghetto had its offices. Exhibits chronicle the camp's cultural life, and tell of the musicians, artists, and writers who continued to work productively. Other exhibits include a reconstruction of a women's dormitory, and graphic drawings of life within the cramped ghetto. Some of the artists paid to produce them were dispatched to the Small Fortress and executed for having perpetrated "propaganda of horror" with their all too realistic drawings.

Small Fortress

The Small Fortress (Malá pevnost) stands on the edge of the town on the other side of the Ohře River. Although there had always been a prison here, beginning in 1940 it became a prison operated by the SS. As

INSIDER TIP:

Despite its grim history, Terezín is still full of life. After visiting the sites, let it all sink in while enjoying traditional dishes at Atypik Café, on the main square.

—PHIL HEIJMANS
Writer & photographer,
The Prague Post

you approach, you see the large Christian and Jewish cemeteries, with their unmarked gravestones. Within the sprawling fortress, you can visit the cramped cell blocks and solitary confinement cells.

Crematorium

The crematorium, located about half a mile (1 km) south of the main museum, was used to dispose of the bodies of the 2,500 individuals who died or were executed in the fortress and at least 30,000 more who died in the ghetto. Alongside the crematorium is a Jewish cemetery on the site of mass graves. When the burial space was full, it became necessary to burn the dead here. ∎

Terezín
🅐 207 D2
🚌 Bus from Prague

Ghetto Museum
✉ Komenského, 41155
☎ 416 782 225
💲 $$$
www.pamatnik-terezin.cz

The Story of Terezín

Although most Jews of central Europe had since the Middle Ages encountered anti-Semitism as an everyday fact of life, anti-Jewish discrimination and persecution were not a prominent feature of Czech life. Jewish communities had been established for centuries throughout Bohemia and Moravia, and synagogues in Prague, Plzeň, and other cities testify to their prosperity by the mid-19th century.

Inevitably the nation could not remain untouched by the political upheavals of the 1930s. The rise of Hitler unleashed the desire of the Sudeten Germans to be incorporated within the Third Reich, and encouraged anti-Semitic feelings.

Even after the invasion of Czechoslovakia in 1939, the mass murders that marked Nazi oppression in Poland remained uncommon here. Instead, the Nazis deported Bohemian and Moravian Jews to the newly created "ghetto" at Terezín (known in German as Theresienstadt).

Beginning in November 1941, the 3,500 people who inhabited Terezín were relocated, and behind its massive fortifications the barracks were converted into a concentration camp. Although this was no extermination camp, conditions were so terrible that some 33,000 of the inmates died of disease and hunger during the war. Despite the overcrowding and prison conditions, the camp was partly self-governing, and the inmates ran schools and cultural activities, largely as a propaganda exercise to show that the Jews were being treated well.

Beginning in October 1942, Terezín was used as a transit camp for 155,000 Jews (105,000 of whom were under the age of 15) from all over Europe. From that point forward, many of those who survived the privations of Terezín were shipped onward to Polish ghettoes such as Łodz or directly to Auschwitz and other extermination camps.

One of the most grotesque features of Terezín was that the Nazis disguised part of it as a show camp. They made a film that depicted the inmates leading a normal life, visiting banks and shops that did not in fact exist, while bands played and tea parties were enjoyed in manicured gardens. It also showed the arrival of Jewish children from Holland and the warm welcome they received from the camp commandant. What this propaganda film did not show was these same children being sent to Auschwitz a few days later.

Scenes of everyday life were staged in June 1944 for the benefit of a Red Cross delegation, which was not shown the barracks where the surviving inmates were housed in squalid conditions. They were shown the Ghetto Elder touring the ghetto in a chauffeur-driven car, but they did not know that the "chauffeur" was an SS officer in disguise. The delegation was fooled and issued a favorable report on the ghetto. When the camp was liberated by Soviet forces on May 8, 1945, there were 17,500 emaciated survivors. Among them were writers Ivan Klíma and Arnošt Lustig, who wrote movingly about the camp and their war experiences. But most of the writers and artists who came to Terezín never left.

A stark Jewish memorial in the cemetery at Terezín

A colossal star of David reminds visitors to Terezín cemetery that most of those who died here were Jewish inmates of the camp.

Even in this dreadful place, Jews managed to maintain a cultural life: Plays and operas were staged, sporting activities took place, and children drew and painted and wrote poems.

So in Terezín there is much to lift the spirits: the unquenchable creativity of people of all ages and from all parts of Europe who knew they would never see their homes again.

Jizerské Hory

In the eastern corner of northern Bohemia, near the Polish border, are the Jizerské hory (Jizera Mountains), which in effect are the western extension of the more dramatic Krkonoše (Giant Mountains) of eastern Bohemia (see pp. 234–237). This is lovely countryside with hillsides clad in spruce forests and flower-sprinkled meadows. Although the area was once deforested by acid rain, it once again attracts hikers, skiers, and weekenders from Prague.

A peaceful remoteness descends on Jizerské in winter.

Although the Jizera Mountains don't reach the heights of their Krkonoše counterparts, some rise to over 3,600 feet (1,100 m). Visitors flock here, both from the Czech Republic and from parts of Poland and Germany just across the borders. For the best view of the region, drive out of Liberec (see p. 215), a once prosperous manufacturing city near the Polish border, and to the top of Mount Ještěd, where you can eat at the revolving restaurant.

Frýdlant

In a valley among the hills north of Liberec is the village of **Frýdlant.** Its melancholy **castle** is believed to have been one of the models for Franz Kafka's novel *Das Schloss (The Castle)*. There's no direct evidence for this, though it is known that Kafka did visit the castle as part of his job when working for an insurance company. It stands on a wooded basalt crag on the edge of town, overlooking the Smědá River.

The castle combines a mixture of elements from several different periods: The 13th-century medieval fortifications and round tower blend in with Renaissance and neo-Gothic buildings. Much of what is visible today is the work of the 16th-century Lombard architect

---

EXPERIENCE: Homestays

Slavs are deservedly well known for their hospitality, and the best way to get to really know your hosts is, of course, to bunk with them and share a dinner table. In Prague, one accommodation agency, **Stop City** (www.stopcity.com), specializes in rooms in flats, but the owners they list don't usually expect to share their lives. For that, a network such as **Couchsurfing** (www.couchsurfing.org) is better set up.

More atmospheric exchanges can be found in the Czech countryside and smaller towns, thanks to a blossoming of agro-tourism/homestay ventures. One worth considering is the **Žofin Goat Farm** (www.kozy-zofin.wz.cz) in Horní Podluží, in the Lužické Mountains nature preserve near Varnsdorf. This family-run dairy specializes in goat milk and cheese, and you're welcome to help with the milking.

Marco Spazzio. It was owned, as were most of the castles in the region, by Albrecht von Wallenstein (Valdštejn), who was made Duke of Frýdlant (see pp. 31–32), and subsequently by the Clam-Gallas family, who renovated the buildings.

There has been a museum in the castle since 1801. The mostly neo-Gothic interior is richly furnished. There is a fine collection of paintings by Bohemian baroque masters, but to get inside, you must join a very lengthy guided tour.

It's also worth stopping in the village center to look at the **Church of the Holy Cross** (Kostel Nalezení sv. Kříže), which contains a magnificent Renaissance tomb by the Dutch sculptor Gerhard Heinrich.

Liberec

Before its German population was expelled in 1945, Liberec was an extremely prosperous industrial city, producing mainly textiles. Its fantastical Flemish-style neo-Gothic **town hall** (radnice) of 1893 is undeniably impressive, though not typically Bohemian. The style is appropriate, since the town was founded in the Middle Ages by Flemish linen weavers. It was

also the hometown of Konrad Henlein, who led the movement for the Sudeten Germans to be united with Nazi Germany.

Liberec's **château** was once owned by the Clam-Gallas family, one of the richest and most powerful in Bohemia. Next to it is the **gallery** of paintings from the collection of Johann Liebig, Liberec's leading textile magnate. The **Museum of Northern Bohemia** (Severočeské muzeum) contains medieval tapestries and interesting exhibits relating to local industries.

Lázně Libverda

In the heart of the hills, some 8 miles (12 km) east of Frýdlant is the small spa of Lázně Libverda. This seems to be one of the few spas Goethe didn't visit, but Carl Maria von Weber wrote part of his opera *Der Freischutz* here in 1821. The location is charming and undeniably tranquil, though it's very low-key. As a social venue, Lázně Libverda can hardly compete with the more famous spas of western Bohemia. It does offer guesthouses, restaurants, springs, and undemanding walks in the hills, however. ∎

Frýdlant

- ⚑ 207 F4
- ✉ 15 miles (23 km) N of Liberec
- 🚆 Train from Liberec

Frýdlant Castle

- 🕐 Closed Mon. & Nov.–March
- 💲 $$–$$$

Liberec

- ⚑ 207 F3
- ✉ 63 miles (106 km) N of Prague on route E65

Visitor Information

- ✉ Náměstí Dr. E. Beneše 1 Liberec
- ☎ 485 101 709
- **www.infolbc.cz**

Museum of Northern Bohemia

- ✉ Masarykova 11
- 🕐 Closed Mon.

A Drive Through České Švýcarsko

In sharp contrast to much of the industrialized north of Bohemia is the delightful national park known as České Švýcarsko (Czech Switzerland). The region acquired its name not from Czech tourism officials, but from Swiss Romantic artists who visited it in the 1770s. Between Hřensko and Česká Kamenice, the hills are pierced by small valleys packed with well-kept villages of half-timbered cottages.

České Švýcarsko National Park

Concealed in the woods are the cliffs and rock pillars and sandstone formations that give the areas around Jetřichovice and Hřensko their drama. When, eons ago, volcanic rock reached the surface, fissures, canyons, and other stunning rock formations were created. Unfortunately, air pollution has hastened the erosion of these natural wonders. But most recently the region is valued as a protected zone for flora and fauna, and it has an outstanding collection of fern species within its boundaries. Today, numerous guesthouses cater to the increasing number of tourists.

České Švýcarsko is best approached from **Hřensko ❶**, north of Děčín. The village sits in a gorge edged by overhanging rocks where it joins the Labe Valley. Hřensko itself is quite a pretty place, with its half-timbered cottages in Germanic style, but unfortunately not enhanced by the profusion of roadside stalls selling cheap souvenirs.

In the woods east of Hřensko, you'll find **Pravčická brána**, the largest natural stone bridge in central Europe, some 85 feet across (26 m) and 68 feet high (21 m), deep. It can only be reached on foo—a 3-mile (5 km) hike from the village. A slightly shorter path is available from Mezní Louka, where you can leave your car; there is ample parking at Hřensko, too. Mezní Louka has a hotel and campsite if you wish to explore farther. A path from the village leads in an easterly direction to another less spectacular stone bridge, the **Malá Pravčická brána**.

From Mezní Louka you can drive a short distance southwest to the hamlet of **Mezná ❷**,

perched above the Kamenice gorge, which can be crossed at this point over a wooden bridge. Hikers often come to Mezná, then return by boat to Hřensko. It's a tranquil place, on grassy slopes among the forests. Even in summer it's not crowded, and there are a handful of rustic guesthouses and restaurants.

Outside the Park

Take the main road east from Mezní Louka to **Jetřichovice ❸**, a charming village where some of the old farmhouses have been converted into simple guesthouses. Continue southward to the town of **Česká Kamenice ❹**, where there is a fine baroque chapel. Another notable rock formation lies 3 miles (5 km) east of here, just beyond Kamenický Šenov. This is the **Panská skála,** thousands of polygonal basalt columns that resemble organ pipes lined up in a row; they formed when molten basalt cooled.

Return to Česká Kamenice and continue toward Děčín via **Benešov nad Ploučnicí ❺**, with two interesting 16th-century **castles**

NOT TO BE MISSED:

Pravčická brána • Mezná • Panská skála • Rose Garden

(closed Mon. May–Sept.; Mon.–Tues. April & Oct.; & Nov.–March, $–$$$). The lower of the two has Renaissance interiors and a collection of furniture, armor, and Oriental art. The upper castle offers changing art exhibitions and some empty rooms with splendid painted ceilings.

České Švýcarsko continues west to Děčín, you'll return here later, so carry on past the town on route 13 to Libouchec, where a road leads north to **Tisá ❻** and the border town

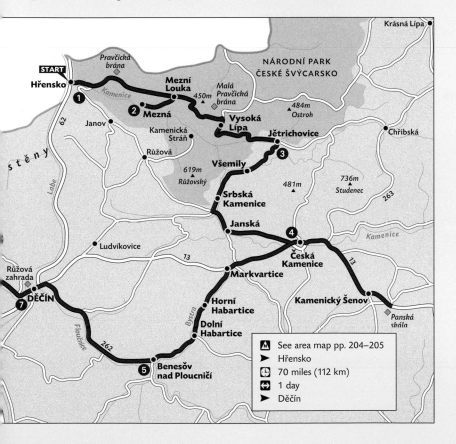

Krásná Lípa

START
Hřensko ❶
Pravčická brána
Mezní Louka
450m
Malá Pravčická brána
NÁRODNÍ PARK ČESKÉ ŠVÝCARSKO
Kamenice
❷ Mezná
Janov
Kamenická Stráň
Růžová
Vysoká Lípa
484m Ostroh
Jětrichovice ❸
Chřibská
stěny
619m Růžovský
Všemily
Srbská Kamenice
481m
736m Studenec
263
Labe
Janská
Ludvíkovice
❹
Česká Kamenice
Kamenice
13
13
Růžová zahrada
DĚČÍN ❼
Markvartice
Kamenický Šenov
Panská skála
Horní Habartice
Bystra
Dolní Habartice
262
Ploučnice
Benešov nad Ploučnicí ❺

See area map pp. 204–205
► Hřensko
🕐 70 miles (112 km)
⬌ 1 day
► Děčín

Remarkable Pravčická brána, east of Hřensko, is the largest stone bridge of its kind in central Europe.

of **Rájec.** Tisá has a distinctive landscape of sandstone boulders (Tiské stěny), accessible by footpath from the village. The other point of interest in this area is the table-topped mountain called **Děčínský Sněžník,** between Děčín and Ostrov. Hiking trails from either town lead up to it.

Drive to Jilově on route 13, and then return to **Děčín ⑦**. Like Ústí nad Labem (see pp. 221–222), Děčín is a heavily industrialized inland port along the Labe River. Its late 18th-century castle spreads along its crag like a cat on a fence; it is

approached through a gateway and by a long ramp. Left derelict after decades of abuse by Czech, German, and Soviet soldiers, the castle is gradually being restored. At the top of the ramp on the right you come to the splendid baroque **Rose Garden** (Růžová zahrada; $), originally planted in the 1670s by Maximilian Thun-Hohenstein, whose family owned the castle until 1932. It's an enchanting spot, perched high above the town and decorated with pavilions, statues, and urns. There is also a small marionette museum *(closed Mon., $).*

More Places to Visit in Northern Bohemia

Jablonec nad Nisou

Jablonec nad Nisou was a very prosperous, German-speaking town until 1945. Its turn-of-the-20th-century villas and grand constructivist municipal buildings from the 1920s and 1930s testify to the success of the local costume jewelry and brass industries. The **Museum of Glass and Jewelry** (Muzeum skla a bižuterie) justifies a visit for its first-rate collections.

🅰 207 F3 ✉ 8 miles (14 km) E of Liberec on route 14 🚊 Tram 11 from Liberec **Visitor information** *www.msb-jablonec .cz* ✉ Mírové náměstí 19, 46751 Jablonec ☎ 483 369 081 🕐 Closed Sun. **Museum of Glass and Jewelry** ✉ U Muzea 4 🕐 Closed Mon. & Oct.–May.

Jablonné v Podještědí

Dominating the town of Jablonné v Podještědí is its large domed **church** with billowing pink-and-white facade, built by the Austrian baroque architect Johann Lukas von Hildebrandt in 1699. In the church's crypt you will find the remains of mummified corpses, but to see them you have to sign up for a guided tour of the monastic complex.

Two miles (3 km) east of town lies **Lemberk,** a castle of 13th-century origin which was remodeled by General Wallenstein (Valdštejn). Its richly furnished rooms can also be visited on a guided tour.

🅰 207 E3 ✉ 13 miles (22 km) W of Liberec via route 35, then route 13 🚌 Bus from Prague's Florenc station, or from Karlovy Vary, and Liberec **Church** 🕐 Closed Mon. Tour: May–Sept. only **Lemberk Castle** 🕐 Closed Mon. May–Sept., Mon.– Fri. April & Oct., & Nov.–March 💲 $

Kadaň

The old double-walled town of Kadaň southwest of Chomutov was severely damaged during the Thirty Years' War. The main square is lined with arcaded houses dating from various periods, grouped around a tall plague column adorned with statuary. An elegant 15th-century white **tower** looks over the square, outclassing the 18th-century **church.** Across the square from the tower is Katová ulička, the Hangman's Lane, a covered passageway almost too narrow for two people to squeeze by each other. Tyršova leads to the frequently restored gray-green **castle.**

🅰 206 B2 ✉ 10 miles (15 km) SW of Chomutov on route 13, then left on route 568 🚊 Train from Prague

Klášterec nad Ohří

Klášterec nad Ohří, with its salmon-pink 17th-century **château** occupying a spur above the Ohře River, lies close to Kadaň.

Coal Mining Changes

Under the Communists, areas of northern Bohemia where coal is abundant were once moonscapes washed over by acid rain. Limits placed on brown coal, or lignite, mining were set during the 1990s, marking the rise of the Czech environmental movement. Progress looks to be in peril again, however: State energy officials have floated the idea of lifting these limits in light of fears that the current supply may run out by 2030 and Russia's repeated threats to curtail the westward flow of natural gas.

One Czech town in particular has become ground zero in the controversy. The historic hamlet of Horní Jiřetín, which sits at the very edge of a rich deposit, is expected to be leveled if mining begins. Watch for impassioned protests to arise if that plan goes forward.

Though greatly altered since it was built, the château contains a large collection of Bohemian porcelain; of equal interest is its park, adorned with statues by the baroque sculptor Jan Brokoff and home to a collection of rare central European trees. The town also has a spa built around a mineral spring; a park—complete with a pond—surrounds this mineral spring.

🅜 206 B2 ✉ 4 miles (6.5 km) W of Kadaň 🚆 Train from Prague **Château** 🕐 Closed Mon.–Fri. & Nov.–March. Guided tours: April–Oct. only 💲 $$

Louny

You enter the walled town of Louny through its commanding late Gothic gate, which along with the church tower is the only building to have survived a devastating fire in 1517. The skyline is pierced by the roof of the **Church of St. Nicholas** (Kostel sv. Mikuláše). The rib vaulting inside is typical of Benedikt Ried, who reconstructed the town in the 1520s. There is also sensational carving on the high altar of 1704, resembling a tropical jungle petrified in wood. The main square is unexceptional, except for one Renaissance house at No. 28 *(tel 0395 652 456)*; from its oriel window the authorities would pronounce the death sentence on unlucky (or criminal) citizens in the 16th and 17th centuries.

🅜 206 C2 ✉ 38 miles (63 km) NW of Prague on route 7 🚆 Train from Prague's Masarykovo nádraží

Most

In 1975 the entire town of Most was demolished and relocated in order to make way for lignite mines. Girdled by steel supports, the 16th-century **Church of the Assumption of Our Lady** (Kostel Nanebevzetí Panny Marie) was shifted on a specially built railroad line 2,750 feet (840 m) from its original location to another site. It was worth saving, for it has a luminous interior filled with interesting examples of religious art roughly contemporaneous with the church. It was designed by Jakob Heilmann, a pupil of Benedikt Ried's, and has spectacular vaulting.

🅜 206 C2 ✉ 67 miles (112 km) NW of Prague via route 7 to Louny, then N on route 28 🕐 Closed Mon.–Tues. 💲 $ 🚆 Train from Prague

Osek

West of Teplice stands the resplendent Cistercian monastery at Osek. It retains its 13th-century chapter house and cloister, but the church itself is a baroque masterpiece by Ottavio Broggio (see pp. 208–209). The stuccoed interior is magnificent, if dilapidated; watch for the superb wooden

---

Czech Glass Struggles

Glassmaking has been a boon to the Czech lands for centuries, thanks to a combination of skilled craftsmen and the fine potash produced by beech trees in northern Bohemia. With Bohemian crystal well established even before Ireland moved into the act, this treasured export can be found all around the world—including the windows of Buckingham Palace. North Bohemian towns such as Jablonec nad Nisou and

Nový Bor are quiet these days, however, as former glass empires have shrunk with modernization and competition.

The global economic crunch that began in 2008 didn't help; one of the country's largest remaining glassmakers, Crystalex, announced that it was being sold and closing its 40-year-old Sklo Bohemia division. Like many older industries, Czech glass is not expected to fare well, thanks to globalization.

and gilt choir stalls. In the 1990s Cistercian monks returned to Osek, finally ending a long exile following their expulsion by the Communists.

🅰 206 C3 ✉ 7 miles (11 km) W of Teplice via route 27 🕒 Closed Sun. a.m. & all Mon. April–June & Sept., & Nov.–March 🚊 $ 🚆 Train from Teplice

Roudnice nad Labem

Near the center of town stands the colossal rust-and-white neoclassical château that once belonged to the Lobkowicz family. It was designed by Francesco Caratti in the 1660s, but, sadly, it has become dilapidated and is closed to the public. The former riding school, outside the château walls, is now a **gallery** containing a major collection of modern Czech art, focused around a

While stemware is relatively recent, Stone Age glass beads have been found in the Czech Republic.

INSIDER TIP:

Although the town of Roudnice nad Labem can hardly compete with the rich offerings of other destinations in Northern Bohemia, its grapes have been winning attention for years. Don't pass up a chance at Château Roudnice wine.

—WILL TIZARD
National Geographic contributor

collection by painter Antonín Slavíček.

🅰 207 D2 ✉ 30 miles (50 km) NW of Prague via E55 **Gallery** 🕒 Closed Mon. 🚊 $

Teplice

A town of astonishing contrasts, Teplice lies close to the German border. You will find entire streets of derelict buildings, blackened with dirt, left empty when the German

population was expelled in 1945. Yet in the core of the town are delightful parks overlooked by elegant spa buildings. Teplice was a spa in the 11th century, if not earlier, but was developed only in the 18th century. Beethoven, Liszt, Wagner, and Ibsen were among its famous visitors. In 1813 the rulers of Austria, Russia, and Prussia met here to sign the "Holy Alliance" against Napoleon. Numerous villas in secession and neoclassical styles testify to the former opulence of the town. On the main square, **Zámecké náměstí,** is an enormous plague column of 1718 by Matthias Braun; the neoclassical castle, now the regional **museum;** and the castle's adjoining church. The square's most handsome mansion has become a hotel, the Prince de Ligne (see p. 315). The castle park offers a useful starting point for many walking trails.

🅰 206 C3 ✉ 52 miles (87 km) NW of Prague via E55, then route 8 🚆 Train from Prague **Museum** www.muzeum-teplice.cz ✉ Zámecké náměstí 14 ☎ 417 537 869, 🕒 Closed Mon. 🚊 $

Ústí nad Labem

Ústí nad Labem is the biggest town in northern Bohemia and the largest port on the Labe River, except for distant Hamburg. The ruinous **castle** on a protruding basalt rock is known as Střekov, and this romantic pile gives Ústí a certain drama. Wagner was inspired to write *Tannhäuser* following a visit here.

The one thing to detain you in this little heavily industrial town is the **cathedral** dating from the early 16th century, its steeple thrown off balance after a bombing raid during World War II, and a **theater** in secession style. The town's reputation was severely damaged in 1999 when the council constructed a wall to separate the Roma people, otherwise known as Gypsies, from the Czech communities. The building of this wall prompted international protests, and also confirmed the Roma's own long-held view that they were being actively discriminated against by certain Czech authorities. A short while later the wall was taken down.

🅰 207 D3 ✉ 54 miles (90 km) N of Prague via E55 🚆 Train from Prague

Strekov Castle 🕒 Closed Mon. & Jan.–March 💲 $

Žatec

Žatec is a faded but dignified little town, surrounded by fields in which the best hops in Bohemia have been grown for centuries (see pp. 186–187). To learn more about the tradition of hops growing and beermaking, visit the **Hops Museum** *(Mostecka 2580, tel 397 626 125)* in town. The often renovated town hall heads the main square and looks onto a plague column reminiscent of petrified profiteroles. Behind the town hall is the hefty medieval **Church of the Assumption of Our Lady** (Kostel Nanebevzetí Panny Marie), which is guarded by a row of baroque statuary. To the left of the church stands one of the medieval town gates, and behind it is what is left of the castle *(hrad),* now a brewery.

🅰 206 B2 ✉ 50 miles (83 km) W of Prague via route 7, then left on route 27 🚆 Train from Prague

It is hard to tell from the pristine interior that, in 1975, Most's entire church was shifted far from its original site, which is now a lignite mine.

Bohemia's winter sports center in the Giant Mountains, with the hills, towns, and castles of Český ráj beckoning in summer

Eastern Bohemia

1729 sundial, Litomyšl castle

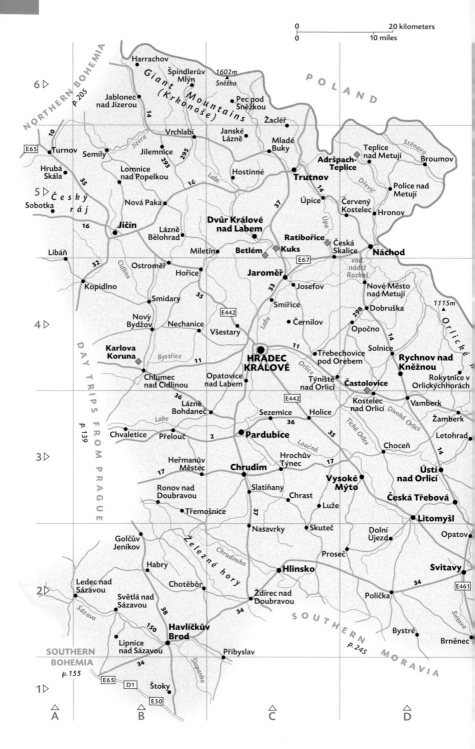

0   20 kilometers

0   10 miles

NORTHERN BOHEMIA
p.205

POLAND

Harrachov

Giant Mountains (Krkonoše)

Špindlerův Mlýn

1602m Sněžka

Jablonec nad Jizerou

Pec pod Sněžkou

Žacléř

Vrchlabí

Janské Lázně

Mladé Buky

Teplice nad Metují

Stěnava

Broumov

E65   Turnov   Semily   Jilemnice

Hrubá Skála

Lomnice nad Popelkou

Hostinné

Adršpach-Teplice

Trutnov

Police nad Metují

5 ▷ Č e s k ý
r á j

Sobotka

Nová Paka

Úpice

Červený Kostelec   Hronov

Dvůr Králové nad Labem

Lázně Bělohrad

Ratibořice

Česká Skalice

Náchod

Libáň

Ostroměř

Miletín   Betlém   Kuks

E67

Hořice

Jaroměř

vod. nádrž Rozkoš

Kopidlno

Smidary

Josefov

Nové Město nad Metují

1115m

Nový Bydžov

Nechanice

E442

Smiřice

Všestary

Černilov

Dobruška

Opočno

Orlické

4 ▷

DAY TRIPS FROM PRAGUE
p.139

Karlova Koruna

Bystřice

HRADEC KRÁLOVÉ

Orlice

Třebechovice pod Orebem

Solnice

Rychnov nad Kněžnou

Chlumec nad Cidlinou

Opatovice nad Labem

Týniště nad Orlicí

Častolovice

Rokytnice v Orlickýchhorách

Lázně Bohdaneč

Sezemice

Holice

Kostelec nad Orlicí

Divoká Orlice

Vamberk

Žamberk

Chvaletice   Přelouč

Pardubice

36

Tichá Orlice

Choceň

Letohrad

3 ▷

Heřmanův Městec

Chrudim

Hrochův Týnec

Vysoké Mýto

Ústí nad Orlicí

Ronov nad Doubravou

Slatiňany

Chrast

Luže

Česká Třebová

Třemošnice

Litomyšl

Nasavrky   Skuteč

Dolní Újezd

Opatov

Golčův Jeníkov

Železné hory

Proseč

Habry

Chrudimka

Hlinsko

Svitavy

Ledeč nad Sázavou

Chotěbor

Ždírec nad Doubravou

Polička

E461

Světlá nad Sázavou

SOUTHERN
MORAVIA
p.245

2 ▷

Sázava

150

Havlíčkův Brod

Bystré

Brněnec

Svitava

SOUTHERN BOHEMIA
p.155

Lipnice nad Sázavou

Přibyslav

1 ▷

E65   D1   Štoky

E50

△ A   △ B   △ C   △ D

Eastern Bohemia

Remote eastern Bohemia has the republic's most spectacular scenery. The northern frontier with Poland is dominated by the Krkonoše mountains, high enough to be a popular skiing resort in winter; in summer you can explore the wilds on hiking trails. More gentle in its contours, but equally popular with Czech visitors and tourists alike, is Český ráj (Czech Paradise) near Turnov, a rolling landscape of ruined castles and strange rock formations.

If you travel farther south in eastern Bohemia, however, the countryside is flatter and frankly not very appealing. This is made up for by the many interesting towns that flourished here. The main one is Hradec Králové, which has all the usual attractions of a Bohemian town—large main square, churches, museums—but was also a center for Czech cubist architecture, much of which has survived. Here, too, is one of the best Czech modern art museums. Litomyšl is the birthplace of the composer Smetana, and it has an especially lovely Renaissance castle. There is much to see in eastern Bohemia, most of it rewardingly eccentric. Kuks was once a large, dramatically sited spa development—a rich man's fancy that evolved into a private resort. But on December 22, 1740, the complex was destroyed overnight by flash floods.

Today only part of the spa remains intact, yet it is a haunting place. Josefov is a rather severe Austro-Hungarian garrison town. Its layout, fortifications, and atmosphere will be familiar to those who have already visited Terezín.

There is no shortage of interesting castles and châteaus to visit in eastern Bohemia. Náchod, Pardubice, Opočno, and Nové Město nad Metují have much to recommend them, and Karlova Koruna is another masterpiece by that baroque genius Santini. The large château at Častolovice is one of the few stately homes in the republic where it is possible to stay, though this trend is set to continue as more and more country mansions and castles are reinvented by their original owners. ■

NOT TO BE MISSED:

Hradec Králové

Hradec Králové was founded in the 14th century and 500 years later was the second most important town in Bohemia. It offers all the attractions of most Bohemian towns, but an abundance of early 20th-century architecture and two notable museums make Hradec Králové particularly interesting. It was a Hussite fortress in the 16th century and fully fortified in the 18th century; although the fortifications were subsequently demolished, traces of the old walls are still visible.

The main square of Hradec Králové, one of the oldest settlements in the Czech Republic

Hradec Králové

🄰 224 C4

✉ 62 miles (100 km) E of Prague via route E67 to end, then route 11

🚆 Train from Prague & Brno. Bus from Prague

Hradec Králové lies along the banks of the Orlice and Labe Rivers. On one side of the Labe stands the tranquil old town on a long ridge, much of which is occupied by Velké náměstí, the large main square. Across the river is the new town, which became a showcase for the best architects of the early 20th century. One end of Velké náměstí is dominated by a huge 16th-century bell tower,

the **White Tower** (Bílá věž). The structure dwarfs even the turreted towers of the lofty Gothic brick cathedral next to it and gives a bird's-eye view over the town. The only medieval furnishings remaining in the cathedral are the tall stone tabernacle of 1497 in the choir and a paneled altarpiece of 1494 in the south aisle. In the north aisle is a painting of St. Anthony by Petr Brandl (about 1730), whose work adorns so many churches in Prague. What makes the main square visually arresting is the sheer variety of buildings, from modest arcaded merchants' houses with shops beneath to the baroque elegance of the bishop's palace of 1716. In the middle of the square is a grandiose plague column of 1717 and a well with a delightfully ornate ironwork grille.

At the other end of the square you'll find the pretty, yellow 17th-century Jesuit church by Carlo Lurago. Its interior features paintings by Brandl. Standing next to it is the Jesuit college.

The **Gallery of Modern Art** (Galerie moderního umění), opposite the Jesuit College, is housed in a gray secession-style building of 1912 by Osvald Polívka, and has an

INSIDER TIP:

In October Hradec Králové hosts "Jazz Goes to Town," a week-long festival showcasing world-famous jazz artists.

—STEPHANIE ROBICHAUX
National Geographic contributor

outstanding collection. There are voluptuous early works by Mucha (1860–1939), which are quite different from the posters for which he became well known. Watch for the arresting portraits and other Cézanne-influenced works by Bohumil Kubišta (1884–1918). Some playful and colorful paintings

by Josef Čapek (1887–1945) are thoroughly representative of his cubist technique. Amid the profusion of works in this museum, try not to miss the surreal abstracts by Josef Šíma (1891–1971) and good cubist works by Emil Filla (1883–1953).

The often remodeled town hall is next to the White Tower, and nearby Ke kopečku leads down to the river, passing the Hotel Bystrica. The hotel was designed by the pioneering architect Jan Kotěra but is now more or less derelict.

Down on the embankment, on Eliščino nábřeží, stands the striking **Museum of Eastern Bohemia,** also designed by Kotěra in 1912. It blends secession pretensions— huge seated statues by Stanislav Sucharda, representing History and Industry, flank the entrance—with a geometric strength and originality of its own. Inside there are fine stained-glass windows by František Kysela, but the actual collections are of little interest, except for the model of the town as it appeared in 1865.

Kotěra also designed the main bridge nearby, which leads into the heart of the new town, much of which was laid out by Josef Gočár, his pupil. Gočár's work can be seen to best advantage in Masarykovo náměstí, where he employed Czech cubist elements yet retained the proportions and gentle coloring of traditional vernacular Czech architecture. Less appealing is the harsh, functionalist stadium he built on the banks of the Orlice River. Václav Rejchl designed the town's railroad station, with its elegant clock tower. ■

Visitor Information

✉ Infocentrum, Gočárova 33, near bus station
☎ 495 534 482
www.ic-hk.cz

White Tower
🕐 Closed Oct.– March
💲 $
www.bilavez.cz

Gallery of Modern Art
✉ Velké náměstí 139
☎ 495 514 893
🕐 Closed Mon.
💲 $
www.galeriehk.cz

Museum of Eastern Bohemia
✉ Eliščino nábřeží 465
☎ 495 512 462
🕐 Closed Mon.
💲 $
www.muzeumhk.cz

Litomyšl

Litomyšl has a knack for making itself known. "Smetanov Litomyšl," the international opera festival held in the town each summer, is a long-standing event. Luckily for Litomyšl, seven European presidents chose the town for a summit meeting in 1994, and the authorities were galvanized into restoring the town's rich collection of noteworthy buildings, which are now in impeccable condition.

The gabled, sgraffitoed château at Litomyšl is one of Bohemia's finest Renaissance palaces.

Litomyšl

◩ 224 D3

✉ 98 miles (164 km) E of Prague. Route 2 to Pardubice, then route 36 to Holice and SE on route 35

🚍 Bus from Prague

A castle was erected here a thousand years ago, and a town was founded around it in 1259. Litomyšl soon acquired importance as the seat of a bishopric, but that came to an end after the Hussite general Jan Žižka captured the town in 1421.

The main square, Smetanovo náměstí, resembles a long, broad, and curved high street, with arcaded houses of all periods lining both sides. Number 61, **At the Knights** (U rytířů), is the most spectacular: Its flamboyant Renaissance facade dates from 1546, statues of knights flank the decorated stone windows, and there is an impressive coffered ceiling inside.

Behind this house, along Boženy Němcové, which runs parallel to the square, are a number of churches, including a large yellow one, by Giovanni

Alliprandi and František Kaňka, on a rampart reached by covered steps from the little square below. Across from the church is the magnificent sgraffitoed and gabled **château,** one of several owned by the Pernštejns, a noble Moravian family who were active and powerful beginning in the late 13th century. It was built by the Aostali brothers in the 1570s. Along one side of the château is a sundial dated 1728 and—a curious feature—windows that look not into rooms but instead into the splendid three-tiered, galleried courtyard. The château still has its perfect little theater, constructed in 1797 and complete with original scenery by Josef Platzer.

The guided tour of the château takes you through elegantly furnished rooms and porcelain collections, and it is worth seeing the theater. The former riding school displays casts—but not originals—of classical antiquities *(closed Mon. & Oct.–April, $).*

Bedřich Smetana's father managed the castle brewery, across from the castle courtyard's portal, and it was here that the composer was born in 1824.

The small **Smetana Museum** commemorates his life.

In addition to these cultural treasures, Litomyšl has more offbeat charms. With the castle to your left, take the first right and walk to Terézy Novákové 75, an outwardly unremarkable house known as the **Portmoneum** (after its owner, Josef Portman). In the 1920s, Portman commissioned artist Josef Váchal, nephew of Mikoláš Aleš, to decorate the interior. He coated the walls with bizarre murals that are full of religious and mystical allusions; he designed the furnishings, too. ∎

INSIDER TIP:

Don't miss the chance to check out Josef Váchal's eerie, primitivist work in the Postmoneum. Considered something of a Czech William Blake, he was a demonically inspired printmaker and poet.

—WILL TIZARD
National Geographic contributor

Visitor Information

☒ Smetanovo náměstí 72
☏ 461 612 161
www.litomysl.cz

Château
☒ Jiráskova 133
🕐 Closed Mon. May–Sept., Mon.–Fri. April & Oct., & all Nov.–March
$ $$–$$$

Smetana Museum
🕐 Closed Mon. May–Sept., Mon.–Fri. April & Oct., & all Nov.–March
$ $

Portmoneum
☒ Terézy Novákové 75
☏ 461 612 020
🕐 Closed Mon. & Oct.–April
$ $

Music Festivals

With warm summer weather come a host of open-air music festivals of all stripes, covering every genre of music—from blues to traditional central European folk to rock. The biggest rock music event of the year is surely the Trutnov Open Air Music Festival *(www.festivaltrutnov.cz),* which takes place every August. Known since 1987 as a kind of Czech Woodstock (complete with thousands of youthful, sometimes muddy, fans), Trutnov is a grand tradition at which every serious local rock band must be seen.

Like rock-and-roll itself, the festival is so tied up with the history of Czech free expression that a Trutnov T-shirt with Václav Havel's image was given to Barack Obama on his visit to Prague in 2009.

Bedřich Smetana

Although Antonín Dvořák may enjoy greater international renown, the Czechs hold Bedřich Smetana in even warmer regard as a composer. In large part this is because he reacted to Habsburg cultural domination by passionately espousing Czech nationalism. Because Czech legends and historical events are the basis for Smetana's operas and other works, he helped forge the cultural identity of the Czech people in the late 19th century.

Costumes for an 1866 production of *The Bartered Bride,* Smetana's best-loved opera

Bedřich Smetana was born in 1824 in Litomyšl (see pp. 228–229), where his father managed a brewery and was an enthusiastic amateur musician. German was the official language of Bohemia from 1784 onward, and German was the first language of the Smetana household. As a child Bedřich had a poor knowledge of Czech, which is ironic given his later role as a champion of Czech nationalism. It soon became clear that young Bedřich had inherited his father's gifts to an even greater degree, proving a fine string and piano player. He pursued his musical studies in Prague and became a much admired music

teacher there. His nationalist views, however, did not endear him to the authorities, and in the late 1850s he moved to Sweden to become conductor of the Gothenburg Philharmonic. Back in Prague four years later, Smetana became a leading advocate of the establishment of a national theater as a showcase for Czech drama and opera, and he later became its principal conductor.

At the same time he was, of course, composing. His best known work is the symphonic poem *Má vlast (My Home)* from 1875, especially its opening movement, which depicts the growth of the River Vltava from a modest stream to a proud river surging through the Czech heartlands. Almost as popular is his comic opera of 1866, *The Bartered Bride*. Set in a Bohemian village, it tackles the familiar theme of a young lady in love with one suitor, but under parental pressure to marry another, richer young man. Smetana seems to have felt some irritation at its enormous success, since he was more proud of his operas on historical and nationalist themes, such as *Dalibor* (1868) and *Libuše* (1881). His operas are regularly performed in Prague and at the music festival held each summer in his native Litomyšl.

Like Beethoven, he was to end his days in total deafness. In the 1870s he began to experience a very high note persistently whistling in one of his ears, a warning of the deafness that was to come. Even the complete inability to hear his own music did not prevent him from composing, and one of his most moving works is the string quartet of 1876 entitled *From My Life*, in which the music is interrupted by a high sustained note on the violin, an echo of the sound that heralded his isolating deafness. There was worse to come: Smetana's health steadily deteriorated and he suffered a stroke; he descended into madness and in 1884 died of syphilis at the age of 60.

Smetana was buried in the cemetery at Vyšehrad, in recognition of his status as a national hero. Ironically, at his death he was revered more for his work in establishing

Bedřich Smetana, even more than Dvořák, is the Czechs' favorite composer, thanks to the nationalist ardor that is expressed in his music.

the National Theater (see p. 121) than for his compositions, only a few of which were regularly performed during his own lifetime. It was Smetana who provided a special composition to be performed at the official opening of the theater in 1883, and when the building was reopened after the site was redesigned in 1983, the occasion was marked, appropriately, with a performance of his opera *Libuše*. The riverfront museum close to Charles Bridge (see p. 94 & below) has become his major memorial in the capital.

Seeing Smetana Scores

As unlikely as it seems, one of Prague's best collections of all things Smetana-related is located on the end of the Lávka pier just upstream of Charles Bridge in Old Town. Original manuscripts, along with the story of the composer's life and musical inspirations, fill the small **Smetana Museum** *(closed Tues., $)*. Although its location is not helped by sharing a building with a buzzy bar and disco (visits by day

are relatively free of competing noise), the reverence for the most important Bohemian composer in the Czech national awakening is unmistakable.

The period décor of these few rooms even manages to transport visitors to the era when Smetana's inspiring arias and chamber pieces filled the sitting rooms of the emerging gentry classes of the 19th century.

Kuks

Kuks, northwest of Jaroměř, is a baroque spa complex completely different from the better known spas in western Bohemia. It was founded by an aristocrat of German origin, Count Franz Anton von Sporck (1662–1738), who inherited the property and a large fortune at the tender age of 17. Finding that waters from a spring on his estate were rich in minerals, he resolved to build a spa complex, a project that began in 1694 and lasted for the next 25 years.

Some of the remaining buildings and Matthais Braun sculptures from the baroque Sporck spa

Kuks

- 224 C5
- 13 miles (20 km) N of Hradec Králové via route 33 to Jaroměř, then N on route 37
- Train from Hradec Králové

The elaborate resort lacked nothing: As well as the baths, hospital, and château, Sporck provided a theater, maze, and racecourse. The spa was completed in 1724 and became an ultrafashionable resort for central European high society, offering cultural diversions as well as the curative waters. There were pageants on the river, hunts, grand fairs, and concerts by Sporck's private orchestra. Johann Sebastian Bach and Petr Brandl were among the many artistic visitors to Kuks.

There was, however, a major design fault in the original layout: Many of the buildings in Kuks faced each other across the Labe

River. They were destroyed by raging floodwaters when the river broke its banks overnight on December 22, 1740. Worse still, the actual spring was found to be beyond repair after the waters receded, so there was no future for the spa. Sporck had died in 1738, and there was little incentive to restore Kuks. In 1901 much of the ruined château was torn down.

Nonetheless, what remains is still impressive. Overlooking the river from a broad terrace are the former **hospital** buildings, now being restored; the **oval chapel** by Giovanni Alliprandi; and the burial **crypt** of the Sporck family. The baroque **pharmacy** retains its original furnishings. But the best feature is the parade of 24 radiant **allegorical statues** (mostly copies; the originals have been taken indoors) by Matthias Braun (1684–1738). These are lined up along the hospital terrace and adorn the dark facades of the buildings. They depict the Vices on one side and the Virtues on the other. Perhaps predictably, the Vices seem more inspired than the Virtues.

Josefov

Not far from Kuks is Josefov, a garrison town on the outskirts of Jaroměř. In the 1780s Josefov was built as a Habsburg fortress on similar lines to those adopted at Terezín (see pp. 210–213). It is a forbidding place, with grim brick fortifications and drab mustard-colored barracks. Military buffs might enjoy taking a candlelit tour of the fort's underground tunnels that formed part of the communications network connecting different parts of the fortress. ■

INSIDER TIP:

If the stunning work of sculptor Matthias Braun here captivates you, be sure to see the original Charles Bridge pieces now residing in Prague's Lapidarium (see p. 136).

—WILL TIZARD
National Geographic contributor

Kuks Hospital & Pharmacy

🕐 Closed Mon. May–Sept., Mon.–Fri. April & Oct., & all Nov.–March

www.kuks-hospital.cz

Josefov

🔺 224 C4

✉ 12 miles (19 km) NE of Hradec Králové via route 33

🕐 Closed Mon. May–Sept.; Mon.–Fri. April & Oct., & all Nov.–March

$ $

Betlém

At Betlém, 2 miles (3 km) to the west of Kuks, Sporck created another park embellished with carvings of biblical scenes which were hewn from the rocks by Matthias Braun. These were completed in 1733 but are now very eroded. In Sporck's day this was a religious grove, with grottoes and hermitages hollowed out from the rocks on the wooded hillside, but many of the statues and buildings were carted off for use as building materials at Josefov and elsewhere. It's well marked with signs from Kuks and can be reached by foot from a parking lot after turning left at Žireč and continuing for 2 miles (3 km). Despite the damaged and eroded condition of the surviving carvings here, Betlém is a unique and moving experience, a rare fusion of art and nature.

Krkonoše

In the northern part of eastern Bohemia, pushing up toward the border with Silesia in Poland, rise the highest mountains in Bohemia, the Krkonoše (Giant Mountains). Sněžka, at 5,255 feet (1,602 m), is the highest peak in the Czech Republic. Much of the area has been protected as a national park since 1963.

Krkonoše mountains cover an immense area of fir-clad slopes and peaks.

Krkonoše

🅰 224 B6, C6

✉ 67 miles (107 km) NE of Prague via route E65 to Mladá Boleslav, E on route 16 to Nová Paka, then N on routes 293 & 195 to Vrchlabí

Most of the Krkonoše massif lies within Bohemia, though the 68 square miles (177 sq km) in Poland have also been protected since 1959. The ranges are fringed on the south by the spa of Janské Lázně and the town of Vrchlabí, and to the north by the resorts of Harrachov and Špindlerův Mlýn. Rivers such as the Jizera and the Labe, whose sources lie here, have carved deep valleys through the mountains, which are characterized by rounded summits rather than conical peaks. From November to April enough snow drapes the rounded ridges and crests of the mountains to make them perfect for winter sports.

Come summer, marked paths traverse the mountains for 625 miles (1,000 km), making this ideal territory for walkers as well. These trails are well supplied with huts (boudy) providing food and shelter. Dozens of stylized signs help to guide hikers and prevent them from getting lost, even in winter, when snow covers the ground. In summer there can be treacherous fogs and low temperatures at higher elevations, so be sure to take warm clothing and a good map. If you do not want to explore the Krkonoše on foot, you can view the mountains from the cable cars and chairlifts that glide up to the summits from Pec pod Sněžkou, Špindlerův Mlýn, and Janské Lázně.

INSIDER TIP:

Spend a night like a commissar in the Communist-era hotel (www.hotelhorizont.cz) at the foot of Sněžka, the Czech Republic's highest mountain. Ski or walk down the next morning.

--CHARLES RECKNAGEL
Radio Free Europe, Prague

One of the most popular walks straddles the ridges that separate Bohemia from Poland. Many visitors cannot resist climbing **Mount Snežka,** which can easily be done from Pec pod Sněžkou, some 2,733 feet (833 m) below the summit. The climb takes five to six hours round-trip.

VISITOR INFORMATION: There are information centers at all the resorts mentioned; they are well supplied with maps and current weather information, and they can usually help find accommodations, which are plentiful. The best centers are at Vrchlabí, on the main road next to the museum (*Dobrovského 3, tel 0438 451111*), and at Harrachov (*Harrachov 150, tel 0432 529600, fax 0432 529425, www.harrach ov.cz*).

EXPERIENCE: Skiing in Krkonoše

Czechs of all ages hit the slopes of the Krkonoše mountains every winter, the more adventurous ones flying down the slopes on snowboards. Those seeking a more communal experience, however, choose to run the hundreds of miles of cross-country trails. **Špyndlerův Mlýn** is the main hub of downhill activity *(http://tiscali.cz/skii/skii_center.html)*, so much so that it can be overrun at peak season time. But the views and invigorating air here make it worth the trip, and the chairlifts sometimes operate in summer so visitors can enjoy the spectacular vantage without necessarily having to rent skis.

Though not on the scale of Alpine ski resorts, this popular spot at 2,350 feet (715 m) above sea level does attract serious competition: The Women's Downhill World Cup was hosted at Špyndlerův Mlýn in 2009. Three speedy chairlifts and five cable lines carry nearly 9,000 skiers per hour, and affordable guesthouses abound in the area.

The most spectacular trail is the **Harrach path,** originally laid out by Count Harrach in 1879, but it is open only during the summer months. Many of the trails offer access to some of the fascinating features of the mountains: peat bogs, rock walls, and waterfalls.

Krkonoše National Park

The national park is of exceptional interest to naturalists, since the mountains are home to 165 species of birds—walking up near the peat bogs you might encounter black grouse or fan-tailed capercaillies.

The 1,300 species of flora found in the park include many rare trees and other plants that thrive in the unusual high peaty pastures characteristic of the Krkonoše. Though once visibly damaged from the acid rain caused by heavy industry pollution, this area is bouncing back and now features organic farms.

In medieval times the Giant Mountains were far more forbidding than they are today because

INSIDER TIP:

With its wellness spa, the eco-friendly Grund Resort *(www.grund resort.cz)* is ideal for a relaxing winter skiing getaway in Krkonoše mountains.

—ANDREA LIŠKOVÁ
CzechTourism USA

they were uninhabited. The forests inspired feelings of awe and apprehension that were often reinforced by the experiences of German and Italian prospectors, who began mining operations in the 16th century, and by farmers who felled some of the woodlands to provide summer pasture for their cattle. The mountains' hostile environment inspired terror of the unknown. This was personified in the form of a supernatural giant, Krakonoš, who was said to be responsible for the natural calamities that were part of the struggle for existence in the harsh climate.

Resort Towns

Only in the late 18th century did the mountains first attract tourists. In those days you needed to be intrepid, because the only accommodations were in mountain huts. In the following century the resorts that flourish today began to develop on the edges of the mountains.

The main and most convenient base for visitors to the area is located just outside the park at **Vrchlabí.** Along the main street are attractive wooden arcaded houses, some of which now contain a regional museum focusing on arts and crafts and the history of local tourism *(closed Mon., $).*

Just inside the park boundaries is the small spa town of **Janské Lázne,** founded in 1677 though not developed until the late 19th century. Compared with the main resorts in the mountains, this is a quiet place. But some may prefer its subdued charms to the raucousness of the other towns.

The road north to Harrachov follows the winding Jizera River, passing through villages and towns with charming wooden houses decorated with white vertical or horizontal lines. These are formed by painting the mortar between logs or by covering the building's sides with a delicate white lattice.

Harrachov *(www.harrachov-info.cz)* 75 miles (125 km) northeast of Prague is more attractive than Vrchlabí. Embedded in the forest, it has been a glass-making town since 1712 as well as a resort. Harrachov has a

festive atmosphere, especially in winter. In bad weather a visit to the **Skiing Museum** here helps while away an hour.

Špyndleruv Mlýn (see sidebar, opposite) and **Pec pod Snežkou** are among the republic's best ski resorts, though neither is a great beauty spot. ■

Skiing Museum

- ✉ Harrachov
- ☎ 481 529 169
- 🕐 Closed Mon.
- 💲 $

The Czech Republic's best winter sports resorts are located in Krkonoše mountains.

Český Ráj

Forested Český ráj, or Czech Paradise, a nature reserve south of Liberec, is a compact area strewn with bizarre rock formations and ancient castles. It typifies the astonishing rapidity with which the landscape can change as you travel in Bohemia. One moment you are among lush fields in a river valley; the next you are plunging through narrow gorges or traversing a high plateau. You'll find various geological wonders here—sandstone formations, stone bridges, and crystal formations.

The dual towers of Trosky Castle dominate the Český ráj.

Český Ráj
- 240; 224 A5–B5
- 50 miles (80 km) NE of Prague via E65 to Turnov

The densely wooded hills and steep slopes of the Český ráj have been a protected area since 1955. Ancient hilltop castles and other fine buildings of historic interest mark the skyline. In summer this small but spectacular area of sandstone hills and basalt outcrops is quite popular with weekending Prague residents and other visitors, but it rarely becomes overcrowded.

Between the northern and southern sections of the park is the town of Turnov, which is a handy if not very appealing base; Jičín, to the southeast, is more attractive but slightly less convenient. In both towns you can easily obtain detailed maps showing all the hiking trails and major geological attractions in the region. **Turnov** has the **Český ráj muzeum** (Skálova 71, closed Mon. May–Sept., Mon.–Fri. Oct. & April, & all Nov.–March, $), a local museum with extensive mineralogical and archaeological collections. On the outskirts of town, just off the road to the glassmaking town of Železný Brod, is the mostly Renaissance château of **Hrubý Rohozec** (closed Mon. May–Sept.; Mon.–Fri. Oct. & April; & all Nov.–March, $), a primrose-colored expanse with fine views from its terraces. The château's interior contains prettily furnished rooms.

From Turnov, a road leads south toward Jičín, forming one of the informal borders of the Český ráj. Just off the road on the right you will come across the restored ruins of the 13th-century **Valdštejn Castle** (Valdštejn hrad), which was partly rebuilt in neo-Gothic style. Its 18th-century stone bridge and statuary have escaped destruction. A few miles farther

south is the village of **Hrubá Skála,** and nearby are the most dazzling of the rock formations, often known as "the rock city." There are about 400 of them, some with fanciful names such as "dragon's tooth," and many can be scrambled up and over with ease. Part of the reconstructed **château** of Hrubá Skála above the village has been converted into a hotel.

Trosky Castle (Trosky hrad) was built on two volcanic pillars—one 154 feet high (47 m), the other 187 feet high (57 m)—which had burst through the sandstone. There are two fantastical lookout towers on these basalt rocks—the lower called Baba (grandmother), the higher Panna (maiden). Both offer spectacular views over the countryside. In the early Middle Ages they formed a medieval fortress and were surrounded by triple walls. After 1620 the castle came into the hands of General Wallenstein (Valdštejn); then it was occupied by Swedish forces in 1648 and burned by the Habsburgs. To reach the castle, go south from Hrubá Skála, then head

Visitor Information

- ✉ Náměstí Českého ráje 26,
- ☎ 481 366 255
- **www.cesky-raj.info**

Valdštejn Castle

- 🕐 Closed Mon.– Fri. April & Oct. & all Nov.– March
- 💲 $

Hiking in Český Ráj

If they ever shot a western in the Czech Republic, it would have to be set in Czech Paradise, or Český ráj, the micro-region of forests, sandstone cliffs, and valleys in eastern Bohemia.

Some 70 square miles (180 sq km) of trails and ruins cover the area between Jičín and Malá Skála. The Prachov formations, the main must-see on any hike through the region, are reachable via a not-too-challenging hike from the parking area at Prachovské skály on the Prachov road

northwest of Jičín. The entrance fee of 50 Czech crowns per adult provides access to a dramatic landscape of buttes and pillars, rising on all sides on the winding trails.

While straying from the paths is not allowed without a permit from the Czech Rockclimbing Association, the stone staircases of this route provide a memorable and tiring workout. Hiking maps with other routes are on hand at each entrance to the area and in bookstores in Jičín and Malá Skála.

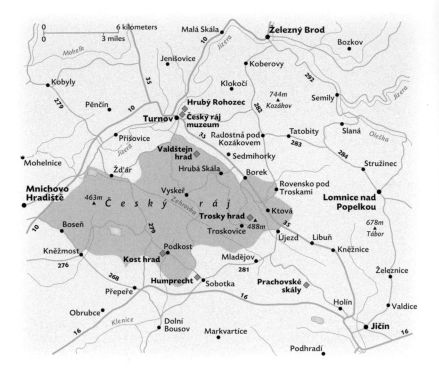

Trosky Castle

🕐 Closed Mon.
May–Sept.;
Mon.–Fri. April
& Oct.; & all
Nov.–March

💲 $

Humprecht Hunting Lodge

🕐 Closed Mon.
May–Sept.;
Mon.–Fri. April
& Oct.; & all
Nov.–March

💲 Guided tour: $

Kost Hrad

🕐 Closed Mon.
May–Sept.,
Mon.–Fri. April
& Oct.; & all
Nov.–March

💲 $$

for Troskovice and leave your car in a parking lot there.

In the west of the Český ráj, overlooking the village of Sobotka, is the remarkable **Humprecht hunting lodge** of 1666. A circular building on a hilltop, it resembles a stumpy moon rocket. Inside, the windowless dining room repeats the circular feature. Head north on the same road for 2 miles (3 km) to the 14th-century fortress of **Kost hrad,** perched on a crag alongside the village of Podkost. A large square keep rises up from the bulk of this well-preserved medieval castle, which houses a collection of Gothic art. Around here, and throughout the Český ráj, there are half-timbered cottages, often painted green.

Between Sobotka and Jičín (and reached by bus from Jičín) are the **Prachov crags** (Prachovské skály), the largest of the region's "rock towns." Neolithic people settled in the pillars, tunnels, cliffs, bridges, and grottoes. Easily accessible, Prachov can get overrun in summer and on weekends, but a visit is still worthwhile.

Southeast of the Český ráj is the town of **Jičín,** which was largely rebuilt by General Wallenstein, who adopted the town as the capital of his duchy of Frýdlant (see pp. 214–215). Here he also founded a hospital, college, and mint, but further plans for the town were brought to a halt by his assassination in 1634 (see pp. 31–32). One of his lasting embellishments is the long avenue of over a thousand linden trees, stretching more than a mile (2 km) alongside the road to Semily. This shaded avenue leads to the gardens of Libosad, created by Wallenstein as a summer retreat, but the site has been neglected. Back in the town itself, you enter the main square through the Valdická Bráma, a tower that was built in the 1570s and can be climbed ($). The 1627 **Church of St. James** (Kostel sv. Jakuba Většího) is on the left, with its set of sea-green altarpieces.

Wallenstein's squat **château** dominates the arcaded square. Built in the 1620s, its bright yellow facade, two lofty courtyards, and great expanses of windows offer a more cheerful aspect than some of his other castles. It was here in 1813 that Emperor Franz I of Austria, Friedrich Wilhelm III of Prussia, and Tsar Alexander I of Russia formed the Holy Alliance that spelled eventual defeat for Napoleon; the treaty was signed in Teplice. The château now houses a gallery and **museum.** At the end of the square a lane leads to Náměstí Svobody and the Gothic **Church of St. Ignatius** (Kostel sv. Ignáce). This pleasant town makes a good base for visiting the Český ráj. ∎

INSIDER TIP:

At the Prachov Rocks, catch the new generation of Czech extreme sport climbers scrambling up and down the cliffs. (Permit required.)

—WILL TIZARD
National Geographic contributor

Jičín

🅰 224 B5

✉ 18 miles (27 km) SE of Turnov via route 35

Visitor Information

✉ Valdštejnovo namésti 1

☎ 493 534 390

www.mujicin.cz

Jičín Museum

🕐 Closed Sat.–Sun.

💲 $

Not a spaceship, but the baroque Humprecht hunting lodge rising from a wooded hilltop

More Places to Visit in Eastern Bohemia

Adršpach-Teplice

Just northwest of Teplice nad Metují, close to the Polish border, lie the Adršpach-Teplice rocks. This small but dramatic region of some 400 sandstone rock formations is similar to the "rock towns" of the České Švýcarsko and Český ráj (see pp. 216–217 and pp. 238–241).
⚠ 224 D5 ✉ 3 miles (5 km) NW of Teplice nad Metují

Častolovice

The 13th-century fortress of Častolovice, remodeled in the late 16th century and then twice more at the end of the 19th century, was returned to the Šternberk family in the 1990s, after confiscation by the Communists in the 1940s. Its park looks as though it is straight from the English countryside. The highlight of the richly furnished interior is the spectacular **Knights' Hall,** with its painted wooden ceiling. Countess Diana Sternbergová-Phipps, the owner, presents the castle as a home rather than a museum, and also rents out rooms.
⚠ 224 D4 ✉ 18 miles (30 km) SE of Hradec Králové via route 11 🕐 Closed Mon. May–Sept, Mon.–Fri. April & Oct., & all Nov.–March 💲 Guided tour: $$

Chrudim

The town of Chrudim has a sinuous baroque plague column and a dark brooding Gothic church. It is best known for its puppet festival, held every July, and its exceptional **Puppet Museum** *(Břetislavova 74, www .puppets.cz, $),* housed in a remarkable 1570s mansion with arcaded galleries. On display you'll find puppets and marionettes from near—Moravia, Bohemia—and far.
⚠ 224 C3 ✉ 8 miles (13 km) S of Pardubice via route 37

Karlova Koruna

The remarkable **château** of Karlova Koruna is located on the outskirts of Chlumec nad Cidlinou. Built in the early 1720s by Giovanni Santini and František Kaňka and set within a large park, the château has been restored to the original owners, the Kinský family. It's a striking building, vaguely star-shaped, with curved facades and dramatic flights of steps. The interior exhibits a fine collection of Czech baroque art and portraits of the Kinský family.
⚠ 224 B4 ✉ 18 miles (30 km) W of Hradec Králové via route 11 🕐 Closed Mon. May–Sept., Mon.–Fri. April & Oct., & Nov.– March 💲 $

Lipnice nad Sázavou

The one claim to fame of the otherwise unremarkable village of Lipnice nad Sázavou is that it was home to the novelist Jaroslav Hašek (1883–1923), who wrote *The Good*

EXPERIENCE: Biking in Eastern Bohemia

Czechs are near-fanatic cyclists and many would rather invest in a set of top-of-the-line gear shifters than stock in Google. A well-developed system of trails, for both hiking and cycling, exists throughout the country, and maps of those in every region are available at their tourist information centers and at sporting goods stores in Prague. Many fall under the spell of eastern Bohemia's trails, and one company, **Sportem** *(www.sportem.info),* has bikes, complete with Trail-Gator tow bars for the kids if needed, plus itineraries for day rides of 15 to more than 35 miles (25–60 km), or multiday rides for cyclists seeking a more intensive experience. Rides through the Hradec woods, and across a nearby 1866 battlefield, are ones you won't soon forget.

Soldier Švejk. Lipnice's medieval **castle** has been partly restored, and you can visit the Gothic chapel and other rooms. Hašek's home, at the beginning of the lane that leads to the castle, is now a commemorative **museum** *(open Tues.–Sun. June–Aug., $),* containing the writer's books, photographs, and memorabilia. His grave lies in an obscure corner of the churchyard reserved for those who had not died in a state of grace.

🔺 224 B2 ✉ 50 miles (80 km) SW of Pardubice via routes 37, 34, 150 and minor roads   **Castle** 🕐 Closed Mon. May–Sept., Mon.–Fri. April & Oct, & Nov.–March 💲 $

INSIDER TIP:

Whether or not you make it to Náchod, the novels of native son Josef Škvorecký make great advance research for a trip to the Czech Republic.

—WILL TIZARD
National Geographic contributor

Moravská Třebová

In Moravská Třebová's spacious central square stands its majestic plague column dating from 1717. The town's **castle,** with its splendid arcaded and galleried courtyard, was once owned by the Liechtenstein family. Its finest feature, which is best viewed from the courtyard, is the three-tiered gateway, built in 1493 and said to be the earliest Renaissance structure in Moravia. The interior is closed to the public.

🔺 225 E2 ✉ 51 miles (85 km) SE of Hradec Králové via route 35

Náchod

Close to the Polish border, Náchod cowers beneath a large sgraffitoed castle on a hilltop. In the center of the main square is the 14th-century **Church of St. Lawrence** (Kostel sv. Vavřinec), with its two squat wooden towers

and, inside, a charming gallery. The most impressive building is the **Hotel U Beránka,** which has a stylish secession interior. It also serves as the town theater. Náchod's sprawling **castle** is Renaissance and baroque. Ferdinand II gave it to Ottavio Piccolomini of Aragon, Wallenstein's bodyguard, in the 1630s, as a reward for his treachery in his general's assassination. It contains a stuccoed chapel and furnishings, tapestries, and paintings. The Czech novelist Josef Škvorecký was born in Náchod in 1924, and the town appears in his novels under the pseudonym of Kostelec.

🔺 224 D5 ✉ 24 miles (38 km) NE of Hradec Králové via route 33 🚂 Train from Prague   **Visitor information** ✉ Kamenice 144 🕐 Closed Sun.   **Castle** 🕐 Closed Mon. May–Sept., Mon.–Fri. April & Oct., & Nov.–March 💲 $–$$

Nové Město nad Metují

Nové Město nad Metují was once a stronghold of the Pernštejn family. The attractive main square is lined with 16th-century houses, a Gothic church of 1519, a gabled 16th-century town hall, and the Pernštejns' **castle,** a Gothic (1501) building subsequently given many overhauls. Approaching the castle along a bridge that crosses the former moat, you pass a series of statues of dwarves by Matthias Braun. These were acquired by textile tycoon Josef Bartoň, who bought the then run-down castle in 1908, and installed them as part of his extensive renovation. The interior is unusual: One hall is vaulted in leather, and there are cubist furnishings alongside Renaissance ones.

🔺 224 D4 ✉ 5 miles (8 km) S of Náchod via route 14 🚂 Train from Náchod   **Castle** 🕐 Closed Mon. 💲 Guided tours: $–$$

Opočno

The Renaissance **château** at Opočno sits high above the Polabí plain. A highlight is the fabulous courtyard, with its magnificent Italianate

Dvůr Kralové Zoo Inspires Novel

Journalist Jonathan Ledgard's multi-textured novel *Giraffe* (Penguin, 2006) was inspired by a small newspaper item he happened across, describing the 1975 shooting of a herd of African reticulated giraffes at the zoo in Dvůr Kralové (20 miles/36 km north of Hradec Králové).

Upon exploring the bizarre secret operation, the Prague-based correspondent for *The Economist* unraveled a tale of cover-ups, paranoia, biological warfare labs, and absurd state security missions.

Tragically, these elements all added up to the demise of the largest herd of captive giraffes in the world—and, as so often under the pre-1989 regime, ultimately for reasons that were never fully explained. These days, the 16-acre (6.5 ha) zoo *(Štefánikova 1029, www.zoodvurkralove.cz, $–$$)* is a happier, modernized place—complete with well-cared-for giraffes.

three-storied loggia. Inside you'll find one of Bohemia's finest armories and a succession of handsome rooms containing Italian paintings and other possessions of the Colloredo family, which once owned the castle.
🅼 224 D4 ✉ 8 miles (13 km) S of Nové Město nad Metují on route 14 to Dobruška, then SW on 298 ☎ 494 668 216 🚌 Bus from Hradec Králové 🕐 Closed Mon. May–Sept.; Mon.–Fri. April & Oct.; & Nov.–March 💲 Guided tours: $–$$

Pardubice

Notorious as the production center for the explosive Semtex, Pardubice prefers to be known for the annual steeplechase. The town was rebuilt by the Pernštejn family after a fire of 1507 destroyed it, but the Thirty Years' War in the 17th century severely damaged it again. The old town is approached from

Náměstí Republiky, where a slightly garish art nouveau **theater** of 1909 faces the charming Gothic **Church of St. Bartholomew** (Kostel sv. Bartoloměje), with its gabled roof, delightful Renaissance north door, and needle-thin spire. The former **Grand Hotel** by Josef Gočár is now a commercial center.

On main square, Pernštejnské náměstí, walk through the 16th-century **Green Gate** (Zelená brána) topped with wildly asymmetrical turrets. Opposite the gate is the busy shopping street of Míru, with its fine trio of secession houses decorated with colorful ceramics. In the center of the square a Marian column of 1695 has a set of statues grouped around it. Among the many handsome Renaissance houses is **Ů Jonáše,** the Jonas House, at No. 50, which has a stucco relief of 1797 showing Jonah being ejected from the whale. To the left, Pernštěnská leads to the walled **castle,** separated from the old town by gardens beneath its walls. Its overall style is sgraffitoed Renaissance, but its Gothic origins are visible in the courtyard. Inside you will find a Gothic hall, rooms with Renaissance murals, a **regional museum** focusing on the Pernštejn family, and a permanent collection of Czech art.
🅼 224 C3 ✉ 12 miles (21 km) S of Hradec Králové via route 37 🚆 Train and bus from Hradec Králové; train from Prague **Visitor information** www.ipardubice.cz ✉ Náměstí Republiky 1 ☎ 466 768 390 **Green Gate** 💲 $ **Castle** 🕐 Closed Mon. 💲 $

Ratibořice

The **château** at Ratibořice is an elegant pink building, originally constructed in 1708, with a curious penthouse. Exhibits here are connected with Božena Němcová, a novelist who wrote about this part of Bohemia in the 1850s. The interior contains early 19th-century furnishings. Much of the surrounding countryside, the Úpa Valley, is now a nature reserve crossed by marked hiking trails.
🅼 224 C5 ✉ 6 miles (10 km) W of Náchod **Château** 🕐 Closed Mon. May–Sept., Mon.–Fri. April & Oct.; & Nov.–March 💲 $

Rolling landscape and vineyards, the perfect Renaissance town of Telč, the fascinating city of Brno, and impressive castles and châteaus

Southern Moravia

Southern Moravia vineyards near Znojmo

Southern Moravia

Southern Moravia probably has more to tempt the visitor than any other region in the republic. Brno offers urban sophistication; Jaroměřice, Buchlovice, Valtice, Kroměříž, and many other places are graced by grand châteaus; and Pernštejn has eerie castles. On the battlefield at Slavkov, the Battle of Austerlitz was fought on December 2, 1805.

After Prague, Brno is the republic's most important and most enjoyable city: urbane, bustling, and rich in culture. On its outskirts is the famous Moravian Karst (Moravský kras), a landscape through which underground rivers have gouged out spectacular caves, some open to the public.

At Zlín, to the east, is another expression of urbanism: a town largely created by one man, shoe manufacturer Tomáš Baťa (1876–1932). The fruits of patronage appear as precedents elsewhere in the region. At Kroměříž, worldly and ecclesiastical ambitions created a great palace and gardens. In Telč, the visions of a powerful 16th-century lord, Zachariáš

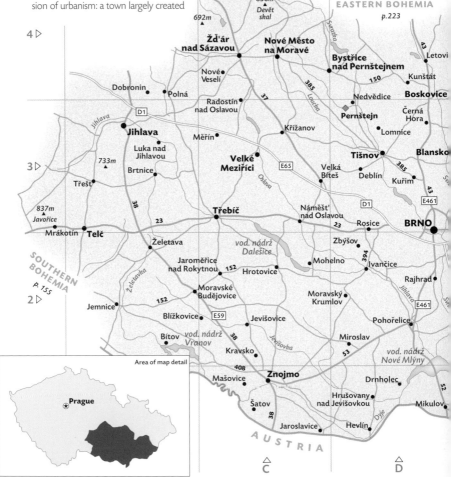

of Hradec, extended not just to his castle but to the entire town. His inspiration produced Telč's square, lined with exquisite arcaded houses.

Great architecture throughout southern Moravia ranges from the Romanesque basilica at Třebíč to the weird and wonderful designs of the most individual master of the Czech baroque, Giovanni Santini, at Žd'ár nad Sázavou.

Churches and monasteries abound here, as do ancient synagogues. For many years the Jewish history of the Czech Republic was suppressed, but that has all changed. The great synagogue in Brno is once again open, and visitors are rediscovering the region's plethora of ancient synagogues and cemeteries.

The region also is home to most of the country's vineyards. ■

NOT TO BE MISSED:

Braving the chill to see mummies in Brno's Capuchin Monastery **249**

Wine tasting in the atmospheric cellars of Valtice **258–259**

The 15th-century synagogue in Mikulov **256–257**

Experiencing Moravian fiddling at the Strážnice Folk Festival **260**

Seeing the clean lines of the one-time Bat'a worker's paradise in Zlín **262**

A stroll through the vaulted library in the fortress at Pernštejn **267**

Wandering the subterranean canals of the Moravian Karst **265–266**

Brno

Two hills, Petrov and Špilberk, dominate Brno: The cathedral stands on top of one; atop the other broods the Špilberk fortress. Even today the grim castle can send a shiver down your spine. Although Brno is a sprawling industrial city, the historic center is fascinating.

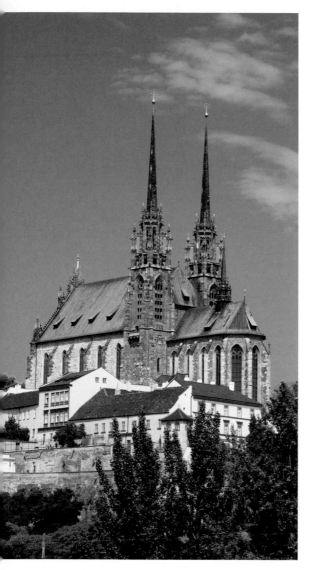

The spires of St. Peter and St. Paul dominate one of the two hilltops of Brno.

Celts settled in the area 2,500 years ago. In the ninth century, Slavs built a castle on what today is Petrov Hill, and from the 11th century on it was the seat of the Margraves of Moravia. In 1641 Brno became the Moravian capital, thus inviting the aggressive attentions of the Swedes and Turks, who inflicted great damage on the city while trying to capture it. Many of the baroque buildings are the work of Mořic Grimm and his brother, the city's best known architects. By 1861, the demolished city were replaced by parks and boulevards.

Industrialization, especially textile manufacture, in the 19th century brought great prosperity to Brno; it also gave its name to the Bren gun, first produced here. By the century's end Brno was the second largest city in the country, and its progressive merchant classes were keen for the city to showcase the latest industrial and commercial design. In 1928 they created the huge trade fair complex, with its innovative architectural styles; it still attracts thousands of international visitors each year.

Petrov Hill

The **Cathedral of St. Peter & St. Paul** (Dóm sv. Petra a Pavla) sits atop Petrov with its spindly spires seen for miles around. After Petrov hill was savaged by Swedish forces in

Venus of Věstonice

Some 80 years ago, remnants of a Stone Age settlement were discovered on the slopes of the Pálava Hills, 30 miles (50 km) from Brno. It belonged to mammoth hunters who developed a culture now dubbed Pavlovian—an early phase of the Gravettian people. Among the ruins, archaeologists uncovered an odd, misshapen clay and ash figurine of a nude woman with sexual features grossly exaggerated—the Venus of Věstonice. She now resides at the Moravské museum in Brno (though she's rarely on exhibit).

Much about these ice age people remains unknown, though their stone and bone tools reveal a civilization with a keen sense of art. Headbands and necklaces have also been found, along with other sculptures of bone and of clay and evidence they made decorative dyes and imprinted textiles. Researchers are still working the site, hoping to learn more. The humble **Mikulov Regional Museum** (*Zámek 1, Mikulov, tel 519 309 013, www. rmm.cz*) near the site tells their story as it now stands.

1645, the cathedral was rebuilt in the baroque style by Mořic Grimm. Then the exterior and entire choir were Gothicized in the early 1900s. More recently, Jiří Marek contributed some striking modernist-expressionist "Stations of the Cross." Next to the cathedral is the Renaissance **Archbishop's Palace** (Biskupská palác, *not open to the public*).

Zelný trh

Steps and cobbled lanes lead down from Petrov to one of Brno's two main squares, Zelný trh, the bustling vegetable market focused around the 1695 Parnassus Fountain by Johann Bernard Fischer von Erlach. The main building on the square, the relatively plain 17th-century **Dietrichstein Palace** (Ditrichštejnský palác), is now the **Moravské muzeum.** Dedicated to Moravian history, the museum contains some craft and folklore exhibits. In the prehistoric finds, the museum's prize possession is

the 27,000-year-old **Venus of Věstonice** (see sidebar above), the earliest known ceramic (or fired-clay) figurine representing the human form.

On leaving the palace, turn right and walk through the iron gates into the Bishop's Courtyard, where the less exciting **Biskupský dvur muzeum** is devoted to Moravian fauna (including a record-breaking collection of cicadas) and coins. Down the slope, in Kapucínské náměstí, is the plain **Capuchin Monastery** (Kapucínský klášter), where some 150 mummified corpses (including that of Mořic Grimm) were deposited clothed and exposed in the crypt. A gruesome sight, but not unusual in central Europe; the practice was stopped on health grounds in 1784. In the last room 24 Capuchin monks are laid out on the bare earth, their heads supported on bricks; some are disconcertingly well preserved after 250 years.

Across Zelný trh from here you can see the complex steeple of the **Old Town Hall** (Stará radnice),

Brno

⬛ 246 D3

✉ 117 miles (195 km) SE of Prague

Visitor Information

✉ Old Town Hall, Radnická 8

☎ 542 427 102

www.ticbrno.cz

Moravské Muzeum

✉ Zelný trh 8

☎ 542 321 205

🕐 Closed Sun.– Mon.

💲 $

www.mzm.cz

Capuchin Monastery

💲 Crypt: $

Old Town Hall steeple

🕐 Closed Oct.–March

💲 $

resembling a series of spiked Ottoman helmets. Anton Pilgram, who later adorned St. Stephen's Cathedral in Vienna with carvings, designed the Gothic portal in 1511, deliberately skewed its central pinnacle as though it were about to topple. Hanging in the arched entryway is the so-called Brno

heaven. Next to the church is the baroque **New Town Hall** (Nová radnice). This was originally the Dominican monastery, designed by the Grimm brothers in the 1690s.

Náměstí Svobody

Opposite New Town Hall, a short street leads down to the

BRVNN
Vulgo Brünn Marchionatus Morauiæ Ciuitas insignis.

In this early 17th-century print, the city is already dominated by the awesome Špilberk fortress.

Dragon (Brněnský Drak), recognizable as a mounted alligator; it was presented by a Turkish delegation to Matthias Corvinus. The people of Brno have a soft spot for this unusual gift, as well as for the cartwheel hanging on the wall. In 1636 Georg Birk, a carter, wagered that he could fashion the wheel from a log and roll it the 35 miles (50 km) from his village to Brno all in one day. He won his bet.

Beyond the Old Town Hall is the 1655 Dominican **Church of St. Michael** (Kostel sv. Michala), which has the usual set of baroque altarpieces and statuary, although the carvings above the pulpit look as though a bomb had detonated in

largest square in the old town, Náměstí Svobody, which is dissected by tramlines. Brno's main street, Masarykova, connects the square to the railway station. Compared with most main squares in Czech cities, Náměstí Svobody is nondescript, and even the plague column is a rigid design. From the top of the square, Jánská leads to the **Minorite church** (Kostel sv. Jana), designed by the Grimms, who studded its broad facade with vigorous statues. The richly decorated interior is enlivened by a baroque organ festooned with putti playing instruments. Opposite the church, along

Minoritská, some fine secession houses and shops have been freshly restored and sparkle with gold leaf. At the other end of Jánská is a glass-paneled former department store called **Centrum,** built by shoe tycoon Tomáš Baťa (see p. 262) in 1928. Continue past Centrum onto **Malinovského náměstí,** where on the left stands the 19th-century **Mahen Theater** (Mahenovo divadlo). It has pretensions to grandeur, with an impressive drive sweeping up to the entrance porch. The interior is sumptuous, including fine staircases, chandeliers, salons for strolling during the intervals, and, of course, a tiered auditorium that is heavily gilded, luxurious yet intimate. In 1882

it was the first theater in Europe to use electric lighting.

Another street leading out of Svobody–Rašinova–takes you to the large Gothic **Church of St. Jacob** (Kostel sv. Jakuba), Brno's parish church, with its lofty belfry. The aisles are sustained by piers so slender they seem incapable of holding the weight of the enormous structure, even aided by a maze of delicate rib vaults. This Gothic elegance is refreshing after so many baroque churches elsewhere in Brno. Continue another block along Rašinova to the **Church of St. Thomas** (Kostel sv. Tomáš), a building noted for a triple-decker pulpit.

Adjoining St. Thomas is the 18th-century **Governor's Palace**

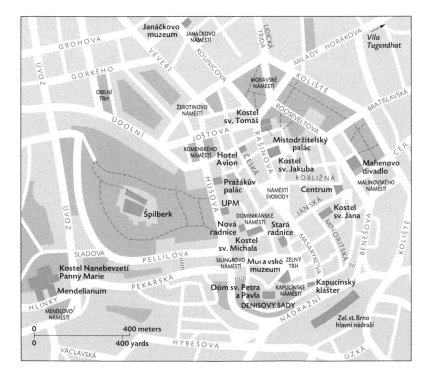

Governor's Palace
⊠ Náměstí Moravské la
☎ 542 321 100
🕓 Closed Mon.–Tues.
💲 $

Pražákův Palác
⊠ Husova 18
☎ 532 169 111
🕓 Closed Mon.–Tues.
💲 $
www.moravska-galerie.cz

Muzeum Romské Kultury/Museum of Romani Culture
⊠ Bratislavská 67
☎ 545 571 798
💲 $

Mendelianum
⊠ Mendlovo náměstí 1
☎ 543 424 043
🕓 Closed Sat.–Sun.
💲 $
www.mendel-museum.com

(Místodržitelský palác), designed by the Grimms. Since 1992 it has housed part of the Moravian Gallery's holdings. The Gothic collection has an abundance of wood carvings and paintings, including a 15th-century panel depicting the martyrdom of St. Osvald. Rubens's vivid snake-strewn portrait of Medusa's head is here, too. There are also good examples of 18th-century paintings by Daniel Gran, Johann Lucas Kracher, Franz Anton Maulbertsch, and Angelica Kauffmann, and 19th-century portraits by Friedrich Amerling and Hans Makart. Down the road from the palace, on the corner of Česká, you come to the **Hotel Avion,** designed by Brno's leading 20th-century architect, Bohuslav Fuchs.

Špilberk Hill

Two branches of the Moravian Gallery are on Husova, near Špilberk. The modern art museum, housed at Husova 18 in the **Pražákův palác,** has impressive cubist paintings by Emil Filla and Antonín Procházka. It's also worth visiting for the portraits by Jan Zrzavý.

INSIDER TIP:

The museum of Roma culture traces Roma history from the migrations out of India. Scheduled events and festivals feature dance and music.

–EMILY THOMPSON
Special Sections editor,
The Prague Post

Across from the palace is the Museum of Applied Arts, known as **UPM,** with works from Gothic times to the present. The comprehensive collection includes ivories, 17th-century glass, and early 19th-century Biedermeier furniture. Following a complete collapse of taste, the secession and the cubist movement breathed new life into furniture design and restored standards of exquisite craftsmanship. Some of the furnishings for Ludwig Mies van der Rohe's Tugendhat House are here.

Opposite these museums is Špilberk hill. The Bohemian king Přemysl Otakar II built a **fortress**

Gregor Mendel

Southwest of Špilberk is the Augustinian priory where the Austrian monk Gregor Johann Mendel (1822–1884) lived. His studies of the inheritance of qualities in the garden pea and beans led to major discoveries in the laws of heredity and the development of the science of genetics. Mendel published the results of his research in scientific journals, but their full significance was overlooked by contemporary scientists. In 1868, disillusioned by the indifference with which his work was greeted, he abandoned scientific research to become the abbot of the monastery. His true greatness was recognized only after his death. His work led to an understanding of the nature and properties of chromosomes and thus the mechanisms of heredity. A museum, the **Mendelianum,** commemorates his achievements, and you can visit the famous priory garden where he conducted his experiments.

Dark dungeons burrow deep beneath the whitewashed walls of the Špilberk fortress.

(Špilberk hrad) here in about 1270, and during the Thirty Years' War it was converted into a fearsome citadel where political opponents of the Habsburgs were incarcerated in its dungeons. Embarrassed by the prison's notoriety, the Habsburgs closed it in the 1850s. In 1880 it was reopened as a tourist attraction. During the Nazi occupation, however, the Gestapo found the fortress ideal for their purposes—many victims were imprisoned, tortured, and executed here. You can visit the **Špilberk dungeons** and torture chambers, and the west side of the fortress is now the city museum ($). It's quite a climb up the hill to the citadel, but the view from the top is terrific.

Other Sites

Leoš Janáček did most of his composing in Brno, and his house is now the **Janáček Museum** (Janáčkovo muzeum).

To reach it from Náměstí Svobody, take Rašinova to the north, then continue along Kounicova, to the museum.

Beyond the town center are the **fairgrounds.** Výstaviště, originally laid it out in 1928. The grounds provided a showcase for the leading Czech architects, then working in a functionalist style.

Another important building, Mies van der Rohe's 1930 **Tugendhat House** (Vila Tugendhat), is set in the suburb of Černá Pole. The stark white villa is revolutionary for its radical design of "free floating space." After the owners fled in 1938, the structure was badly damaged by the Nazis and Soviets. After World War II, it was a dance school and a rehabilitation hospital for children. Finally restored in the 1980s, the home was declared a UNESCO World Heritage site in 2001. An extensive restoration began in early 2010. ∎

UPM
- ✉ Husova 14
- ☎ 532 169 111
- ⏰ Closed Mon.–Tues.
- 💲 $

Špilberk Dungeons
- ☎ 542 123 611
- ⏰ Closed Mon. & Nov.–March
- 💲 $
- www.spilberk.cz

Janáček Museum
- ☎ 541 212 811
- ⏰ Closed Fri.–Sun.
- 💲 $

Tugendhat House
- ☎ 542 123 611
- ✉ Černopolní 45
- ⏰ Closed Mon.–Tues.; reservations required
- 💲 Guided tours: $, $$
- www.tugendhat.eu

Znojmo

The ancient hilltop town of Znojmo lies close to the Austrian border. A thousand years ago Bohemia's Prince Břetislav I built a citadel here to defend an important trading route. The Přemyslid king Otakar II was buried in a monastery near the town in 1278, and in 1437 Emperor Sigismund breathed his last here. Its military usefulness diminished over the centuries, and Znojmo became a tranquil regional center marred by industrial outskirts.

Znojmo is known for its churches and wine.

Znojmo

- 246 C1
- 33 miles (56 km) SW of Brno

Visitor Information

- Obroková 10
- 515 222 552

www.znojmocity.cz

Some of the town's fortifications have survived. It has two principal squares: Horní náměstí is situated higher up, while the larger Masarykovo náměstí is flanked by the town hall. The old town hall was destroyed by the Nazis, but the remarkable pinnacled tower, built in 1445,

has survived. Just off Horní náměstí on Slepičí trh, you can join a 40-minute guided tour to the **underground tunnels** (*podzemí*), which were used both for defensive and storage purposes. The square was severely damaged during World War II and is now a hodgepodge of buildings, the best being the House of Art (Dům umění) at No. 11. The courtyard is arcaded, and the buildings are used as an art gallery.

From the town hall Mikulášská leads to the tall, elegant Gothic **Church of St. Nicholas** (Kostel sv. Mikuláše), which is furnished with an exuberant baroque pulpit. Behind it, the tiny 16th-century **Chapel of St. Wenceslas** (Orthodox kaple sv. Václava) forms part of the town ramparts. A terrace nearby offers views onto the Dyje River Valley below.

The Castle

It's a short stroll from here to what's left of the castle. Within its precincts stands a small Romanesque rotunda that dates from the early 11th century. The precious 12th-century frescoes decorating it are the most complete, best preserved examples from the period in the Czech Republic. The lower tier depicts scenes from the life of the Virgin, while those above illustrate the legendary Libuše and the Premyslid kings. The Premyslids themselves commissioned this remarkable cycle in 1134. Also within the castle is the **South Moravian Museum** (Jihomoravské muzeum), with varied archaeological and natural history collections. The castle is now a brewery, a very Czech solution to conservation. Wine also holds sway here: Each September, Znjomo commemorates the 1327 visit of King Jan Lucemburský with the Historical Vintage Festival.

Outside Znojmo

There are two worthwhile attractions on the outskirts of town. A mile (2 km) out on the road to Mašovice is the baroque **Church of St. Hippolytus** (Kostel sv. Hypolita); it sits on the site of the original ninth-century Znojmo, which switched to its present hilltop two centuries later. Frescoes in the dome are

INSIDER TIP:

Harvest season's the best time to visit Znojmo. Catch the jousting tournaments during the Historical Vintage Festival (Sept.).

—WILL TIZARD
National Geographic contributor

by Austrian artist Franz Anton Maulbertsch, whose work also adorns Kroměříž (see pp. 263–264). And just south of Znojmo, off the Vienna road, is **Louka,** where the Premonstratensian monastery was founded in the 12th century. The monastery's Philosophical Library was moved, in its entirety, to Strahov monastery in Prague (see pp. 83–84). The baroque buildings, larger than many a palace, were long used as a barracks and are derelict, but the plain church of 1689 has been restored. In the courtyard stands a black cross wreathed in barbed wire, and an inscription honors the "victims of Stalinist Bolshevism 1945–1989." ∎

Town Hall Tower
🕐 Closed Sun. April & Oct. & Sat.–Sun. Nov.–March
💲 $

Underground Tunnels
🕐 Closed Mon. April–Sept. & Sat.–Sun. Nov.–March
💲 $

Rotunda
🕐 Closed Mon. June–Sept.; Mon.–Fri. May & Oct.–April; & all Nov.–March
💲 Guided tour: $$

South Moravian Museum
✉ Přemyslovců 8
☎ 515 282 211
🕐 Closed Mon. May–Sept., & Mon.–Fri. Oct.–April
💲 $
www.znojmuz.cz

Jewish Moravia

Although the Jewish synagogues and cemeteries of Prague have been attracting visitors for decades, the republic's other Jewish centers are only recently being rediscovered. There was already a substantial Jewish community in the Czech lands in early medieval times, and in 1254 King Přemysl Otakar II offered royal protection in a charter. It wasn't always effective—Jews suffered from the same discrimination and attacks as elsewhere in Europe.

Despite the expulsions and occasional pogroms, the Jewish culture managed to thrive. By 1938 the Jewish population of Bohemia and Moravia was around 120,000; the sheer scale of the main synagogue in Brno gives some idea of the size and wealth of the local community. World War II and the Holocaust reduced that community to tatters; well over half the population perished. Many of those who survived emigrated after the war ended, and more left the country in 1968 when the Soviet invasion extinguished hopes of liberalization. Numbers for the Jewish population today are hard to come by, but one estimate is about 6,000. During the communist years the community kept a low profile, but since 1989 Bohemia and Moravia have taken pride in the remnants of a once vital culture. Most synagogues were

destroyed by the Nazis or converted for other uses, but a few survive, as do cemeteries, many of which contain gravestones dating back three centuries. Hardly a town in Moravia is without its Jewish traces, and here are a few highlights:

Boskovice

At Boskovice, north of Brno, there's a cemetery with graves dating back to the 17th century. The graves lie in lines across a wooded slope, a tranquil and haunting spot. (A key is available from the information center in the town hall.) Plačkova street retains several Jewish houses.

Holešov

In Holešov, north of Zlín, the synagogue *(closed Mon., $)* is on Striční, two blocks behind the information office on the main square, Náměstí E. Beneša. This is the Šachova synagóga, named after its most celebrated rabbi. The building dates from 1560, but the lovely interior is essentially 18th century, from the Hebrew inscriptions on the walls to the fine ironwork around the bima. The gallery has been adapted into a small museum. Behind Striční, on Hankého, is the entrance to the Jewish cemetery, a few recent graves a welcome reminder that the Jews of Moravia were not entirely wiped out by 1945. Hundreds of older gravestones, dating back to the 17th century, lie in random order.

Mikulov

There has been a Jewish community in Mikulov, south of Brno close to the Austrian border, since at least 1369, rising to 3,500 in

The Jewish cemetery at Třebíč is the largest in the republic.

Šachova synagóga in Holešov is one of Moravia's most beautiful synagogues.

number during the 19th century. Two rare survivals are the 15th-century synagogue at Husova 13 (closed Mon. & Oct.–April) and the overgrown Jewish cemetery on Brněnská.

Třebíč

Not far from the basilica of St. Procopius, which stands on a hill overlooking Třebíč,

is the former Jewish quarter. Together, the basilica and the quarter were named a UNESCO World Heritage site in 2003. Two synagogues—one from 1639 on Tiché náměstí, the other at Bohuslavova 42—still exist. North of the former is the republic's largest Jewish cemetery, outside Prague, with 3,000 headstones dating back to the 1640s.

Valtice & Lednice

Valtice and Lednice are two of the vast Moravian châteaus owned by the Liechtenstein family, one of the most powerful families of the Austro-Hungarian Empire. Although situated quite close to each other, they are entirely different in style and atmosphere. Valtice is probably the more interesting house, but Lednice is set on very beautiful grounds, which can also be visited. The châteaus were named a UNESCO World Heritage site in 1996.

The baroque château of Valtice looks out over formal gardens dotted with statues.

Valtice

 247 E1

✉ 40 miles (64 km) S of Brno via route E65, Břeclav exit

🚆 Train from Mikulov or Břeclav

The Liechtensteins owned two enormous palaces in Vienna and dozens of estates in Moravia, where they became landowners in the 14th century. In 1945, the family was accused of collaboration with the Germans and fled the country as the Soviets advanced. Their estates were confiscated; the family was still negotiating with Czech authorities for the return of their properties as late as 2009, when the Principality of Liechtenstein established diplomatic relations with the Czech Republic.

Valtice

Valtice is a pompous baroque château festooned with coats

of arms, statues, and military emblems. There was a castle here in the 12th century, but it was frequently altered and rebuilt. Its present appearance dates from the early 18th century.

Part of the château is now a hotel, but some state rooms are open to the public. Valtice has a certain grandeur, the opulent high baroque chapel being notable. The wood-paneled Gold Chamber adjoining the princess's bedroom is another exquisitely ornamented room. Many of the rooms are almost bare, however, because after the château was expropriated in 1945, it was stripped of its furnishings.

Valtice has its own wine estate; the **cellars,** which can be visited, date from the 1430s. In August, a baroque music festival held at Valtice includes open-air performances of both opera and ballet.

Lednice

Lednice is quite different. Where Valtice is about power, Lednice's endearing neo-Gothic fantasy is playful, an attempt to dress up in history. The Liechtensteins lost interest in Valtice in the 18th century and concentrated on Lednice. The existing structure was built by Jiří Wingelmüller in 1856, the latest in a succession of rebuildings of the château owned by the family since the mid-13th century. Guided tours of the château show you the brightly colored and heavily paneled interior. It is impressively lavish, if hardly the epitome of good taste.

The Park

The park between the châteaus boasts three lakes created in the 17th century, as well as a larger natural lake strewn with islets. With so much water around, the park is a haven for waterfowl. Over the centuries pavilions, summerhouses, a mock-ruined castle, and, most curious of all, a huge Turkish-style minaret of 1802 were added. You can walk the 4 miles (7 km) from one château to the other, along an avenue of lime trees. ■

Visitor Information

- ✉ Náměstí Svobody 4, Valtice
- ☎ 519 372 978

Valtice Château

- 🕐 Closed Mon. May–Sept.; Mon.–Fri. April & Oct.; & all Nov.–March
- 💲 $–$$

Valtice Cellars

- 🕐 Closed Mon. & Oct.–April

Lednice

- ⬛ 247 E1
- ✉ 38 miles (61 km) S of Brno
- 🚆 Train from Břeclav

Visitor Information

- ✉ Zámecké náměstí 68
- ☎ 519 340 986

Lednice Château

- 🕐 Closed Mon. May–Sept.; Mon.–Fri. April & Oct.; & all Nov.–March
- 💲 $$–$$$

Mikulov

Six miles(10 km) west of Valtic is Mikulov (*Náměstí 7, tel 519 512 200, www.mikulov .cz*) worth a stop for its castle and wonderful churches. The **castle** *(closed Sat.– Sun. Nov.–March, $)* is essentially a modern reconstruction. This newness is thanks to the Nazis, who blew up the original Dietrichstein castle in 1945. The cellars hold a 17th-century cask, probably Europe's largest wine barrel, with a capacity of 26,680 gallons (101,300 l). In fact, Mikulov is also known as one of Moravia's centers of white wine production.

Near the town's main square stands the 15th-century **Church of St. Wenceslas** (Kostel sv. Václava), with a belfry and enchanting rococo interior. It was built on what was once the site of a 12th-century church. The pompous 1840s facade of the **Church of St. Anna** (Kostel sv. Anny) conceals the church and mausoleum *(closed Nov.–March, $)* of the Dietrichsteins. The 44 coffins, some of them highly elaborate, date back to Renaissance times.

Strážnice's Folk Festival

Folk festivals, typically held in the summer months, are enormously popular throughout the country. Perhaps the most famous of all is Strážnice's boisterous festival in late June, established in 1946. The event draws thousands of visitors each year to this easygoing town, 12 miles (19 km) south of Uherské Hradiště.

Traditional fiddlers strike up a tune in the fields around Strážnice.

It has to be recognized, however, that many so-called "folkloric" events lack authenticity. With religious practice severely discouraged by the Communists, there were fewer outlets for the almost universal desire to enjoy feasts and festivals. In some cases traditional observances were retained without their religious overtones; in others, a somewhat bogus return to national roots was seen as a way of keeping the people entertained while at the same time fostering a national consciousness without nationalist overtones. Traditional costumes and melodies were put at the service of the state during May Day parades and other glorifications of the communist way of life. Books and posters can still give the impression that the countryside in the Czech lands is filled with smiling peasantry in brightly patterned national costumes. In truth, such

costumes are rarely glimpsed, except during these festivals.

A new musical tradition was also created, since the puritanical Communist authorities took a dim view of jazz and rock and roll, which were associated with the depravities of the West. In their place were brass bands, folk dance ensembles, and musical contests. Naturally, the more wily composers and performers devised satirical or subversive songs in the guise of traditional music. Membership in folkloric ensembles was often little more than a cover for trips out of the country, a form of travel restricted to the privileged few until 1989.

In **Strážnice** (*Vinohradská 35, tel 578 325 721*), as in other towns with a similar tradition and identity—including Domažlice (see pp. 200–201), in western Bohemia, and Buchlov (see p. 272)—folklore and marketing join hands. Workshops in the town manufacture hand-painted ceramics with folkloric themes, and the castle museum features displays of local folk art.

The town has lost most of its fortifications, although two Renaissance gateways survive. The **castle** (*closed Mon. & Nov.–April, $*) was originally built in the 13th century, but the present structure is an 1850s reconstruction in a Renaissance style. An attractive **skansen** (*closed Mon. & Nov.–April, tour $*), an open-air museum of folk architecture, sits the edge of town. Most of the structures here date from the 19th century; they include a winery, smithy, and decorative beehives.

Strážnice's three-day festival is billed as international, though it focuses mostly on local traditions in music, dance, and costume. The performances take place on the castle grounds, and there are also parades within the town, with a strong emphasis on children's participation. Huge quantities of food, wine, and beer are consumed.

Velehrad

Six miles (9 km) northwest of Uherské Hradiště, in pretty hill country, stands the immense monastery of Velehrad. It's not only the 18th-century church with its two tall steeples that is impressive, it's also the whole complex of yellow-and-white monastic buildings surrounding it.

The first Cistercian monastery in Moravia was built here in the early 13th century, but Hussites partly destroyed it in 1421. It lied in ruins until the remains were incinerated in 1681. Reconstruction got under way rapidly, with Giovanni Tencalla as the principal architect. Work was completed in 1710; the present church was consecrated in 1735. Beneath the church is a lapidarium, where the **crypt** and some remains of the original church can still be seen, showing its size—clearly built on a very large scale. Vestiges of the Romanesque church remain in the apses at the west end.

Velehrad is an important pilgrimage church—tens of thousands of worshipers visit each year. One reason it attracts so many pilgrims is its dedication to the Apostles of the Slavs, Saints Cyril and Methodius (see p. 25). Some therefore conclude, falsely, that it was the site of St. Methodius's bishopric.

In 863 the two priests were dispatched from Constantinople as missionaries. In Moravia they preached in the vernacular, winning the admiration of the populace. They returned to Rome, but Methodius returned to Moravia, enduring hardships and imprisonment, thanks to the jealous interventions of other clergy. He rose to become a bishop. While once believed that he died here in 885, but this is now questioned.

Nevertheless, pilgrims come here in droves on July 5, a state and church holiday. More than 150,000 worshipers flocked here in 1985 for the 1,100th anniversary of Methodius's death, despite Communist authority disapproval. When Pope John Paul II paid homage to the two saints at Velehrad in April 1990, an estimated half a million worshipers were present.

The 18th-century building is baroque, but the interior, with its immense length and serene atmosphere, retains impressive

Velehrad

🗺 247 F3
🚌 Bus from Uherské Hradiště

Crypt

🕐 Closed Mon. April, May, Sept., & Oct.; & all Nov.– March
💲 $

INSIDER TIP:

If around Uherské Hradiště in late July, don't miss the Letní Filmová Škola (*www.lfs .cz*). International indie films screen, some on the square.

—MARK BAKER
National Geographic Traveler
magazine writer

Romanesque proportions. Note the delightful, if faded, trompe l'oeil frescoes, the pink and eggshell-blue paintwork, carved choir stalls (1700), and succession of side altars, each with differing stucco decoration. Seek out the 1745 organ, festooned with cherubs. ∎

Zlín

Zlín is a factory town—with a difference. When the Baťa footwear factory was constructed here, Tomáš Baťa built not only his own villa but also an entire company town. The company was founded in 1894; as it prospered, Zlín grew from a small town of a few thousand people to a city sprawling along a verdant valley with almost 100,000 inhabitants. Baťa made his fortune during World War I, outfitting the millions of soldiers in the Austro-Hungarian forces with boots.

Zlín

⛰ 247 G3

🚌 Bus from Uherské Hradiště & Brno. Train from Olomouc & Brno

Visitor Information

✉ Náměstí Míru 12

☎ 577 630 222

www.zlin.eu

Shoe Museum

☎ 577 522 225

🕐 Closed Mon. April–Oct., Sat.–Sun. Nov.– March

💲 $

www.muzeum-zlin.cz

Castle

☎ 577 004 611

🕐 Closed Mon.

💲 $

After the war, the company continued to expand. When Baťa died in a plane crash in 1932, it was the world's largest shoe manufacturer. In 1938 his son, also called Tomáš, saw there was no future for the Baťas in Moravia and immigrated, together with a substantial part of his workforce, to Canada, where the company expanded further.

It may be decried as old-fashioned paternalism, but Baťa wanted to provide his workforce with good housing and prestigious educational and cultural amenities.

Shoe King

Known for his social conscience, one of the first mass producer of shoes, native son Tomáš Baťa's (1876–1932) entrepreneurial spirit lives on in shoe stores around the world.

He brought in the finest architects of the day, including Frenchman Le Corbusier (1877–1965), as well as the Czech Jan Kotěra, who built Baťa's villa. Le Corbusier's designs for the new town didn't satisfy Baťa, who gave the commission to Kotěra's pupil František Gahura (1891–1958). The principal building was the shoe factory; later called the Svít Corporation, it now houses

a comprehensive **museum** about shoes and their manufacture. The factory's most remarkable feature was a glass elevator that had a dual role as Baťa's mobile office, allowing him to work on each floor of the building. Opposite the factory are a department store, the Moskva Hotel, and a cinema, all part of the original town plan. So is the large square called Masarykovo náměstí, with one of the town schools and the concert hall.

Zlín is not particularly beautiful, but its buildings are functional and well designed, and most have aged well. Like many grand town plans, Gahura's was never completed; moreover, much was destroyed during World War II. The modernized Renaissance **castle**, a square yellow block near the factory, is of interest for its excellent museum. The collection features 20th-century Czech art (with representative paintings by Filla, Kubišta, Josef Čapek, and Antonín Procházka, as well as by contemporary artists), plus exhibits on southeast Moravia.

From 1949 to 1990 the town was called Gottwaldov after Communist leader Klement Gottwald. Famous natsives of Zlín include playwright Tom Stoppard and Ivana Trump, ex-wife of tycoon Donald Trump. The town is also known for film studios specializing in animated films. ■

Kroměříž Palace

The old town of Kroměříž was almost destroyed during the Thirty Years' War—only a single tower remained of the Renaissance Bishop's Palace. The prince-bishops of Olumouc reconstructed it, from 1686 onward, on the grandest scale. Not only did they build a palatial residence, but they laid out elaborate Italian gardens, all of which survive, as does the fine gallery attached to the palace. Even in a country rich in palaces, this one is just about unrivaled in its pomp and opulence.

Fountains, romantic tree alleys, and small lakes are just some of the charms of the palace gardens.

The present complex, which stands just north of the main square, was almost entirely rebuilt by Prince-Bishop Karl Eusebius von Liechtenstein-Kastelkorn. He appointed the Italian architects Filiberto Lucchese and Giovanni Tencalla to draw up plans for his new palace. They came up with a somewhat intimidating early baroque design. Italian craftsmen, including Baltasare Fontana, decorated the interior and carried out the stuccowork. The prince-bishop also established a court orchestra.

The only way to visit the palace is by guided tour, which takes 90 minutes. There is also a tour that takes you to the top of the lofty tower, but this is of less interest. The original interior was destroyed by fire in 1752, and the

Kroměříž

 247 F3

 40 miles (64 km) E of Brno

Train from Brno, change at Kojetín. Bus from Brno & Prague

Visitor Information

✉ Velké náměstí 50/45

☎ 573 334 191

🕐 Closed Sun. in winter

www.mesto-krome riz.cz

Kroměříž Palace

☎ 573 502 011

🕐 Closed Mon. May–Sept.; Mon.–Fri. April & Oct.; & all March–Dec.

💲 $$$. Gallery: $$

artists commissioned to repair the damage were Franz Anton Maulbertsch and Josef Stern. The colorful style of Stern's frescoes, on the theme of Parnassus, a Greek sacred mountain, contrasts with the austere exterior of the palace. In the 1770s the Diet Hall (Sněmovní sál) was lavishly painted by František von Freenthal.

The stupendous **library** holds more than 50,000 volumes, plus a collection of globes and an extensive musical archive, including scores by Mozart and Haydn. A collection of coins and medals reflects the fact that there was a mint at Kroměříž between 1613 and 1760. On the tour you also

INSIDER TIP:

The palace gardens in Kroměříž were an inspiration for baroque landscape design all over central Europe. A picnic there won't soon be forgotten

—MARK BAKER
National Geographic Traveler
magazine writer

visit the Hunting Hall, the Throne Room, the Audience Hall, and the Tsar's Hall, where Emperor Franz Josef I and Tsar Alexander III met in 1885.

You'll need a separate ticket to visit the **picture gallery,** which is housed on the second floor of the palace where you tour without a guide. The art collection, the largest in the Czech Republic outside

Prague, is based on the acquisitions of Karl von Liechtenstein, who astutely bought up other private collections. The gallery has masterpieces that include religious works by the Master of Kroměříž and Lucas Cranach the Elder. The Italian paintings include Veronese's fragmentary "Apostles," a cycle by Jacopo Bassano on the story of Noah, and a 1571 masterpiece by Titian: "The Flaying of Marsyas by Apollo," a brooding and unsettling visualization of the gruesome scene. There are also works by Jan and Pieter Breughel, and a tender double portrait by Anthony van Dyck of the English king Charles I and his queen, Henrietta.

Surrounding the palace, the beautiful **gardens,** extending to the banks of the Morava River, contain many lakes and waterways. Attractions include a Chinese Pavilion, an aviary, and a menagerie.

To visit the rest of Kroměříž, return to the main square (Velké náměstí). From here, Jánská leads to the sinuous baroque **Church of St. John the Baptist** (Kostel sv. Jana Křtitele), and Jánska itself contains houses for the church's officials. From the Church of St. John the Baptist, walk up Pilarova to the 13th-century **Cathedral of St. Maurice** (Chrám sv. Mořice); though it's one of the few surviving medieval buildings in town, its interior is disappointing. The Jewish **town hall** *(Radnice)* at Moravcova 9 is the only surviving example outside Prague.

Don't miss the prince-bishop's other splendid **flower garden** *(Kvetná zahrada),* west of the town on Svobody. ∎

Moravian Karst

Sixteen miles (25 km) north of Brno is a fascinating region of Devonian limestone hills known as the Moravian Karst (Moravský kras). Some 4 miles wide (6 km) and 16 miles long (25 km), it's a forested area of spectacular rock formations and deep ravines, which also is home to countless miles of mysterious caves and tunnels. Many of these caves have been carved out by an underground river, the Punkva.

Of the thousand or so caves in the region, only four are open to the public. Many of the caverns have been explored only recently for the first time. The **Punkevní caves** (Punkevní jeskyně; *www.punkevni-jeskyne.cz, $$$*) are the most spectacular and popular, with long lines forming in summer. Arrive early to avoid a tedious wait or a sellout for the rest of the day. Along with the Kateřinská caves, they are best reached by taking the road from Blansko toward **Rock Mill** (Skalní Mlýn) nature reserve *(tel 516 413 575)*. You'll find a parking lot and hotel at Skalní Mlýn. From here it is a short walk to the Kateřinská caves and a mile-long (2 km) walk to the Punkevní caves. A small train also shuttles spelunkers back and forth *($)*.

The hour-long tour of Punkevní passes through five large caves, glistening with stalactites and stalagmites formed by the steady drip of rainwater through the limestone, and emerges at the lake at the foot of the Macocha Abyss. This chasm is 453 feet deep (138 m), created when the rock roof of an immense cave collapsed. The abyss is filled with luxuriant vegetation, owing to the exceptionally warm and moist microclimate of the chasm.

A ride on the underground Punkva River is just one highlight of the Punkevní cave tour.

Moravian Karst
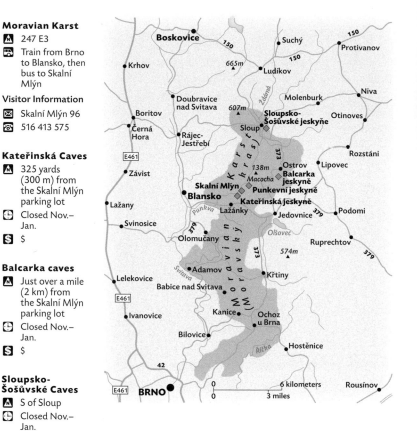
🅰 247 E3
🚆 Train from Brno to Blansko, then bus to Skalní Mlýn

Visitor Information
✉ Skalní Mlýn 96
☎ 516 413 575

Kateřinská Caves
🅰 325 yards (300 m) from the Skalní Mlýn parking lot
🕐 Closed Nov.–Jan.
💲 $

Balcarka caves
🅰 Just over a mile (2 km) from the Skalní Mlýn parking lot
🕐 Closed Nov.–Jan.
💲 $

Sloupsko-Šošůvské Caves
🅰 S of Sloup
🕐 Closed Nov.–Jan.
💲 $

If you want to see how the chasm looks from the top, take a cable car (buy a ticket before entering the caves, $) to the crest of the abyss, where there is a restaurant. You can also get there by road: Take the Ostrov direction from Skalní Mlýn, and turn left after just over a mile (2 km). The tour then continues by boat—a 1,640-foot-long (500 m) ride on the underground Punkva River.

Much less crowded are the **Katerinská caves** (Kateřinská jeskyně). They have a remarkable collection of stick stalagmites in two vast caverns (30-minute tour). In summer, concerts are held in

this amazing setting. The **Balcarka caves** (Balcarka jeskyně), east of the Macocha Abyss, are smaller, but they have colorful stalactites and stalagmites (45-minute tour).

Linked by domed chambers and galleries, the **Sloupsko-Šošuvské caves,** just south of the hamlet of Sloup, are the spookiest. Many fossils have been discovered here, and in 1966 the remains of a Neanderthal man were found nearby, as well as vestigial prehistoric wall paintings.

For a change from the subterranean wonderland, the wooded hills of the Moravian Karst can be easily explored along walking trails. ∎

Pernštejn

Overlooking the Svratka River and the little town of Nedvědice is the amazing castle of Pernštejn. Originally a 13th-century fortress, it grew to become one of the country's largest and best-preserved castles as the Pernštejn family gradually converted their stronghold into an isolated palatial residence. The oldest sections are the ramparts and the round tower.

By 1596, the family had fallen on hard times and were forced to sell the castle. It changed hands several times until it was purchased in 1818 by the Mitrovic family, who owned it until 1945. The most celebrated feature is the wooden bridge, with a perilous drop beneath, that links two of the keeps. There are many defensive machicolations, so the building gets fatter but more angular and more elaborate as it rises. It is baffling to imagine how such a complex structure could have been constructed on this rocky and vertiginous spur. Unsurprisingly, with such a dominant position, the castle was never conquered.

If you don't arrive at the castle by car, you can reach it by taking the train from Brno to Nedvědice. From the train station, it's a 1-mile (1.6 km) walk or short taxi ride to the castle. You embark on the 80-minute tour through one set of walls and gateways after another—the outer walls shelter a restaurant and pub. Gradually the amazing sight of the top-heavy castle comes into full view. The initially Renaissance interior was adapted and decorated in the 18th and 19th centuries, and its staid, and occasionally over-pretty state, is a bit disappointing after the high drama of the exterior. But there are older parts that have not been altered to the same extent—notably the chapel of 1570, the baroque Knights' Hall with its stucco swags, and the library. Some of the later decorations are quite successful, including the low-ceilinged Hall of Conspirators, with its neo-Gothic furnishings and painted coats of arms. ∎

Pernštejn

🅰 246 D3

✉ 25 miles (40 km) NW of Brno via routes 43 and 387

🕐 Closed Mon. May–Sept.; Mon.–Fri. April & Oct.; & Nov.– March

💲 $$–$$$

Sitting astride a craggy spur, Pernštejn was never conquered.

Czech Wine

Bohemia understandably became world famous for its beer, but few know about Czech wine. Winemaking dates back to the third century, when Romans grew grapes in the Palava region near Mikulov, in southern Moravia on the Old Amber Trail. Archaeologists found a vintner's knife for cutting vines at the site of the camp. In 1358 winemaking received royal patronage under Charles IV, who had been educated in the French court.

Hobby winemaking: stirring up the fermenting grapes in a private cellar

When the king returned home, he began importing Burgundy grapes from France, thereby turning Prague into a major viticulture center. You'll find vineyards along the Elbe River in Bohemia and along the Danube River in Moravia, though it's the latter region, the larger of the two, that is most lauded. The region around Mikolov especially (see p. 259), with its cool microclimate and warm, south-facing slopes, remains one of the most productive wine regions in the Czech Republic. It's not surprising that

the wines here bear a resemblance to their Austrian brethren, grown across the border in a region known as the Weinviertel. As in Austria, white wines are favored—about 75 percent of Czech wines are white—and the grape varieties are similar: Ryzlink Rýnský (Riesling), Ryzlink Vlašský (Welschriesling), Müller-Thurgau, Tramín (Gewürztraminer), Rulandské bílé (Pinot Blanc), and the often excellent Veltlinské zelené (Grüner Veltliner).

The Czech reds can range from good to excellent, though they are quite different

INSIDER TIP:

One way to sample Moravia's
best vintage is on a tour of the
National Wine Center in Valtice
(www.vinarskecentrum.cz), where
they keep more than 100
award winners. A sommelier
is on hand to answer your
questions and refill your glass.

—EMILY THOMPSON
Special Sections editor, The Prague Post

from French or Spanish wines, since many of
the grapes used are different. The best reds
often come from the Velké Pavlovice region
of Moravia. Among the leading varieties,
resembling those found in neighboring Austria,
are Frankova (Lemberger, Blaufränkisch), Svato-
vavřinecké (St. Laurent), and Zweigelt.

Many of the wines produced in the Czech
Republic are made from grape varieties such as
Müller-Thurgau, which are best enjoyed young.
A notable quantity of sparkling wine is also
produced here. Under communist rule, almost
all wine production fell into the hands of
cooperatives, which valued volume over quality,
thereby assuring the downfall of the fine wines
once grown in Czechoslovakia. Today many
of those cooperatives have become private

companies that dominate the market. There
are also a number of private producers, including the Lobkowicz family in Mělník in Bohemia,
and many smaller growers in Moravia who
are aiming for higher quality. Assisted by the
Viticultural Law, passed in 1995 to govern and
standardize the industry, it's assured that Czech
wines are making a strong comeback.

Czech wine producers have followed several
tasting events to identify the country's best
growers. Their wines are available for tasting
and purchase in the wine cellars at Valtice in
Moravia (see pp. 258–259).

Award-Winning Vintages

Foreign oenophiles have been following the
columns and reviews of British expatriate
wine aficionado Helena Baker *(www.baker
wine.cz)* for over a decade. Her knowledge
of the best vintages, techniques, and ter-
roires in Bohemia and Moravia have made
her coverage in *The Prague Post* and other
publications required reading.

Most recently, she praised the Patria 2007,
a unique blend of berries Chardonnay and
Gewürztraminer, from the Patria Kobylí winery.
Another winner to look for in specialty wine
shops is Patria 2007 late harvest blend of St.
Laurent, André, and Pinot Noir varieties. Both
fared well against even award-winning Chilean
wine at a recent competition of experts.

EXPERIENCE: Biking in Wine Country

A great way to take in the Moravian
wine country while staying in shape is to
pedal a bicycle on the **Greenways Wine
Tour** *(www.gtc.cz/tour_wine.htm).* This
admittedly ambitious guided ten-day
journey starts in nearby Vienna and
covers the Czech vineyards in Znojmo,
Mikulov, Valtice, Pavlov, and Strážnice,
among others. Aside from learning which
growers are bottling the finest Pinot
Gris, or Rulandské šede, as it's known in

Moravia, the tour takes in charming
châteaus, historic exhibits, traditional
music, and Podyjí National Park.

Greenways Travel Club, which was
established in 1999 in Mikulov, promotes
ecologically sustainable tourism. The
company also offers shorter rides, walking, and multisport tours around the
Czech Republic. They specialize in small
groups and provide accommodation in
family-owned pensions.

Telč

The exquisite town of Telč, located in the western part of the region, is understandably popular with visitors. Built by the Lords of Hradec in the 14th century, it relied economically on the fishponds that dot the surrounding countryside. These large ponds, linked by a canal that traverses the castle grounds, give the town a shimmering, aquatic appearance that greatly adds to its charm.

The loveliest town square in the Republic is surely Telč's gentle span of arcaded houses and shops.

Telč

⚑ 246 B3

✉ 54 miles (87 km) W of Brno via route 23

Visitor Information

✉ Town hall, Náměstí Zachariáše z Hradce

☎ 567 112 407

 www.telc.eu

A devastating fire in 1530 destroyed much of Telč, but its Gothic churches survived. In 1992 the town was made a UNESCO World Heritage site. At the top of the square named after Zachariáš of Hradec you'll find the Renaissance **château.** An existing stronghold was rebuilt for Zachariáš of Hradec by Antonio Vlach and Baldassare Maggi in the 1560s and '70s. The lovely gardens, magnificently

decorated halls, and gorgeous chapel reflect the sumptuous Italianate taste of the family. The château remained in their hands until 1712, when it passed to the Liechtensteins.

Visitors are offered two tours. Tour A, the better of the two, takes an hour and gives access to the beautifully decorated Renaissance-style rooms, some of which have delicate sgraffito decoration. In complete contrast is the African

INSIDER TIP:

Feeding the ducks in Štěpnický pond behind Market Square is a good way to relax and appreciate the beautiful town as blithely as the locals do.

—EMILY THOMPSON
Special Sections editor,
The Prague Post

Hall, where hunting and safari trophies are displayed. The intricately stuccoed chapel was built around 1580 as the burial place of Zachariáš and his wife, Kateřina, who are represented in pious effigies. Attached to the castle is the small **gallery** *(closed Dec.–Feb.)* devoted to the work of the surrealist and landscape painter Jan Zrzavý (1890–1977). The shorter Tour B visits the rooms decorated after Zachariáš's time.

But it's the main square, **Náměstí Zachariáse z Hradce,**

that makes Telč so irresistible: Long rows of arcaded gabled houses, hardly any two alike, are painted in pastel colors, and between them is an expanse of cobbles, interrupted only by fountains and a twisting plague column of 1720. The most delightful house perches on the corner of U Masných krámů, with its recently restored sgraffito and frescoes and Renaissance oriel. A medieval survival is the **Church of St. James** (Kostel sv. Jakuba), near the castle.

At the squares' other end is the oldest church in Telč, the 13th-century **Church of the Holy Spirit** (Kostel sv. Ducha), whose tower *(closed Sun., $)* provides views of the town. Down Palackého from the square you will find the **Great Gate** (Velká brána), from which you can reach the remaining fortifications. At the far end of the square, take the lane to the right before the gallery to the town's other medieval gateway, the **Little Gate** (Malá brána), leading into the castle's park. ∎

Château
🕐 Closed Mon. & Nov.–March
💲 $$–$$$

Jihlava

North of Telč, 45 miles (72 km) west of Brno, the medieval silver-mining town of Jihlava *(Masarykovo náměstí 19, tel 567 308 034)* has a sloping main square adorned with a 1679 plague column and fountains. Next to the Church of St. Ignatius (Kostel sv. Ignáce), you can access the so-called catacombs *(closed Jan., $)*, underground tunnels used for storage and refuge during the Thirty Years' War. At No. 58 two Renaissance houses now contain the town's museum *(closed Mon., $)*, which has mostly natural history collections. The building itself is more rewarding.

The remaining fortifications lie south of Masarykovo náměstí, the main square, and the Church of the Assumption (Kostel Nanebezetí Panny Marie), with its Gothic frescoes, stands 200 yards (180 m) west of it. The composer Gustav Mahler (1860–1911) grew up here. His connections with the town are honored in a museum *(Kosmákova 9, closed Mon. April–Oct., & all Nov.–March, $)*, just off the lower main square. For fun, there's a zoo a short walk from the main square, with a good collection of cats, including snow leopards, as well as monkeys and hippos.

More Places to Visit in Southern Moravia

Bítov

At Bítov, high on a crag along the southern border with Austria, stands a medieval **castle,** much expanded over the centuries. Although impressive from the outside, the mostly neo-Gothic interior is less interesting, with exhibits focusing on the castle's history. **⚠** 246 B2 ✉ 24 miles (38 km) NW of Znojmo. NW on route 38 for 3 miles (5 km), then NW on route 408, at Desov S on route 411 🚌 Bus from Znojmo 🕐 Closed Mon. May–Sept.; Mon.–Fri. April & Oct.; & Nov.–March 💲 $$

Buchlovice

The gorgeous, early 18th-century **château** of Buchlovice lies within a beautiful English-style park. Its design is usually attributed to Domenico Martinelli. The château faces an equally majestic pavilion, the curved facade of each building complementing the other, with balustrades, gravel terraces, and parterre gardens separating the two. The cozy rococo interior is beautifully furnished. The whole design feels ambitious yet essentially modest: Everything seems perfectly in place.

Continue toward Brno for 3 miles (5 km), and there's a sharp turn to **Buchlov,** a thick-walled and compact 13th-century **castle,** from which there are splendid views.
⚠ 247 F2 ✉ 6 miles (10 km) W of Uherské Hradiště via route 50 🚌 Bus from Brno **Buchlovice château** 🕐 Closed Mon. May, June, & Sept.; Mon.–Fri. April & Oct.; & Nov.–March 💲 $ **Buchlov castle** 🕐 Closed Mon.–Fri. April & Oct., & Nov.–March 💲 $

Bučovice

To the east of Slavkov rises the moated Renaissance château of Bučovice, once owned by the Liechtensteins. Although it has a rather unimaginative exterior, there's a superb galleried courtyard and a beautifully decorated interior designed in the late 16th century. One entire room is bizarrely painted with hares exacting vengeance upon their foes, human and canine, and the royal hare couple enjoying a banquet.
⚠ 247 E2 ✉ 6 miles (10 km) E of Slavkov via route 50 🚌 Train from Brno **Château** 🕐 Closed Mon. May–Sept.; Mon.–Fri. April & Oct.; & Nov.–March 💲 $

Jaroměřice nad Rokytnou

North of Znojmo is the village of Jaroměřice nad Rokytnou, with its vast **château.** Commissioned in 1711 by Count Questenberg, the building took 25 years to complete. The château contains a theater, as the count was a great patron of music: The first Czech opera,

---

EXPERIENCE: The Old West, Czech Style

Visitors from North America are sometimes stunned to see just how passionate citizens of the former Eastern bloc are about Westerns. The former Czechoslovakia produced its own, in fact, the musical melodrama known as *Lemonade Joe* or *Limonádový Joe aneb Konská* opera, in 1964, a classic still known to all ages. In that spirit, the **Western Park Boskovice** (www.westernove-mestecko.cz) opened in 1993, and has since expanded into cabaret shows, shoot-outs, rodeos, and oldtime dances billed as "country balls." It's all to be taken with a grain of salt (depictions of Native Americans would not go down well with those being celebrated), but it does provide an insight into the power of the myth of the cowboy to central Europeans. It's a fantasy that has grown since the first letter arrived from cousins who settled in Praha, Texas.

The charming château at Buchlovice stands in contrast to Moravia's more overblown country houses.

O původu Jaroměřic by František Václav Míča, received its premiere here in 1730, and a music festival is still held in summer.

🅰 246 C2   ✉ 22 miles (35 km) N of Znojmo via route 38   🚌 Bus from Brno **Château** 🕐 Closed Mon. May–Sept., Mon.–Fri. April & Oct., & Nov.–March   💲 $–$$

Křtiny

A lofty white pilgrimage **church,** designed by Giovanni Santini in the early 18th century, completely dominates this village. The interior is essentially one vast domed expanse, exuberantly frescoed in high-baroque style. Rolling woodlands around make for a lovely setting, and opposite is a restaurant.

🅰 247 E3   ✉ 10 miles (16 km) NE of Brno via route 373   🚌 Bus from Brno

Luhačovice

Northeast of Uherské Hradiště, the grand spa of Luhačovice lies among wooded hills. Its briny mineral springs are said to benefit respiratory ailments. Slovak Dušan Jurkovič (1868–1947) designed many of the sanatoria in a folksy secessionist style. There are more impressive spas, but anyone with an interest in European domestic architecture will not be disappointed.

🅰 246 G2   ✉ 18 miles (29 km) NE of Uherské Hradiště. E on route 50 to Uherský Brod, then N on route 492   🚌 Bus from Brno

Moravský Krumlov

Midway between Znojmo and Brno, Moravský Krumlov contains yet another **castle,** rebuilt during the Renaissance and grouped around a tiered and arcaded courtyard. One wing of the castle houses a gallery devoted to Alfons Mucha (1860–1939), who was born close by. His reputation lies with his art nouveau posters, but here the most striking exhibits are his rich historical paintings. Mucha spent nearly two decades creating this series of 20 monumental canvases, which is known as the "Slav Epic."

🅰 246 D2   ✉ 20 miles (32 km) SW of Brno on route E65, then S on route 394   🚌 Bus from Brno   **Castle** 🕐 Closed Mon. May–June & Sept.–Oct., & all Nov.–March   💲 $

Slavkov u Brna

On December 2, 1805, in what was to become known as the Battle of Austerlitz, Napoleon delayed his advance on the enemy until the optimal moment, thereby thrashing the Austrians and Russians in one of his most defining moments. The site, due east of Brno at Slavkov u Brna (Austerlitz), and in between the two towns, is now commemorated with a scattering of sites. At the top of the Pratzen hill (Pracký kopec), on route 417 between Slavkov and Brno, is Josef Fanta's **Monument of Peace,** commissioned in 1912 by the three combatant countries.

A **museum** *($)* marks this crucial event. Napoleon stayed at the colossal **Slavkov Castle,** built for the Kaunitz family by Domenico Martinelli in the 18th century. Inside its neoclassical bulk, stuccoed salons display exhibits devoted to Napoleon and his influence on the country.

🅐 247 E3 ✉ 10 miles (16 km) E of Brno via E462, W on route 50 🚍 Bus from Brno **Visitor information** ✉ Palackého náměstí 1 ☎ 544 220 988 **Slavkov Castle** *www.zamek-slakov.cz* ☎ 544 221 204 🕐 Closed Mon. April–May & Sept.–Nov.; & all Dec.–March 💲 $–$$

Tišnov

Near Tišnov in the valley of the Svratka River is the Cistercian **Abbey of Porta Coeli,** founded in 1233 and built in Romanesque style. It has a superb, if overrestored, west portal, richly carved, and fine cloisters.

🅐 246 D3 ✉ 15 miles (24 km) N of Brno via routes 43 and 385 🚍 Train from Brno

Třebíč

It's worth pausing at Třebíč to visit the magnificent **Basilica of St. Procopius** (Kostel sv. Prokopa). Built in granite between 1240 and 1260, it sports a superlative Romanesque porch (Gate of Paradise), and a chapel in the choir contains rare 13th-century frescoes. The lovely maze of a crypt is forested with stubby columns. The conventual buildings house a **museum** of Christmas crèches *(closed Mon., $).*

🅐 246 C3 ✉ 35 miles (56 km) W of Brno via E65, exit at Rosice, W on route 23 **Visitor information** ✉ Karlovo náměstí 56 ☎ 568 896 120

Uherské Hradiště

Uherské Hradiště is best known for its excavations of Velká Morava, **Great Moravia,** the oldest Slav settlement in the Czech Republic: Follow the signs to "Památník." At the museum *(closed Dec.–March, $),* an English guidebook explains the significance of the excavations and skeletons, weaponry, jewelry, and other exhibits.

🅐 247 F2 ✉ 40 miles (64 km) E of Brno via route E462, then W on route 50 🚍 Bus from Brno

Vranov nad Dyjí

Dramatically located on a crag above Vranov nad Dyjí is the town's **château,** largely rebuilt in the 1690s by the Austrian architect Johann Bernard Fischer von Erlach. The present building is a hodgepodge of baroque and neoclassical styles. The chateau's interior includes the domed Hall of the Ancestors, lavishly frescoed.

🅐 246 B2 ✉ 14 miles (22 km) W of Znojmo via routes 38, 408, 398 🚍 Bus from Znojmo **Château** 🕐 Closed Mon. May–Sept.; Mon.–Fri. April & Oct.; & Nov.–March 💲 $$–$$$

Žd'ár nad Sázavou

Just north of Žd'ár nad Sázavou you'll discover a striking Cistercian monastery. With the original monastery having been destroyed during the Hussite wars in the 15th century, the present complex was mostly built by Giovanni Santini (1677–1723). His style is a curious hybrid, often placing Gothic forms within a supple baroque framework, a style evident also at the nearby pilgrimage **Church of St. John of Nepomuk** (Kostel sv. Jana Nepomuckého). The church is decorated with motifs associated with the saint. The design is unique: Not only pentagonal but also encircled by a zigzag of continuous arcades, making this one of the most eccentric expressions of central European baroque. There is a fine book museum in the monastery stables.

🅐 246 C4 ✉ 40 miles (64 km) NW of Brno 🚍 Train from Prague and Brno **Church of St. John of Nepomuk** 🕐 Closed Mon. May–Sept.; Mon.–Fri. April & Oct.; & Nov.–March 💲 $$

From the Jeseníky mountains to the mining town of Ostrava to the university town of Olomouc

Northern Moravia

Mount Praded lookout tower

Northern Moravia

Three cities in northern Moravia are industrial but have much of interest, while the remote Jeseníky mountains are popular with skiers. Olomouc is a beautiful central European city, while the country's most impressive *skansen*, an open-air museum of vernacular architecture, provides a glimpse into the past.

The northern area near the Polish border is historically part of Silesia. To the west, also bordering Poland, the Jeseníky mountains are home to a number of old-fashioned ski resorts. Like northern Bohemia, this area has bounded back since industrial pollution has ceased. Easily the most interesting of northern Moravian cities is Olomouc, with its two handsome squares and many churches, museums, and institutions. It makes a good base for exploring the region.

Less rich in castles than eastern Bohemia, northern Moravia nonetheless has some winners when it comes to eccentricity at Bouzov and Plumlov. Visitors head to Rožnov pod Radhoštěm to see the largest and most impressive of the Czech Republic's *skansens*. The town is also a good center for exploring Moravian Wallachia, one of the most durable of the regional subcultures.

Moravia pays homage to its distinguished offspring in various places. At Hukvaldy, museums and memorials are devoted to the great composer Leoš Janáček (1854–1928), and the achievements of the athlete Emil Zátopek (1922–2000) are celebrated in Kopřivnice (this town also boasts the Tatra Museum, deservedly popular with car enthusiasts). Curiously, the town of Příbor has been slow to honor its most famous native, Sigmund Freud (1856–1939), father of psychoanalysis. ■

Area of map detail

Prague

0   20 kilometers
0   10 miles

NOT TO BE MISSED:

Seeing the proletarian heroes on the town hall in Olomouc **278–279**

The magnificence and flora and fauna of the Jeseníky mountains **284–285**

The Teutonic fortifications of Bouzov **288**

Checking out pre-war motoring at Kopřivnice's Tatra Museum **290**

Drinking in the newly revived nightlife in Ostrava **290–291**

The 13th-century chapel in Šternberk **292**

Osoblaha

Jindřichov

Mesto Albrechtice

Karlovice

Krnov

POLAND

Opavice

Opava

45

57

untál

Horní Benešov

11

Koběřice

46

N í z k y

Litultovice

Opava

56

Kravaře

Opava

Hlučín

468

Odra

vod. nádrž ská Harta

Hradec nad Moravicí

11

Bohumín

Orlova

Karviná

Dvorce

ravský roun

vod.nádrž Kružberk

46

Moravice

57

Klimkovice

OSTRAVA

Havířov

Olše

67

e s e n í k

Vitkov

Bilovec

47

Ostravice

56

11

Česky Těšín

Fulnek

Studénka

58

Odra

Frýdek- Místek

Brušperk

O d e r s k é

Odry

Příbor

E462

Dobra

Trinec

E75

995m

v r c h y

Potštát

57

Kopřivnice

Hukvaldy

Frýdlant nad Ostravicí

Guty

Bystřice

11

ubočky
35

Nový Jičín

48

Rybí

Frenštát pod Radhoštěm

1323m

Jablunkov

Slezské Beskydy

řšice

Hranice

Hodslavice

Štramberk

M o r a v s k o s l e z s k é

1067m

Lipník nad Bečvou

47

Bečva

B e s k y d y

Přerov

Valašské Meziříčí

Rožnov pod Radhoštěm

35

Horní Bečva

F

55

57

V s e t í n s k e

912m

Velké Karlovice

Jablůnka

v r c h y

SLOVAKIA

UTHERN MORAVIA

Vsetín

Nový Hrozenkov

p. 245

Halenkov

Hovězí

E

69

49

Senice

57

Francova Lhota

C

D

Olomouc

The seventh century marked the first settlement at Olomouc; it was Moravia's capital until 1641. Now it's a thriving industrial and university town of broad avenues lined with old seminaries, solid 19th-century apartment houses, leafy parks, baroque fountains, and stately university buildings.

The Renaissance town hall dominates Olomouc's large main square in the city center.

Olomouc became the seat of a bishopric in 1063. It prospered during the 16th century but then suffered during the Thirty Years' War. Despite losing its capital status to Brno, Olomouc remains an important and lively city.

The heart of the Old Town beats in two bustling squares, Horní náměstí and Dolní náměstí. The vast Horní náměstí encircles the Renaissance **town hall** (*radnice*), a complex, much altered structure with a Gothic oriel window, double staircase, tower, loggia, and portal. Its famous astronomical clock was reconstructed after it was destroyed during World War II. When the hour strikes, a procession of proletarian figurines (the communist version of saints) parades past.

The town hall vies for attention with the colossal **Trinity column,** culminating at a height of 115 feet (35 m) in an obelisk from which carved angels seem to tumble. Built in 1754, it is the largest of the thousands of such columns throughout the Czech Republic. The neoclassical **theater,** designed by Josef Kornhäusel in 1830, is where the young composer Gustav Mahler worked in 1883.

Adjoining Horní náměstí is Dolní náměstí, with its own pair of fountains and a Marian column. Among the Renaissance mansions here, the **Hauenschild Palace** at No. 27 boasts a double-height oriel window on the corner. The Gothic **Church of St. Maurice** (Kostel sv. Mořice) has a somewhat grimy exterior and fortresslike tower. Inside, the usual baroque and neo-Gothic furnishings can't conceal the soaring Gothic piers and vaults, even though the ribs have been painted a dirty pink. The church is celebrated for its 1745 organ, and an organ festival is held here each September. On the other side of Horni náměstí, the **Church of St. Michael** (Kostel sv. Michala) may be drab outside, but inside you find a three-domed baroque extravaganza. Nearby, the tiny 20th-century **Sarkander chapel,** like a small domed baroque temple, honors the Catholic priest Jan Sarkander, who was tortured to death in 1620.

The early 18th-century Jesuit **Church of Our Lady of the Snows** (Kostel Panny Marie Sněžné) overlooks Náměstí Republiky. The former Jesuit college here faces two museums: The **Art Museum** (Muzeum umění; *closed Mon., $*) displays exhibits relating to Olomouc's history and 16th- to 18th-century Dutch paintings; the **Vlastivědné muzeum** contains a natural history collection.

In the **Archbishop's Palace** (Arcibiskupský palác), a graceful building of the 1600s, the teenage Franz Josef was proclaimed emperor of Austria in 1848.

The Romanesque origins of the **Cathedral of St. Wenceslas** (Dóm sv. Václava; *closed Mon. & Oct.–March*) are obscured by the drastic 1880s restoration that expanded the baroque cathedral. The famous treasury is housed in the reliquary-filled crypt.

Adjoining the cathedral are the remains of the old **Bishop's Palace** *(closed Mon.).* Excavations revealed Romanesque double windows, a Gothic cloister, and

INSIDER TIP:

For surreal fun, crack an overpriced can of Gambrinus at Letka (Legionářská ulice), a Soviet commercial airliner that has been converted into a bar.

—EMILY THOMPSON
Special Sections editor,
The Prague Post

a chapel with 16th-century frescoes. The Romanesque work is of outstanding quality. Opposite the cathedral is the deanery; here the last Přemysl king, Václav III, was murdered in 1306. Don't overlook the north wall with its unique late-Gothic-style paintings. ∎

Olomouc

- 🔼 276 B2
- ✉ 170 miles (274 km) E of Prague
- 🚆 Train and bus from Prague

Visitor Information

- ✉ Town hall, Horní náměstí
- ☎ 585 513 385

www.olomouc-tourism.cz

A Walk Around Olomouc

Busy Olomouc is a city in which the ancient and youthful blend well together, and it's small enough to be easily and enjoyably explored on foot. This walk takes you through the two important squares at the heart of the Old Town, through the university area, and on to the cathedral. The energetic may like to continue out to the Premonstratensian monastery at Hradisko.

Around Horní náměstí

Start on Horní náměstí by the Renaissance **town hall** (radnice) ❶ and admire its slender tower and Italianate loggia and portal. Time your walk so that you are by the town hall when the astronomical clock strikes the hour. It draws large crowds with its procession of proletarian figurines.

Walk past the **Trinity column** (Sousoší Nejsvětější trojice), and the **theater** where the young composer Gustav Mahler served a

NOT TO BE MISSED:

Town hall • Horní náměstí
• Dolní náměstí • Bishop's Palace

three-month stint as musical director in 1883. The comfortable Café Mahler is across the square. Its rival, Café Caesar, occupies the prestigious site of the first-floor vaults of the town hall, and in summer terraces at both establishments spill out on to the square.

Go south from Horní náměstí to Dolní náměstí, lined with Renaissance mansions, notably the ornate **Hauenschild Palace** (Hauenschilduv dům) ❷, on the corner at No. 27. You can pause in summer for a snack at the open-air beer hall in the middle of the square.

Return to Horní náměstí, bear right past the clock tower, and follow Opletalova to the Gothic **Church of St. Maurice** (Kostel sv. Mořice) ❸. Pop inside to admire the soaring piers and vaults. For a view of Old Town, you can climb the church tower. In December you can see traders selling live carp outside the supermarket next to the church. Go back to Horní náměstí again, turn left after Café Mahler, then immediately right on Michalská. This leads to the domed baroque **Church of St. Michael** (Kostel sv. Michala) ❹, attached to a Dominican friary. Past the church, bear left, and after 55 yards (50 m) you'll see the tiny circular **Sarkander chapel** (Kaple sv. Jana Sarkander).

Walk back to the Church of St. Michael and follow the sign on the left to the restored **Villa Primavesi** (Vila Primavesi) ❺, which now

An elaborate astronomical clock adorns the side of the town hall. Its mosaics depict valorous laborers.

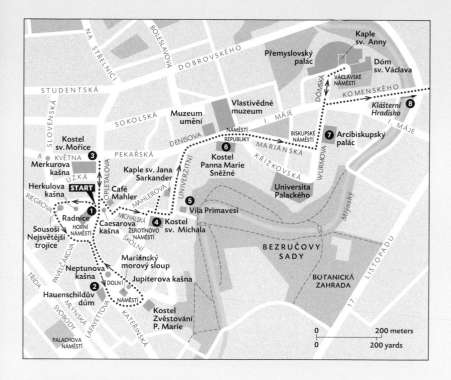

houses a restaurant *(www.primavesi.cz)*, offices, and apartments. Continue down Univerzitní, passing a palatial 17th-century seminary before reaching Denisova and the overbearing early 18th-century Jesuit **Church of Our Lady of the Snows** (Kostel Panny Marie Sněžné) ❻. It overlooks Náměstí Republiky, where the former Jesuit college faces two museums.

Bishop's Palaces & Cathedral

From the post office on Náměstí Republiky, Mariánská leads to the **Archbishop's Palace** (Arcibiskupský palác) ❼, flanked by other baroque and reconstructed palaces and now part of Palacký University. Bear left on Wurmova and then take Dómská to the **Cathedral of St. Wenceslas** (Dóm sv. Václava). Adjoining the cathedral are the remains of the **Bishop's Palace** (Přemyslovský palác) that once stood here. Opposite the cathedral is the deanery, now also part of the university.

🅰	See area map p. 276
►	Horní náměstí
🕒	3 miles (4.5 km)
↔	3–4 hours
►	Monastery of Hradisko

North of Olomouc

North of Olomouc is the vast former Premonstratensian **Monastery of Hradisko** (Klášterní Hradisko) ❽. The monastery is about a one-mile (1.6 km) hike from the cathedral. Take Komenského, the eastward extension of Denisova, in the direction away from the Old Town, cross two bridges, then take a left along an unnamed road. Soon you will see looming ahead the yellow and white of this baroque monastery. It is now a hospital and therefore not open to visitors, but you can usually walk into the courtyard to admire its sheer size.

Rožnov pod Radhoštěm
& the Wallachians

Rožnov pod Radhoštěm is the site of the splendid *skansen,* or open-air museum, of Wallachia that dominates this small town. Many of the exhibits—churches, houses, schools—have been collected from Wallachian villages in the nearby Beskydy mountains.

Three villages at Rožnov's open-air museum depict Wallachian life and cultural traditions.

Rožnov pod Radhoštěm

- 🅰 277 D2
- ✉ 35 miles (56 km) E of Olomouc
- 🚌 Bus from Olomouc, Prague, & Brno

Regional Visitor Information

- ✉ Municipal Information Center, Burian Museum, Závličí 456, Štramberk
- ☎ 556 852 240
- 🕒 Closed Mon.

The Wallachians were a nomadic sheep-rearing people with a strong cultural tradition of their own. Nobody knows exactly where the Wallachians came from, but these herdsmen and woodsmen were possibly related to the Romanian Vlachs. With their distinctive customs and traditions, they were evidently considered outsiders, and much of their culture was wiped out by the Habsburgs in the 17th century. Even today the Wallachian people still preserve their own dialect and local customs.

Their heartland is in the Beskydy mountains northeast of Rožnov pod Radhoštěm. In villages such as **Štramberk,** dozens of traditional wooden cottages are still inhabited. Despite their timeless appearance, many of these cottages were built in a range of styles in the early 19th century and are in varying states of repair. You can get an excellent view over the Wallachian countryside from the reconstructed Gothic castle tower at Štramberk *(closed Nov.–March, $).*

Other Wallachian villages that remain relatively unspoiled include **Velké Karlovice,** with its wooden church, town hall, and farmhouses, and Nový Hrozenkov, Hovězí, and Halenkov. The fiery plum brandy known as *slivovice* is not unique to Wallachia, but this region remains a center of production, with a large distillery at Vizovice.

Rožnov's Skansen

The skansen at Rožnov was the first to be opened to the public, in 1925, and it is still the largest, an assembly of more than 90 structures, from churches to shepherd's huts dating from the 17th to 20th centuries (some are replicas). The dark logs of the houses look splendid in this wooded setting.

There are three sections to the skansen, each of which can be visited separately. The first site is the **Wooden Village** (Dřevěné městečko; *closed Nov., $*), the original part of the museum. If you only have time to visit only one of the three sites, this is the one to choose. The most impressive exhibits here are the wooden town hall of Rožnov, dating from 1770, followed by a fine reconstruction of a 17th-century timber church from Větřkovice, a family house from 1750, and a collection of carved beehives—beekeeping was important in Wallachia's rural economy. Be sure to watch for these, as they are highly unusual, with lively sculptured scowling faces. The pubs are fully operational at the Wooden Village, and light food as well as beer are served.

The second skansen is the **Wallachian Village** (Valašská dědine; *closed Oct.–April, $*), which shows what village life was like here in the past. The cattle are still raised as they would have been by Wallachian herdsmen. Horse-drawn carriages and musical ensembles featuring violins and dulcimers enliven the scene. A Wallachian carnival is staged here in February to celebrate the end of winter, and in July there are folkloric performances at Rožnov. In early July Texans of Czech descent pour into the town for a boisterous week of cook-offs and rodeos.

The most recent addition to the museum is **Mill Valley** (Mlýnská dolina; *closed Oct.–April, $*); it is the only one that has to be visited on a guided tour. Here you are shown around a water mill, a sawmill, and a flour mill, in the company of cheerful guides in Wallachian peasant costumes. A combined ticket *($$)* is available to visit all three villages. ■

Rožnov Visitor Information

 Masarykovo náměstí 128

☎ 571 652 444

www.roznov.cz

Wallachian Architecture

The Wallachians' distinctive rustic architecture aptly illustrates their tradition of melding sturdy, unpretentious utility with the charm of hand-crafted woodwork. These buildings, generally constructed of local pine and fir, feature gaps filled in with clay—humble homes that provided affordable, warm, weather-tight shelters for generations of rural folk. Often built with a single door and small windows to protect residents from the long, cold, wet Czech winters, these buildings, reminiscent of American log cabins, still survive in many places. Some of the larger ones have been renovated with modern conveniences into enchanting country homes and are in high demand.

Jeseníky Mountains

North of Šternberk rise the Jeseníky mountains (Hrubý Jeseník), the highest in Moravia, stretching eastward across the Polish border. The mountains are popular with hikers; in winter this is a highly regarded area for cross-country skiing. In addition, there are some small spas.

Grand hotels cater to visitors in Karlova Studánka and other Jeseníky resorts.

Jeseníky Mountains

🗺 276 B4

🚆 Train from Olomouc or Opava to Jeseník

Visitor Information

✉ Masarykovo náměstí 1/167, Jeseník

☎ 584 498 111

www.jesenik.org

Most visitors approaching the region do so from the textile-producing town of **Šumperk.** There is very little to see here, though there is a plague column in the main square. On its southern outskirts at **Bludov,** however, an immense square château has two turrets capping either end of the facade. Originally a Renaissance structure, it was given a thorough baroque face-lift in 1708.

From Šumperk continue north to the more prepossessing resort and spa town of **Velké Losiny,** which is a good starting point for mountain hikes. At the entrance to the village, dominating a beautiful park, is a splendid sgraffitoed Renaissance **château** with a three-tiered, galleried courtyard; it was owned by the wealthy Žerotín family until they were ejected after the Battle of White Mountain in 1620. During the Counter-Reformation, witch trials were conducted here over a 15-year period; 56 perfectly innocent people, their "confessions" extracted by torture, were dispatched to the stake.

From Velké Losiny the road north climbs past sawmills to a mountain pass. From here the road traverses hairpin bends along the way to Jeseník in the heart of the main Hrubý Jeseník range. From either side of the road you can see the principal summits, rising to 4,892 feet (1,491 m); some of them can be reached by walking trails that start at the top of the pass, Červenohorské sedlo, which itself is 3,314 feet high (1,010 m). The villages along the way are filled with low wooden cottages, usually painted green and topped by huge gabled roofs with large overhanging eaves. The landscape has suffered badly from acid rain; bleak moors, easily seen from the pass, exist where trees once thrived.

Spa Towns

Jeseník is above the little spa town of **Lázně Jeseník,** founded in 1826. From here there are fine views of the mountains. Most of the extant buildings date from the early 20th century. The natural springs are dispersed around the spa, and you'll find numerous walks along the trails through the pleasant countryside.

An even smaller spa lies a little farther to the west: **Lipová-Lázně.** Follow route 60 north to the caves known as **Jeskyně na Pomezí** (closed Mon.& Nov.–March, $), with their bizarre stalactite and stalagmite formations, then continue north to reach the village of **Žulová,**

where a fortress was converted into a church tower in the 19th century.

South of Jeseník

South of Jeseník, a particularly beautiful road (route 450) traverses the forests to the region's most enticing old spa: **Karlova Studánka.** Founded in 1785, it is noted for cold springs with a high iron content. This is easily the best of the mountain resorts, with its broad main street, handsome wooden buildings, and pleasant gardens. At 2,543 feet high (775 m), it's an excellent base for hiking to the Praděd (4,892 feet/1,491 m), the region's highest peak, and the Bílá Opava River's waterfalls.

INSIDER TIP:

Many trails run through these mountains. The S Koprníčkem, "around the mountain," trail is suitable for children.

—KATEŘINA PAVLŮ
Head of Information Centre
Jeseník

In the lower reaches of the mountains lies **Bruntál.** Its huge yellow-and-white baroque **château** (closed Mon. & Nov.–March, $–$$) has an entrance portal on a palatial scale from the 1760s and a lavishly furnished and frescoed interior. The charming arcaded courtyard, with its irregular shape, dates from the 16th century. ■

Velké Losiny Château

🕐 Closed Mon. May–Sept., Mon.–Fri. April & Oct., & Nov.– March

$ Guided tour: $

The Roma Plight

Nobody knows for certain how the Roma (Gypsies) ended up in central Europe, but they seem to have originated in India and migrated west during the late Middle Ages. Their nomadic way of life, communal ways, and distinctive clothing and customs cut them off from the rest of society from the start, and through the centuries they have been discriminated against and even persecuted for their dissimilarities.

Roma women and children don their finery for a festival at Brno.

Persecution of the Roma

In modern times, troubles for the Roma arose in 1927, when the Czechoslovak government passed the Law on Wandering Gypsies—forcing them to apply for identification and permission to stay the night. But the greatest tragedy came with World War II, when the Nazis established punitive labor camps for "Gypsies and other wandering individuals." These camps were replaced later by concentration camps at Lety u Písku in Bohemia and Hodonín u Kunštátu in Moravia, where many Roma died of starvation, malnutrition, disease, and brutality. Those who survived the concentration camps were subsequently transported to Nazi death camps. In the end, out of the prewar population of 6,500 Roma in Bohemia and Moravia, only 300 remained— a blight treated after the war with an embarrassed silence by the Czech nation.

Communist Re-education

Attempts were made during the communist era to integrate the Roma into society, to re-educate the Roma in the communist image—meaning, their language was suppressed and their nomadic way of life discouraged. They were forced out of their traditional occupations as weavers, musicians, and blacksmiths and drafted as unskilled construction workers. They were moved from rural settlements to tenement housing in the city. At the same time, although they were at the lower end of the socioeconomic system, they were partially incorporated into the fabric of society, often forced to go to school and jobs and to participate in the greater community.

Post-Communist Challenges

Since the fall of communism in 1989, the Roma have been left without any kind of social safety net to espouse their cause. Roma children are often denied access to normal schools. Few employers will offer adults steady work, let alone a career. Their unemployment rate is estimated to be about 70 percent. Public opinion polls show that most Czechs view the Roma minority as thieves and drunks. Racially motivated, physically violent crimes against them are commonplace. In response, many Roma have abandoned their homeland and immigrated to Canada or western Europe.

Human Rights & the Roma

It wasn't long ago that the Czech Republic found itself embarrassed over the issue of Roma integration. In 1998, a wall was erected in Ústí nad Labem to separate members of this minority ethnic group from non-Roma people in the town. That act, conceived by the Ústí mayor, did not hold for long, but there is still much progress to be made, according to human rights groups.

Assaults on Roma by neo-Nazi groups are at an all-time high in both the Czech Republic and Slovakia and many have questioned whether police and prosecutors take the issue seriously. The Roma organization Dženo issued a study in 2009 that indicated that,

Artistic talent flowers within the Roma community.

while support for Roma culture and language has been a positive development, housing and labor conditions have deteriorated and "extremism has risen alarmingly."

Ivan Veselý of the European Association of Roma Civic Initiatives in the Czech Republic says the state is primarily to blame. He cites a rise of Roma ghettos and anti-Roma statements made by government officials as proof of this assertion.

Prague human rights organizer Gwendolyn Albert also points to research by the Czech Education Ministry, showing that, even after much attention has been given to school integration, "one-third of all Roma are educated in schools for the mentally disabled, often due to faulty diagnoses of their mental ability."

Albert argues that at a time when much of Europe is celebrating two decades of freedom and hard-won civil rights since the fall of the Berlin Wall, it would seem that one group has been notably left behind.

Bouzov & Plumlov

In a country rich in castles, Bouzov and Plumlov stand out. They are fascinating for very different reasons: Bouzov (northwest of Olomouc), because of its history as a favorite Nazi residence during World War II, and Plumlov (just west of Prostejov), for its sheer architectural weirdness.

Bouzov
- 🅰 276 A3
- ☎ 585 346 202
- 🕑 Closed Mon. April–Oct., Mon.–Fri. Nov.– March
- 💲 $$$
- 🚌 Bus from Olomouc

www.hrad-bouzov.cz

Plumlov
- 🅰 276 B2 & 247 E3
- ☎ 774 302 163

www.zomek-plumlov.cz

Bouzov

Bouzov is a frenzy of towers and turrets, steeply pitched orange-red roofs, chimneys and gables, balconies over precipitous drops, and a drawbridge, all huddled around an immense round tower.

The 14th-century fortress became a royal property under George of Poděbrady. In 1696 it became the headquarters of the Hospitallers' Order of the Grand Masters of the Teutonic Knights, a ferociously anti-Slav organization. The Knights restyled the castle in neo-Gothic in the late 19th and early 20th centuries. The order was abolished in 1939; Bouzov was taken over by Nazi occupiers, who found the Teutonic pomposity irresistible.

Three tours of the castle are offered. The best option is the hour-long Tour 1; although Tour 2 is more detailed, it is also much longer. Tour 3 just visits the tower.

The interior is a medieval dream, with suits of armor, heavy wooden furniture, and wooden ceilings such as the barrel-vaulted Knights' Hall. Some bedrooms are amazingly sumptuous. The enormous bed and other furnishings in the grand master's bedroom are riotously carved.

Plumlov

About 20 miles (32 km) southeast of Bouzov is another extraordinary building, the vertiginously tall château at Plumlov *(closed Mon. July–Aug., Mon.–Fri. April–June & Sept.–Oct.).* The 17th-century architect, Prince-Bishop Karl Eusebius von Liechtenstein-Kastelkorn, was a member of the owning family. The slablike château—only one of the four projected wings was built—has so little depth that it seems like a strong wind could blow it over. The facade consists of three colossal stories, each lined with rows of columns. It is utterly repetitive, quite mad, and unforgettable. Exhibitions on Plumlov's history are the main offering inside, but are light on English. ∎

Only one wing of Plumlov château was ever completed.

EXPERIENCE: Visiting a Coal Mine

The role of coal in Czech history is a central one, for better or worse. Lignite played a key part in the region's rise from rural backwater to most advanced industrial power among the eastern provinces of the Austro-Hungarian empire by providing for much of Bohemia's and Moravia's wealth and political bargaining power at a critical time. And, in the 1930s, the growing Nazi war machine looked hungrily at Czech coal and steel production to meet its vast needs.

Heritage vs. Fuel

As is the case worldwide, in countries rich with resources of coal, profits and utility long trumped concerns over preserving cultural heritage and maintaining a healthy, natural environment. To this day, controversies rage over plans to move or destroy historic towns such as Horní Jeřetín to make way for mining. Before the Velvet Revolution, the state had little trouble with such obstacles and managed to liquidate dozens of villages and towns if they were deemed to stand in the way of industrial progress.

Russia has increased the frequency of its threats to cut off natural gas flows into Europe whenever Moscow feels slighted or piqued by political developments not to its liking. This, combined with advances in clean coal and carbon capture technology, has only driven the appetite for the deep lodes of lignite remaining in the Czech lands.

Many Czechs, now busy building their own careers and providing for growing families, seem to have lost interest in the fight against destructive mining practices. The shocking images of devastated moonscapes in north Moravia and around Litvínov in Bohemia are few and far between in news coverage these days.

Anselm Mine

A visit to the now closed Anselm mine of the coal giant OKD in Ostrava offers not just a sense of the grim and dangerous work that put food

INSIDER TIP:

The Anselm mine museum opened on December 4, 1993, St. Barbara's Day. The patron saint of miners, Barbara's name also graces the cathedral in the mining town of Kutna Hora.

—WILL TIZARD
National Geographic contributor

on the table for thousands but also a frisson of the realpolitik of energy security in central and Eastern Europe.

Trundling down the mine shaft in a groaning elevator to the quarter mile of tunnels at the **Mining Museum OKD** (*Pod Landekem 64, Ostrava-Petřkovice, 3 miles/5 km from downtown Ostrava, tel 596 131 803, www.muzeumokd.cz, $$$*), the sense of claustrophobia

is almost inevitable—and only heightened when you see the crawlspaces in which workers sometimes toiled all day. This unique exposition, first opened to the public in the early days of democracy in 1993 when industrial giants were still shutting down all over the country, is, ironically, in a setting far cleaner and greener than it has looked for centuries. This region has been a rich source of cheap coal energy and fuel since 1782 and the scale that production eventually reached is evident from the monster machinery visitors can see, some still operational.

Displays and commentary explain the science of coal seams and geological strata, along with chilling descriptions of the risks of fire in the mines and the massive bulkheads installed to help contain outbreaks.

The Anselm mine, once dubbed Ferdinand by the archdiocese in Olomouc, added deep tunnels in 1835; it was the first in the Ostrava region to reach significant depths. Mining here ended in 1991. When the museum opened on the feast day of the patron of miners, St. Barbara, the former operation was christened as a cultural monument.

More Places to Visit in Northern Moravia

Fulnek

Badly damaged during World War II, Fulnek has been restored with sensitivity. The main square is lined with pretty houses, many of them clearly modern but built to blend in. The Czech nationalist philosopher Jan Komenský (Comenius) taught at a Lutheran college here from 1618 to 1621, and the college has been reconstructed. On one side of the square is a baroque **church** set elegantly among the greenery of a wooded hillside. Atop the hill is the town's tall but somewhat shabby baroque **castle,** which was renovated in 1810 after a major fire.

◪ 277 D3   ✉ 12 miles (20 km) S of Opava via route 57

Hradec nad Moravicí

A fortress has overlooked the town of Hradec nad Moravicí since the tenth century. The princely Lichnowsky family has owned Hradec since 1777, and in its heyday composers Beethoven, Liszt, and Paganini all stayed at the lime-green neoclassical **château.** In the 19th century the town was encircled by red-brick crenellated walls, complete with portcullis, rather like a Victorian prison. A Beethoven music festival is held here every June.

◪ 277 D3   ✉ 5 miles (8 km) S of Opava via route 57   **Château** ⏺ Closed Mon. May–Sept., Mon.–Fri. April, Oct., & Dec. **Visitor information** www.hradecnamoravci.cz ✉ Opavská 265 ☎ 553 783 992,

Hukvaldy

The remarkable Czech composer Leoš Janáček (1854–1928) was born in Hukvaldy, a pretty, well-maintained hillside village, with a deer park below the ruins of a medieval **castle.** Though his birthplace was the village school where his father taught, the little **museum** dedicated to Janáček is housed in the building where he spent his final years, having lived most of his life at Brno. Find it

by turning left at the castle entrance and walking down a lane for 325 yards (300 m). It contains some of Janáček's furniture and the lectern on which he composed while standing, as was his custom.

◪ 277 E2   ✉ 4 miles (6 km) E of Příbor. E on route 48, then S on route 486   **Castle** ⏺ Closed Mon. May–Sept., Mon.–Fri. April & Oct., & Nov.–March   🅂 $ **Janácek Museum** ⏺ Closed Mon. May–Sept.; Mon.–Fri. April & Oct, & Nov.–March   🅂 $

Kopřivnice

North of Rožnov pod Radhoštěm (see pp. 282–283) is the unattractive industrial town of Kopřivnice, mainly taken up by the huge plants that have manufactured Tatra cars and trucks since 1897. The citizens of Communist Czechoslovakia grew used to seeing sleek black Tatra limousines, reserved for the state's favored few, overtaking their Trabants and Ladas. The **Tatra Museum** (www.tatramuseum.cz) is a striking, angular, blue-and-white structure consecrated to the history of the Tatra enterprise and to the achievements of Olympic athlete Emil Zátopek, a native of the town (1922–2000).

◪ 277 D2   ✉ 12 miles (19 km) N of Rožnov pod Radhoštěm via route 58 **Tatra Museum** ✉ Záhumenní 367 ⏺ Closed Mon.   🅂 $

Nový Jičín

West of Příbor (see p. 292) is Nový Jičín, situated in the heart of the region known as the Kuhlander, once a German-speaking agricultural area specializing, as its name suggests, in cattle raising. The sprawling town has a charming arcaded main square, with a plague column of 1710 in the center. In the much rebuilt Renaissance **castle,** nearby on Lidická, are a number of museums, one of which is devoted to the hat, a sartorial item in which the town has specialized since 1799.

The **Hat Museum** (Kloboučnické muzeum) displays examples worn by such famous Czechs as President Masaryk.
🔺 277 D2 ✉ 8 miles (13 km) W of Příbor via route 48 🚌 Bus from Prague and regular services from Olomouc   **Hat Museum** 🕐 Closed Mon.   💲 $

Opava

Opava is the former capital of Silesia, first Austrian and then Czech. Both the Thirty Years' War and World War II inflicted enormous damage on this industrial city. Near Horní náměstí, the main square, is the rather ugly, and much altered, 14th-century brick **parish church,** typical of Silesian Gothic. The town hall tower dates from 1618. Two blocks behind the church is Masarykova, lined with patrician mansions; these include the shabby, buff-colored, baroque Blücher Palace, now a branch of the Silesian Museum, and the beautifully restored playful facade of the Sobek Palace, now a bank. With typical

architectural insensitivity, the Communist regime attached concrete apartment blocks to this lovely building. Opposite is the **Church of the Holy Ghost** (Kostel sv. Ducha), with an interesting pink-and-green baroque facade resembling Dutch stepped gables, and the neoclassical Minorite convent. The main **Silesian Regional Museum,** founded in 1814, is on the outskirts of the old town.
🔺 277 D4 ✉ 20 miles (32 km) NW of Olomouc on route 46 via Šternberk
🚆 Train from Olomouc   **Silesian Regional Museum** ✉ Tyršova 1 🕐 Closed Mon.

Ostrava

Near the Polish border sprawls the large industrial city of Ostrava. After coal was found here in the 1760s, mines were tunneled under the city, with foundries being built perilously close to the city center. By the late 1990s most, but not all, had been closed down, and pollution levels, once dangerously high, have diminished. Many buildings, however, are still prone to subsidence.

A visit to Kopřivnice to tour the splendid Tatra Museum is a must for car enthusiasts.

Apart from the town hall tower (1687) in the main square, Masarykovo náměstí, there is little that's compelling in the center, even though it is the third largest city in the republic. However, the **Mining Museum OKD** (Hornické muzeum) is of surprising interest. It is situated in the northern suburb of Pod Landekem, and based in a former colliery; visitors can even go down to the coal face itself (see feature p. 289). One of Ostrava's best known natives is the tennis star Ivan Lendl, who was born here in 1960.

🅜 277 E3   ✉ 100 miles (160 km) NE of Brno via E462, then route 47. Train and bus from Prague   **Visitor information** *www.ostra vainfo.cz* ✉ Jurečkova 12   ☎ 596 123 913   **Mining Museum** *www.muzeumokd.cz* ✉ Pod Landekem 64   ☎ 596 131 803 $ Guided tour: $$$

INSIDER TIP:

It's easy to miss the house of Sigmund Freud's birth in Příbor, on the street formerly named Zamečnická. The address, Freudova 177, is not the street number but a second municipal number.

—WILL TIZARD
National Geographic contributor

Příbor

Příbor is the **birthplace of Sigmund Freud** (1856–1939), the father of psychoanalysis, at Freudova 117. The town was strangely reticent about the fact until recently, not honoring him until 1994. Then a bust was placed between the main square and the former college, where the town **museum** is housed. The room devoted to Freud contains little more than familiar photographs and books, but the infant Freud left Příbor at the age of three and the Freud museums in Vienna and London have had first pick of

letters and memorabilia. In the late 1990s the town finally got around to naming its pleasant main square after its most famous son.

🅜 277 D3   ✉ 19 miles (33 km) SW of Ostrava via route 58   **Museum** 🕘 Closed Mon., Wed., & Fri.–Sat. $ $

Šternberk

North of Olomouc lies Šternberk and its **castle,** which was founded in the 13th century by the eponymous family. It was largely rebuilt in a cramped neo-Gothic style in the 1880s, though vestiges of the medieval fortifications and a tall Gothic chapel, complete with Gothic murals and a fine statue of the Madonna, remain. The interior is sparsely furnished, but it contains medieval artifacts from Olomouc.

🅜 276 B3   ✉ 10 miles (15 km) N of Olomouc via route 46   **Castle** *www.hrad-stern berk.cz* ✉ Horní náměstí 6   ☎ 585 012 935   🕘 Closed Mon. May–Sept., Mon.–Fri. April & Oct., & Nov.–March $ $–$$

Svatý Kopeček

Just off route 46, the road from Olomouc to Šternberk, is Italian architect Giovanni Tencalla's 17th-century **church** at Holy Hill (Svatý Kopeček). With its broad two-story facade topped with a row of statues, it resembles a baroque palace as much as a church. The interior of this fine yellow and white pilgrimage church is a feast of lilac marble, coarse stucco, and crowded ceiling frescoes. The galleried dome is impressive, and the organ gallery has a riot of decorative musical cherubs. Along the outer side of the church an array of little cafés and snack bars caters to pilgrims. You can also buy religious knickknacks and even plastic budgerigars. For the more secular-minded, there's a small zoo. The view from this hill stretches a great distance but there is not much to see in the surrounding countryside.

🅜 276 C3   ✉ 3 miles (5 km) NE of Olomouc via route 46

Travelwise

Prague tram

TRAVELWISE

PLANNING YOUR TRIP
When to Go

Prague has become a year-round destination. Late spring and summer are, in many ways, the best time to visit. The climate is generally warm, occasionally hot, and you can take advantage of the city's many summer terraces in restaurants and cafés. If you enjoy music and the performing arts, you might consider visiting Prague during the annual Prague Spring Music Festival, in the second half of May. If you plan to do this, make your bookings well in advance.

But there are drawbacks to visiting Prague in the summer. The first is that it becomes extremely crowded. It is a small city, and its proximity to the German and Austrian borders has led to a steady influx of visitors from those countries. In summer, you will need to plan your stay well in advance, securing hotel reservations as early as possible. Once you have arrived, you are likely to find that the best or most fashionable restaurants are also booked up days ahead. Most visitors, especially those on day or weekend trips from Germany, crowd into the same narrow streets and squares. The crush can be fatiguing, as can the heat. And unfortunately, there are often downpours in July and August.

The great advantage of visiting Prague out of season is that you will not be jostling with quite so many other tourists. You can also take advantage of low-season hotel rates, which in general apply from November through March. There are performances of operas and symphony concerts in the city's main opera houses and concert halls year-round, but the height of the cultural program is in the fall

and winter. The drawbacks of coming to Prague out of season are the drop in temperature and the short days, which limit sightseeing time.

As for the rest of the country, it does not make much sense to plan a trip through the Bohemian and Moravian countryside in the late fall and winter. Quite apart from the vagaries of the climate, many tourist attractions will be closed. Castles, châteaus, and other major sites are usually open daily from May through September, and on weekends only during April and October. Most sites are closed to the public from November to March, with a handful of exceptions such as Karlštejn. Snow and ice are common in the countryside from December to February, making a tour of the country by car quite hazardous during winter.

Christmas in Prague can be great fun, with open-air markets, clowns and pranksters in the streets, and the welcome possibility of crunchy snow underfoot. On the other hand, the city can become as crowded as during the height of summer, and many hotels charge their highest rates over Christmas and New Year's.

Climate

The climate of the Czech Republic is varied, owing to the length of the country from east to west and variations in altitude. Local microclimates are of great importance, and climatically the republic is a distinct patchwork. Generally speaking, the climate becomes more continental as you move eastward into Moravia, whereas Bohemia has a more moderate maritime climate, comparable to that of southern Germany. Summers can be quite hot, extending into delightful falls, but winters are occasionally severe.

Rainfall also varies, again as a result of elevation. Annual precipitation in Prague is 20 inches (510 mm), with July and August being the wettest months and February the driest. Prague enjoys a particularly mild climate, with an average temperature throughout the year of 48°F (8°C). Even in the winter the temperature does not usually drop far below freezing point, although it can remain at that chilly level for many days at a time. Cold weather can set in by late October, and January and February in particular are often chilly. In July the average temperature is 64°F (18°C); in February 34.7°F (1.5°C).

The Moravian climate is distinct. The north is considerably wetter than Bohemia due to the lack of high mountains to shelter the region. The south is notably mild, with a long, warm fall that makes the region ideal for viticulture.

What to Take

Prague is a modern city with modern shops. Nevertheless, if you need special medication, be sure to take it with you. Medication that may be available over the counter in your own country may be on prescription only in the Czech Republic. While most hotels stock electronic adaptors (220V) for computers, hair dryers, etc., it is wise to buy them in your home country. As for clothing, be prepared for extremes, especially in winter, when the temperatures vary from mild to very cold. Take footwear that can withstand rain and slush. In summer light slacks or skirts and T-shirts should be sufficient.

Insurance

Although travel in the Czech Republic will not expose you to unusual risks or dangers, it is best to take out travel insurance. Your travel agent will be able to help, but the prices may not be competitive, so shop around. If your bookings are made using a major credit card, such as American Express, you will probably be covered for basic risks and losses, but check the coverage carefully.

Theft & Loss
In the event of theft or other crime, make an immediate report to the police, and be sure to get a copy of the report; it will be essential in processing any claim you subsequently make.

Medical
Similarly, keep copies of all bills for any medical treatment you receive while abroad. The Czech Republic provides free emergency medical care for all foreigners. You will be charged for medical problems not classified as emergencies, though, so it is sensible to take out medical insurance.

Car
If you are driving your own car, you should obtain a green card (usually free) from your insurer as proof of insurance before leaving your country of residence.

Entry Formalities
You need a valid passport to enter the Czech Republic and stay for up to 90 days. Make sure that the validity of your passport extends for at least six months from your date of entry. At present, citizens of the United States, the European Union, and some other countries do not require visas; Canadians now do, however. Check with your travel agent or Czech consulate well in advance of your journey, as visas cannot be issued at your point of entry.

Further Reading
If you think that the work of Franz Kafka will prove an ideal literary introduction to Prague, you will find you are wrong. Instead, if you are not familiar

with their works, try the novels and stories of Milan Kundera, Josef Škvorecký, Ivan Klíma, and the late Bohumil Hrabal, whose *I Served the King of England* is a modern Czech classic. An older Czech classic is *The Good Soldier Švejk*, a celebrated novel by Jaroslav Hašek; for many readers it is the definitive delineation of the wily Czech character.

Václav Havel is not only the country's former president but also its most distinguished playwright and essayist. Volumes such as *Letters to Olga*, written during Havel's 1979–1982 imprisonment, offer unique insight into Czechoslovakia under the Communists. Timothy Garton Ash is the best modern chronicler of the politics of central Europe *(The Magic Lantern)*, and Peter Demetz's *Prague in Black and Gold* gives a detailed cultural history of the city.

HOW TO GET TO PRAGUE & THE CZECH REPUBLIC
By Air
Most visitors arrive by air at Ruzyně, 12 miles (19 km) from Prague city center. For flight information in English, call 220 113 314 or try the Czech Airlines website, www.csa.cz. The airport has been modernized, and you are unlikely to meet serious delays at immigration or in the baggage hall.

The Czech national carrier is Czech Airlines (ČSA), but many airlines provide regular service from European cities to Prague. There are regular, though not daily, flights on ČSA to Prague from New York and Newark, or on Continental from Newark. All other airlines connect through British and European airports.

Getting to the City Center
Čedaz (tel 220 114 296, www .cedaz.cz) will take you to Náměstí Republiky, close to the city center, for 120 Kč. Tickets are

available at the airport newsstand. When you book your room, check to see if the hotel offers minibus or limousine service from the airport. You can also take local bus 119 to the terminus at Dejvická, from where it's a short metro ride into the city. Tickets at the metro station are 26 Kč for a transfer ticket (this allows you to travel on all forms of public transportation) or 18 Kč for a single ride (maximum 15 minutes). This is the cheapest option by far, but it can be slow and tiring if you have a lot of luggage.

The quickest way into town from the airport is by taxi, but drivers are notoriously dishonest. Be sure to agree on a fare beforehand; expect to pay about 300 Kč for a one-way trip. Reputable English-speaking companies include City Taxi (tel 257 257 257) and AAA (tel 14014).

By Train
Prague has four train stations: Nádraži Holešovice, Hlavní nádraži (the main station), Masarykovo nádraži, and Smíchovské nádraži. All are on metro lines. If you arrive by train from another European city, check your ticket to see where you will arrive. For train information, call 221 111 122.

By Car
If you drive into Prague, bear in mind that parking in the city center is strictly regulated and signs are not always fully comprehensible to non-Czech readers. Many hotels have parking lots or access to secure parking close by; expect to pay $10–$18 per day for parking.

By Coach
For U.K.-based travelers one of the cheapest ways to get to Prague is by coach. Student Agency *(www.studentagencybus .com)* offers coach trips six days a week, and the journey takes just

under a day. The Prague office can be contacted at 841 101 101, or e-mail info@studentagency bus.com.

GETTING AROUND Prague

By Public Transportation

Prague has an extensive and efficient public transportation system employing metro, trams, and buses. Almost all the places you are likely to visit are easily accessible by frequent trams and metro trains. At night a limited tram service operates, so you will rarely be completely dependent on taxi drivers.

It is crucial to have a valid ticket before you travel. Plain-clothes inspectors check tickets often and will impose an on-the-spot fine of 700 Kč if you are traveling without a valid ticket. Ticket prices vary according to whether or not you wish to transfer from one conveyance to another. Tickets are valid for between 60 and 90 minutes only and must be punched as you enter a metro station or board a tram or bus. Buy tickets from tobacconists and station booking offices. Alternatively, a 24-hour pass costs 100 Kč and a 120-hour pass 500 Kč. Metro and tram maps are displayed at all stations and are available at some station offices.

Metro

There are three lines (see map inside back cover): A (Green), B (Yellow), and C (Red). Trains are frequent and clean; they run from around 5 a.m. to midnight.

Trams

Unlike metro lines, the trams run through the night. But the night trams, numbered 51–58, are crowded and offer limited, less frequent service. Lines such as the 22 are very useful.

Buses

Buses often run from metro terminuses and provide access to suburban destinations such as the airport, Troja, and Star Castle. You can find bus information on www.dpp.cz or call 800 191 817.

By Taxi

Use taxis as a last resort. Inquire at your hotel about acceptable rates for trips you are planning; then, agree with drivers about rates before setting off, or insist that they run their meters (most are disinclined to do so). Discourage overcharging by asking your driver for a receipt with the company's name on it. Try City Taxi (tel 257 257 257) or AAA (tel 14014).

On Foot

Prague is a small city—the fastest way to get somewhere in the center often is by walking. It is a 15-minute stroll from the Castle to the Old Town, and about the same from the Old Town Square to the National Museum.

Czech Republic

By Bus & Train

The Czech Republic has a well-developed train and bus system linking the major cities, but trains in particular can be very slow. Finding accurate timetables and fares can be frustrating and time-consuming. Buses can be good for day trips from Prague to places such as Kutná Hora, but are not recommended as a way of exploring the whole country. If you plan to crisscross the republic for a week or more, look into the available passes. Students, teachers, and those under 26 are eligible for the Czech Flexipass. For information, see Čedok, Na Příkopě 18, tel 800 112 112, www.cedok.com.

By Car

If your license does not include a photograph, obtain an International Driving Permit. In addition, you should carry a green card and your vehicle registration document if you are driving your own car (not necessary for rental cars).

Outside major cities, traffic is lighter and roads are maintained well, making driving largely stress-free—except when you are stuck behind slow-moving trucks. Driving is on the right side of the road, and drivers should know it is not acceptable to have any alcohol in the blood.

Speed limits range from 20 to 30 mph (30/50 kph) in urban areas to 55 mph (90 kph) on country roads and 68 to 80 mph (110/130 kph) on highways. Seat belts must be worn, and during the winter months you must keep your headlights turned on. In towns with tramlines, remember that trams always have the right-of-way.

If you plan to use the country's few highways, you must display a special sticker. Such items are inexpensive and can be bought at gas stations and post offices. Most rental cars are provided with them. Always lock the car, don't leave valuables within view, and keep your luggage in the trunk if possible. Car theft and break-ins are not common, but opportunist crime does occur.

Breakdown & Accidents

If an accident occurs, the police should be notified as soon as possible. It is advisable to contact the Czech automobile club, UAMK, for emergency phone numbers before setting out. UAMK headquarters are at Na štrzi 9, Nusle, Prague 4 (tel 261 104 111), but you may find it easier to contact your own automobile association, with which UAMK may have a reciprocal agreement.

Car Rental

If you plan to spend much time exploring the country, car rental is your best option. It is advisable to make reservations when you book your vacation. All the major international rental companies have offices in main towns and

in such hotels as Prague's Inter-Continental. You will find local companies that are considerably cheaper (from $20 per day, including insurance), but the language barrier may prove to be a difficulty.
Hertz Karlovo náměstí 15, Prague 2, tel 225 345 021, www.hertz.com
Avis Klimentská 46, Prague 1, tel 221 851 225, www.avis.com
National Masarykovo nábřeží 4, Prague 2, tel 224 923 719, www.nationalcar.com

Gas
Gas (benzin) is cheaper than in most Western European countries, and the republic is well supplied with large and well-equipped gas stations, many open 24 hours.

PRACTICAL ADVICE
Communications
Cell Phones
Cellular telephones brought from other countries in Europe or from Australia will probably work in the Czech Republic, but check with your service provider to ensure they will allow calls to and from your number. Cell phones brought from North America normally use a different frequency; they will not work in the Czech Republic unless they have a tri-band frequency option.

Post Offices
Post offices are open Monday to Friday from 8 a.m. to 5 p.m., and on Saturday from 8 a.m. to noon. The main post office in Prague (Jindřišská 14) is open 24 hours. Stamps and phone cards are available at many newsstands.

Telephones
The easiest way to make phone calls, both local and international, is to use a phone card. Hotel-room phone charges can be exorbitant. The entire domestic telephone system has been overhauled in recent years and many phone numbers have changed. Numbers in older guides and listings may be invalid.

Conversions
1 kilo = 2.2 pounds
1 liter = 0.2642 U.S. gallon
1 kilometer = 0.62 mile
1 meter = 1.093 yards

Women's Clothing

U.S.	6	8	10	12	14	16
Czech	34	36	38	40	42	44

Men's Clothing

U.S.	36	38	40	42	44	46
Czech	46	48	50	52	54	56

Electricity
Electricity in the Czech Republic is 220 volts. Plugs have two round pins. If you bring electrical equipment from the U.S. or the U.K., you will need an adapter, plus a transformer for 110/120-volt appliances.

Etiquette
Etiquette does not differ greatly from that expected in other European countries. It is customary to say "good day" (dobrý den) on entering an office or shop, and to say "goodbye" (na shledanou) on leaving. If you visit a private home, it will be much appreciated if you bring a small gift, such as a bunch of flowers or an item from your own country. In some homes you will be politely asked to remove your shoes. In pubs and simpler restaurants, you are expected to share tables during busy times.

Media
Newspapers
The Prague Post is a weekly newspaper published in English. Its "Night & Day" supplement (and www.praguepost.com) has very useful listings and reviews. Various free publications can be found in hotel lobbies, but they are essentially advertisements for restaurants and clubs. Non-Czech newspapers are easy to obtain in major cities, but difficult elsewhere. European editions of the Guardian, USA Today, and the International Herald Tribune are more widely available, as are magazines such as Time and Newsweek.

Radio
Czech radio runs the gamut from pop music to jazz to classical. English-language programs can be found on several stations, including the BBC at 101.1 FM. Radio Prague can be found at 92.6 FM and 102.7 FM, on medium wave within the Czech Republic at 1287, 1233, or 1071 KHz, and on shortwave around the world. It broadcasts programs in English Monday through Friday at 1:30 p.m. and 7:30 p.m., and on Saturday and Sunday at 1:30 p.m. and 8:30 p.m. The BBC World Service broadcasts on several SW and FM frequencies, but many of the programs are in Czech.

Television
There are two state-owned television channels, and at least two commercial channels. Česká Televize's Channel 2 shows news transmissions in English at 8 a.m. weekdays, 7 a.m. weekends.

Money Matters
Czech currency is based on the koruna (plural: koruny), abbreviated to Kč and known in English as crowns. Each crown is divided into 100 hellers, but do not get stuck with these—they have been phased out. Money can be changed easily, especially in Prague, where there are dozens of bureaus. Try to avoid changing money at the airport or border crossings; commission rates are often a steep 5 percent. Equally, beware of bureaus that offer "no commission"; exchange rates can be very unfavorable.

Outside major towns and cities, your best bet is to use an ATM.

Most banks have currency-changing desks and charge a minimal fee, but the process can be time-consuming.

There is a marked contrast in expense between Prague and the rest of the country. It is hard to find a double room in Prague for under 3,000 Kč, which in most small towns would buy you the best suite in town. Similarly, Prague restaurants that have French chefs or cater to foreigners (there are tens of thousands of foreign residents as well as visitors) charge prices comparable to those of other European cities. Restaurants with a local clientele charge much less, simply because the average Czech cannot afford Berlin or Paris prices.

Major credit cards are widely accepted in Czech hotels, restaurants, and shops. Nonetheless, there are exceptions, so it is wise to carry a reasonable amount of Czech currency.

National Holidays

There are relatively few national holidays. The most important are:
January 1 (New Year's Day)
Easter Monday
May 1 (May Day)
May 8 (National Liberation Day)
July 5 (Sts. Cyril and Methodius)
July 6 (Jan Hus Day)
September 28 (St. Václav's Day or Czech Statehood Day)
October 28 (Foundation of the Czechoslovak Republic, 1918)
November 17 (Student's Day)
December 24–26 (Christmas).
Most castles and some museums are closed on national holidays and the day following.

Opening Times

Opening times are irregular, but, generally, shops, offices, and banks are open from 8 a.m. to 5 p.m. or 9 a.m. to 6 p.m. Some close at lunchtime. In general, small shops and banks are closed on Sunday and holidays, and often on Saturday afternoons. A few shops offer later opening times, and even 24-hour "nonstop" hours. Pharmacies are open from 7:30 a.m. to 6 p.m. on weekdays; in major cities there will be one or two 24-hour pharmacies. Most restaurants are open for lunch and dinner, seven days a week, and do not have the variable day off that is common in countries such as France and Germany. Many churches are open all day, especially when they are in use for regular services, but others have more quirky opening times. Some are open only during services (usually early morning and late afternoon); others close for a number of hours during the day.

Places of Worship

Many churches are tourist attractions as well as places of worship. Times of services are normally posted on the door. They are also listed in the classified section of *The Prague Post*. No formal dress is required, except for yarmulkes in synagogues and at the Jewish cemeteries (paper ones are usually available at the synagogues). Many churches also function as concert halls. In some cases, the only way you can see inside a church without paying is to attend a service.

Rest Rooms

Public rest rooms are usually clearly marked "WC"; a small charge (around 5 Kč) is levied for admission and some sheets of toilet paper. Standards vary, but most rest rooms are clean and properly maintained. Women should look for the words *Dámy* or *Ženy;* men for *Páni* or *Muži* (however, be aware that paní means "women" and is sometimes used on WC doors). Additional facilities, sometimes free and better maintained, are available at many metro stations, department stores, museums, restaurants, and cafés.

Safety

There was a time when an evening stroll down Václavské náměstí (Wenceslas Square) required you to be fully alert to the attentions of roaming gangs of pickpockets. Those days are over, and Prague is no more threatening or dangerous than any large European city.

Pickpockets are still at work in the metro, and on trams and at tramstops. Trams 22 and 23 are popular with tourists—and with pickpockets. Tourist attractions such as the Charles Bridge are also prime spots. Speaking English or German is enough to draw attention to yourself. Keep wallets in front pockets; close purses and hold them near the body. Similarly, be careful when withdrawing cash from an ATM.

Unsavory characters, including drug addicts, often congregate at the main railway station, the park in front of it, and the Florenc bus terminal, especially late at night. So take care if you find yourself at these locations, although they are not in themselves dangerous.

Time Differences

The Czech Republic runs on CET (Central European Time), one hour ahead of GMT (Greenwich Mean Time), six hours ahead of New York, and nine hours ahead of Los Angeles. Clocks change for daylight saving on the last Sunday in March (one hour forward), and go back one hour the last Sunday in October.

Tipping

In general Czechs do not tip, but they do round up the bill in restaurants. For example, if your bill comes to 282 Kč, you might hand the waiter 300 Kč in notes and tell him to keep the change. If it comes to 235 Kč, you could ask for 50 Kč back.

Travelers with Disabilities

Special provisions for the disabled are still the exception rather than the rule, but Prague hotels, restaurants, and museums are becoming increasingly aware of the need to cater to such special needs. Some of the hotel listings that follow indicate wheelchair accessibility. The major problem for people with disabilities arises when using public transportation. You cannot get a wheelchair onto a tram.

The Prague Wheelchair Association publishes *Accessible Prague,* a guide to facilities for the disabled. Contact them at Benediktská 6, Staré Město, Prague, tel 224 827 210. The travel agency Accessible Prague also offers assistance at www.accessibleprague.com.

Visiting Castles & Châteaus

In Czech, a castle is known as a *hrad;* a *zámek* denotes a building akin to a French château, i.e., the country residence of an aristocratic family, varying in scale from a modest mansion to a palace. Opening times of castles and museums vary considerably. Except for the most popular attractions, all such places are closed on Monday, national holidays, and the days following national holidays. Though a castle may advertise its open hours as 9 a.m. to 5 p.m. in summer, there is often a lunch break from noon to 1 p.m. Also, if the site can be visited only on a guided tour, the last tour is likely to leave an hour before the official closing time. Guided tours range in duration from 45 to 90 minutes.

The more popular attractions offer guided tours in languages other than Czech, usually German and English. The admission fee is usually double that for a tour in Czech, but well worth the extra cost, for obvious reasons. Some larger châteaus offer as many as three separate tours, each focusing on different features of the building.

Visitor Information

Visitors to the Czech Republic are served well by information bureaus, which are readily identifiable by a large, bright-green, lowercase letter i. There is scarcely a provincial town of any interest that does not have such an office, usually in the main square or within or near the town hall. Some bureaus are extremely useful, and can assist with hotel and campsite bookings. Others are essentially glorified sales outlets for local postcard producers. Overall, however, they are mines of information, offering maps, booklets, and verbal guidance.

In Prague the main visitor information centers are located at the main station, Hlavní nádraží at Na Příkopě 20, and in the Old Town Hall (Staroměstské náměstí). If you are planning an excursion out of Prague, it is worth visiting the latter, where staff have access via their computers to the opening times of all castles and museums throughout the republic. The Prague information center has a useful website at www.pis.cz.

EMERGENCIES
Embassies in Prague
United States
Tržište 15, Prague 1, tel 257 530 663. Open Mon.–Fri. 8 a.m.–4:30 p.m. (consular hours 9 a.m.–12 p.m.).

Canada
Muchova 6, Prague 6, tel 272 101 800. Open Mon.–Fri. 8 a.m.–4 p.m.

United Kingdom
Thunovská 14, Prague 1, tel 257 402 111. Open Mon.–Fri. 9 a.m.–noon.

Emergency Phone Numbers
Police 112
Prague Police 112
Fire 112
Ambulance 112
Automobile emergencies 1230

Health
If you think you need a doctor during your stay, consult your hotel reception desk. For minor ailments, go to any pharmacy *(lékárna);* if the language problems can be overcome, you can often obtain advice and inexpensive medicines there. Most pharmacies close at 6 p.m. but some remain open 24 hours: Palackého 5, Prague 1, near Můstek metro station, tel 224 946 982. Belgická 37, Prague 2, near Náměstí Míru metro station, tel 222 519 731. Štefaníkova 6, Prague 6, near Andel, tel 257 320 918.

By Western European and North American standards, charges for non-emergency treatment and medication are low. If you do not have health insurance, you can apply for short-term coverage from the VZP insurance office, Orlická 4, Prague 3 (tel 221 751 111).

In Prague, the recommended clinic is the Na Homolce Hospital, Roentgenova 2, Smíchov, Prague 5, tel 257 271 111, which has English-speaking staff. If you have a dental emergency, go to Palackého 5, tel 224 946 981 (24 hours). The Canadian Medical Center (24 hours) is at Veleslavínská 1, Prague 6, tel 235 360 133; after hours tel 724 300 301 (general practice) and tel 724 300 303 (pediatrician), www.cmcpraha.cz.

Lost Property
Prague's central lost property office is at Karoliny Světlé 5, Prague 1, tel 224 235 085. Open weekdays 8 a.m.–noon, 12:30 p.m.–5:30 p.m.

If you lose your credit card, telephone the relevant provider:
American Express
tel 222 412 241
Visa/Eurocard/Mastercard
tel 800 111 055
Diners Club
tel 267 197 450

Hotels & Restaurants

Prague restaurants and hotels have come up by leaps and bounds in the last few years: The city now has Michelin-star dining at the Four Seasons Hotel, and designer accommodation is not unusual—and often surprisingly affordable. Czech cuisine is general of high quality, but Asian and Mediterranean eateries now offer equally excellent alternatives (at least at sit-down eateries).

Accommodations

Prague has hundreds of hotels and guesthouses, but at certain times of the year a room is very difficult to find; it's best to make reservations well in advance if possible. Czech tourist offices provide fairly complete lists of hotels in Prague, and local tourist offices outside the capital usually have information about accommodations in their regions.

Standards are high, especially in Prague, where almost all rooms have bathrooms and basic facilities such as telephones and televisions. While you can assume rooms will be comfortable and clean, don't always expect light, airy rooms with modern furnishings in Prague or the Czech Republic: Decor and furniture tend to be traditional, which means dark and heavy.

You will find a huge price differential between hotels in Prague and those outside the city. For 2,000 Kč you may get a large, comfortable room in the provinces, but this will pay only for rock-bottom accommodations in the capital. Prices should include all taxes, but it's sensible to check before making a reservation. The room rate often includes breakfast. Major credit cards are accepted in all but the smallest and most remote hotels.

Price ranges indicated in the listings below are official "rack rates." Except during the high season, it is usually possible to negotiate a discount, especially at some of the luxury hotels that have high overhead costs and, out of season, when occupancy rates are fairly low.

There is little clear difference between a hotel and a pension.

Indeed, the City Hotel in Prague manages to be both. A pension will usually be family-run, and it may not have a reception desk; guests are provided with a key to the front door as if to a private house.

If you are planning a stay of a week or more, it is worth considering a "residence" or private accommodations. A residence provides a fully furnished apartment, often centrally located, with cooking facilities. Prices vary enormously, depending on location, quality of facilities, and the degree of independence and privacy.

A few agencies specialize in locating accommodations in private apartments. Try Ave Travel at the main train station (Hlavní nádraží, tel 251 551 011, www.ave travel.cz) or the Stop City agency (Vinohradská 24, tel 222 251 234, www.stopcity.com).

Restaurants

A *restaurace* is a proper restaurant, sometimes formal and relatively expensive, but not necessarily so. For simpler food a *pivnice, hostinec,* or *hospoda* (all essentially pubs) will usually be adequate; if you wish to drink wine with your meal rather than beer, look for a *vinárna* (wine bar). In practice, beer and wine are equally available in a *restaurace* and a *vinárna,* but the latter should offer a better range. You can get snacks at *bufets.*

In simpler establishments, cooked dishes may be rudimentary—sausages or stews—and you often get better value from *chlebíček,* open sandwiches made from sausage, ham, other meats, and cheese, usually topped with sour cream, gherkins, radishes, and other garnishes. Some of the grander coffeehouses *(kavárna)* also serve simple meals. The quality and hygiene are generally better than you will find at roadside stands. Fast-food chains are sadly becoming more common in all the towns, but there seems little point in coming all the way to Prague or Brno to end up eating a Big Mac.

Dining Etiquette & Times

Understanding the local etiquette makes eating out simpler. In basic restaurants and pubs it is not unusual to share a table—a good way of meeting local people, if you can find a common language.

Lunch is served from about 11:30 a.m. on; Czechs tend to eat their evening meal around 7 p.m. Except in the cities and tourist centers, it can sometimes be difficult to order hot meals after 9 p.m.

Menus

The menu *(jídelní lístek)* can be an obstacle. A few standard terms stand out: *Vepřové* means "pork," *hovězí* "beef," *klobása* "sausage," and *hranolky* "French fries" or "chips." Cooking terms include *na roštu* (roasted), *smažený* (fried), and *řízek* (breaded). But the dish descriptions in which these staple terms are embedded are often unfamiliar, and either denote special methods of preparation or are fanciful terms invented by the chef. Even with a basic command of Czech culinary terms, you will almost certainly need to ask the waiter for advice. And waiters tend to recommend the more expensive dishes, and those, like schnitzel or steak, that are likely to be familiar. Thus the chances of sampling original cooking, where it is available, are remote.

Fortunately almost all restaurants, except the most basic establishments such as country pubs, have menus in German and sometimes English. Even though translations are not always reliable, they will certainly help you make your choice.

Privatization has led to an improvement in overall quality. Under the state-owned system, service was poor, menus were indecipherable, and cooks had no incentive to excel. Meals were often dull and marred by mediocre ingredients. Today the problem is very different, since some modern cooks try to bring together all kinds of ingredients in an attempt at originality or exoticism, with sometimes chaotic and indigestible results.

Outside Prague, most visitors will find a great deal of similarity among restaurants. Establishments vary in comfort, decor, and quality of food and service, but their menus tend to focus on the same types of dishes, with a few of the chef's own concoctions. Some may offer specialties such as fish or game. There is also very little variation in price. On the other hand, quality is usually dependable.

In Prague, however, the situation is different. In the working-class suburbs, and even in the city center, you will find smoky pubs that serve basic food to hordes of regular lunchtime customers. Such establishments are not focused on foreign visitors, so the menus may be in Czech only. You can eat very cheaply, but you may not feel particularly welcome.

In contrast, the tourist-frequented areas such as the Little Quarter (Malá Strana), Old Town (Staré Město), and the Jewish Quarter (Josefov) have numerous restaurants that are expensive by Czech standards, but some of them are very high-quality, serving international dishes to international standards. There should be no problem with communication with the waiting staff, and the selection of drinks is wide. Such restaurants can be excellent, but over a long period they will be a drain on most budgets. In smart residential districts such as Vinohrady, visitors will find a plethora of small, cozy, neighborhood restaurants serving up mostly Czech dishes with a modest selection of beers and wines. These places are inexpensive, and the food is usually delicious and served in generous portions. Plenty of restaurants offer pasta, French, and even Indian dishes as well.

Paying for Your Meal

Unfortunately, many waiters in Prague feel it is their patriotic duty to cheat foreign customers. In modest establishments such as pubs, the waiter will tot up the bill on a slip of paper and present it to you. Close scrutiny will often reveal that the bill has been padded. Have an idea of what your bill should be before you ask for it; if there's a clear discrepancy, check it. You may be charged extra for accompaniments that are in fact included in the cost of the meal. Often the sums involved are trifling, but these attempts to defraud are perpetuated because many visitors will not challenge questionable calculations.

Be aware that there is no "service charge" in any Czech restaurant, although many that cater to foreigners try to rip their customers off by imposing one. The size of the charge varies and can be as high as 20 percent. Refuse to pay the charge. Instead, slip some money to the waiter or waitress in person, as you can be sure that any "service charge" will not end up in the pockets of the restaurant's owner.

Notes

The hotels and restaurants listed here have been grouped by area (in Prague) or region (in the Czech Republic). They are then listed alphabetically by price category. The postal address Prague 1 covers the central part of the city—the Castle District, Little Quarter, and Old Town. Visitors with disabilities should ask the establishment about facilities.

Abbreviations:

L = lunch
D = dinner

AE American Express
DC Diner's Club
MC MasterCard
V Visa

PRAGUE

■ CASTLE DISTRICT & LITTLE QUARTER

Hotels

🏨 **ALCHYMIST GRAND**
🍴 **HOTEL & SPA**
$$$$$
TRŽIŠTĚ 19
PRAGUE 1
TEL 251 286 111
FAX 251 286 017
www.alchymisthotel.com
This palatial pile next to the American embassy features kingly rooms with timbered ceilings, a gourmet restaurant serving continental cuisine, and a pool and spa specializing in massage, aromatherapy, and wraps. Service is top-notch, with a concierge standing by to help with hard-to-acquire event tickets and tips for what's going on in the city.
ℹ️ 46 Ⓜ Malostranská 🅿 🚇
📺 ⚙ All major cards

🏨 **HOFFMEISTER**
🍴 **$$$$$**
POD BRUSKOU 7

PRAGUE 1
TEL 251 017 111
FAX 251 017 120
www.hoffmeister.cz
The Hoffmeister, Prague's only Relais & Châteaux group member, offers luxury and excellent service. The rooms are very richly furnished, with heavy draperies, but the location along a busy tramline beneath the castle may not be ideal. There's a fine and tasteful restaurant, the **Ada,** and the terrace is delightful in summer.
🛏 41 🚇 Malostranská 🅿 ⬗
🔌 🎴 All major cards

🛏 SAVOY
🍴 $$$$$
KEPLEROVA 6
PRAGUE 1
TEL 224 302 430
FAX 224 302 128
www.savoyhotel.cz
This is an art nouveau building near the Strahov Monastery. Its elegant public rooms include a lobby bar, with curved banquettes, where you can have a wide range of snacks and light meals, and the glass-roofed **Hradčany** restaurant. The bedrooms are among the largest in the city, with complimentary minibars and spacious marble bathrooms. Guests have free use of the fitness center. The hotel is extremely popular with celebrities, but the location at some distance from the city center may be a disadvantage for most visitors to Prague.
🛏 61 🚇 Malostranská 🅿 ⬗
🔌 🔌 🎴 🎴 All major cards

🛏 U TŘÍ PŠTROSŮ
🍴 $$$$$
DRAŽICKÉHO NÁMĚSTÍ 12
PRAGUE 1
TEL 257 288 888
FAX 257 533 217
www.utripstrosu.cz
The Three Ostriches, in the shadow of the Charles Bridge,

is one of Prague's best-established luxury inns. It was the city's first coffeehouse, and until the 1960s was run by the Dundr family, who regained possession in the 1990s. The interior retains precious Renaissance features including a painted wooden ceiling. The U Tří Pštrosů restaurant offers a good selection of fish, including carp filets and salmon with caviar sauce. Game dishes, such as leg of boar with rosehip sauce, traditional Czech dishes, and ostrich specialties are also on the menu. There's a cheaper lunchtime selection.
🛏 18 🚇 Malostranská 🅿
🎴 All major cards

SOMETHING SPECIAL

🛏 U ZLATÉ STUDNĚ
🍴 $$$$–$$$$$
U ZLATÉ STUDNĚ 4
PRAGUE 1
TEL 257 011 213
FAX 257 533 320
www.goldenwell.cz
Tucked away in a cul-de-sac beneath the castle, this 16th-century mansion, once the property of Rudolf II and astronomer Tycho Brahe, was skillfully converted in 2000 into a luxury hotel. It's certainly among the best of Prague's top hotels. All rooms are furnished differently and to the highest standards, with a Jacuzzi in every bathroom. The equally luxurious restaurant offers a short menu of dishes that often blend different European cuisines. The decor is essentially modern, and in summer a roof terrace adjacent to the Ledebur Gardens has what is surely the best view of all the roofs of the Little Quarter.
🛏 19 🚇 Malostranská 🅿 🔌
🎴 All major cards

<table>
<tr><td colspan="2">**PRICES**</td></tr>
<tr><td colspan="2">**HOTELS**</td></tr>
<tr><td colspan="2">An indication of the cost of a double room in the high season is given by $ signs.</td></tr>
<tr><td>**$$$$$**</td><td>Over $200</td></tr>
<tr><td>**$$$$**</td><td>$130–$200</td></tr>
<tr><td>**$$$**</td><td>$80–$130</td></tr>
<tr><td>**$$**</td><td>$50–$80</td></tr>
<tr><td>**$**</td><td>Under $50</td></tr>
<tr><td colspan="2">**RESTAURANTS**</td></tr>
<tr><td colspan="2">An indication of the cost of a three-course meal without drinks is given by $ signs.</td></tr>
<tr><td>**$$$$$**</td><td>Over $35</td></tr>
<tr><td>**$$$$**</td><td>$25–$35</td></tr>
<tr><td>**$$$**</td><td>$15–$25</td></tr>
<tr><td>**$$**</td><td>$10–$15</td></tr>
<tr><td>**$**</td><td>Under $10</td></tr>
</table>

🛏 THE AUGUSTINE
🍴 $$$$
LETENSKÁ 12
PRAGUE 1
TEL 266 112 233
FAX 266 112 234
www.theaugustine.com
Newly opened in a former monastery and one of the city's most venerated beer halls, this atmospheric hotel features a fine dining restaurant that combines fresh designer style with classic Old Europe woodwork and high ceilings. Rooms, some with spectacular views, feature elegant but comfortable modernist designs and pampering amenities.
🛏 101 🚇 Malostranská 🅿
⬗ 🔌 🎴 All major cards

🛏 SAX
$$$$
JÁNSKÝ VRŠEK 3
PRAGUE 1
TEL 257 531 268
FAX 257 534 101

🛏 Hotel   🍴 Restaurant   🛏 No. of Guest Rooms   🪑 No. of Seats   🅿 Parking   🚇 Metro   🔌 Closed   ⬗ Elevator

www.hotelsax.cz
This discreet hotel is located
on a quiet square off Vlašská
in the heart of the Little
Quarter. The retro-style rooms
have won design awards,
and the stylish lobby bar in a
courtyard atrium is decorated
with modern art.

🛏 22 🖼 Malostranská 🅿 ⬍
💳 All major cards

🛏 **U PÁVA**
$$$$
U LUŽISKÉHO SEMINÁŘE 32
PRAGUE 1
TEL 257 533 360
www.romantichotels.cz
U Páva is located on a quiet
square just a short distance
from the Charles Bridge.
Ask to see the rooms before
making a reservation; some
can be a bit gloomy, especially
in winter. The dark wood
furnishings and heavy drapery
are not to everyone's taste,
but the rooms are sumptuous.
It is worth investigating the
suites, which are only slightly
more expensive than the
double rooms.

🛏 27 🖼 Malostranská 🅿 ⬍
💳 AE, MC, V

🛏 **ZLATÁ HVĚZDA**
$$$$
NERUDOVA 48
PRAGUE 1
TEL 257 532 867
FAX 257 533 624
www.hotelgoldenstar.com
The grand Zlatá Hvězda in
the heart of the Little Quarter
occupies a magnificent 1730s
baroque building. It was
reconstructed in 2000, but
original features such as the
ornate plasterwork were not
disturbed. The rooms vary
in size, and all have period
wooden furnishings.

🛏 26 🖼 Malostranská 🅿 ⬍
💳 AE, MC, V

🛏 **PENSION**
🍴 **DIENTZENHOFER**
$$$
NOSTICOVA 2
PRAGUE 1
TEL 257 311 319
FAX 257 320 888
www.dientzenhofer.cz
The birthplace of architect
Kilián Ignác Dientzenhofer,
close to Kampa Island, now
flourishes as a small hotel
and restaurant. The location
is appealing and quiet, but
the rooms, although quite
spacious, need a makeover.
There is wheelchair access, and
a pleasant garden terrace.

🛏 9 🖼 Malostranská 🅿 ⬍
💳 All major cards

Restaurants

🍴 **U MALÍŘŮ**
$$$$$
MALTÉZSKÉ NÁMĚSTÍ 11
PRAGUE 1
TEL 257 530 318
FAX 257 530 000
www.umaliru.cz
The restaurant claims to date
back to 1543. The food leans
French except for the Menu
Bohemia, which includes veni-
son terrine and roast goose.
Good selection of pricey
French wines.

🍴 60 🖼 Malostranská 🅿 ⬍
💳 AE, MC, V

🍴 **KAMPA PARK**
$$$$
NA KAMPĚ 8B, PRAGUE 1
TEL: 296 826 112
www.kampagroup.com
Consistently the toast of *New
York Times* critics, Kampa Park
has been the fine dining spot
for taking in views of the
Charles Bridge since the early
90s. Outstanding seafood,
Asian accents and Bohemian
classics go with the top service
and wine list.

🍴 160 🖼 Malostranská
💳 All major cards

🍴 **U ZLATÉ HRUŠKY**
$$$$
NOVÝ SVĚT 3/77
PRAGUE 1
TEL 220 941 244
FAX 220 512 608
www.uzlatehrusky.cz
The restaurant occupies three
wood-paneled rooms on the
first floor of an old house.
In summer you can eat in the
garden. Most of chef Karel
Brázda's dishes are inter-
national, but there are also
local specialties such as tripe
cooked in Bohemian style,
a stew served as an appetizer,
and venison roulade with pear
purée. All dishes are freshly
prepared, so you may have
a wait of 20–50 minutes. The
desserts are solidly Bohemian,
from noodles with poppy seed
and curd to dumplings with
plum sauce. The international
wine list is less exciting than
the menu.

🍴 70 💳 AE, MC, V

🍴 **COWBOYS**
$$$
NERUDOVA 40
PRAGUE 1
TEL 296 826 107
FAX 257 534 848
www.kampagroup.com
Formerly known as Bazaar,
this rambling collection of
cellars leading to a fine terrace
overlooking the city is now
an accomplished specialist at
steaks, something near and
dear to meat-loving Czechs.
The western theme and
seafood offerings add interest
and service is sharp, as at all
restaurants in the local Kampa
Group's stable.

🍴 180 🖼 Malostranská
💳 All major cards

🍴 **U MALÉ VELRYBY**
$$$
MALTÉZSKÉ NÁMĚSTÍ 15,
PRAGUE 1
TEL: 257 214 703

www.umalevelryby.cz
From the seared scallops on spinach to the lobster pasta, Chef Jason LeGear invariably charms his guests while whipping up international dishes with dash in this intimate eatery. Street tables expand capacity in warm months.

🏨 20 🚇 Malostranská
🗝 All major cards

🍴 U MALTÉZSKÝCH RYTÍŘŮ
$$$
PROKOPSKÁ 10
PRAGUE 1
TEL 257 530 075
FAX 257 531 324
www.umaltezskychrytiru.cz
With its medieval cellars and piano bar, this small, cozy restaurant has a devoted following. The menu is sensibly short, featuring Continental dishes such as Chateaubriand steak for two, lamb fillets, duck, quail, and sole.

🏨 30 🚇 Malostranská
🗝 AE, MC, V

🍴 U ŠEVCE MATOUŠE
$$$
LORETÁNSKÉ NÁMĚSTÍ 4
PRAGUE 1
TEL 220 514 536
This is a grand Czech restaurant, located in vaulted chambers, with staid furnishings. The menu is enormous, and so are the helpings. Chicken and steak are prepared in a number of different ways, but the wine list is limited.

🏨 45 🚇 Malostranská
🗝 All major cards

🍴 WALDŠTEJNSKA HOSPODA
$$$
TOMÁŠSKA 16
PRAGUE 1
TEL 773 139 519
www.waldstejnska hospoda.com

This Czech restaurant specializes in game, but also serves some international dishes. The specialty is the "Valdštejn sword"—various meats skewered onto a sword, for two people or more. Try the steak with port wine sauce. Most of the wines are Moravian. The decor of the three rooms is traditional, with dark wooden banquettes.

🏨 100 🚇 Malostranská 🗝 MC, V

🍴 U LABUTI
$$–$$$
HRADČANSKÉ NÁMĚSTÍ 11
PRAGUE 1
TEL 220 511 191
FAX 220 511 190
www.ulabuti.com
The U Labuti is based in a historic building that has over the years been home to Johannes Kepler, Tycho Brahe, and the young Madeleine Albright, former U.S. secretary of state. It has two rooms—one, the principal restaurant, focuses on international cuisine, while the other, more like a pub in atmosphere, offers Czech cuisine and Plzeň beer. The house specialty is the Old Prague Platter, which consists of duck, rabbit, smoked pork, red and white cabbage, and three kinds of dumplings. The vaulted rooms, pretty tapestry chairs, and pink tablecloths make for an elegant setting. The wine list is international.

🏨 100 🚇 Malostranská
🗝 All major cards

🍴 GITANES
$$
TRŽIŠTĚ 7
PRAGUE 1
TEL 257 530 163
www.gitanes.cz
A homey little place for Dalmatian and Montenegrin flavors and hearty red wine, well-situated on one of the district's quieter streets but

just a block off the main square. Familial service and a relaxed but capable waitstaff have made Gitanes a favorite of locals and regular visitors to the city.

🏨 44 🚇 Malostranská
🗝 All major cards

■ OLD TOWN

Hotels

🏨 BUDDHA BAR HOTEL
🍴 $$$$$
JAKUBSKÁ 8
PRAGUE 1
TEL 221 776 300
FAX 224 776 310
www.buddha-bar-hotel.cz
Leave Old Prague behind for a taste of mod-Orientalism at this hotel version of Paris's hyper-hip nightclub, located right in the heart of Old Town. Dark woods, red accents, low lighting, and incense and Buddha beat music add to its mystical, romantic charm. Turndown service includes chocolates and an orchid (and a pillow menu). If you don't stay overnight, at the very least come for a meal at Siddartha café, with its chi-chi Asian fusion cuisine, or a drink at the super chic eponymous bar.

🏨 39 🚇 Náměstí Republiky
🔲 🎭 🗝 All major cards

🏨 KEMPINSKI HYBERNSKÁ PRAGUE
$$$$$
HYBERNSKÁ 12
PRAGUE 1
TEL 226 226 111
www.kempinski.com
Housed in a retrofitted 15th-century baroque palace just steps from the Powder Tower and Municipal Hall, this business hotel on the edge of Old Town features contemporary decor in generously sized units that feel more apartment than hotel with separate bedroom,

---

🏨 Hotel 🍴 Restaurant 🏨 No. of Guest Rooms 🏨 No. of Seats 🅿 Parking 🚇 Metro 🕐 Closed 🛗 Elevator

living area, and kitchenette. Exquisite service.

(i) 75 Náměstí Republiky
All major cards

PAŘÍŽ
$$$$–$$$$$
U OBECNIHO DOMU 1
PRAGUE 1
TEL 222 195 195
FAX 224 225 475
www.hotel-pariz.cz
This gorgeous secessionist hotel was renovated to combine comfort with beauty. Public rooms include the Café de Paris, with its art nouveau light fittings. Look for the lovely ironwork on the staircase.

(i) 94 Náměstí Republiky
All major cards

UNGELT
$$$$–$$$$$
MALÁ ŠTUPARTSKÁ 7
PRAGUE 1
TEL 224 745 900
FAX 222 745 901
www.ungelt.cz
The Ungelt hotel, behind the Týn church, offers spacious apartments. All have a kitchenette. Some have two bedrooms, sleeping four.

(i) 10 Náměstí Republiky
All major cards

CENTRAL
$$$$
RYBNÁ 8
PRAGUE 1
TEL 224 812 041
FAX 222 315 386
www.central-prague.com
Built in 1931, the Central, near Náměstí Republiky, was renovated in the 1990s. Rooms are simply furnished. The best and priciest, on the top floors, have balconies with views over the city. There's an attractive lobby bar.

(i) 68 Náměstí Republiky
MC, V

RESIDENCE ŘETĚZOVÁ
$$–$$$$$
ŘETĚZOVÁ 9
PRAGUE 1
TEL/FAX 222 221 800
www.retezova.com
Centrally located in the maze of streets in the Old Town, this renovated 15th-century building offers a range of accommodations in self-catering units. This is a good choice if you are staying in Prague for more than just a few days.

(i) 9 Staroměstská
All major cards

HOTEL JOSEF
$$$
RYBNÁ 20
PRAGUE 1
TEL 221 700 111
FAX 221 700 999
www.hoteljosef.com
This designer hotel, created by Czech-U.K. architect Eva Jiřiáná, has won critical praises since it opened in 2002. Though rooms are small, glass walls and interior decor with clean lines improve things, along with the sharp service and affordability.

(i) 109 Náměstí Republiky
AE, MC, V

U ČERVENÉ ŽIDLE
$$$
LILIOVÁ 4
PRAGUE 1
TEL 296 180 018
FAX 221 700 999
EMAIL u-cervene-zidle@prague-spot.com
This guesthouse in a 15th-century building offers charm galore. The rooms, which range from singles to quads, have spare, tidy furnishings and all have private baths. It's situated in the historic heart of the city, close to Charles Bridge. Buffet breakfast.

(i) 15 Můstek
AE, MC, V

ČERNÁ LIŠKA
$$$
MIKULÁŠSKÁ 2
PRAGUE 1
TEL 224 232 250
FAX 224 232 249
www.cernaliska.cz
Considering its location right on Staroměstské náměstí, the Black Fox, as its name translates, is a cozy, classy old-fashioned option with notably attentive service and competitive rates. Rafters, wood floors and cushy sofas fill out this (thoroughly but tastefully modernized) 14th-century building.

(i) 12 Staroměstská
All major cards

UNITAS
$$$
BARTOLOMĚJSKÁ 9
PRAGUE 1
TEL 224 221 802
FAX 224 230 532
www.unitas.cz
This is a clean but spartan budget choice, with twin and triple rooms and some dormitory-style rooms in what used to be convent cells. All bathroom facilities are shared at Unitas, and the rooms are hardly spacious, but the location, just a short walk from the Charles Bridge and the Old Town, is good.

(i) 34 Národní třída
None

Restaurants

BELLEVUE
$$$$$
SMETANOVO NÁBŘEŽÍ 18
PRAGUE 1
TEL 222 221 443
FAX 222 220 453
www.bellevuerestaurant.cz
The cooking is Continental, and primarily French. Dishes include New Zealand lamb, turbot, and venison—all richly prepared and very expensive. Guests

---

Nonsmoking   Air-conditioning   Indoor Pool   Outdoor Pool   Health Club   Credit Cards

appreciate the spacious views of Hradčany. Live jazz on Sunday.
⚽ 120 🔳 Staroměstská
🔲 AE, MC

🍴 V ZÁTIŠÍ
$$$$–$$$$$
BETLÉMSKÉ NÁMĚSTÍ, LILIOVÁ 1
PRAGUE 1
TEL 222 221 155
FAX 222 220 629
www.vzatisi.cz
This exceptionally pretty and acclaimed restaurant occupies several rooms, with mottled Provençal decor. The menu, which changes regularly, is international, but there are also Bohemian specialties such as goose, and venison with foie gras. House specialties include New Zealand lamb chops, duck, and John Dory. The strength of the wine list lies in good Czech wines. Service is excellent.
⚽ 105 🔳 Národní třída 🔲
🔲 AE, MC, V

🍴 RYBÍ TRH
$$$$
TÝNSKÝ DVŮR 5
PRAGUE 1
TEL 224 895 447
FAX 224 895 449
The tanks arranged round the restaurant's two rooms are a clear indication of what to expect on the menu here: live lobster, octopus, squid, cod, halibut, and tuna. Steamed mussels, bouillabaisse, sushi, and oysters all feature. The location is in the smart Ungelt courtyard. In summer you can eat in the garden.
⚽ 60 🔳 Náměstí Republiky
🔲 All major cards

🍴 ANGEL
$$
V KOLKOVNÉ 7
PRAGUE 1
TEL 773 222 422
www.angelrestaurant.cz
Local celeb chef Sofia Smith

oversees this inspired, arty dining room that blends Southeast Asian food with expert culinary handling of fresh spices, meats and intoxicating sauces. Don't miss the house special cheesecake by any means.
⚽ 48 🔳 Staroměstská 🕐 Closed Sun. 🔲 All major cards

🍴 BRASILIERO
$$
U RADNICE 8
PRAGUE 1
TEL 224 234 474
www.ambi.cz
This invariably packed steakhouse shows off the Czech affinity for tender grilled beef, mixed with authentic Brazilian butchery, all set in an atmospheric stone cellar beneath Old Town's main square.
⚽ 56 🔳 Staroměstská
🔲 All major cards

🍴 DEBRUG
$$
MASNÁ 5
PRAGUE 1
TEL 724 122 994
Offering a zesty break from Czech cuisine, this classic darkpaneled Belgian restaurant, serves up authentic mussels and fruit and nut beers. Debrug has won over regulars with fleet service. In warm months, its streetside tables are buzzing.
⚽ 65 🔳 Náměstí Republiky
🔲 All major cards

🍴 KOLKOVNA
$$
V KOLKOVNÉ 8
PRAGUE 1
TEL 224 819 701
www.kolkovna.cz
All the Old World Czech classics in a charming wood-and-brass interior but with modern service and speed. The recipe, along with excellent Pilsner pours, has made this place so

popular it's best to try early or late.
⚽ 104 🔳 Staroměstská
🔲 All major cards

🍴 KLUB ARCHITEKTŮ
$$
BETLÉMSKÉ NÁMĚSTÍ 169/5A
PRAGUE 1
TEL 224 401 214
www.klubarchitektu.com
This is a basement restaurant with bare stone walls and wooden tables. The large menu includes odd dishes such as chicken with peaches, plus Thai dishes, burritos, and BBQ. A good selection of wines from individual growers.
⚽ 100 🔳 Národní třída
🔲 MC, V

🍴 MONARCH
$$
NA PERŠTÝNÉ 15
PRAGUE 1
TEL 224 239 602

www.monarch.cz
The Old Town district's best source of international wines is mainly about sipping fine vintages in grand wine bar style. But the Monarch's menu of beef Tartar, locally made sausages, excellent cheeses, salads and duck, shrimp and soups make for a nice light meal too.

🔁 55 🚇 Národní třída
🏧 All major cards

🍽 RED HOT & BLUES
$$
JAKUBSKÁ 12
PRAGUE 1
TEL 222 314 639
Simply furnished, this large restaurant with many rooms offers a home-away-from-home to hundreds of (mostly American) expats who can't get enough of its burgers and Creole and Tex-Mex dishes. Live jazz every evening; filling brunches over the weekend.

🔁 130 🚇 Náměstí Republiky
🏧 AE, MC, V

🍽 U SUPA
$$
CELETNÁ 22
PRAGUE 1
TEL/FAX 224 227 800
www.restauraceusupa.cz
Behind the facade along Celetná are two spacious vaulted halls that have long been a popular traditional restaurant. U Supa is very much on the tourist trail, but the food is authentic and excellent. Such staples as cabbage soup and duck with red cabbage are rich and tasty. If you are part of a large group, consider ordering the house specialty a day in advance: whole suckling pig. Service is swift and professional, but check your bill for extra "service charges."

🔁 160 🚇 Náměstí Republiky
🏧 None

🍽 COUNTRY LIFE
$
MELANTRICHOVA 15
PRAGUE 1
TEL 224 213 366
One of Old Town's few vegetarian options, this affordable, friendly cafeteria-style place is lined with surreal woodcarving and serves up fresh salads, smoothies and grain-and-veggie-based baked goods, along with nutritious soups.

🔁 48 🚇 Můstek 🏧 None

JOSEFOV

Hotel

🏨 INTERCONTINENTAL
🍽 **$$$$$**
NÁMĚSTÍ CURIEOVÝCH 43/5
PRAGUE 1
TEL 296 631 111
FAX 224 811 216
www.icprague.com
Quite a few of the international chains have hotels in Prague, but this has the best location: on the river just a few minutes' walk from Josefov. As well as having all the restaurant and business facilities one expects from a hotel of this caliber and price (most notably the rooftop restaurant, **Zlatá Praha**), the hotel has wheelchair access and a Casa del Habano cigar shop.

🛏 364 🚇 Staroměstská

🏧 All major cards

Restaurants

🍽 PRAVDA
$$$$$
PAŘÍŽSKÁ 17
PRAGUE 1
TEL 222 326 203
FAX 222 312 042
www.pravdarestaurant.cz
Right next to the Old-New Synagogue, this fashionable restaurant offers "specialties of the global villages"—

from Vietnam to Mexico. Highlights include pea and leek soup with fresh oysters; tea-smoked Atlantic scallops with bell pepper and orange sauce; and baked lamb loin with sweet corn, tomatoes, and goat's cheese. Pravda occupies a vaulted room in a corner building. One arm is a well-stocked bar; the other, the restaurant. There's a good range of French wines and champagnes.

🔁 100 🚇 Staroměstská
🏧 All major cards

🍽 BAROCK
$$$$
PAŘÍŽSKÁ 24
PRAGUE 1
TEL 222 329 221
FAX 222 321 933
www.barockrestaurant.cz
Owned by the same group that created Pravda a few doors farther up the road, Barock places the emphasis on Asiatic cuisine, notably sushi and sashimi. The restaurant's walls are plastered with photographs of supermodels, which tells you a bit about the market it is targeting. The front of the restaurant also functions as a bar, and in summer there's extra seating in the garden.

🔁 50 🚇 Staroměstská
🏧 All major cards

🍽 LE CAFÉ COLONIAL
$$$$
ŠIROKÁ 6
PRAGUE 1
TEL 224 818 322
www.lecafecolonial.cz
This Josefov restaurant offers eclectic cooking and a chic ambience. Starters may be duck carpaccio and marinated seafood; main courses include elaborate salads, pasta dishes, satay, fondue, fresh fish, chicken curry, and steaks. The setting is informal, with cane chairs and low lighting.

It's a popular place for breakfast, but prices, even by Prague standards, are quite high.

🍽 85 🚇 Staroměstská
💳 All major cards

🍽 **KING SOLOMON**
$$$
ŠIROKÁ 55
PRAGUE 1
TEL 224 818 752
FAX 274 864 664
www.kosher.cz
This grand and elegant all-kosher restaurant has been a hit since its opening in the early 1990s, with specialties such as delicate caviar malossol and gefilte fish. A well-stocked wine cellar goes along with the top service.

🍽 60 🚇 Staroměstská
💳 All major cards

■ **NEW TOWN**

Hotels

🏨 **JALTA**
🍽 **$$$$$**
VÁCLAVSKÉ NÁMĚSTÍ 45
PRAGUE 1
TEL 222 822 111
FAX 222 822 833
www.jalta.cz
Built in the 1950s, the Jalta has successfully converted from a fairly soulless place to a comfortable four-star hotel. The rooms are well appointed and spacious, although the public areas lack charm. There is a good Japanese restaurant within the hotel for those with a craving for sushi.

ⓘ 94 🚇 Můstek 🅿 🔁
💳 AE, DC, JCB, MC, V

🏨 **AMBASSADOR ZLATÁ HUSA**
$$$$–$$$$$
VÁCLAVSKÉ NÁMĚSTÍ 5–7
PRAGUE 1
TEL 224 193 876
FAX 224 226 167

www.ambassador.cz
The Ambassador's location on Wenceslas Square is hard to beat, and the guest rooms are comfortable and well equipped, although the public rooms are lacking in atmosphere. The hotel adjoins the nightclub and casino.

ⓘ 160 🚇 Můstek 🔁 🚫 🔁
💳 All major cards

🏨 **CITY HOTEL MORAN**
$$$$–$$$$$
NA MORÁNI 15
PRAGUE 2
TEL 224 915 208
FAX 224 920 625
The rooms in this attractive building are spacious and well equipped, though bland. Just off Charles Square, it is a good choice in this location.

ⓘ 57 🚇 Karlovo Náměstí 🅿
🔁 🔁 💳 All major cards

🏨 **PALACE PRAHA**
$$$$–$$$$$
PANSKÁ 12
PRAGUE 1
TEL 224 093 111
FAX 224 221 240
www.palacehotel.cz
This 1906 secessionist building is perfectly located just off Wenceslas Square. One of Prague's first luxury hotels, it is still holding its own. It's expensive, but has personality, and is very well equipped and effortlessly comfortable. Many of the rooms are individually decorated; all are stylish, with fine-quality fabrics for curtains and bedspreads.

ⓘ 124 🚇 Můstek 🅿 🚫 🔁
💳 All major cards

🏨 **EVROPA**
🍽 **$$$**
VÁCLAVSKÉ NÁMĚSTÍ 25
PRAGUE 1
TEL 224 228 117
FAX 224 224 544

www.evropahotel.cz
An old building, only partly renovated, Europa has lots of character—though the 18th-century (Louis XVI–style) furnishings in some rooms clash with the art nouveau structure. Rooms with bathrooms are spacious; avoid the rooms without bathrooms, which are dreary and can be hot. The café downstairs is a perfect gathering place; the location is as good as it gets.

ⓘ 92 🚇 Můstek 🅿 🔁
💳 AE, MC, V

🏨 **HOTEL ELITE**
🍽 **$$$**
OSTROVNI 32
PRAGUE 1
TEL 224 932 250
FAX 224 930 787
www.hotelelite.cz
This former baroque barracks is one of Prague's best values, especially considering the unique decor of each room, restored in period style, the excellent reputation for service and the location just a block from Old Town.

ⓘ 76 🚇 Národní třída 🅿 🔁
💳 All major cards

🏨 **CITY BELL**
$–$$
BELGICKÁ 10
PRAGUE 2
TEL 733 722 856
FAX 222 522 422
www.hotelcitybell.cz
The City Bell, a five-minute walk from náměstí Miru, is one of the few bargains in the city center. The rooms are large and bright, but sparsely furnished. The cheaper rooms have separate, shared bathrooms. Service is exceptionally helpful.

ⓘ 24 🚇 Náměstí Miru 🅿
🔁 💳 All major cards

🏨 Hotel 🍽 Restaurant ⓘ No. of Guest Rooms 🍴 No. of Seats 🅿 Parking 🚇 Metro 🕐 Closed 🔁 Elevator

Restaurants

🍴 OLIVA
$$$
PLAVECKA 4
PRAGUE 2
TEL 222 520 288
www.olivarestaurant.cz
With a zesty Mediterranean menu, this intimate bistro is warming in winter. It's well worth hunting down any time of year, though, for its inspired menu, from seafood fennel chowder to lamb with sweet and sour aubergine and tempting paellas.
🔲 65 🔲 Karlovo Náměstí 🕐 Closed Sun. 🐾 All major cards

🍴 BUFFALO BILL'S
$$
VODIČKOVA 9
PRAGUE 1
TEL 224 948 624
FAX 296 238 083
www.buffalobill.cz
The ribs, tacos, burritos, and country music served up at this Tex-Mex hangout are popular with expats.
🔲 65 🔲 Můstek 🐾 AE, MC, V

🍴 JÁMA
$$
V JÁMĚ 7, PRAGUE 1
TEL 224 222 383
www.jamapub.cz
The pre-eminent expat bar and social center of Prague, this comfortable, plank-floored establishment also does Czech classics along with its top-ranked burgers and brunches. Patio seating out back adds to capacity in warmer months.
🔲 74 🔲 Můstek 🐾 MC, V

🍴 PIZZERIA DI CARLO
$$
KARLOVO NÁMĚSTÍ 30
PRAGUE 2
TEL 222 231 381
www.dicarlo.cz

In addition to pizza, this popular basement with its summer garden offers a full range of pasta dishes. Portions are generous and the salads impressive. Busy at lunchtime with local office workers.
🔲 120 🔲 Karlovo Náměstí 🐾 AE, MC

🍴 U ČÍŽKŮ
$$
KARLOVO NÁMĚSTÍ 34
PRAGUE 2
TEL 222 232 257
U Čížků, with its cozy wood-beamed interior, offers good Moravian wines and rich Czech cooking such as pig's trotter in beer. There are also vegetarian dishes.
🔲 100 🔲 Karlovo Náměstí 🔳 🐾 AE, MC, V

🍴 U KALICHA
$$
NA BOJIŠTI 12–14
PRAGUE 2
TEL/FAX 296 189 600
www.ukalicha.cz
Josef Švejk and the novelist Jaroslav Hašek, who created him, have made this pub famous. It is extravagantly Czech, serving goose, pork knuckle, and steaks, and specializing in large platters for groups. It is decorated with Švejk memorabilia, and its walls are scribbled with signatures of celebrities. The menu is in 22 languages. Music in the evening.
🔲 240 🔲 I. P. Pavlova 🐾 AE, DC, V

🍴 U PINKASŮ
$$
JUNGMANNOVO NÁMĚSTÍ 16,
PRAGUE 1
TEL 221 111 150
www.upinkasu.cz
A rollicking local pub with a capable Bohemian cuisine kitchen since 1843, this three-story oasis of the Old World is

often overlooked even though it stands just off the bottom of Wenceslas Square. Costumed waiters hoist Pilsner mugs till the late hours but dining is just till 10pm.
🔲 145 🔲 Můstek 🐾 All major cards

FARTHER AFIELD

Hotel

🏨 MÖVENPICK
$$$
MOZARTOVA 261/1
PRAGUE 5
TEL 257 151 111
FAX 257 153 131
www.moevenpick-prague.com
Pink and starkly modern, Mövenpick is in one of the city's least attractive districts, but there is little choice in this area. This hotel is especially useful for travelers with cars, because access is easy and there is ample parking. Moreover, prices are fair. The rooms have modern furnishings and the beds have thick mattresses and luxurious duvets.
ⓘ 434 🔲 Andel 🅿 🔳 🔳
🔳 🐾 All major cards

Restaurants

🍴 AROMI
$$$
MÁNESOVA 78, PRAGUE 2
TEL 222 713 222
www.aromi.cz
Prague's standard bearer for Italian cuisine attracts up and coming Czechs, expats and not a few residents of the boot itself with stunning seafood, top-notch presentation, a thoughtfully done winelist and a relaxed, rustic atmosphere. The house veal on saffron risotto is something to celebrate.
🔲 88 🔲 Jiřího z Poděbrad 🐾 All major cards

🔳 Nonsmoking 🔳 Air-conditioning 🔳 Indoor Pool 🔳 Outdoor Pool 🔳 Health Club 🐾 Credit Cards

🍴 CAFÉ SAVOY

$$$

ZBOROVSKÁ 68, PRAGUE 5

TEL. 251 511 690

www.ambi.cz

For a glimps of pre-war Prague, try a café table at this excellent venue where aproned table staff glide amid art nouveau wood paneling, serving Mediterranean cuisine, delicate deserts and an excellent light breakfast along with fine espresso. Just west of the Legionnaire's Bridge (Most Legií) from Old Town.

🔧 82 🚇 Malostranská

🃏 All major cards

🍴 MOZAIKA

$$

NITRANSKÁ 13

PRAGUE 2

TEL/FAX 224 253 011

www.restaurantmozaika.cz

The international menu at this comfortable cellar dining room is brought off with confidence, not pretense, earning it a loyal local following. Risotto and duck in Asian-inflected variations are the strong suits.

🔧 40 🚇 Jiřího z Poděbrad

🃏 All major cards

■ DAY TRIPS FROM PRAGUE

KUTNÁ HORA

🏨 ZLATÁ STOUPA

🍴 $$

TYLOVA 426

TEL 327 511 540

FAX 327 513 808

The hotel is located close to the city center, and facilities include a restaurant and wine bar. All rooms are equipped with a safe, minibar, and satellite TV. Secure parking is available.

ℹ️ 25 P 🃏 All major cards

🍴 U GROŠE

$

KOLLÁROVA 313

TEL 327 515 330

This Czech restaurant occupies a much renovated medieval building in the historic center of town. The menu is extensive; dishes to try include trout and, for dessert, pancakes.

🔧 70 🃏 None

MĚLNÍK

🏨 U RYTÍŘŮ
🍴 $$$

SVATOVÁCLAVSKÁ 17

TEL 315 621 440

FAX 315 621 439

www.urytiru.cz

Located next to the castle, this renovated old building offers comfortable accommodations with kitchenettes. Some rooms have four beds, making the hotel a useful option for families. In summer ask for a room with a terrace. The hotel has a restaurant, which has a terrace for dining al fresco in summer, and a less formal café.

ℹ️ 5 🃏 All major cards

PODĚBRADY

🏨 BELLEVUE-TLAPÁK
🍴 $$

NÁMĚSTÍ MASARYKA 654

TEL 325 623 111

FAX 325 614 584

www.bellevue.cz

The Bellevue has the best location in town, overlooking the park. It's a comfortable hotel, with a restaurant and a wine bar. The rooms are not lavishly decorated, but they are modern; each comes with a shower or bath and has satellite TV.

ℹ️ 60 P 🃏 All major cards

<table>
<tr><td colspan="2">PRICES</td></tr>
<tr><td colspan="2">HOTELS
An indication of the cost of a double room in the high season is given by $ signs.</td></tr>
<tr><td>$$$$$</td><td>Over $200</td></tr>
<tr><td>$$$$</td><td>$130–$200</td></tr>
<tr><td>$$$</td><td>$80–$130</td></tr>
<tr><td>$$</td><td>$50–$80</td></tr>
<tr><td>$</td><td>Under $50</td></tr>
<tr><td colspan="2">RESTAURANTS
An indication of the cost of a three-course meal without drinks is given by $ signs.</td></tr>
<tr><td>$$$$$</td><td>Over $35</td></tr>
<tr><td>$$$$</td><td>$25–$35</td></tr>
<tr><td>$$$</td><td>$15–$25</td></tr>
<tr><td>$$</td><td>$10–$15</td></tr>
<tr><td>$</td><td>Under $10</td></tr>
</table>

CZECH REPUBLIC
■ SOUTHERN BOHEMIA

ČESKÉ BUDĚJOVICE

🏨 GRAND HOTEL ZVON
🍴 $$$

NÁMĚSTÍ PŘEMYSLA OTAKARA 11, 28

TEL 381 601 601

FAX 381 601 605

www.hotel-zvon.cz

This well-established hotel is on the main square and offers a number of restaurants and snack bars. Try to get one of the rooms that face onto the square; they have some of the best urban views in Bohemia. Several rooms have four-poster beds. The kitchens produce the rich cakes that are sold in the hotel's excellent pastry shop—which may explain why the hotel is especially popular with

sweet-toothed Austrians.
Other facilities here include
a business center.

☐ 75 ▣ ⬗ 🅢 All major cards

🏨 BOHEMIA
🍴 $–$$
HRADEBNÍ 20
TEL/FAX 386 360 691
www.bohemiacb.cz
On the edge of the old town,
the Bohemia occupies two
renovated buildings. Though
rooms have antique touches,
all come with bathroom,
minibar, and satellite TV. The
hotel offers good value and
a restaurant; you can park your
car safely in the courtyard.

☐ 16 🅢 All major cards

🍴 PANSKÝ SENK
$$
PLACHÉHO 10
www.panskysenk.cz
The Panský Senk (Lords' Inn)
set in vaulted 13th-century
rooms with a medieval ambience, specializes in game.

☐ 80 🅢 None

ČESKÝ KRUMLOV

SOMETHING SPECIAL

🏨 HOTEL RŮŽE
$$$$
HORNÍ 154
TEL 380 772 100
FAX 380 713 146
www.hotelruze.cz
Without question, this is the
best hotel in town, and one
of the best in all of southern
Bohemia. It's away from the
main tourist throng in a very
beautiful sgraffitoed Renaissance building that was once
a Jesuit college. It has been
exquisitely renovated, and
its Renaissance character has
been maintained. Rooms are
furnished with dark wooden
beds, heavy draperies, and in
some cases, beamed wooden
ceilings and brass chandeliers.

There's a delightful and spacious terrace high above
the river with a café and live
music in summer. The hotel
can arrange sporting activities
such as cycling and rafting in
the surrounding region.

☐ 81 ▣ 🏊 🅦 🅢 All
major cards

🏨 DVOŘÁK
$$$
RADNIČNÍ 101
TEL 380 711 020
FAX 380 711 024
www.hoteldvorak.com
Although it's in the city
center, the Dvořák spreads
along the banks of the River
Vltava. The rooms come
with marble bathrooms, and
some are furnished with
antiques. A treasured feature
is the terrace overlooking
the river, a lovely spot for
a summer drink.

☐ 20 ▣ ⬗ 🅦 🅢 All
major cards

🍴 NA OSTROVĚ
$$
NA OSTROVĚ 171
TEL 380 727 708
FAX 380 731 436
www.naostroveck.cz
Avoid the touristy restaurants
on the main streets of town
and instead come straight to
this inexpensive fish restaurant
just beyond the castle viaduct.
Don't expect elegantly presented food or refined service;
the emphasis is on good fresh
ingredients and simple cooking. The menu features carp,
eel, trout, and other fish.

☐ 80 🅢 None

🏨 THE OLD INN
🍴 $$
NÁMĚSTÍ SVORNOSTI 12
TEL 380 772 500
FAX 380 772 550
www.hoteloldinn.cz
This hotel has been created

from three old houses in the
main square, and it has access
to the facilities of the costlier
Hotel Růže (see above). Some
of the rooms have plain furnishings, but the pricier
ones are more luxurious,
with antique-style beds and
dressers. Although parking is
not available at the hotel, the
staff will park your car and
retrieve it for you. The restaurant spills out onto the square,
and there's a beer cellar dating
back to the 13th century.
Guests are also entitled to use
the Růže's pool and fitness
center, just a few minutes'
walk away—all of which makes
this hotel quite a bargain.

☐ 52 ▣ ⬗ 🏊 🅦 All
major cards

FRYMBURK

🏨 VLTAVA
$$
FRYMBURK 45
TEL 380 735 605
FAX 380 735 603
www.hotel-vltava.com
The Vltava fronts the main
square of this pretty little
resort, but terraces behind the
building extend to the shore
of the lake. In summer you
can eat outdoors. The rooms
are bright and cheerful, and
there are a few apartments
that have kitchenettes.
The staff will help to arrange
excursions and various sporting activities. Massages and
sauna add to the relaxation.

☐ 25 ▣ ⬗ 🏊 🅢 All
major cards

JINDŘICHŮV HRADEC

🏨 BÍLÁ PANÍ
🍴 $$
DOBROVSKÉHO 5
TEL/FAX 384 363 329
www.hotelbilapani.cz
This tiny, family-run hotel is

close to the castle and has a restaurant. The atmosphere is pleasant, but ask to see the rooms before you commit to staying here; some are more comfortable than others.

[1] 11 [P] [&] All major cards

GRAND HOTEL
$

NÁMĚSTÍ MÍRU 165
TEL 384 361 252
FAX 384 361 251
www.relaxhotel.cz
The Grand Hotel is well situated on the town's main square and has been here for centuries. Although it doesn't quite live up to its name, the rooms are adequate for a night or two. It also has a restaurant and wine bar.

[1] 29 [P] [&] All major cards

PÍSEK

HOTEL ART
$$

FRÁNI SRÁMKA 158
TEL 773 994 959
www.hotelart.cz
This renovated small hotel, centrally located and decorated with original art work, is a charming option. It has a capable dining room specializing in freshwater fish; rates include breakfast. Hotel Art also offers a range of anti-stress massages.

[1] 18 [P] [&] All major cards

PRACHATICE

PARKÁN
$$

VĚŽNÍ 51
TEL/FAX 388 311 868
www.hotelparkan.cz
This reconstructed hotel in the city center occupies a renovated medieval house. The rooms are equipped with shower, satellite TV,

and refrigerator. There's a pleasant summer terrace, and the friendly staff can help you organize hiking and other activities in the nearby Šumava mountains.

[1] 17 [&] All major cards

TÁBOR

U KALICHA
$

SVATOŠOVA 25
TEL 381 251 927
Set in a large vaulted room near the church, U Kalicha (At the Chalice) offers diners a fairly sophisticated version of Czech cooking.

[🕘] Closed Sun. [&] None

TŘEBOŇ

ZLATÁ HVĚZDA
$$–$$$

MASARYKOVO NÁMĚSTÍ 107
TEL 384 757 111
FAX 384 757 200
www.zhevzda.cz
This fine Renaissance house stands on the main square. Although the decor is not exciting, the rooms are well equipped. The restaurant features both local and Continental cuisine.

[1] 48 [P] [&] All major cards

BÍLÝ KONÍCEK
$$

MASARYKOVO NÁMĚSTÍ 97
TEL/FAX 384 721 213
www.hotelbilykonicek.cz
The Bílý Koníćek, or White Little Horse, is in one of the oldest buildings on the main square (it dates from 1544). It also offers the best deal in town. Some of the rooms here are small, but all have bathrooms. You can rent bikes here, and a restaurant serves typical Czech dishes.

[1] 23 [P] [&] None

ŠUPINKA
$

VALY 56/155
TEL 384 721 149
www.supina.cz
This small restaurant, situated well away from the crowds of the square, specializes in fish. The Šupina restaurant facing it serves an identical menu. Despite their location off the well-beaten track, both restaurants are popular and are often full.

[P] [&] All major cards

■ WESTERN BOHEMIA

CHEB

HVĚZDA
$$

NÁMĚSTÍ KRÁLE JIŘÍHO Z PODĚBRAD 4–6
TEL 354 422 549
FAX 354 422 546
www.hotel-hvezda.cz
In an excellent location on the main square, the Hvězda is the best place to stay in Cheb. Ask for one of the rooms with a private bathroom; the slight extra cost is worthwhile.

[1] 42 [P] [&] All major cards

DOMAŽLICE

CHODSKY HRAD
$$

CHODSKÉ NÁMĚSTÍ 96
TEL 379 720 424
This spacious and lively restaurant adjoining the castle serves typical Czech food. The pork dishes are a good option.

[🔜] 100 [&] All major cards

FRANTIŠKOVY LÁZNĚ

BOHEMIA
$$

KLOSTERMANNOVA 92
TEL 354 403 811
FAX 354 403 844

[📠] Hotel [🍴] Restaurant [1] No. of Guest Rooms [🔜] No. of Seats [P] Parking [🚇] Metro [🕘] Closed [🔌] Elevator

The bustling Bohemia, on the edge of the spa gardens, is just a few minutes' walk from the spa and casino and offers good spa packages. The rooms are modern and very clean, and the restaurant is friendly and informal.

🛈 29 **P** 🉐 None

🍴 GOETHE
$$

NÁRODNÍ 1

Located within the casino, this opulent restaurant offers mostly Czech dishes in a sumptuous setting—with prices to match.

🉐 All major cards

KARLOVY VARY

SOMETHING SPECIAL

🏨 GRANDHOTEL PUPP
$$$$$

MÍROVÉ NÁMĚSTÍ 2
TEL 353 109 111
FAX 353 266 638
www.pupp.cz

This immense and luxurious hotel is *the* place to stay in Karlovy Vary. It was founded in 1701, though the present buildings date mostly from the 19th century. As a gathering place for the rich and famous in times past—guests from earlier days include J. S. Bach, Ludwig van Beethoven, Franz Liszt, Karl Marx, Franz Kafka, and Rita Hayworth—it was built to impress. Its palatial halls can be intimidating, but the rooms are richly furnished and is as luxurious as any hotel in Prague. If the prices are too daunting for you, consider the annex, **Parkhotel Pupp**, where 140 rooms are done up in a slightly less opulent manner; rates there are generally lower than those at the Grandhotel.

🛈 110 **P** 🍴 🉐 All major cards

🏨 DVOŘÁK
$$$–$$$$

NOVÁ LOUKA 11, 36021
TEL 353 102 111
FAX 353 102 119
www.hotel-dvorak.cz

A grand and well-equipped hotel with comfortable rooms, near the Grandhotel Pupp, the Dvořák is very popular option with visitors who are taking spa treatments in Karlovy Vary.

🛈 120 **P** 🉐 🉐 All major cards

🏨 OSTENDE
🍴 $$$–$$$$

STARÁ LOUKA 60
TEL 353 585 216
FAX 353 585 230
www.ostende.cz

Deceptively plain from the outside, the Ostende is a small but luxurious hotel that offers spa treatments as well as comfort. The rooms, furnished in an old-fashioned style, are ideal for long-term stays; they are equipped with fully fitted kitchenettes. The restaurant has a pleasant terrace facing the museum. The Ostende is located near the Grandhotel Pupp.

🛈 20 **P** 🉐 🉐 All major cards

🏨 INTERHOTEL CENTRAL
🍴 $$$

DIVADELNÍ NÁMĚSTÍ 17, 36003
TEL 353 182 630
FAX 353 321 522
www.interhotel-central.cz

This spacious hotel is in a relatively tranquil setting close to the springs and the town center. While the Central cannot be described as chic, the rooms are spacious and are painted in attractive pastel shades. It has a pleasant outdoor café and two restaurants.

🛈 84 **P** 🉐 🉐 All major cards

🏨 EMBASSY
🍴 $$–$$$

NOVÁ LOUKA 21

TEL 353 221 161
FAX 353 223 146
www.embassy.cz

This is a small, perfectly located, family-run hotel with comfortable rooms and a few apartments. It has an attractive restaurant, which is decorated with old stoves and painted alcoves and offers traditional Bohemian cooking and beers.

🛈 18 **P** 🉐 All major cards

🏨 PALACKÝ
$$–$$$

STARÁ LOUKA 40
TEL 353 222 544
FAX 353 228 122
www.hotelpalacky.cz

Well located near the Spring Colonnade, this modest hotel has spacious and comfortable rooms. The hotel can arrange for spa treatments and will provide special dietary meals.

🛈 7 **P** 🉐 🉐 All major cards

🏨 PROMENÁDA
🍴 $$–$$$

TRŽIŠTĚ 31
TEL 353 225 648
FAX 353 229 708
www.hotel-promenada.cz

The charming Promenáda has pleasant rooms and its restaurant, which occupies an inner atrium, serves both international and Czech cuisine. Very good wine list.

🛈 21 **P** 🉐 All major cards

🏨 HOTEL BOSTON
🍴 $$

LUČNÍ VRCH 9
TEL 353 362 711
FAX 353 221 602
www.boston.cz

Handily located just off Karlovy Vary's riverside promenade, the Boston offers good value for simple rooms with courteous service. Dozens of restaurants and spas surround the pink-facaded hotel.

🛈 16 **P** 🉐 🉐 All major cards

🉐 Nonsmoking 🉐 Air-conditioning 🉐 Indoor Pool 🉐 Outdoor Pool 🍴 Health Club 🉐 Credit Cards

MARIÁNSKÉ LÁZNĚ

🏨 **BOHEMIA**
$$–$$$
HLAVNÍ 100
TEL 354 610 111
FAX 354 610 555
www.hotelbohemia.net
This grand, old-fashioned
hotel epitomizes the appeal of
the spa: luxurious, but with an
emphasis on health-enhancing
treatments. The rooms have
satellite TV, minibar, safe, and
shower room. Some of the
rooms have balconies that
overlook the spa garden.

ℹ️ 77 🅿️ 🦽 All major cards

🏨 **VILLA BUTTERFLY**
$$–$$$
HLAVNÍ 655
TEL 354 654 111
FAX 354 654 200
E-MAIL villabutterfly@
badmarienbad.cz
Kitsch comes to Marienbad, as
the skinny nudes gesticulating
from the hotel roof confirm.
Despite the flamboyant
exterior, the rooms are conventional, with large beds and
desks. Some of the pricier ones
have Jacuzzis and Internet
access. Villa Butterfly also has
a coffeeshop and a chic lobby
bar that provides snacks as
well as drinks.

ℹ️ 96 🅿️ 🍴 🦽 All major cards

PLZEŇ

🏨 **CONTINENTAL**
$$
ZBROJNICKÁ 8
TEL 377 235 292
FAX 377 221 746
www.hotelcontinental.cz
Originally built by the Plzeň
brewery in 1895, this hotel has
a location that's hard to beat,
just off the main square. The
rooms have been redecorated,
though the interior decor and
furnishings have deliberately
been kept old-fashioned so as
to harmonize with the turn-

of-the-20th-century exterior.
Not all rooms have WCs, so be
sure to specify when making
a reservation.

ℹ️ 21 🅿️ 🦽 All major cards

TEPLÁ

🏨 **KLÁŠTER TEPLÁ**
🍴 **$$**
KLÁŠTER TEPLÁ 10
TEL 353 392 264
FAX 353 392 312
www.hotelklastertepla.cz
When the monks returned to
this vast Premonstratensian
foundation in the 1990s, they
reconstructed a wing of the
ancient monastery with the
aim of providing simple but
comfortable accommodations.
All the rooms have private
bathrooms but are not lavishly
fitted out. On the premises are
a restaurant and tavern, and a
golf course is nearby.

ℹ️ 65 🅿️ 🔁 🦽 All major cards

◼ NORTHERN BOHEMIA

DĚČÍN

🏨 **HOTEL ESKÁ KORUNA**
$
MASARYKOVO NÁMĚSTÍ 7
TEL 412 516 104
FAX 412 519 086
www.hotelceskakoruna.cz
A good, clean option on the
main square, with simple,
modern rooms that represent
the standard for economic
accommodation in central
Europe. Comfortable enough
as a base for exploring.

ℹ️ 43 🦽 All major cards

HŘENSKO

🏨 **PRAHA**
$$
HŘENSKO 37
TEL 412 554 006

FAX 412 554 162
An old resort hotel in this
touristy village, the skillfully
modernized Praha is the
best place to stay. Rooms are
comfortable, and the terrace
is popular in summer. There's
a sauna to relax in after a day's
hiking. Wheelchair access.

ℹ️ 34 🅿️ 🔁 🦽 All major cards

LIBEREC

🏨 **PRAHA**
🍴 **$$**
ŽELEZNÁ 2
TEL 485 102 655
FAX 485 113 138
www.hotelpraha.net
The hotel is in an exceptionally well restored, impressive
1905 art nouveau building.
Its excellent facilities include a
restaurant, coffee bar, casino,
and nightclub. Staff will help
organize sporting and tourism
activities. Wheelchair access.

ℹ️ 62 🅿️ 🔁 🦽 All major cards

PRICES

HOTELS
An indication of the cost of
a double room in the high
season is given by $ signs.

$$$$$	Over $200
$$$$	$130–$200
$$$	$80–$130
$$	$50–$80
$	Under $50

RESTAURANTS
An indication of the cost of
a three-course meal without
drinks is given by $ signs.

$$$$$	Over $35
$$$$	$25–$35
$$$	$15–$25
$$	$10–$15
$	Under $10

🏨 Hotel   🍴 Restaurant   ℹ️ No. of Guest Rooms   🔀 No. of Seats   🅿️ Parking   🚇 Metro   🕐 Closed   🔁 Elevator

LITOMĚŘICE

⊞ SALVA GUARDA
⋔ $–$$
MÍROVÉ NÁMĚSTÍ 12
TEL 416 732 506
FAX 416 732 798
www.salva-guarda.cz
The rooms in this remarkable Renaissance house dating from 1560 are not stylish, but the comfortable apartments have good-size bathrooms. A few rooms have four beds and are ideal for families. Salva Guarda also offers a good restaurant and wine bar.

ⓘ 16 🅿 ⚜ All major cards

TEPLICE

⊞ PRINCE DE LIGNE
⋔ $$–$$$
ZÁMECKÉ NÁMĚSTÍ 136
TEL 417 514 111
FAX 417 537 727
www.princedeligne.cz
Completely renovated in 1991, this 1824 building is situated near the spa and gardens—the most pleasant corner of a town that sees more people visiting on business than on holiday. If you feel like a splurge, ask for the suite done out in sumptuous 18th-century style. Worth a try are the Italian Leone Venezia restaurant, and the smaller Cabana Mexicana.

ⓘ 32 🅿 ⊟ ⚜ All major cards

ŽATEC

⊞ U HADA
⋔ $
NÁMĚSTÍ SVOBODY 155
TEL/FAX 415 711 000
www.uhada-zatec.cz
The town's only real draw for visitors is its fame as the source of the world's best hops. If you come to attend its hop festival, you will find the U Hada conveniently situated

on the main square. It is a well-restored, ancient building—be careful not to bang your head on the low wooden beams—with a restaurant and wine bar. Parking is secure.

ⓘ 21 🅿 ⛉ ⚜ All major cards

■ EASTERN BOHEMIA

HRADEC KRÁLOVĚ

⊞ U JANA
⋔ $
VELKÉ NÁMĚSTÍ 137
TEL 844 223 113
U Jana, attractively located on the main square, has been renovated in an unusually minimalist and elegant style. The hotel's restaurant specializes in fish and Czech cuisine.

ⓘ 9 🅿 ⚜ All major cards

⋔ SPORT CAFÉ
$
VELKÉ NÁMĚSTÍ 151
TEL 495 514 202
www.sport-cafe.cz
This is just the spot when you tire of Bohemian food and fancy pizza, chili, or pasta instead. In summer, enjoy the terrace jutting out onto the square. The café is deservedly popular with town residents and visitors alike for its friendly service and reliable food.

⚜ All major cards

HRUBÁ SKÁLA

⊞ ŠTEKL
$
HRUBÁ SKALÁ, TURNOV, 51101
TEL 481 389 684
www.hotel-stekl.cz
The Štekl occupies a former castle in the middle of the Český ráj (see pp. 238–241). Its location is exemplary, making it a perfect base for exploring the region. Rooms are basic, but the Štekl has the

merit of being inexpensive. Some of the cheapest rooms have shared bathrooms. Some rooms have Wi-Fi. Breakfast is included.

ⓘ 29 🅿 ⚜ All major cards

JANSKÉ LÁZNĚ

⊞ LESNÍ DŮM
⋔ $
KRKONOŠSKÁ 208
TEL 499 875 167
FAX 499 875 167
www.lesnidum.cz
Though just a modest chalet hotel, the Lesní Dům has a good deal of charm. Service is friendly and hospitable. The hotel also offers a decent and inexpensive restaurant, a summer terrace, a tennis court, and a sauna.

ⓘ 21 🅿 ⚜ None

LITOMYŠL

⊞ ZLATÁ HVĚZDA
⋔ $$
SMETANOVO NÁMĚSTÍ 84
TEL 461 615 338
FAX 461 615 091
www.zlatahvezda.cz
This stylish hotel on the main square is reasonably priced, with efficient and helpful staff. The management makes much of the fact that President Havel once stayed here. Ask for a room with a view of the castle. Serious Czech and Oriental cooking is served in the somber dining room.

ⓘ 29 🅿 ⊟ ⛉ ⚜ All major cards

NÁCHOD

⊞ U BERÁNKA
⋔ $$
NÁMĚSTÍ TGM 74
TEL 222 532 534
The hotel dates from 1914, which explains its essentially

secessionist decor. The rooms have parquet flooring and are high-ceilinged and airy. The restaurant has a splendid pristine secessionist interior. Given the hotel's small size, it is impressive that there is 24-hour room service. Overall, the Beránka has much more character than most Czech hotels.

🏨 57 🄿 🄴 🅂 All major cards

🏨 U MĚSTA PRAHY
🍽 $

NÁMĚSTÍ TGM 66
TEL 491 421 817
A good choice for the budget traveler, this hotel offers simple rooms, a popular restaurant and wine bar, and a terrace on the square in summer.

🛏 10 🄿 🅂 None

TURNOV

🏨 KORUNNÍ PRINC
🍽 $$

NÁMĚSTÍ ČESKÉHO RÁJE 137
TEL 481 313 520
FAX 481 313 522
www.korunniprinc.cz
The Korunní Princ enjoys an excellent central location in a town that is a popular base for visiting the Český ráj. The rooms are comfortable if not luxurious. The restaurant offers a wide range of dishes, specializing in fish and game.

🛏 24 🄴 🅂 None

VRCHLABÍ

🏨 LABUT
🍽 $

KRKONOŠSKÁ 188
TEL 499 406 220
FAX 499 421 700
www.hotellabut.cz
Vrchlabí is an excellent base for visiting the Krkonoše mountains, and the Labut has perfectly adequate accommo-

dations. Its spacious restaurant presents international as well as Czech dishes, and there's an attractive courtyard where you can enjoy a beer after a day's hiking.

🛏 24 🄿 🄴 🅂 All major cards

■ SOUTHERN MORAVIA

BRNO

🏨 GRAND HOTEL
🍽 $$$

BENEŠOVA 18
TEL 542 518 111
FAX 542 210 345
www.grandhotelbrno.cz
This is the city's leading international hotel, offering health club, sauna, hairdresser, all laundry requirements, and room service. The cheerful bedrooms all have minibars, satellite TVs, safes, and telephones. As well as a restaurant and grill room, the hotel has its own nightclub and casino. The Grand is located right on the edge of the Old Town, with parking immediately outside.

🛏 105 🄿 🄴 🍽
🅂 All major cards

🏨 INTERNATIONAL
🍽 $$$

HUSOVA 16
TEL 542 122 111
FAX 542 210 843
www.hotel.international.cz
Well located opposite the Špilberk hill, this modern hotel offers reasonably sized, brightly furnished rooms and a range of services and facilities that includes two restaurants, a casino, a hairdresser, a fitness center, and a car repair shop. There's a car rental facility on the premises.

🛏 252 🄿 🄴 🍽 🅂 All major cards

🏨 SLAVIA
🍽 $$

SOLNIČNÍ 15
TEL 542 321 249
FAX 542 211 769
www.slaviabrno.cz
The Slavia is in a 19th-century building on the edge of the old town, not far from the Špilberk fortress, and has been here for over a century. It has high-ceilinged, spacious bedrooms, and the public rooms include a restaurant, wine bar, and coffee bar.

🛏 82 🄿 🄴 🅂 All major cards

🏨 AVION
$–$$

ČESKÁ 20
TEL/FAX 542 214 055
www.avion-hotel.cz
A famous building designed in 1928 by Brno's leading modernist architect of the day, Bohuslav Fuchs, the Avion offers reasonably priced rooms. It's in a pedestrian zone, so reasonably tranquil, but there is no easy parking.

🛏 35 🄴 🅂 All major cards

🍽 POD ŠPILBERKEM
$$

HUSOVA 13
TEL 543 211 669
Typical and unpretentious, this Czech inn is perfectly located should you need reviving after a tour of the Špilberk or the Moravian galleries.

🛏 80 🄿 🅂 None

🍽 ŠPALÍČEK
$$

ZELNÝ TRH 13
TEL 542 211 526
This straightforward city-center restaurant serves hit-and-miss traditional Czech food. In summer there's a terrace at the top of the square.

🅂 None

🏨 Hotel 🍽 Restaurant 🛏 No. of Guest Rooms 🄴 No. of Seats 🄿 Parking 🚇 Metro 🕐 Closed 🄴 Elevator

TAJ
$$
BĚHOUNSKÁ 12/14
TEL 542 214 372
www.tajbrno.cz
When dumplings pall, it's worth considering this fairly authentic, light and airy Indian restaurant in the city center. You can also enjoy a drink at the thatched bar.
🅂 🅂 All major cards

KROMĚŘÍŽ

BOUČEK
$-$$
VELKÉ NÁMĚSTÍ 108
TEL/FAX 573 342 777
www.hotelboucek.cz
The Bouček enjoys an excellent location on the main square, and the rooms are cozy. No-smoking rooms are available. Parking can be a problem during the day, but there is short-term, meter parking outside.
ⓘ 11 🅂 🅂 All major cards

MIKULOV

HOTEL ELISKA
$
PIARISTŮ 4
TEL/FAX 519 513 073
www.hoteleliska.cz
The popular Hotel Eliska is a simple, no-frills hotel that fills up fast in the summer. A bonus is the Irish pub on the ground floor.
ⓘ 53 🅿 🅂 None

SLAVKOV

SOKOLSKÝ DŮM
$
PALACKÉHO NÁMĚSTÍ 75
TEL 544 221 103
FAX 544 227 737
www.hotelsokolskydum.cz
Half an hour's drive from Brno, this modern, clean, pleasant hotel on the main street is an excellent option for those who would prefer not to stay in the big city. Rooms are very comfortable and offer good value for the money. Service is friendly and efficient. It's best to reserve ahead for a summer visit. The restaurant offers good steaks and a few Mexican dishes.
ⓘ 20 🅿 🅂 None

STRÁŽNICE

FLAG HOTEL
STRÁŽNICE
$
PŘEDMĚSTÍ 3
TEL 518 332 059
FAX 518 325 069
The building is dull and the rooms are standard, but the hotel is right in the town center. It is the best base for those planning to visit the annual folk festival (see p. 260)—as long as you can get a room. A restaurant and wine bar are on the premises; parking is secure.
ⓘ 57 🅿 🅂 🅂 All major cards

TELČ

ČERNÝ OREL
$$
NÁMĚSTÍ ZACHARIÁŠE Z HRADCE 7
TEL 567 243 222
FAX 567 243 221
www.cernyorel.cz
This 16th-century building right on the main square has been a hotel since 1907 and is now the top choice in Telč. A few of the rooms don't have private bathrooms, so check when making a reservation. There's a restaurant serving traditional Czech fare, but, like the bedrooms, it lacks any real atmosphere or style. Rates include breakfast, parking, and Wi-Fi.
ⓘ 33 🅿 🅂 🅂 All major cards

HOTEL TELČ
$-$$
NA MŮSTKU 37
TEL 567 243 109
FAX 567 223 887
E-MAIL hotel.telc@tiscali.cz
This small hotel is perfectly adequate, but the rooms are sparsely furnished.
ⓘ 10 🅿 🅂 All major cards

U ZACHARIÁŠE
$$
NÁMĚSTÍ ZACHARIÁŠE Z HRADCE 33
TEL 567 243 672
On the main square, the cozy Zachariáše serves fish, beef, and pork, all in generous portions. The menu often includes imaginative dishes such as sliced steak stewed with white asparagus. Regent beer is on tap.
🅂 60 🅂 All major cards

VALTICE

APOLLON
$
PETRA BEZRUČE 720
TEL 519 352 625
FAX 519 352 009
www.hotel-apollon.cz
Located in a quiet spot on the outskirts of the town, the Apollon is nevertheless within walking distance of the center and the château (see pp. 258–259). The hotel offers simply furnished and comfortable rooms, a pleasant restaurant, and a summer terrace.
🅂 22 🅿 🅂 All major cards

NORTHERN MORAVIA

KARLOVA STUDÁNKA

DŽBÁN
$
KARLOVA STUDÁNKA 12
TEL 554 772 014

🅂 Nonsmoking 🅂 Air-conditioning 🅂 Indoor Pool 🅂 Outdoor Pool 🅂 Health Club 🅂 Credit Cards

www.hoteldzban.cz
The unique feature of the centrally situated Džbán is that it offers experienced mountain guides. Rooms are comfortably if cheaply furnished. There are a few rooms that have four beds, which are ideal for families or groups.

🛈 25 **P** 🛡 🕸 All major cards

OLOMOUC

🏨 **GEMO**
🍴 **$$$–$$$$**
PAVELČÁKOVA 22
TEL 585 222 115
FAX 585 231 730
www.hotel-gemo.cz
This modern hotel is just a few steps from the main square. Rooms are attractive, decorated mostly with modern pine furnishings and brightly colored floral and abstract fabrics. The Gemo also has a good, if pricey, seafood restaurant.

🛈 100 **P** 🔄 🕸 All major cards

🏨 **PALÁC**
$
1 MÁJE 27
TEL 585 224 096
This may look like a grim Stalinist exercise in hospitality from the outside, but the Palác's rooms are clean and reasonably spacious, and the location, near the cathedral, is excellent. A good option for the budget traveler.

🛈 24 **P** 🔄 🕸 All major cards

🍴 **CAESAR**
$
HORNÍ NÁMĚSTÍ 583
TEL 585 225 587
This lively Italian restaurant is in a splendid setting in the undercroft of the town hall. Pizzas are the most popular choice, but there is also a wide selection of pasta dishes.

🔄 120 🕸 All major cards

🍴 **U CERVENÉHO VOLKA**
$
DOLNÍ NÁMĚSTÍ 39
TEL 585 226 069
This restaurant is on one of the town's two main squares, next to Hauenschild Palace. It serves mostly Czech food and some Italian and Chinese dishes. The conservatory-style room is an attractive setting.

🔄 100 🕸 All major cards

OSTRAVA

🏨 **POLSKÝ DŮM**
🍴 **$**
PODĚBRADOVA 53
TEL 596 122 001
E-MAIL polskydum@volny.cz
It may not be in the most salubrious location, but this art nouveau mansion has been beautifully restored. Most of the rooms are large and comfortable. The restaurant offers a small discount to hotel residents and serves large portions of typical Czech food. Secure parking is available.

🛈 20 **P** 🔄 🕸 All major cards

ROŽNOV POD RADHOŠTĚM

🏨 **EROPLÁN**
🍴 **$$**
HORNÍ PASEKY 451, ROŽNOV
TEL 571 648 014
FAX 571 648 222
www.eroplan.cz
The Eroplán is a large, modern, chalet-style hotel close to the *skansen* (see pp. 282–283). It is comfortable and offers excellent facilities and services. All rooms have bathrooms and Internet connections. The complex includes a restaurant and snack bar, as well as a fitness center with a sauna and solarium. Some evenings feature live music and dancing. Secure parking is available.

🛈 39 **P** 🔄 🕑 🛡 🕸 All major cards

VELKÉ LOSINY

🏨 **PRADED**
$$
LÁZEŇSKÁ 4
TEL/FAX 583 248 215
The Praded is very close to the spa center in this attractive resort town. The rooms are decorated in bright and cheerful colors. The staff can help to arrange sporting activities such as tennis and mountain biking.

🛈 32 **P** 🕸 All major cards

🏨 Hotel 🍴 Restaurant 🛈 No. of Guest Rooms 🔄 No. of Seats **P** Parking 🚇 Metro 🕑 Closed 🔄 Elevator

Shopping

The Czech Republic is hardly a shopper's paradise, but even through the communist era it continued to produce the items for which it has always been well known—notably crystal glassware and garnets. The quality of clothing before 1990 was dire; however, in recent years there has been a resurgence of design, and a few boutiques are now selling high-quality products of local design and manufacture. The price of beer is kept low because the local population demands it, so beer remains a tremendous bargain (assuming you are able to take it home with you).

Antiques

Prague has plenty of antique shops, varying in content from junk to fine-quality furniture and clocks. If you are serious about finding bargains, take a preliminary tour of the Dorotheum auction house to get an idea of the going price for desirable items, and seek specialized advice about the most reliable antique dealers. Some luxury hotels, such as Růže in Český Krumlov, incorporate antique shops; outside Prague it is worth inquiring at the front desk of your hotel about local antique shops where you just might find something rare or interesting. Book collectors can pass many fascinating hours browsing in one of the country's many *antikvariát* (secondhand bookshops).

Antikvariát Galerie Mustek Národní třída 40, Prague 1, tel 224 949 587. Open Mon.–Fri. 10 a.m.–1 p.m., 2 p.m.–7 p.m., & Sat. 10 a.m.–2 p.m. One of the best secondhand bookshops in the city, with an excellent selection of art books.

Antiques & Auction House Slezská 24, Prague 2 (opposite "Vinohrady" Pavilion), tel/fax 222 512 512. Open Mon.–Fri. 10:30 a.m.–6 p.m. This shop specializes in paintings and furniture from the 18th to the 20th century.

Art Deco Michalská 21, Prague 1, tel 224 223 076. Open Mon.–Fri. 2 p.m.–7 p.m. As well as clothing from the art deco period, there is usually a fine and affordable collection of costume jewelry.

Dorotheum Ovocný trh 2, Prague 1, tel 224 222 001. Open Mon.–Fri. 10 a.m.–7 p.m. & Sat. 10 a.m.–5 p.m. Carries crystal, glass, jewelry, pictures, furniture, and more.

Beer

Prices of bottled beer are a fraction of those charged for the same products elsewhere in Europe. The best buys are the classics such as Pilsner Urquell and Budvar (see pp. 186–187); also watch for Krušovice, Radegast, Regent, and other labels. Just about any beer that you sample on tap in a pub will be available in a bottled version, so just follow your personal tastes when stocking up.

CDs

These can be good value, especially recordings of classical music and ethnic Czech music on the local Supraphon label. But in recent years prices in Europe and the United States have become highly competitive, so CDs are not the bargains they once were.

Kafkovo kuihkupectví Staroměstské nám 606/12 (Old Town Square), tel 222 321 454. Open Mon.–Fri. 10 a.m.–7 p.m. This has an interesting selection of ethnic music, as well as classical and jazz. It also has good books.

Philharmonia Pařížská 13, Prague 1, tel 222 324 060. Open Mon.–Fri. 10 a.m.–6 p.m. This shop has a big selection of classical, jazz, ethnic, and folk music; it is affiliated with Prague Philharmonic orchestra.

Clothing

Fashionable streets such as Pařížská in Prague are lined with clothes boutiques, but you are unlikely to find anything that is not available at home. However, some local workshops are now beginning to produce clothing and accessories of good quality.

Army shop Ripská 22, Prague 3, tel 224 251 232. Open Mon.–Fri. 9 a.m.–6 p.m. This Vinohrady shop sells army surplus items, especially clothing, at low prices.

Klára Nademlýnská Dlouhá 7, Prague 1, tel 2481 8769. Open Mon.–Fri. 10 a.m.–7 p.m. & Sat. noon–6 p.m. This Czech designer is based in Paris, but her designs, many of them haute couture, are on sale in this sumptuous shop.

Piano Betlémské náměstí 6, Prague 1, tel 222 220 210. Manufactures and sells stylish handbags and leather goods. Fairly expensive.

Taiza Na Příkopě 31, Prague 1, tel 221 613 308. Open Mon.–Sat. 10 a.m.–8 p.m. & Sun. 1–6 p.m. The Cuban-born designer Osmany Laffita produces extravagant and expensive women's wear. There is also a branch in Karlovy Vary, Vridelní 57, tel 353 224 828.

Crystal

The Czech Republic produces glassware that is high quality and widely available. Indeed, for many visitors Bohemia is synonymous with crystal. There are glassware shops in every major town, but the best selection and most competitive prices are in Prague. Commercial streets such as Karlova have countless glass shops. Most Bohemian crystal is cut glass and often colored, too. With such a vast range available, you are bound to find something that suits your taste—unless you are looking for classic, unadorned wine glasses. Many shops will pack and dispatch your purchases.

Celetná Crystal Celetná 15, Prague 1, tel 222 324 022. Open Mon.–Thurs. 10 a.m.–8 p.m. & Fri.–Sun. 10 a.m.–10 p.m. This large shop offers a classic selection of good-quality Bohemian crystal, displayed in attractive surroundings.

Moser Na Příkopě 12, Prague 1, tel 224 211 293; fax 224 228 686. Also Malé náměstí 11. Since 1857, when the firm was founded in Karlovy Vary, Moser has been the leading producer of fine Bohemian glassware. Prices are very high, but the products are handmade. Even if you have little interest in crystal, it is worth visiting the showrooms on the first floor. This building was once the home of Bohumil Bondy, a rich industrialist who decorated his mansion in lavish 19th-century style, and the wood paneling, wood inlays, and chandeliers here are all immaculately preserved.

Moser Tržiště 7, Karlovy Vary. The firm's leading showroom in this spa town. To learn more about the glassmaking process, visit the factory and museum in Karlovy Vary at Jaroše 19, tel 353 416 111. Also visit www.moser-glass.com. Open Mon.–Fri. 8 a.m.–5 p.m. & Sat. 9 a.m.–3 p.m.

Moser Náměstí Svobody 15, Brno, tel 542 514 300. Same stock, different city.

Delicatessen

The range of both Czech and imported food products available in Prague has expanded and improved in quality over recent years, and visitors will find plenty to tempt them.

Ocean Zborovská 49, Prague 5, tel 9000 1517. Open Mon.–Sat. 10 a.m.–8 p.m. This fish shop flies in fresh fish and shellfish twice weekly. Quality and prices are high.

Garnets

These semiprecious stones come from Turnov in northern Bohemia and are very decorative and relatively inexpensive. Modest in size, they rarely exceed two carats;

larger stones are imported from India. Color does not affect the value of garnets as it does with other precious and semiprecious stones. There are many garnet shops in Prague.

Granát Turnov Dlouhá 30, Prague 1, tel 222 315 612, www.granat-cz.com. Also Panská 1. Open Mon.–Fri. 10 a.m.–6 p.m. & Sat. 10 a.m.–1 p.m. This factory store is the best place in Prague to buy garnets: Buyers can be sure they're getting Bohemian (Czech) garnets, not stones from elsewhere. The company, a cooperative based in Turnov, produces an evolving range of 3,500 items, with garnets set in silver or gold. There are other branches of this company in the following towns:
České Budějovice: Dr. Stejskala 9
Český Krumlov: Latrán 53
Liberec: Náměstí E. Beneše 12/4
Turnov: Náměstí Ceského ráje 4.

Marionettes

Marionette theaters have been popular in the Czech lands since the 17th century, and to this day puppets are crafted with sophistication and humor. Unfortunately, you will find mostly mass-produced examples for sale. Though perfectly acceptable if chosen as an inexpensive souvenir, they give little idea of the refinement of the best handmade marionettes. To find out more about marionette making, including where to go to make your own, see p. 52.

Wine

The quality of Bohemian and Moravian wine is improving. Most towns have at least one wine shop with a fair selection of local bottles, and there is a growing number in Prague. Many stock wines from all over the world as well as from the Czech Republic. (If you order the house red, you'll get Frankovka; the most common white is Ryzlink.) The best Czech wines tend to come from small growers with limited production

and distribution. Some labels worth watching for are Baloun, Znovín, Znojmo, Tomáš, Krist, Sonberk, and Petr Skoupil Winery.

Monarch Na Perštýně 15, Prague 1, tel 224 239 602. This shop has a fine selection of Czech, French, and Italian wines.

Vinotéka Carrefour Mall, Plzeňská 8, Prague 5, tel 257 329 257. This shop carries a large range of reasonably priced Czech wines from good producers.

Wine Shop Ungelt Týnský dvůr 7, Prague 1, tel 224 827 501, fax 224 895 449. An extensive international range, and some good Moravian white wines, too; prices are high.

Activities & Entertainment

The Czech Republic has always been a hotbed of cultural activity. The love of music is profound; dozens of festivals feature classical music, jazz, and folklore. Nightclubs and jazz clubs are common in every major town. Czechs are enthusiastic about sports; Prague and the Czech Republic offer a wide variety of sporting and other recreational activities. There is something to suit all tastes, ranging from spectator sports such as horse racing or ice hockey to active sports—for example, cycling or hiking in the Český ráj region. The country boasts a network of well-marked hiking trails; skiing is also popular.

PRAGUE

Entertainment

The English-language weekly *The Prague Post* is invaluable for checking all listings.

Classical Music & Opera

Lovers of classical music and opera are well served, especially in the fall and winter (there are few performances during the summer months). The city has two first-rate orchestras, the Czech Philharmonic and the Prague Symphony, and a renowned annual music festival.

Music lovers enjoy the many concerts held in Prague's churches and chapels, in the beautiful Chapel of Mirrors at the Klementinum (see pp. 94–95), and, in summer, in the gardens of some of the city's loveliest palaces. Opera is performed regularly at Prague's two opera houses, **Státní Opera** *(State Opera, Wilsonova 4, Prague 1, tel 224 227 266)*, and **Národní divadlo** (National Theater), *(Narodní 2, Prague 1, tel 224 901 668)*. The National Theater also administers the **Stavovské divadlo** *(Estates Theater, Ovocný trh 1, Prague 1, tel 224 215 001)*. Another notable theater is **Klementinum,** *(Zrcadlová kaple, Mariánské náměstí, Prague 1, tel 272 766 902)*. For general information about concerts, also see www.pis.cz.

Theater & Mime

Language may be an obstacle to enjoying theatrical performances abroad, but this does not apply to the celebrated multimedia **Laterna Magika** productions at the National Theater in Prague (see p. 121), nor to the many puppet theater companies across the country. Best known in Prague are the **National Marionette Theater** *(Žatecká 1)*, and **Spejbl and Hurvínek** *(Dejvická 38, Prague 6, tel 224 316 784)*. Many puppet productions are ideal for children; they tend to be mounted at a sophisticated level, so adults enjoy them, too. Mime is another strong Czech tradition (see p. 56).

Prices for cultural events are reasonable, even inexpensive. Tickets can be obtained from **TicketPro** *(Rytířská 31, tel 221 610 162, www.ticketpro.cz)*; **Bohemia Ticket International** *(Malé náměstí 13)*; and box offices.

Nightlife

Prague has the most vibrant nightlife in the republic, with a good selection of discos and jazz clubs, as well as clubs where live music can be heard until the early hours of the morning. A large and popular disco is **Retro** at Francouzská 4, Prague 2, a complex combining a large dance floor, casino, pub, café, and steak house. The **Reduta** *(Národní 20, Prague 1, tel 224 933 487)* is the city's best-known jazz club (performances start at 9 p.m.), along with **AghaRTA Jazz Club** *(Železná 16, Prague 1, tel 224 239 697, open 3 p.m.–1 a.m.)*. Theme nights can provide some unintended entertainment as the crowds dress up in their finest approximations of Western cowboy gear. Better music and a wilder clientele can be found at clubs such as the **Rock Café** *(Národní 20, Prague 1, tel 224 933 945)*. **Roxy,** *(Dlouhá 33, Prague 1, tel 224 826 296, www.roxy.cz)*, combines music, a gallery, performing arts, and film with an Internet café. The gallery and café open from 1 p.m. until 1 a.m., the club from 8 p.m. until 5 a.m. Other clubs include **Radost FX** *(Belehradská 120, Prague 2, tel 224 254 776)*, which is a vegetarian restaurant with very late hours in addition to one of the city's most popular dance club despite its small size; the gallery and café at street level are popular all day with students.; and **Palác Akropolis** *(Kubelíkova 27, Prague 3, tel 296 330 913)*. The club situation is very volatile, with new ones opening as swiftly as others close.

Coffeehouses have returned to Prague and other main cities. Some, such as **Slavia** *(Národní trida 1, Prague 1)* and **Kavárna,** Obecní dům in Prague, are in the Viennese mold—places to talk, snack, drink coffee, and read newspapers; others are closer in style to Italian espresso bars. Internet cafés have sprung up in most Czech towns, but are often gloomy basement dives. In Prague there's also **Bohemia Bagel** *(Masna 2, Prague 1)*, which is popular with U.S. visitors and expats.

Festivals & Events

April–July

AghaRTA Prague Jazz Festival
Running on-and-off April through July, this club-organized concert series brings jazz giants such as

the Pat Metheny Group and John Scoield to intimate venues (Lublaňská 57, tel 222 511 858, www.agharta.cz).

May
Prague Spring International Music Festival The biggest and best-known music festival of the year; it was first held in 1946 (Hellichova 18, Prague 1, tel 257 312 547, www.festival.cz).

June
Prague Writer's Festival Started in London in 1980, nowadays this festival draws names such as Alain Robbe-Grillet, Jiří Gruša, and Ludvík Vaculík (Kremencova 7, Prague 1, ww.pwf.cz).

July
ECM Prague Open Tennis Championship In mid-July WTC tennis is played on the I. CLTK clay courts, the oldest tennis club in Prague (www.pragueopen.cz).

October
4 + 4 Days in Motion This popular multi-venue festival of movement theater brings some of the most innovative artists and companies from around the world to Prague's funkiest theaters (Celetná 17, tel 224 809 116, www.ctyridny.cz)

December
Eve of St. Nicholas (Dec. 5). People dressed as angels and devils tease children and give them sweets. Prague's Old Town Square is a good place to be, although most of the festivities take place at home. St. Nicholas Day (Dec. 6) is comparatively quiet.

Activities
Golf
There is a 9-hole course in Prague's 5th district (Plzenská, tel 257 216 585, www.gcp.cz.).

Health & Fitness
Fitness centers and gyms are

spreading like wildfire. Some of the best-equipped clubs in Prague are at the **Hilton Hotel** (Pobřežní 1, Prague 6, tel 224 841 111), the **Crown Plaza** at Dejvice (tel 296 537 111), and the **Intercontinental Hotel** (Námestí Curieovych 43/5, Prague 1, tel 296 631 111). Non-residents can pay to use the facilities. Other clubs advertise widely on the metro and buses.

Horse Racing
In the Prague suburb of **Radotín,** about 3 miles (5 km) south of the city, various types of races take place at the Velká Chuchle track (tel 257 941 431, www.chuchle.cz) from May through October. To get there from the city center, take the metro in from Smíchovské nádraží, then bus 129 or 172.

Ice Hockey & Skating
Ice hockey has become a popular sport, especially since the Czech team has triumphed at an international level. National league games usually take place on Tuesday & Friday, and sometimes on Sunday afternoons. The best stadia are the **Tesla Arena** in Holešovice, close to Vltavská metro station, and **Slavia Praha** winter stadium (U Slavia, Vršovice, Prague 10, www. slavia.cz). Ice rinks are also used for skating (Oct.–April).

Soccer
This is the republic's most popular sport. Most matches are played on Sunday, September through November and April through June. The two leading Prague-based teams, Sparta Praha (tel 220 570 323) and Slavia Praha (tel 233 081 751), are bitter rivals. The most important games are played at the **Generali stadium** in Prague, which is easily accessible from Hradčanská metro station.

Sports Complexes
Southeast of Prague, the **Club Hotel** (Plzenská, Prague 5) on the Prague–Plzeň road has a

golf course and facilities for tennis, riding, squash, badminton, and other activities. Fees for the use of recreational facilities are very reasonable.

Squash
Squash is very popular in Prague, especially with young executives resident in the city. There are courts available at the **Arebes** (Arbesovo náměstí 15, Smíchov, tel 257 326 041), which stays open until 11 p.m. Slightly cheaper but on the edge of town is **Hotel Squash sportcentrum** in Radotín (K Cementárně 1a , Prague 5, tel 257 912 024, www.hotelsquash.cz), with courts open 9 a.m.–9 p.m.

Swimming
Plavecký Stadion Podolí (Podolská 74, Prague 4, tel 241 433 952) has modern indoor and outdoor facilities. The **Aquacentrum** pool (Tupolerova 665, Prague-9-Letnany, tel 283 921 799) has waterslides and children's pools, as well as a fitness center.

Tennis
The Czechs have excelled at tennis for decades, producing champions such as Ivan Lendl, Martina Navratilova, Jana Novotna, and the late Jaroslav Drobny. The **I. CLTK** club, on Štvanice island opposite Old Town's north side, has 14 outdoor clay courts and six indoor courts (Štvanice Ostrov 38, Prague 7, tel 222 316 317, www. cltk.cz). For further information, contact the **Czech Tennis Federation** (Ostrov Štvanice 38, Prague 7, tel 224 810 108, www.cztenis.cz).

CZECH REPUBLIC
Entertainment
Classical Music, Opera, & Theater
Ostrava and Olomouc have their own orchestras, and Olomouc and Brno hold music festivals. Many smaller festivals, held in châteaus, specialize in baroque

music or the works of individual composers such as Janáček, Smetana, and Beethoven. In many towns, including Brno and Plzeň, delightful 19th-century theaters have been restored; they offer a wide repertoire of drama, opera, and ballet. Brno is home to the National Theater *(Dvořákova 11, tel 542 158 111)* and Janáčkovo divadlo *(Rooseveltova, tel 542 158 254).* Puppet and mime theater companies are found in many towns across the republic.

Nightlife

In the smaller towns people tend to go home early, so don't expect late-night carousing outside the cities. Since nightspots come and go all the time, look for detailed listings in local newssheets and promotional brochures.

Today even small towns are likely to have casinos, which may be incorporated into local hotels. Smaller casinos, called *herna,* are ubiquitous and remain open until dawn. They consist of little more than slot machines and a bar.

Festivals & Events

April

Flora Olomouc international garden exhibition, Olomouc. This weekend-long exhibition has been running since the early 1980s; indoor and outdoor displays *(www.flora-ol.cz).*

May

Beer festival, Karlovy Vary.
Janáček International Music Festival, Ostrava. Some lesser-known works by Janáček can be heard at this festival held near his native village of Hukvaldy *(Masná 10, 70200 Ostrava, tel 558 431 524, www.janackovy-hukvaldy.cz).*
Olomouc Beer Festival, Olomouc. A four-day festival of beer olympics and music ranging from jazz to blues, rock, and folk. Most of the major breweries are represented, and it's all free *(www .pivnifestival.cz).*

June

International Festival of Records, Curiosities, and Budvar Beer, Pelhřimov. Enjoy beer as you watch people vie for a place in the *Guinness Book of Records (Agency Dobrý den Pelhrimov, Slovanského bratrství 1664, 39301 Pelhrimov, tel 565 321 226, www.dobryden.cz).*
Music in Gardens and Châteaus, Kroměříž. A summer series of concerts *(Kovárská 1, 76701 Kromeríž, tel 573 331 473, www .hudba-kromeriz.cz).*
Smetanova Litomyšl International Opera Festival, Litomyšl. This open-air classical festival, held over two weekends at the castle in Smetana's hometown, is one of the republic's oldest *(www.smetanovalitomysl.cz).*
Strážnice International folk festival Held the last weekend of June, this has been attracting folk dancers, singers, and musicians from all over the Czech Republic and the rest of the world since the 1940s *(Ústav lidové kultury, tel 518 306 611, www.straznice-mesto.cz).*

July

Karlovy Vary International Film Festival The most important film festival in central and Eastern Europe, the ten-day Karlovy Vary festival dates to the mid-20th century. It usually attracts lots of famous faces *(tel 221 411 011, www.kviff.com).*
Puppet festival, Chrudim. A week-long festival is presented by the city's Puppet Museum *(tel 469 620 310, www.puppets.cz).*

August

Brno Grand Prix motorcycle race This is part of the World Championship of Road Motorcycles *(Automotodrom Brno, Ostrovice 201, 664 81 Brno venkov, tel 5191 406 6260, www.brnograndprix.com).*
Chodské slavnosti, Domažlice. This folk festival is devoted to the Chod people and their traditions.
International Bagpipe Festival (dudácký festival), Strakonice. Bagpipers, singers, dancers, and

artists come from all over Europe to perform *(tel 383 311 530, www .dudackyfestival.cz).*

September

Hop festival, Žatec. Celebrates the Czech Republic's most famous product—beer *(Tourist Information Office, Náměstí Svobody 1, tel 415 736 156, www.mesto-zatec.cz).*

October

Moravsky podzim international music festival, Brno. The two-week "Moravian Autumn" festival of classical music has a good showing of Czech composers *(www.mhf-brno.cz).*
Jazz Goes to Town, Hradec Králové. An international jazz festival *(tel 495 211 081, www .jazzgoestotown.com).*
Pilsnerfest, Plzeň. This two-day festival is the granddaddy of all beer festivals, put on by Pilsner Urquell brewery *(tel 377 062 888, www.pilsnerfest.cz).*
Velká pardubická steeplechase, Pardubice (second Sunday in October). This world-famous cross-country steeplechase has been running for over a century *(tel 466 797 111, www.pardubice-racecourse.cz).*

November

Blues-Alive international blues festival, Šumperk. Three days of blues from around the world *(www.bluesalive.cz).*

Activities

Boating

Lakes such as Lipno provide good boating and windsurfing. Contact the **Czech Yachting Union** *(Atletická 100/2, Prague 6, tel 220 513 656, www.sailing.cz)*. At the same address is the **Czech Canoeing Union** *(www.kanoe.cz).*
See also p. 99

Cycling

Mountain bikes may be rented at many resorts in the Český ráj or Krkonoše mountains. It can also be pleasant to rent a bicycle and explore the gentler terrain of southern Bohemia and Moravia, on mostly uncrowded roads.

Details of facilities and competitive events for serious cyclists are available from the **Czech Cycling Union,** Nad Hliníkem 4, Prague 5, tel 257 214 613. For cycling routes, contact *www. czeskysvazcyklistiky.cz.*

Fishing
Lakes, mountain streams, and major rivers provide excellent opportunities for fishing. Besides trout, there are catfish, common walleye, perch, carp, pike, and river eels. Fishing permits, available from many tackle shops and the Czech Fishing Association, are required, and regulations determine seasons and the size of the catch. Contact: **Czech Angling Union** *(Nad Olšinami 31, Prague 10, tel 274 811 751, www.rybsvaz.cz).*

Golf
The best golf courses are at Mariánské Lázně (where a large, comfortable hotel adjoins), Karlovy Vary, and Ostrava. There is a 9-hole course at Pardubice. The latest 18-hole course to open is at Karlštejn *(tel 311 684 716 or 311 684 717).* The game is becoming increasingly popular, so book in advance. For more information, contact the **Czech Golf Federation** *(Strakonická 510, Prague 5, tel 5415444, fax 544586).*

Health & Fitness
Many hotels in larger towns are equipped with fitness centers and gyms. Alternatively, your hotel concierge should be able to tell you about local health clubs.

Hiking
Most of the republic is hilly or mountainous, and there are ample opportunities for hiking. Some of the many parks offer inexpensive accommodations in *chaty* (hostels) and *horské hotely*

(mountain hotels; check with the local information office). Many prefer the comfortable base offered by a spa, from which well-marked trails explore the surrounding hills and woods. Regions such as the Český ráj (Czech Paradise) and České Švýcarsko (Czech Switzerland) are popular. Detailed maps of hiking trails are available from most bookstores. For more information contact **Klub Česýck turistů,** the Czech Hiking Club *(Jaromírova 9, Prague 2, tel 235 514 529).* Experienced hikers seeking details of more challenging activities should contact the **Czech Orienteering Association** *(Strahov, Prague 6, tel 354679).*

Horse Racing
The major event in the Czech Republic is the Grand Steeple-chase at Pardubice, which has been in existence since 1874 (see p. 323). There are 39 jumps, making it a race that both horses and jockeys find extremely demanding. The most notorious jump is the Taxis Ditch, which many an experienced horse and jockey fail to clear. Increasing awareness about animal welfare issues has led to improvements that should make the course less dangerous for horses.

Horse Riding
There are stables in Poděbrady, Třeboň, Karlovy Vary, and other towns. You can obtain further information from the **Czech Equestrian Federation** *(Zátopkova 2, Prague 6, www.cjf.cz).*

Hunting
During the Habsburg empire, the Austrian nobility maintained hunting lodges in Bohemia and farther east. Game birds may be less plentiful nowadays, but there is good year-round sport for those with a license. Game includes pheasant, wild duck, deer, wild boar, and hare. For further information, contact **Pragolov**

(Nad Kazankou 31, Prague 8, tel 233 554 797). This private company organizes permits and accommodations.

Ice Hockey & Skating
Almost every town has a winter stadium *(zimn stadion),* where ice hockey matches are held. In the winter months ice rinks are also used for skating; there is good outdoor skating in rural areas when some reservoirs freeze over.

Motor Sports
Two outstanding events are the Motorcycle Grand Prix in Brno *(www.brnograndprix.com),* which takes place in August, and the Golden Helmet Speedway Race in Pardubice a month later.

Sports Complexes
Every town has a sports complex, a beneficial legacy of the Communist era. One of the largest sports complexes in the Czech Republic, at Roudnice, north of Prague, also has a good hotel and restaurant. Reasonable fees.

Swimming
Most towns have swimming pools. Sometimes standards of cleanliness and hygiene may be suspect, so in summer it is often preferable to head for the lakes and reservoirs. Many have excellent sandy beaches—for example, **Slapy reservoir,** south of Prague on the River Vltava.

Tennis
Many hotels, especially in spa towns, have courts for casual players. In Prague, you'll find first-class clay courts at **Tenisové Haly Uhríneves** *(Prague 10, tel 267 711 440 to reserve a court).* Also contact the **Czech Tennis Federation** *(Ostrov Štvanice 38, Prague 7, tel 222 333 444, www.cztenis.cz).*

Language Guide & Menu Reader

Czech belongs to the Slav family of languages and, as such, is highly inflected. Even if you learn a good deal of vocabulary, you still will find it difficult to speak or understand the language effectively without some knowledge of its grammatical structure. Nonetheless, even a limited knowledge of the language can prove helpful.

Most English-speakers find pronunciation a problem, but the system of accents should make it clear. Acute accents (or in the case of "u," ů) lengthen the vowel. The stress usually falls on the first syllable. There are some clear differences from "English-style" pronunciation:

á = as in far
c = *ts* as in cats
č = *ch* as in cheek
ch = *ch* as in loch
ě = *ye* as in yet
é = *ea* as in pear
í and ý = *ee* as in see
j = *y* as in yawn
ň = *ny* as in banyan
ř = as in bourgeois (combined rolled r and ž sound)
š = *sh* as in shabby
ú and ů = *oo* as in zoo
y = *j* as in fit
ž = *zh* sound as in measure

General Conversation
Good day/hello *dobrý den*
Goodbye *na shledanou*
Please *prosím*
Thank you *děkuji*
Yes *ano*
No *ne*
Good/OK *dobře*
Sorry/Excuse me *prominte*
Where? *kde je?*
When? *kdy?*
Why? *proč?*
Large/Small *velký/malý*
More/Less *více/méně*
Hot/Cold *horký/studený*
Here/There *tady/tam*
Right/Left *vpravo/vlevo*
Straight ahead *jděte přímo*

Signs
vchod entrance
východ exit
otevřeno open

zavřeno closed
pozor danger
toalety rest rooms
muži/páni men/gentlemen
ženy/dámy women/ladies

Time
Today *dnes*
Tomorrow *zítra*
Yesterday *včera*
Morning *ráno*
Afternoon *odpoledne*
Evening *večer*
Night *noc*

Shopping
Cash desk *pokladna*
Post office *pošta*
Bank *banka*
Supermarket *potraviny*
Chemist *lékárna*
Expensive/Cheap *drahý/levný*
How much is it? *Kolik to stoji?*

Transportation
Airport *letiště*
Railway station *nádraží*
Bus station *autobusové nádraží*
Metro station *stanice*
Aeroplane *letadlo*
Train *vlak*
Bus *autobus*
Tram *tramvaj*
Seat *místo*
Ticket *lístek*
One-way *jednosmeřnou*
Return *zpáteční*

Geography & Places
Tourist office *informační centrum*
Theater *divadlo*
Garden *zahrada*
Church *kostel*
Museum *muzeum*
Bridge *most*
Avenue *třída*
Square *náměstí*
Street *ulice*
Castle *hrad*

Château *zámek*
Mountain *hora*
River *řeka*

Hotels
Hotel *hotel*
Room *pokoj*
Breakfast *snídaně*
Key *klíč*
Reservation *mistenka*
Toilet *toaleta*
Bath *koupelna*
Shower *sprcha*

Emergencies
Help! *pomoc!*
Doctor *doktor/lékař*
Dentist *zubní lékař*
Hospital *nemocnice*
Police Station *policie*

Numbers
1 *jeden*
2 *dva*
3 *tří*
4 *čtyři*
5 *pět*
6 *šest*
7 *sedm*
8 *osm*
9 *devět*
10 *deset*
15 *patnáct*
20 *dvacet*
25 *dvacet pět*
50 *padesát*
100 *sto*
1000 *tisíc*
1,000,000 *jeden milión*

Days of the Week
Monday *pondělí*
Tuesday *úterý*
Wednesday *středa*
Thursday *čtvrtek*
Friday *pátek*
Saturday *sobota*
Sunday *neděle*

Months of the Year & Seasons
January *leden*
February *únor*
March *březen*
April *duben*
May *květen*
June *červen*
July *červenec*
August *srpen*
September *září*
October *říjen*
November *listopad*
December *prosinec*

Spring *jaro*
Summer *léto*
Autumn *podzim*
Winter *zima*

Menu Reader
General Terms
restaurant *restaurace*
menu *jídelní lístek*
table *stůl*
lunch *oběd*
dinner *večeře*
appetizer *předkrmy*
main meal *hlavní jídlo*
side dish *přílohy*
dessert *moučník*
wine list *nápojový lístek*
the bill *účet*

Basics
bread *chléb*
butter *máslo*
sugar *sukr*
eggs *vejce*
cheese *sýr*
cream *smetana*
fruit *ovoce*
meat *maso*
vegetables *zeleniny*
soup *polévka*
salt *sul*
pepper *pepr*
vinegar *ocet*
oil *olej*

Cooking Methods
grilované grilled
piněné stuffed
pečené baked
smažené fried

uzený smoked
špíz skewered
vařené boiled

Meats
drůbež poultry
kuře chicken
husa goose
kachna duck
bažant pheasant
krocan turkey
hovězí beef
vepřové pork
teleci veal
šunka ham
králik rabbit
játra liver
klobása sausage
vepřový řízek schnitzel
Bepřové koleno pork knee

Seafood
ryby fish
uzený losos smoked salmon
kapr carp
pstruh trout
treska cod
tuna tuna
krevety prawns

Side Dishes
brambory potatoes
knedlíky dumplings
rýže rice
hranolky french fries
bramborová kaše mashed potatoes
salát salad

Fruit
jablko apple
banán banana
pomeranč orange
citrón lemon
jahody strawberries
hrozny grapes
hruška pear
ananas pineapple
rozinky raisins

Vegetables
hrášek peas
rajčata tomatoes
špenát spinach
cibule onion
česnek garlic
okurka cucumber
karotka carrot

zelí cabbage
žampiony mushrooms
květák cauliflower

Desserts
palačinky pancakes
zmrzlina ice cream
závin strudel
dort cake
buchty curd cakes
čokoláda chocolate

Drinks
voda water
minerální voda mineral water
  nešumivá still
  šumivá sparkling
mléko milk
čaj tea
káva coffee
pomerančový džus orange juice
červené víno red wine
bílé víno white wine
pivo beer

Other
chlebíček open sandwiches
omeleta omelette
smažený sýr fried cheese

INDEX

ACKNOWLEDGMENTS

The author and National Geographic wish to thank the Czech Tourism Authority *(www.czechtourism .com)*; Miloš Čuřik, Arts & Music Travel *(arts.music@volny.cz)*; and Roz Hoagland, Hoagland Art Travel, *(rlhoagland@cox.net)*.

ILLUSTRATIONS CREDITS

2-3, Barbara Noe; 4, Index Stock/Alamy; 8, Vladimir Wrangel/Shutterstock; 11, PeterSVETphoto/Shutterstock; 12, Richard Nebesky/Getty Images; 13, Lee Malis/Spectrum Pictures, Prague; 14-15, Nikada/ iStockphoto.com; 16, S. McBride/AA Photo Lib; 18, Sean Gallup; 21, Hana Bilikova/iStockphoto. com; 22-23, Pavel Kosek/Shutterstock; 24-25, AKG London; 27, BESTWEB/Shutterstock; 29, J. Wyand/AA Photo Lib; 30-31, AKG London; 33, Robert Bremec/iStockphoto.com; 34, AKG London; 39, AKG London; 40-41, Nathan Benn/National Geographic Society; 43, Novosti/Rex Features; 45, Dan Breckwoldt/Shutterstock; 46, Earl & Nazima Kowall/CORBIS; 49, Robert Harding Picture Lib; 50, AKG London; 52, Lance Bellers/Shutterstock; 54-55, Chris Fredriksson/Alamy; 57, Lucy Nicholson/AFP/ Getty Images; 58-59, Barbara Noe; 61, C.Sawyer/ AA Photo Lib; 64, T. Souter/AA Photo Lib; 69, Barbara Noe; 73, Barbara Noe; 74, Jeff Whyte/ Shutterstock; 75, Barbara Noe; 76, Franta Toth/ Spectrum Pictures, Prague; 78, Zdenek Thoma/ Spectrum Pictures, Prague; 82, S. McBride/AA Photo Lib; 85, Sofron/Shutterstock; 87, Roman Sigaev/ iStockphoto.com; 90, Robert Harding Picture Lib; 93, Jiri Foltyn/Shutterstock; 95, Zdenek Thoma/ Spectrum Pictures, Prague; 96, Nataliya Hora/ Shutterstock; 98, S. McBride/AA Photo Lib; 100, David Aleksandrowicz/Shutterstock; 101, The Art Archive/Mozart Museum Villa Bertramka Prague/ Dagli Orti; 102, Matt Trommer/Shutterstock; 105, S. McBride/AA Photo Lib; 106, janprchal/Shutterstock; 107, S. McBride/AA Photo Lib; 108, Oldrich Karasek, Prague; 113, Jan Gottwald/iStockphoto. com; 114, J. Wyand/AA Photo Lib; 116, Scott Waymouth; 119, Zdenek Thoma/Spectrum Pictures, Prague; 122, Rex Features; 123, Zdenek Thoma/ Spectrum Pictures, Prague; 124, Petr Koudelka/ iStockphoto.com; 126, Frantisek Preucil/Spectrum Pictures, Prague; 128, PjrTravel/Alamy; 130, Sean Gallup/Getty Images; 132, J. Wyand/AA Photo Lib; 134, Wrangel/iStockphoto.com; 135, AKG London/Bridgeman Art Lib; 137, AKG London; 140, C. Sawyer/AA Photo Lib; 142, Pavel Dosoudil/ Spectrum Pictures, Prague; 144, Sean Gallup; 146, Pavel Dosoudil/Spectrum Pictures, Prague; 152-153, BESTWEB/Shutterstock; 154, Shutterstock; 155, Petr Student/Shutterstock; 158, Ionia/Shutterstock;

162, Pedro Salaverría/Shutterstock; 164, IFA/A1Pix; 165, J. Wyand/AA Photo Lib; 166, Pavel Dosoudil/ Spectrum Pictures, Prague; 168, Robert Harding Picture Lib; 170, Oldrich Karasek, Prague; 172, Oldrich Karasek, Prague; 174, AKG London; 175, AKG London; 176, J. Wyand/AA Photo Lib; 179, Pavel Dosoudil/Spectrum Pictures, Prague; 181, Jan Matoška/Shutterstock; 182, Kletr/Shutterstock; 184, Manfred Gottschalk/A1Pix; 186, Sean Gallup; 188, Gunther Grafenhain/A1Pix; 190, Lee Malis/ Spectrum Pictures, Prague; 193, Rex Features; 194, Andrea Seemann/Shutterstock; 196, Toriru/Shutterstock; 199, Palis Michalis/Shutterstock; 200, Zdenek Thoma/Spectrum Pictures, Prague; 202, Pavel Dosoudil/Spectrum Pictures, Prague; 204, Daniel Prudek/Shutterstock; 205, Matt Ragen/ Shutterstock; 208, Milan Vasicek/Shutterstock; 210, Oldrich Karasek, Prague; 212, J. Wyand/AA Photo Lib; 213, Robert Harding Picture Lib; 214, CZfoto/ Shutterstock; 218, Frantisek Preucil/Spectrum Pictures, Prague; 221, Boris Karpinski/Alamy; 223, skvoor/Shutterstock; 226, Alexei Fateev/Alamy; 228, Pavel Dosoudil/Spectrum Pictures, Prague; 230, Mary Evans Picture Lib; 231, Smetana Muzeum, Prague/Bridgeman Art Lib., London; 232, Michaela Dusíková/Alamy; 234, Thomas Boettger/A1Pix; 237, Lubomir Stiburek/Alamy; 238, Antonin Vodak/ Spectrum Pictures, Prague; 241, Zdenek Thoma/ Spectrum Pictures, Prague; 245, Richard Semik/ Shutterstock; 248, Pavelka/Shutterstock; 250, AKG London; 253, Pavel Dodoudil/Spectrum Pictures, Prague; 254, Ivan Tihelka/Shutterstock; 256, Sean Gallup; 257, Sean Gallup; 258, Pavel Dosoudil/ Spectrum Pictures, Prague; 260, Zdenek Thoma/ Spectrum Pictures, Prague; 263, Pavel Dosoudil/ Spectrum Pictures, Prague; 265, Oldrich Karasek, Prague; 267, Zbynek Burival/Shutterstock; 268, Hana Jakrlova/Spectrum Pictures, Prague; 270, Robert Harding Picture Lib; 273, Robert Harding Picture Lib; 275, Ales Nowak/Shutterstock; 278, Robert Harding Picture Lib; 280, Rex Features; 282, Zdenek Thoma/Spectrum Pictures, Prague; 284, Zdenek Thoma/Spectrum Pictures, Prague; 286, Robert Harding Picture Lib; 287, Lee Malis/Spectrum Pictures, Prague; 288, Pavel Dosoudil/Spectrum Pictures, Prague; 291, Zdenek Thoma/Spectrum Pictures, Prague; 293, Loic Bernard/iStockphoto.com.

National Geographic
TRAVELER
Prague &
the Czech Republic

Published by the National Geographic Society
John M. Fahey, Jr., *President
and Chief Executive Officer*
Gilbert M. Grosvenor, *Chairman of the Board*
Tim T. Kelly, *President, Global Media Group*
John Q. Griffin, *Executive Vice President;
President, Publishing*
Nina D. Hoffman, *Executive Vice President;
President, Book Publishing Group*

Prepared by the Book Division
Barbara Brownell Grogan, *Vice President
and Editor in Chief*
Marianne R. Koszorus, *Director of Design*
Barbara A. Noe, *Senior Editor*
Carl Mehler, *Director of Maps*
R. Gary Colbert, *Production Director*
Jennifer A. Thornton, *Managing Editor*
Meredith Wilcox, *Administrative Director,
Illustrations*

Staff for This Book
Caroline Hickey, *Project Editor*
Kay Kobor Hankins, *Art Director*
Linda Makarov, *Designer*
Rob Waymouth, *Illustrations Editor*
Paula Kelly, *Text Editor*
Mike McKey, *Map Coordinator*
Mapping Specialists, *Map Production*
Jane Sunderland, *Editorial Consultant*
Al Morrow, *Design Assistant*
Connie Binder, *Indexer*
Steven Gardner, Nicholas Rosenbach, Stephanie
Robichaux, *Contributors*

Manufacturing and Quality Management
Christopher A. Liedel, *Chief Financial Officer*
Phillip L. Schlosser, *Vice President*
Chris Brown, *Technical Director*
Nicole Elliott, *Manager*
Rachel Faulise, *Manager*

Cutaway illustrations drawn by Maltings Partnership,
Derby, England

**National Geographic Traveler: Prague & the Czech
Republic (Second Edition)
ISBN: 978-1-4262-0635-1**
1st ed. ISBN 0-7922-4147-9

The National Geographic Society is one of the world's largest nonprofit scientific and educational organizations. Founded in 1888 to "increase and diffuse geographic knowledge," the Society works to inspire people to care about the planet. It reaches more than 325 million people worldwide each month through its official journal, *National Geographic,* and other magazines; National Geographic Channel; television documentaries; music; radio; films; books; DVDs; maps; exhibitions; school publishing programs; interactive media; and merchandise. National Geographic has funded more than 9,000 scientific research, conservation and exploration projects and supports an education program combating geographic illiteracy. For more information, visit nationalgeographic.com.

For more information, please call 1-800-NGS LINE (647-5463) or write to the following address:

National Geographic Society
1145 17th Street N.W.
Washington, D.C. 20036-4688 U.S.A.

Visit us online at www.nationalgeographic.com

For information about special discounts for bulk purchases, please contact National Geographic Books Special Sales: ngspecsales@ngs.org

For rights or permissions inquiries, please contact National Geographic Books Subsidiary Rights: ngbookrights@ngs.org

The information in this book has been carefully checked and to the best of our knowledge is accurate. However, details are subject to change, and the National Geographic Society cannot be responsible for such changes, or for errors or omissions. Assessments of sites, hotels, and restaurants are based on the author's subjective opinions, which do not necessarily reflect the publisher's opinion.

Printed in China

11/TS/02

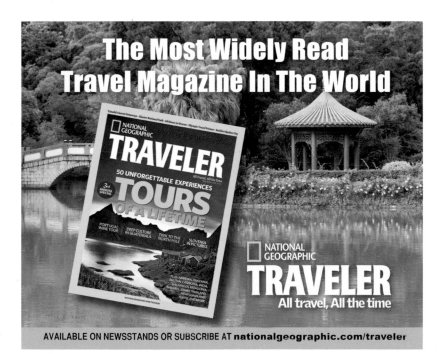